ESSENTIAL READINGS IN
HUMAN SEXUALITY

EDITED BY JAN CAMPBELL

REVISED FIRST EDITION

cognella
academic publishing

Bassim Hamadeh, CEO and Publisher
Michael Simpson, Vice President of Acquisitions
Jamie Giganti, Managing Editor
Jess Busch, Graphic Design Supervisor

First published in the United States of America in 2013 by Cognella, Inc.

Trademark Notice: Product or corporate names may be trademarks or registered trademarks, and are used only for identification and explanation without intent to infringe.

Cover photography by Eric Campbell

Printed in the United States of America

ISBN: 978-1-62131-924-5

www.cognella.com   800-200-3908

CONTENTS

PREFACE

JAN CAMPBELL

An examination of the human sexuality discipline takes many years of study. One may spend a lifetime exploring and uncovering the layers and depths of this theme. It is literally lifelong learning. As humans, we spend our lives as sexual beings. It seems only natural that we should study it. The complexities and intricacies of sexuality necessitate that we learn more about ourselves. We spend more time and effort on buying goods and services than we do learning about how to function.

Human sexuality is an integral part of who we are as males and females. It is like pieces of a pie. There are parts related to: decision-making about choosing an intimate; reducing risk-taking regarding sexually transmitted infections/diseases; communication; gender roles; sexual orientation; learning about issues like deviance; sexual assault and the sale of sex; reproduction; and, of course, human anatomy, physiology, and sex itself. No one part of the pie is more important than the other parts, and each one is interrelated to the others. People sometimes think that human sexuality and intimacy is just about sex. But, we know that intimacy is really about unmasking and being who we really are, as opposed to only being sexually intimate.

After teaching Human Sexuality courses for over thirty years, it is my opinion that we don't know much, as a human collective, about how we function. We don't know much about our own understanding of these various parts of the "pie." The changes and contributions to the development of sexuality are interesting to explore, since our development as a new nation over two hundred and forty years ago. Even if we look at the last one hundred years, there have been vast, dynamic changes in how we see sexual and social norms. With all of the contributing factors like technology, travel, trade, and the way in which the world seems smaller, we are still grappling with how to communicate with one another, what traits make a good partner, and how to deal with certain behaviors and atrocities by people who would choose to exploit human sexuality.

This book of readings is intended to raise consciousness, foster healthy debate, and provide a unique look at issues in human sexuality. The authors who contributed to this anthology have provided thoughtful writings to help us see the discipline from different vantage points. Hopefully, it produces discussion and promotes life-long academic learning of this discipline.

Many thanks go to Jaime McLendon, Melissa Accornero, Amy Wiltbank, Jennifer Bowen, and Toni Weeks for their contributions to the development of this anthology. Thanks also to my colleagues and students for teaching me about how much there is yet to learn. And thanks to my family, who are always there to help me realize how fortunate I am.

Happy reading,
Jan Campbell

INTRODUCTION TO: DESIRE, DEMAND, AND THE COMMERCE OF SEX

JAN CAMPBELL

In this article, Bernstein and Schaffner portray a graphic yet compelling view of the sex industry as a commodity. In relating how market-mediated, variant sexual encounters are described by patrons of the trade, the authors give us a comprehensive picture of how this industry works. Rationales and theories are used to describe the motivations of these patrons, and two unique tendencies—burgeoning consumption and state intervention—are discussed. The authors show how encounters can be anything from purchasing a fantasy, a streetwalker, or a call girl to, more recently, the GFE (Girlfriend Experience) or something more than a commercial transaction where the paid relationship is akin to a non-paid encounter.

The authors present information on client reeducation programs, such as "John Schools," that have recently been developed to offer alternatives to arrest and prosecution. However, they are quick to report that equal punishment of both the prostitute and the client are neither applied nor enforced. Cross-cultural views of decriminalization and also prosecution of the client are presented. Even in the U.S., many cities, according to the authors, have been broadcasting on cable TV the names and photos of male clients who have been arrested.

Bernstein and Schaffner point out that "commercial sexual consumption is simultaneously being *normalized* and *problematized*."

DESIRE, DEMAND, AND THE COMMERCE OF SEX

ELIZABETH BERNSTEIN AND LAURIE SCHAFFNER

Suddenly, the car takes off. We're moving again, but I'm not quite sure whom we're following. Apparently, a woman has gotten into the car ahead of us with a date. We proceed at full speed about a block or two, over train tracks, to a deserted stretch of territory with few cars or people. Indeed, the area is completely barren save for a few abandoned warehouses. Despite the gleaming California sunshine, the atmosphere is tense.

Everything happens in a flash. In mere minutes, it's all over; we slam the brakes on, and two of the officers hop out. They motion for me to join them.

The other members of the Street Crimes Unit are already on the scene. They stopped a blue Chevrolet truck and handcuffed the driver, a large but trembling man who is trying to be obsequious in spite of being terrified. Two of the officers have their guns pointed toward him. In addition to the arresting officer, the sergeant and another policeman also surround the suspect. Meanwhile, the female officers beckon the passenger, Carla, from her seat and begin to talk to her.[2] They are trying to get her side of the story so that they can use it as evidence. Carla is high on drugs and rather weary, but still lucid. She is apparently one of the numerous street prostitutes whom the officers know by name, because she has been arrested repeatedly during the 10 or so years that she has been working. But today she is not the main focus of their attention.

I hover in the background, absorbing the drama of the surrounded man, the drawn guns, the momentary displays of power and fear. My heart pounding, I try to listen, feeling vaguely guilty about being a part of this. The arresting officer delivers a rapid-clip, tough-guy, made-for-TV monologue:

I want you to tell me what happened. ... Remember, we've spoken to her so we know. ... What were you thinking? ... Did you use a condom? ... No? So you came in her mouth? ... Did you even look at her? Did you see that disgusting shit she has on her hands? Now it's all over your wee-wee. ... Do you have a wife or girlfriend? Now you're going to go home and give whatever you just got to her. Every man's thought of it, but you don't need to take chances. Next time you're feeling horny, why don't you just buy some porn and jack off?

Before releasing their detainee, the officers issue him a written citation and a court date.

Much later that same evening, I arrive at a famed "erotic theater" with a friend, tired but intrigued. The theater has a reputation for being one of the most upscale of the 14 legal sex clubs in the area, where striptease, lapdances, and, in recent years, hand jobs and blow jobs are widely, if unofficially, available for purchase. We wade through the small crowd of Asian businessmen standing outside and make our way to the entrance. A middle-aged man with glasses politely takes our money ($45 each) with no perceptible surprise that we should choose to come here—even though we are obviously the evening's only female customers. A basket of condoms sits prominently by the door.

Again in straightforward fashion, an employee proceeds to give us a tour and to describe the various shows. The rooms have names like the "VIP Club" and the "Luxury Lounge." The premises are dimly lit but clean, orderly, and rather spare. The floors are bare yet spotless. We head over to the main stage in the back room, where a young, tanned, and toned woman in a sparkly thong bikini is doing a dance to the accompaniment of strobe lights and disco. She twists and turns, gyrates and thrusts, opens and closes her legs. Her featured partner is a long, silver pole that protrudes upright from the floor. As the male customers watch the show, I watch them. They crane their necks to get a better view of the dancer. All of the seats are filled and it's standing room only. "Imagine coming home to that," *gushes a 40-something white man in a dark business suit and red tie to one of his colleagues. The performance concludes with the dancer making her way into the audience and sidling up to individual customers who caress the surface of her body and push $20 bills under her garter.*

Many of the customers are extremely young: under 25, perhaps under 20, white, baseball-capped, and sporting casual attire. These contingents have clearly come in groups. The 30- and 40-something, suited, white businessmen seem to comprise another category, and also cluster together in groups of three or four. Then there are the loners— again, typically under 50 years of age, predominantly white, with a sprinkling of Blacks and Latinos. All are able-bodied, of average looks and builds. By mere appearances, they certainly belie the stereotype that the sex industry is geared toward older men who can't find partners.

In a room called "Amsterdam Live," a central stage is encircled by a sunken ring of little cubicles, each partitioned off from the performance area by fine, black mesh curtains. This design allows the heads and bodies of the customers to protrude through to the stage, and for the women to protrude back through to the booths in the other direction. A surrounding wall of mirrors above the cubicles means that each customer can see every other customer, as well as the performers. Two young, beautiful women come out, both with gleaming, waist-length hair and very high heels, naked but for black and white midriff corsets that leave their breasts and genitals exposed. They perform a highly choreographed and stylized sex act together, kissing and licking. Then, despite an earlier staff person's admonishment that body parts must remain within the booths, the women come over to each booth to ask if anyone would like a "show." Both of them soon descend into the dark cubicles where they are grasped by eager hands, momentarily disappearing from our line of vision.

[Fieldnotes, San Francisco Bay Area, May 1999]

Feminists and other scholars have debated theoretically what is "really" purchased in the prostitution transaction: Is it a relationship of domination? Is it love, an addiction, pleasure? Can sex be a service like any other? But they have scarcely tackled this question empirically. This chapter draws upon field observations of and interviews with male clients of sex-workers and state agents entrusted with regulating them in order to probe the meanings ascribed by different types of consumers to commercial sexual exchange and to situate such exchanges within the broader context of postindustrial transformations of culture and sexuality.[3]

I begin with the two paradoxical ethnographic images above. The first describes the new and growing phenomenon of the arrest of heterosexual clients of female street prostitutes, an unprecedented strategy of direct state intervention in the expression of male sexual desire. In the late 1990s, for the first time ever, U.S. cities such as San Francisco and New York began to boast arrest rates of male customers that approached those of female prostitutes, reversing a historical pattern that feminists have long criticized (Pheterson 1993; Lefler 1999).[4] The second takes us to a local sex club where sex acts are—legally, and to some extent, culturally—consumed as relatively unproblematic instances of sexual entitlement and male bonding.

In Western Europe and the U.S., recent state efforts to problematize heterosexual male desire—rising client arrests and re-education via diversion programs such as "John School," vehicle impoundment, stricter domestic and international laws on the patronage of underage prostitutes and the possession of child pornography—have occurred in the face of an increasingly unbridled ethic of sexual consumption. During the last 30 years, demand for commercially available sexual services has not only soared, but become ever more specialized, diversifying along technological, spatial, and social lines. The scope of sexual commerce has thus grown to encompass live sex shows; all variety of pornographic texts, videos, and images, both in print and online; fetish clubs; sexual emporiums featuring lap-dancing and wall-dancing; escort agencies; telephone and cyber-sex contacts; drive-through striptease venues; and organized sex tours of developing countries (Kempadoo and Doezema 1998; Weitzer 2000a; Lopez 2000). Sexual commerce has become a multifaceted, multi-billion-dollar industry, produced by and itself driving developments in other sectors of the global economy, such as hotel chains, long-distance telephone carriers, cable companies, and information technology.[5] Just as the availability of hardcore pornographic films on videocassettes led directly to the introduction of the home VCR, pornography on CD-ROM and over the Internet has been responsible for the acceptance and popularization of these new technologies (Schlosser 1997; Lane 2000). According to Internet research firms, a full one-third of the people who surf the Internet visit a pornography site (typically during workday hours) and, as late as 1997, almost all paid content sites on the Web were pornographic (Learmonth 1999; Prial 1999; "Sex, News, and Statistics" 2000).

These contradictory social developments reveal a tension between sex-as-recreation and the normative push for a return to sex as romance, a cultural counterpart of which can be found in the simultaneous emergence of Viagra and 12-step languages of masculine sexual addiction. "Sex" as cultural imperative and technical quest, now freed from the bounds of emotionality and romance, and the casting of nonrelationally bound erotic behavior as a pathological "addiction" are products of the same place and time. My goal in this chapter is to unravel this paradox.

Some have attributed recent attempts to reform male sexuality to the gains of second-wave feminism, and even described a shift in social stigma from the seller to the buyer of sexual services (Kaye 1999). Yet the influence of larger, structural factors has been neglected in most discussions. In fact, state interventions in (a typically lower-class tier of) male heterosexual practices, and the regendering of sexual stigma in certain middle class factions can both be linked to some of the broader transformations that produced the burgeoning demand for sexual services in the first place. In the industrializing nineteenth and early twentieth centuries, the "wrong" in prostitution was seen to reside in the female prostitute herself,[6] and in the classical writings of social science, prostitution as a social institution was portrayed as the supreme metaphor for the exploitation inherent in wage labor (Marx [1844] 1978; Engels [1884] 1978; Simmel [1907] 1971). In the late twentieth century, however, with the shift from a production-based to a consumption-based economy, the focus of moral critique and political reform is gradually being displaced: The prostitute is normalized as either "victim" or "sex-worker,"[7] while attention and sanction is directed away from labor practices and toward consumer behavior.

In what follows, I first sketch a brief genealogy of the academic and political discourses surrounding male sexual desire and consumer demand that have developed over the past century. I next take the reader to a variety of settings in which commercial sexual consumption takes place and to the smaller subset of arenas in which the state forcefully intervenes to redirect or contain it, in order to explore the meanings and motivations that contemporary clients ascribe to their own activities. In the final section, I contrast these framings with recent attempts by state agencies to reshape demand in the wake of a booming and diversifying sexual marketplace. My discussion throughout is based upon 15 in-depth interviews with male sexual consumers, 40 in-depth interviews with male and female sex-workers, a review of local sex newspapers and other print and electronic media, and ethnographic fieldwork in sexual markets carried out in six northern California and Western European cities over the course of five years.

EXPLAINING COMMERCIAL SEXUAL DEMAND

Like social policy, the scholarly literature on prostitution has typically grasped the varied phenomena of sexual commerce through a narrow focus on the etiology, treatment, and social symbolism of the female prostitute. Although the purity crusaders in the late nineteenth-century United States sought to problematize male sexuality, their campaign to replace the prevailing double standard with a single female standard that would be encoded into state policy met with little success (Luker 1998). After the Progressive Era, far less social or scholarly attention was paid to prostitution as functionalism and psychoanalysis reinscribed the double standard and rendered prostitution not only unproblematic for the male clientele, but structurally integral to the institution of marriage (Davis 1937; Greenwald 1958). In the 1970s and 1980s, both the sociology of deviance and feminist theory saw the prostitute (but not the client) as a symbolically laden precipitate of larger social currents. Although some second-wave feminists critiqued the lack of attention to male clients (McIntosh 1978; Hobson 1990; Høigård and Finstad 1986), as well as the sexual double standard that underpinned it, it is only during the last decade that a body of empirical literature has emerged with a sustained focus on male sexual clients.

In the past 15 years, a small but growing number of qualitative studies of client behavior have been undertaken by a new generation of feminist social researchers.[8] Meanwhile, building on Kinsey's influential—if methodologically flawed—work (1948), as well as heeding feminist calls to render male sexual clients visible, quantitative researchers have begun to correlate men's proclivity to visit prostitutes with other sociodemographic patterns. Analyzing data from the 1993 University of Chicago National Health and Social Life Survey, researchers Elliot Sullivan and William Simon found factors such as age cohort, military experience, education, and racial and ethnic background to be statistically significant predictors of commercial sexual purchase (Sullivan and Simon 1998). Commercial sexual proclivity has been shown to vary systematically with a variety of attitudinal dispositions, including "socio-emotional problems," as measured by reported feelings of emotional and physical dissatisfaction, feeling unwanted and sexually unsatisfied, and, most interestingly, by "not hav[ing] sex as an expression of love" (Sullivan and Simon 1998, 152). It has also been correlated with a "commodified" view of sexuality, as measured by number of sexual partners, use of pornography, and the belief that one needs to have sex immediately when aroused (Monto 2000).

Finally, client behavior has increasingly been featured as a key component of broader qualitative studies on commercial sexual exchange (Høigärd and Finstad 1986; McKeganey and Barnard 1996; Flowers 1998; O'Connell Davidson 1998). Drawing upon field data and interviews, these scholars have generated typologies of clients and consumer motivations. Whereas research on female prostitutes has been driven by questions of etiology (how did she get that way, why would a woman do that?), this research highlights differences between men, but typically takes their status as purchasers for granted. The primary motivations identified by these authors include clients' desire for sexual variation, sexual access to partners with preferred ages, racialized features and physiques, the appeal of an emotion-free and clandestine sexual encounter, loneliness, marital problems, the quest for power and control, the desire to be dominated or to engage in exotic sex acts, and the thrill of violating taboos. While provocative and insightful, this literature has often failed to explain client motives with any degree of historical specificity, or to link these motives to social and economic institutions that might themselves structure the relations of gender domination implied by many of the explanatory categories mentioned previously. In general, typologies are presented as if based on distinct attributes of a transhistorical and unwavering masculinity. Two exceptions to this tendency are recent works on client behavior by anthropologist Anne Allison (1994) and sociologist Monica Prasad (1999).

In *Nightwork*, an ethnography of a Tokyo hostess club where beautiful young women serve businessmen drinks and light their cigarettes, keep the banter flirtatious, and make their bodies available for groping, all at corporate expense, Allison draws on Frankfurt-school theory to argue that "the convergence of play and work and player and worker, supposed and presupposed by the institution of company-paid entertainment, is a feature of any society progressing through the late stages of capitalism" (1994, 23). According to Allison, the nightly participation of Japanese businessmen *in the mizu shobai*, or erotic nightlife, as well as their emotional distance from their wives and families, epitomizes this historical trend. Meanwhile, in "The Morality of Market Exchange," an article based on phone interviews with male sexual customers that engages the classic distinction articulated by Karl Polanyi and Marshall Sahlins between market and premarket societies, Prasad argues that the prostitution exchange contains within itself a form of morality specific to mass-market societies. Her interviews reveal that [c]ustomers conduct the prostitution exchange in ways that are not very different from how most market exchanges are conducted today: information about prostitution is not restricted to an elite but is widely available; social settings frame the interpretation of this information; the criminalization of prostitution does not particularly hinder the exchange; and whether the exchange continues is often dictated by how well the business was conducted. In short, according to these respondents, in late-capitalist America, sex is exchanged almost like any other commodity. (1999, 188) Noting that her interviewees "praise 'market exchange' of sex for lacking the ambiguity, status-dependence, and potential hypocrisy that they see in the 'gift exchange' of sex characteristic of romantic relationships," Prasad goes on to conclude that, in the "fervently free-market 1980s and 1990s, romantic love might sometimes be subordinated to, and judged unfavorably with, the more neutral, more cleanly exchangeable pleasures of eroticism" (1999, 181, 206).

Unlike many treatments of sexual clients, the contributions of Allison and Prasad situate sexual consumption within the context of an expanded and normalized field of commercial sexual practices. Their analyses begin to reveal a shift from a relational to a *recreational* model of sexual behavior, a reconfiguration of erotic life in which the pursuit of sexual intimacy is not hindered but facilitated by its location in the marketplace.[9]

THE SUBJECTIVE CONTOURS OF MARKET INTIMACY

I'm by myself a lot, used to it, but sometimes I crave physical contact. I'd rather get it from someone I don't know because someone I do will want more. You get lonely. There's this girl right now I'm seeing. I like the attention. But that's it, in a nutshell. I find [prostitution] exciting, kind of fun. It's amazing that it's there. More people would participate if it weren't illegal. A lot of frustration in both sexes could be eliminated.

Don, *47,* house painter

I feel guilty every time I cheat on my wife. I'm not a psychopath. I try to hide it as much as possible. I had a nonprofessional affair once. It was nice, and intimate, and I didn't have to pay! But I felt more guilty about that, messing with someone else's life, even though she knew I was married. You don't ever have to worry about that when you pay for it. I'm conservative by nature, but I believe in freedom of choice. If a woman wants to do it, more power to her! She's providing a service. I'm not exploiting her. Exploitation would be finding some hot 25-year-old who doesn't know any better and taking her to lunches, then to bed.

Steve, 35, insurance manager

My wife has never understood my desire to do this. I have no problem with my wife. We have a good sexual relationship. There's a Vietnamese restaurant on 6th and Market that I love, but I don't want to eat there every day. …

Rick, 61, data processor

I started seeing escorts during a time when I didn't have many venues to meet women. I felt isolated. My friends had moved away, and I was lacking motivation. It's more real and human than jacking off alone. My first preference was to pick up women for casual sex. Since that wasn't happening, I got into the habit. It was so easy.

Dan, 36, research analyst

Amid the disparate themes that animate the accounts clients gave me of their motivations for purchasing sexual services runs one counterintuitive thread. As Monica Prasad and Anne Allison found, for increasing numbers of men, erotic expression and the ethos of the marketplace are by no means antithetical. Indeed, contemporary client narratives of sexual consumption challenge the key cultural opposition between public and private that has anchored modern industrial capitalism.

Theorists of gender have sometimes regarded the recent growth of the commercial sex industry as a reactionary reassertion of male dominance in response to the gains of second-wave feminism (O'Connell Davidson 1998) or as compensation for men's economic disempowerment in the postindustrial public sphere (Kimmel 2000). In such scenarios, the role of commercial sex is to provide the male client with a fantasy world of sexual subservience and consumer abundance that corrects for the real power deficits he experiences in his daily life. While not disputing such accounts, I would like to suggest that men's quest for market-mediated sexual intimacy is guided by an additional set of historical transformations.

Compensatory arguments of the sort put forth by O'Connell Davidson, Kimmel, and others rest upon the implicit premise that commercial sex caters to needs that would more preferably and fulfillingly be satisfied within an intimate relationship in the private sphere of the home. Yet for many sexual clients, the market is experienced as enhancing and facilitating desired forms of nondomestic sexual activity. This is true whether what the client desires is a genuine but emotionally bounded intimate encounter, the experience of being pampered and "serviced," participation in a wide variety of brief sexual liaisons, or an erotic interlude that is "more real and human" than would be satisfying oneself alone. The platitudinous view that sexuality has been "commodified"—and by implication, diminished—like everything else in late capitalism (e.g., Lasch 1979) does not do justice to the myriad ways in which the spheres of public and private, intimacy and commerce, have interpenetrated one another and thereby been mutually transformed, making the postindustrial consumer marketplace a prime arena for securing varieties of interpersonal connection that circumvent this duality.

For many clients, one of the chief virtues of commercial sexual exchange is the clear and bounded nature of the encounter. In prior historical epochs, this bounded quality may have provided men with an unproblematic and readily available sexual outlet to supplement the existence of a pure and asexual wife in the domestic sphere. What is unique to contemporary client narratives is the explicitly stated preference for this type of bounded intimate engagement over other relational forms. Paid sex is neither a sad substitute for something that one would ideally choose to obtain in a noncommodified romantic relationship, nor the inevitable outcome of a traditionalist Madonna/whore double standard. Don, a 47-year-old, never-married man from Santa Rosa, California, described the virtues of the paid sexual encounter this way:

> I really like women a lot, but they're always trying to force a relationship on me. I'm a nice guy, and I feel this crushing thing happen. Right now, I know a woman; she's pretty, nice, but if I make love to her, she'll want a relationship. But I'm really used to living by myself. I go and come when I want, clean when I want. I love women, enjoy them; they feel comfortable around me. I've always had a lot of women friends. I flirt and talk to them, but I don't usually take the next step, because it leads to trouble!

Much is lost if we try to subsume Don's statements under pop-psychologizing diagnoses such as "fear of intimacy," or even a more covertly moralistic social-psychological descriptor like "techniques of neutralization" (Sykes and Matza 1957). In Don's preference for a life constructed around living alone, intimacy through close friendships, and paid-for, safely contained sexual encounters, we also see evidence of a disembedding of the (male) individual from the sex-romance nexus of the privatized nuclear family. This is a concrete example of the profound reorganization of personal life that diverse social analysts (Swidler 1980; Giddens 1992; Hochschild 1997) have noticed occurring during the last 30 or so years.[10] Demographic transformations such as a decline in marriage rates, a doubling in the divorce rate, and a 60 percent increase in the number of single-person households during this period have spawned a new set of erotic dispositions, ones which the market is well poised to satisfy.[11]

An additional advantage of market-mediated sexual encounters was articulated by Steve, a married, 35-year-old insurance manager from a middle-class California suburb. Frustrated that sexual relations with his wife had been relatively infrequent since the birth of their child, Steve had decided to look for sex elsewhere. Although elements of Steve's story invoke the sexual double standard of eras past, his reasoning during our interview betrayed a decidedly new twist. For Steve, the market-mediated sexual encounter is morally and emotionally preferable to the "nonprofessional affair" because of the clarifying effect of payment. Though he characterized himself as "conservative by nature," Steve had incorporated a fair amount of sex-worker rights rhetoric into his own discourse, describing the professional choice of his paid service providers with tangible awe. Having grappled with feminist critiques of male sexual indulgence as exploitative, he concluded that true exploitation resided in the emotional dishonesty of the premarket paradigm of seduction, rather than in the clean cash-for-sex market transactions that he participated in.

Other clients were insistent that their patronage of the commercial sexual economy did not in any way result from problems or deficits in their primary sexual relationships. Rick, a 61-year-old data processor from San Francisco, emphasized that his sexual relationship with his wife was just fine, and likened his desire to pay different women for sex to other, less socially problematic consumer experiences: "There's a Vietnamese restaurant … that I love, but I don't want to eat there every day." Rick's statement may be read as a variant of the classic argument that prostitution is an expression of the male "natural appetite"—a perspective which, like Steve's, is of course premised upon a notion of the sexual double standard. As Carole Pateman (1988, 198) points out, in such arguments, "the comparison is invariably made between prostitution and the provision of food." Significantly, however, Rick's explicit justification for patronizing prostitutes is less one of essential, biological drives than it is one of simple consumer choice. Rick's stated preference for variety presumes an underlying model of sexuality in which sexual expression bears no necessary connection to intimate relationship, and in which a diversity of sexual partners and experiences is not merely substitutive but desirable in its own right.

In the same vein, Stephen, a 55-year-old writer from San Francisco, described an exciting and sexually adventurous life at home with his female domestic partner of eight years. He chose to supplement this with once-a-month, paid sexual encounters involving female exotic dancers and transgender prostitutes that were "fun" and "intriguing." "Sometimes it's a really nice contact, how they touch me, how they move, but it's not for something I can't get at home," he explained. Stephen went on to elaborate upon some of his motivations for patronizing prostitutes:

> When I grew up, I was younger and shorter than everyone else, convinced I wasn't sexually desirable to anyone. I was two years ahead in school, a total nerd. The notion that these glamorous women want to persuade me to have sex with them is incredible. I understand that it's not because of my looks. I could never get this many women who are this gorgeous to be sexual with me if I didn't pay.

Interviewees like Stephen and Rick challenge the second-wave feminist presupposition that prostitution exists chiefly to satisfy sexual demands that nonprofessional women find unpleasant or feel inhibited to participate in (Rosen 1982, 97). If commercial sex is compensation for anything, it is not for something lacking in men's primary domestic relationships. Rather, it is for the access to multiple attractive partners that, in the wake of the historical shift from the family-based good provider role to the unfettered, consumeristic Playboy philosophy many male sexual clients feel they are entitled to (Ehrenreich 1983). Within the terms of this new cultural logic of male dominance, clients conjure the sexual marketplace as the great social equalizer, where consumer capitalism democratizes access to goods and services that in an earlier era would have been the exclusive province of a restricted elite.[12]

Here is another man's account of his commercial sexual activity, this time from an Internet chat room for patrons of strip clubs:

> I finally got to spend some quality time in the city by the Bay, compliments of my employer, who decided that I needed to attend a conference there last week. So, armed with a vast array of knowledge regarding the local spots, I embarked on a week of fun and frolicking. Unfortunately, I ended up spending too much time with conference-goers so I only made three trips to clubs. I had an absolutely incredible time at both places. …
>
> At the first club, I adjourned to the Patpong Room with Jenny, who asked me what I was interested in. I said that a couple of nude lap dances were on the agenda and I inquired as to her price: $60 each. Okay, no problem. I forked over the cash. After the two long dances she offered me a blowjob for another $120. I said that that would be heavenly and handed her the money. … It was an absolutely fabulous experience. I spent $30 on cover charges, $10 on tips, $240 with Jenny, and $300 with another girl named Tanya for a total of $580. Not bad for just over two hours of illicit fun. I'm used to paying that for decent outcall so this was a nice change of pace.[13]

Like Rick and Stephen, this man is unselfconscious about depicting his experience as a form of light and unproblematic commercial consumption ("two hours of illicit fun," "a nice change of pace"). For this client, prostitution is primarily a pampering diversion financed by and casually sandwiched in between a week's worth of requisite, and presumably less pleasurable, professional activities.

Yet the paid sexual encounter may also represent to clients something more than just an ephemeral consumer indulgence. In their 1982 article, "The Phenomenology of Being a John," Holzman and Pines (1982) argued that it was the fantasy of a mutually desired, special, or even romantic sexual encounter that clients were purchasing in the prostitution transaction—something notably distinct both from a purely mechanical sex act and from an unbounded, private-sphere romantic entanglement. They observed that the clients in their study emphasized the warmth and friendliness of the sexworker as characteristics that were at least as important to them as the particulars of physical appearance. The clients I interviewed were also likely to express variants of the statement that "If her treatment is cold or perfunctory, then I'm not interested." In Web-based client guides to commercial sexual services such as "The World Sex Guide," reviewers are similarly critical of sex-workers who are "clock watchers," "too rushed and pushy," who "don't want to hug and kiss," or who "ask for a tip mid-sex-act."

Although patrons of different market sectors expressed variants of these sentiments, those who frequented indoor venues enjoyed the benefit of an arrangement that was structured to more effectively provide them with the semblance of genuine erotic connection. For example, interactions with escorts as opposed to streetwalkers are typically more sustained (averaging an hour as opposed to 15 minutes), more likely to occur in comfortable settings (an apartment or hotel room, rather than a car), and more likely to include conversation as well as a diversity of sexual activities (vaginal intercourse, bodily caresses, genital touching, and cunnilingus, rather than simply fellatio) (E. Bernstein 1999; Lever and Dolnick 2000). The fact that street prostitution now constitutes a marginal and declining sector of the sex trade means a transaction that has been associated with quick, impersonal sexual release is increasingly being superseded by one which is configured to encourage the fantasy of sensuous reciprocity, a fantasy safely contained by the bestowal of payment.

In recent years, one of the most sought after features in the prostitution encounter has become the "Girlfriend Experience," or GFE. In contrast to commercial transactions premised upon the straightforward exchange of money for orgasm, clients describe the GFE as proceeding "much more like a nonpaid encounter between two lovers," with the possibility of unhurried foreplay, reciprocal cuddling, and passionate kisses. As with other forms of service work, successful commercial sexual transactions are ones in which the market basis of the exchange serves a crucial delimiting function (Hochschild 1983; Leidner 1993) that can also be temporarily subordinated to the client's fantasy of authentic interpersonal connection, as the following client's description of an encounter in a commercial sex club illustrates:

> At the club, I had a memorable experience with a light-skinned black girl named Luscious ... we adjourned to the backstage area for one full-service session during the course of my visits. This time I brought my condoms. We began with the usual touchy-feely. ... I could feel she was just soaking, an indication her moans were not faked. Several minutes later I shot my load and used the conveniently located Kleenex dispenser to wash up. The most unusual aspect of this encounter is that Luscious didn't ask for money up front, which is a first for a place of this type. I tipped her $60.

Even when the encounter lasts only minutes, from the client's perspective it may represent a meaningful and authentic form of interpersonal exchange. Clients are indeed seeking a real and reciprocal erotic connection, but a precisely limited one. For these men, what is (at least ideally) being purchased is a sexual connection that is premised upon *bounded authenticity*. As with the previous client's invocation of the physical tangibility of Luscious's desire, other clients boasted of their ability to give sex-workers genuine sexual pleasure, insisted that the sex-workers they patronized liked them enough to offer them freebies or to invite them home for dinner, and proudly proclaimed they had at times even dated or befriended the sex-workers they were seeing.

The repeated claims about authentic interpersonal connection are particularly striking to consider in light of the fact that the vast majority of sex-workers I spoke with imposed very rigid emotional boundaries between their customers and their nonprofessional lovers. For sex-workers, the former almost always constituted a thoroughly de-eroticized category of identity that was rarely if ever transgressed. One of the few sex-workers I spoke with who admitted to occasionally looking for lovers among her client pool said that she had given up the practice of offering her preferred clients bargain rates or unpaid sexual arrangements because it inevitably met with dire results:

> They pretend to be flattered, but they never come back! If you offer them anything but sex for money they flee. There was one client I had who was so sexy, a tai chi practitioner, and really fun to fuck. Since good sex is a rare thing, I told him I'd see him for $20 (my normal rate is $250). Another guy, he was so sexy, I told him "come for free." Both of them freaked out and never returned. The men want an emotional connection, but they don't want any obligations. They don't believe they can have no-strings-attached sex, which is why they pay. They'd rather pay than get it for free.

Christopher, a male sex-worker who had also once tried to redefine his relationship with a client, recounted similarly: "I called a trick once because I wanted to have sex with him again … we agreed in advance that it was just going to be sex for sex's sake, not for pay, and that was the last time I ever heard from him!" Critics of commercialized sex may misconstrue clients' desire for bounded authenticity if their implicit point of reference is the modernist paradigm of romantic love, premised upon monogamous domesticity and intertwined life trajectories. Thus, Carole Pateman (1988, 199) asks why, if not for the sake of pure domination, would "15 to 25 percent of the customers of the Birmingham prostitutes demand what is known in the trade as 'hand relief,'" something which could presumably be self-administered. Yet, as one client insisted, after explaining to me that he studied and worked all the time, and consequently didn't have much opportunity to even meet women, let alone to pursue a romantic relationship, "it's more real and human than jacking off alone." This client reveals an underlying sexual paradigm that is not relational but recreational, compatible with the rhythms of his individually oriented daily life, and increasingly, with those of other men with similar white, middle-class sociodemographic profiles.

It's 9 A.M. on a Saturday morning. In one of the only occupied rooms of the San Francisco Hall of Justice, I am seated in the back row of "John School," the city's pretrial diversion program for men who have been arrested for soliciting prostitutes. The city is proud of its program and boasts a low recidivism rate of less than one percent for first-time arrestees, who, for a mere $500, can have their records cleared. There are approximately 50 to 60 men in the room this morning, of diverse class and ethnic backgrounds (three of the men around me are accompanied by translators: one Spanish, one Arabic, one Cantonese). More striking still is that there are nearly equal numbers of arrested Johns and media people in the room. By the end of the first hour, I have been introduced to journalists from TV-20, the London Times, *and* Self *Magazine. "There are representatives from different media organizations here each month," announces Evelyn, the program's feisty director, to the men. "I never do this class without media coverage." In stark contrast to the Johns, the media people are predominantly 30-something, stylish, educated women, acutely and evidently fascinated by the spectacle of so many sheepish and docile men before them, and by the feminist fantasy of having the gender tables turned (now these men are quiet and still, and, at least until 5 P.M. this evening, they will be forced to remain that way and listen). Although I am perhaps more conscious than they that it is as much class advantage as feminist victory that permits this witnessing, I notice too the superficial similarity between these women and me.*

Table 1-1.		*The Sexual Addiction Screening Test, distributed at the San Francisco First Offender Program*	
– yes	– no	1. Were you sexually abused as a child or adolescent?	
– yes	– no	2. Have you subscribed or regularly purchased sexually explicit magazines, such as *Playboy* or *Penthouse!*	
– yes	– no	3. Did your parents have trouble with sexual behavior?	
– yes	– no	4. Do you often find yourself preoccupied with sexual thoughts?	
– yes	– no	5. Do you feel that your sexual behavior is not normal?	
– yes	– no	6. Does your spouse [or significant other(s)] ever worry or complain about your sexual behavior?	
– yes	– no	7. Do you have trouble stopping your sexual behavior when you know it is inappropriate?	

– yes	– no	8. Do you ever feel bad about your sexual behavior?	
– yes	– no	9. Has your sexual behavior ever created problems for your family?	
– yes	– no	10. Have you ever sought help for sexual behavior you did not like?	
– yes	– no	11. Have you ever worried about people finding out about your sexual activities?	
– yes	– no	12. Has anyone been hurt emotionally because of your sexual behavior?	
– yes	– no	13. Are any of your sexual activities against the law?	
Table 1-2.		*The Sexual Addiction Screening Test, distributed at the San Francisco First Offender Program* (**Continued**)	
– yes	– no	14. Have you made promises to yourself to quit some aspect of your sexual behavior?	
– yes	– no	15. Have you made efforts to quit a type of sexual activity and failed?	
– yes	– no	16. Do you have to hide some of your sexual behavior from others?	
– yes	– no	17. Have you attempted to stop some parts of your sexual activity?	
– yes	– no	18. Have you ever felt degraded by your sexual behavior?	
– yes	– no	19. Has sex been a way for you to escape your problems?	
– yes	– no	20. When you have sex, do you feel depressed afterwards?	
– yes	– no	21. Have you felt the need to discontinue a certain form of sexual activity?	
– yes	– no	22. Has your sexual activity interfered with your family life?	
– yes	– no	23. Have you been sexual with minors?	
– yes	– no	24. Do you feel controlled by your sexual desire?	
– yes	– no	25. Do you ever think your sexual desire is stronger than you are?	

Yet according to the Johns I chat with during the coffee breaks, very few are passively absorbing the information presented to them, and they are far from being persuaded of the error of their ways. The men say that John School is even worse than Traffic School—an all-day ordeal in a stuffy room with a whole procession of equally stuffy speakers. "This is bullshit." "I was trapped." "These people are so hypocritical." "Prostitution should be legalized." "They act like it's something special, but all men do it … Men and women just think differently. Men will fuck sheep, boys, anything. They are dogs."

The first presentation is led by an assistant district attorney and is entitled "Prostitution Law and Street Facts." Although John School is officially available to all men arrested for soliciting a prostitute, the structure of the program demonstrates that those who do get arrested comprise only a small and special subgroup. This program is clearly geared for heterosexual men who shop the streets. During his presentation, the DA, trying to get the group to engage, asks, "How many of you were picked up in the Tenderloin? How many of you were picked up in the Mission?" (two of San Francisco's historically low-income and newly gentrifying neighborhoods where street prostitution is concentrated). He does not bother to ask how many were picked up at the local erotic theater, or with an escort, or while cruising for a sex-worker online, or even on Polk Street (where male and transgender street prostitutes work).

The DA's objective is to scare the men out of their established patterns of behavior by gruesomely cataloguing the potential legal repercussions of what they are doing—what it's like to get booked, to be herded into the paddywagon, to spend the night in jail, or to be forced to take an HIV test—all likely consequences of a second arrest. He shows the class a brief video reviewing the laws. I am at first confused by the last image in the sequence: the captionless depiction of a man hunched over a computer screen. The DA's final words to the men are even more remarkable: "Next time you're thinking of going out on the street, do like this guy: Go on the Internet if you have to—but stay away from minors!" The final presentation before the lunch break features a former street prostitute and ex-heroin addict who now runs a program to help prostitute women transform their lives and get off the streets. Seated beside her is a panel of three other former homeless and drug-addicted streetwalkers. Now clean and sober, well scrubbed, well fed, and conservatively attired, their appearances are not much different from other 30- to 40-year-old professional women. Only their scathing and effusively expressed anger betrays a difference.

For the men, this is no doubt the most riveting panel of the day. At last, their attention is focused, as they sit tense and upright in their chairs. From their facial expressions and inclining postures, some even seem to be vaguely aroused. The rhetorical tactic employed by the women is a combination of shock therapy and a firm reassertion of the primacy of marital domesticity. "Most of the women I have worked with started turning tricks as children or teens," says one woman in a harsh, accusatory voice. "I learned a long time ago that it's not pedophiles involved in that, but the men that sit here in this room." Through teary eyes and clenched teeth, another panelist tells the men her own story of early sexual abuse, addiction, and rape. Her tale, gripping and theatrical, ends with the following admonition:

Once, I remember being crusty and dope sick, wearing yellow shorts, and walking around with blood caked on my thighs for two days. No one asked me what was wrong. I felt like a fallen woman that God, society, and my family would never forgive. … We're not out there because we like to suck dick, and you're not out there because you like us. You're the cause of our suffering, and you can become statistics yourselves. Try and realize, if you have to go back out—these women were hurt! A lot of you men are husbands, fathers, and grandfathers. What did you tell your significant others today? Hopefully, someday soon you'll learn how to have healthy relationships— with your wives.

In the afternoon, there are three additional presentations: one featuring representatives from organized neighborhood and merchant groups, another with a sergeant from the vice squad on the dynamics of pimping, and the final presentation by a therapist on "Sexual Compulsivity and Intimacy Issues." The neighborhood groups are represented by two men and a woman, white residents and small shopkeepers from the Tenderloin district. Together with the Vice cop, they paint the Johns as aggressors against family, community, and—rather ironically—business.[14] The harms that the Johns are held responsible for are both symbolic and material. "Do you have sex in front of your children?" they ask. "Little boys in my neighborhood blow up condoms like balloons! You hear about victimless crimes, but our whole neighborhood is a victim! Fifteen-year-old girls turn tricks and 20 minutes later deliver babies. Millions of dollars pass through these girls, but at the end of the day they have nothing. All the way through this business, there are victims." The final session, led by a licensed marriage and family counselor, relies upon a 12-step sexual addiction model of client behavior. The counselor is a white, middle-class, casually dressed man in his late thirties, an exemplar of northern California therapeutic culture and soft-spoken masculinity. He begins his presentation with a definition: "Sex addicts have trouble thinking of sex and love together, in the same relationship. They say, 'I love my wife, but I have sex with a prostitute.' The challenge is to do them together, to learn how to nurture relationships. This is not just a woman's job. "After distributing a "Sexual Addiction Screening Test" (see Table 1-1) to the members of the class (with questions such as "Do you often find yourself preoccupied with sexual thoughts?" and "Has your sexual activity interfered with your family life?"), the therapist tries to enlist them in a discussion about why men visit prostitutes. "Stress," volunteers one man. "Curiosity," says another. "Anger? Loneliness?" offers the therapist, and some of the men agree.

Finally, one John rouses himself out of boredom to protest. "Come on already! It should just be legalized! Guys need a place to get relief." The police officer who is seated to my left leans over to me and whispers in my ear: "I agree. Anyway, I bet most of these men will now just go indoors, where they don't have to worry about any of this."

[Fieldnotes, San Francisco, May 1999]

Feminists have bemoaned, but also taken for granted, the sexual double standard in the treatment of prostitution by the criminal justice system. As recently as 1993, the scholar and prostitutes' rights activist Gail Pheterson (1993, 44) could righteously argue that [o]f course, the customer is also party to prostitution transactions and in countries where sex commerce is illegal; he is equally guilty of a crime. But such laws are not equally applied to customer and prostitute. ... Nowhere is equal punishment enforced, however, partly because law officials are either customers themselves or they identify with customers. Prostitutes have numerous stories of the sexual demands of police, lawyers, judges, and other male authorities.

Pheterson and other critics would never have predicted that, by the mid-1990s, municipal and national governments might actually intervene to challenge and reconfigure patterns of male heterosexual consumption, and even mobilize feminist arguments in the service of such interventions. Nor did they foresee that, despite a shared gender and sexual identification with customers, male authorities would be beholden to other social forces and political interests that might lead them to curtail the prerogatives of heterosexual desire. And they did not anticipate how programs such as "John School" and the expanding and diversifying market in commercial sexual services might represent what only seem to be paradoxical facets of interconnected social trends.

During the last five years, John Schools, First Offender Programs, and Client Re-education Projects have sprung up in American cities as diverse as San Francisco and Fresno (California), Portland (Oregon), Las Vegas (Nevada), Buffalo (New York), Kansas City (Kansas), and Nashville (Tennessee), as well as in Toronto and Edmonton (Canada), and Leeds (United Kingdom). Numerous other cities throughout the U.S. and Western Europe are currently considering implementing similar programs.[15] After decriminalizing prostitution in the late 1960s, in 1998 Sweden became the first national government to unilaterally criminalize the purchase of sexual services by male customers (E. Bernstein 2001). In the U.S., although sporadic and fleeting gestures toward the arrest of male clients date back to the 1970s, contemporary client re-education programs must be seen as part of a new strategy of state intervention in male sexual behavior.

In both Oklahoma City and Kansas City, for example, city officials have begun to broadcast the photos and names of male clients arrested by police for prostitution-related offenses on cable television (Hamilton 1999; Weitzer 2000b). In Huntington Woods, Michigan, the police have released the names of 16,000 alleged prostitution customers on CD-ROM ("Names" 1999; "Suburban Detroit" 1999). Police in various municipalities have also arranged for the names of arrested clients to be published in local newspapers, including *The Hartford Courant* in Connecticut, *The Brockton Enterprise* in Massachusetts, and *The Kentucky Post* in Kentucky (Lewis 1999). Perhaps the most provocative (though not state-run) recent example of John "outing" is "Webjohn," an online database organized by concerned community members, featuring Johns caught on video picking up or communicating with a known prostitute. The site's mission statement notably posits Johns, not prostitutes, as vectors of disease, and declares two official aims: "to deny Johns their anonymity" and "to offer any residential or business communities in North America a cost-free and law suit-free mechanism to suppress street-level prostitution in their area." Taken together with a revision of legal codes to facilitate client arrests and to stiffen criminal penalties, "public outings" in the mass media, vehicle impoundment, and revocation of driver's licenses, as well as stricter prohibitions against the patronage of child prostitutes and the possession of child pornography, the new spate of social policies that seek to regulate male heterosexual behavior is historically unprecedented (Lefler 1999; Weitzer 2000b).

Allison, Prasad, and other sociologists such as Castells (1996) and Kempadoo and Doezema (1998) have rightly pointed to the burgeoning demand for commercial sexual services as paradigmatic of various key features of late capitalism: the merging of public and private, the extension in depth and breadth of the service sector, the individualization of sex, the preference for the neatly bounded commodity over the messy diffuseness of nonmarket exchange. Missing from these accounts is a recognition that commercial sexual consumption is simultaneously being *normalized* and *problematized,* and that these two phenomena are linked. Underlying the lack of attention to the recent criminalization of consumer behavior is the neglect of some other key features of late capitalist society: the relationship between postindustrial poverty and gentrification, as well as the normative push on the part of some feminists to retain a modernist model of relationally bound sexual intimacy.

John schools are the outcome of an alliance between feminist anti-prostitution activists, organized groups of predominantly lower-middle-class community residents and small-scale merchants, and politicians and big businesses with interests in gentrifying neighborhoods such as San Francisco's Tenderloin and Mission districts—neighborhoods that are home to the city's principal streetwalking strolls and the most socially marginal sectors of the commercial sex trade, yet close to the business district and highly valuable real estate. Although the three groups indicated have disparate ideological and material agendas, they have joined forces to target the male patrons of prostitution's most publicly visible domain. In contrast to the moral wars of a century ago, contemporary campaigns against prostitution are chiefly concerned with cleaning up the gritty underbelly of an industry that is basically left alone so long as it remains behind closed doors, or, more preferably still, online (Weitzer 2000b). Attempts to eradicate the most "problematic" segments of the industry implicitly serve to legitimize the *unproblematic* parts that remain.

The district attorney's advice to the attendees of John School to get out of their cars and turn on their computers can in this way be rendered decipherable as an important step toward cleaner streets and gentrified neighborhoods. Thus, in 1994, when the San Francisco Board of Supervisors assembled a Task Force to investigate revisions to the city's prostitution policy, the primary and explicitly stated impetus was community and merchants' objections to disruptions on their streets (San Francisco Task Force on Prostitution 1994). In its *Final Report*, the Task Force noted that

> Despite their concerns about noise, traffic, etc., most residents [of the Tenderloin and Mission districts] supported decriminalization or legalization of prostitution. ... Residents' valid concerns about quality of life, yet support for decriminalization, was a conflict more apparent than real. The conflict could be resolved by focusing on the complaints: not against prostitution itself, but by the perceived fallout or side effects of street prostitution. (San Francisco Task Force on Prostitution 1996, 27, 29)

Although police representatives and municipal politicians continue to frame their street-focused enforcement strategy as being in accordance with the preponderance of citizens' complaints, the effect of their policies is clearly to divert sex-workers and customers into indoor and online commercial sex markets.

The new social policies targeting male sexual conduct and commercial consumption are not, however, completely absent of moral focus or content. The various strands of the ideological agenda behind programs such as John School, like the interest groups behind it, are multiple but interweaving. Many contemporary feminist activists, like their feminist forerunners, are keen upon challenging the male half of the sexual double standard. Given the emergence of the sexually consumeristic Playboy ideal in the 1960s (Ehrenreich 1983), the deregulation and normalization of pornography in the 1970s (Juffer 1998), and other predominantly male benefits of the sexual revolution, the reassertion of sexual domesticity and marital fidelity is experienced as particularly crucial. Responding to a similar constellation of concerns, lower-middle-class residents and small-scale merchants can be seen as participating in both a material and a symbolic "crusade" against the incursion of market forces into a longed-for protected sphere of family, neighborhood, and community.

CONCLUSION

The two historically unique and contradictory tendencies that I have documented here, namely burgeoning consumption and increasing state intervention, should be understood within a broad array of economic and cultural transformations that have unfolded over the last 30 years. The pursuit of *bounded authenticity* that is encapsulated in the demand for sexual commerce has been augmented by the shift from a relational to a recreational model of sexual intimacy, by the symbiotic relationship between the information economy and commercial sexual consumption, by the ways in which tourism and business travel facilitate the insertion of men into the commercial sexual marketplace, and, more generally, by the myriad mergings and inversions of public and private life that are characteristic of our era.

At the same time, the corresponding phenomena of postindustrial poverty and the gentrification of the inner city have led to an overlapping of ambitions between municipal politicians, developers, and feminist anti-prostitution activists who are jointly interested in "cleaning up" the male desires that contribute to the sullying of city streets. John Schools, as well as other measures that penalize a subgroup of the male clients of commercial sex-workers, have emerged out of the confluence of these disparate political agendas. The recent crackdowns on Johns and the normalization of other forms of commercial sex go hand in hand because state regulatory strategies around prostitution are deeply embedded in struggles over the allocation of urban space. Both the state policing of the street-level sex trade and the normalization of the sex business reveal a shared set of underlying economic and cultural interests: the excision of class and racial Others from gentrifying inner cities, the facilitation of the postindustrial service sector, and the creation of clean and shiny urban spaces in which middle-class men can safely indulge in recreational commercial sexual consumption.

DISCUSSION QUESTIONS

1. What were the main traditional obstacles to the sociological study of sex commerce? What has changed in the past 20 years to stimulate such research?
2. What do the authors mean by the term "bounded authenticity"?

3. Why, historically, have sex consumers (i.e. "Johns") been treated less harshly by the justice system than prostitutes themselves? How does this fit in with the authors' discussion about the "shift in social stigma" regarding the roles of the "buyer" and "seller"?

NOTES

1. I am grateful to Kerwin Kaye, Laurie Schaffner, Loi'c Wacquant, Kristin Luker, Paul Willis, Lucinda Ramberg, Will Rountree, Lawrence Cohen, and Myra Marx Feree for their support, comments, and suggestions. An earlier version of this piece appeared in *Ethnography* in September 2001. Reprinted by permission of Sage Publications.

2. All of the names and identifying details of individuals and specific commercial venues have been changed or omitted to protect their anonymity. Geographical locations, when included, have been left unmodified in order to respect the locational specificity of the events I describe.

3. My focus is on heterosexual male desire and consumption patterns—increasingly the primary, if not the exclusive, commercial sex market in which the state in tervenes. In touristic urban centers, heterosexual prostitution is estimated to comprise approximately two-thirds of the overall market, while paid encounters between men constitute approximately one-third (Leigh 1994). Although there is a growing literature on the emergence of women as consumers of pornographic images (Juffer 1998), and on the recent phenomenon of female sex tourism to the Caribbean (O'Connell Davidson and Sanchez Taylor, this volume), there is scant evidence that any significant number of female clients of prostitutes—either lesbian or heterosexual—exists domestically. I have thus not sought to include any female sexual clients in my sample. The lack of such a market reveals a great deal about the persistently gendered nature of commercial sexual consumption.

4. The first arrests of clients in the U.S. (which were intermittent and few in number) followed a 1975 ruling brought by the American Civil Liberties Union before a California State Court, which noted "the plain unvarnished fact ... that men and women engaged in proscribed sexual behavior are not treated equally" (MacDonald 1978). On the increase in client arrest rates in mid-1990s San Francisco, see Marinucci (1995a) (describing a 25% increase in client arrest rates) and Marinucci (1995b) (quoting SFPD statistics indicating a dramatic surge in prostitution-related arrests of male clients to 1,000 of 4,900 total). On the emergence of a similar phenomenon in New York City as part of Mayor Rudolph Giuliani's "Quality of Life" campaigns, see Pierre-Pierre (1994) and Nieves (1999).

5. As Eric Schlosser (1997, 141) has pointed out, "most of the profits being generated by porn today are being earned by business not traditionally associated with the sex

industry—by mom and pop video stores; by long-distance carriers like AT&T; by cable companies like Time Warner and Tele-Communications, Inc.; and by hotel chains like Marriott, Hyatt, and Holiday Inn that now reportedly earn millions of dollars each year supplying adult films to their guests."

6. Despite the fact that male prostitution was also prevalent in urban centers during this period, male prostitutes were typically subsumed under the new and more socially salient banner of "homosexuals" in scholarly, medical-psychological, and political discourses (Weeks, [1981] 1997).

7. It is ironic that prostitutes' rights movements have sought legitimacy under the banner of "sex-work" (Jenness 1993), considering that, for Marx and other early socialist critics, what was wrong with wage labor as work was precisely that it resembled prostitution (Marx [1844] 1978, 103).

8. The relevant studies include Mansson 1988, Prieur and Taksdahl 1993, Hart 1994, Allison 1994, Prasad 1999, and Frank 2002.

9. In the *Social Organization of Sexuality*, Laumann et al. use the terms *relational* and *recreational* to designate distinct normative orientations toward sexual be havior (1994). I use the terms both to distinguish between different normative models and to indicate successive, historically specific configurations of sexual and emotional life. Social historians have linked the relational model (also referred to as "amative" or "companionate") to the rise of modern romance and the nuclear family under capitalism, contrasting it with the prototypically *procreative* orientation of pre-industrial society (Fass 1977; D'Emilio 1983a; Luker 1984). Some social theorists have pointed to an emergent second shift in paradigms of sexuality, occurring roughly around the 1970s, in which sexuality derives its primary meanings from pleasure and sensation, and is no longer the exclusive province of marital or even durable relationships. This second shift to what I am calling a *recreational* paradigm of sexuality has been variously described as the "normalization" of sex (Castells 1996), "unbounded eros" (Seidman 1991), "the postmodern erotic revolution" (Bauman 1998), and the "fun ethic" (Bourdieu 1984). In contrasting recreational sexuality with relational sexuality, I seek to distinguish the former from the romantic residues and extrasexual associations that typically accompany the notion of a relationship, but I do not mean to suggest that it must lack a meaningful intersubjective component.

10. Giddens's *Transformation of Intimacy* (1992) employs a compensatory model of men's participation in commercial sex, while also describing more general reconfigurations in late capitalist paradigms of intimacy. Giddens introduces the term "plastic sexuality" to refer to a new paradigm of eroticism that is nonreproductive, in principle reciprocal and egalitarian, and subjectively experienced as a property of the self. Plastic sexuality is the erotic counterpart of the pure relationship, a relationship entered into for the sake of the intimacy it affords both partners. Unlike the model of recreational sex that I present here, Giddens's plastic sexuality is still essentially connected to a

notion of private sphere, durable romantic relationships. Giddens uses the term "episodic sexuality" to refer to what for him is a less significant, if more troubling, cultural offshoot. Episodic sexuality is gendered masculine, compulsive in nature, and aims to neutralize the anxieties that are stimulated by the threat of intimacy contained in the pure relationship and the relative emancipation of women. As such, episodic sexuality typically finds expression in practices of commodified sex such as the consumption of pornography.

11. By 1988, nearly a third of American households consisted of a single individual. In Western European countries, single-person households have been the most rapidly growing household type since the 1960s, with from 25 percent (in the United Kingdom) to 36 percent (in Sweden) of the population living alone. In the U.S., the percentage of unmarried adults rose from 28 percent to 37 percent between 1970 and 1988 (for a fuller account of recent changes in U.S. and Western European social demography, see U.S. Bureau of the Census 1989, 1992, 2000; Sorrentino 1990; and Kellogg and Mintz 1993).

12. Marx was the first to note the ironic leveling capacity of market transactions, though in lament rather than celebration: "That which is for me through the medium of *money*—that for which I can pay (i.e., which money can buy) that am I, the possessor of the money. The extent of the power of money is my power. Money's properties are my properties and essential powers—the properties and powers of its possessor. Thus, what I *am* and *am capable of is* by no means determined by my individuality. I am ugly, but I can buy for myself the most *beautiful* of women" (Marx [1844] 1978, 103).

13. Although prostitution (i.e., genital-oral or genital-genital contact in exchange for payment, which are criminal acts under California state law) has been well documented in San Francisco's legal sex clubs by the clients and sex-workers I interviewed, by clients in online chat rooms, and by the local press, the clubs officially deny that illegal activities take place on their premises (Brook 1998).

14. Ruth Rosen observed a similar split between the interests of large and small-scale business owners earlier in the century, when large-scale business interests (real estate agents, landlords, and owners of saloons and breweries) supported organized brothel prostitution, whereas small shopkeepers opposed it (Rosen 1982).

15. See, for example, Marinucci 1995a and b, Kilman and Smyth 1998, Symbaluk and Jones 1998, Lefler 1999, Monto 2000, Nieves 1999, and Weitzer 2000b.

REFERENCES

Allison, Anne. 1994. *Nightwork: Sexuality, Pleasure, and Corporate Masculinity in a Tokyo Hostess Club*. Chicago, IL: University of Chicago Press.

Allison, Anne. 1994. *Nightwork: Sexuality, Pleasure, and Corporate Masculinity in a Tokyo Hostess Club.* Chicago, IL: University of Chicago Press.

Bauman, Zygmunt. 1998. "On Postmodern Uses of Sex." *Theory, Culture, and Society* 15(3): 19–34.

Bernstein, Elizabeth. 1999. "What's Wrong with Prostitution? What's Right with Sex-Work? Comparing Markets in Female Sexual Labor." *Hastings Women's Law Journal* 10(1): 91–119.

Bernstein, Elizabeth. 2001. *Economies of Desire: Sexual Commerce and Post-Industrial Culture.* Ph.D. Dissertation, Department of Sociology, University of California, Berkeley, CA.

Bourdieu, Pierre. 1984. *Distinction: A Social Critique of the Judgment of Taste.* Cambridge, MA: Harvard University Press.

Castells, Manuel. 1996. "The Net and the Self: Working Notes for a Critical Theory of the Informational Society." *Critique of Anthropology* 16(1): 9–38.

D'Emilio, John. 1983a. "Capitalism and Gay Identity." In *Powers of Desire: The Politics of Sexuality,* Ann Snitow, Christine Stansell, and Sharon Thompson, eds. New York: Monthly Review Press, pp. 100–117.

Davis, Kingsley. 1937. "The Sociology of Prostitution." *American Sociological Review 2:* 744–755.

Ehrenreich, Barbara. 1983. *The Hearts of Men: American Dreams and the Flight from Commitment.* New York: Doubleday.

Engels, Friedrich. [1884] 1978. "The Origin of the Family, Private Property, and the State." In *The Marx-Engels Reader,* Robert Tucker, ed. New York: W.W. Norton, pp. 734–760.

Fass, Paula. 1977. *The Damned and the Beautiful: American Youth in the 1920s.* Oxford, UK: Oxford University Press.

Flowers, Amy. 1998. *The Fantasy Factory: An Insiders View of the Phone Sex Industry.* Philadelphia, PA: University of Pennsylvania Press.

Frank, Katherine. 2002. *G-Strings and Sympathy: Strip Club Regulars and Male Desire.* Durham, NC: Duke University Press.

Giddens, Anthony. 1992. The Transformation of Intimacy: Sexuality, Love, and Eroticism in Modern Societies. Stanford: Stanford University Press

Greenwald, Harold. 1958. *The Elegant Prostitute: A Social and Psychoanalytic Study.* New York: Ballantine Books.

Hamilton, Arnold. 1999. "Lurid Tactics: Oklahoma City Threatens Prostitution Participants Glare of TV Publicity." *Dallas Morning News,* March 18. 33A.

Hart, Angie. 1994. "Missing Masculinity? Prostitutes' Clients in Alicante, Spain." In *Dislocating Masculinity: Comparative Ethnographies,* Andrea Cornwall and Nancy Lindisfarne, eds. New York: Routledge. pp. 48–66.

Hobson, Barbara. 1990. *Uneasy Virtue: The Politics of Prostitution and the American Reform Tradition.* Chicago, IL: University of Chicago Press.

Hochschild, Arlie Russell. 1997. *The Time Bind.* New York: Metropolitan Books.

Hoigard, Cecilie, and Liv Finstad. 1986. *Backstreets: Prostitution, Money, and Love.* University Park, PA: Pennsylvania State University Press.

Holzman, Harold, and Sharon Pines. 1982. "Buying Sex: The Phenomenology of Being a John." *Deviant Behavior A:* 89–116.

Jenness, Valerie. 1993. *Making It Work: The Prostitutes' Rights Movement in Perspective.* New York: Aldine de Gruyter.

Juffer, Jane. 1998. *At Home with Pornography: Women, Sex, and Everyday Life.* New York: New York University Press.

Kaye, Kerwin. 1999. "Male Sexual Clients: Changing Images of Masculinity, Prostitution, and Deviance in the United States, 1900–1950." Unpublished manuscript on file with author.

Kellogg, Susan, and Steven Mintz. 1993. "Family Structures." In *Encyclopedia of American Social History,* Vol. Ill, M.C. Cayton et al., ed. New York: Scribner. pp. 1925–1941.

Kempadoo, Kamala, and Jo Doezema, eds. 1998. *Global Sex Workers: Rights, Resistance, and Redefinition.* New York: Routledge.

Kilman, Lisa, and Kate Watson-Smyth. 1998. "Kerb Crawlers Offered Aversion Therapy Course." *Independent,* August 3:5.

Kimmel, Michael. 2000. "Fuel for Fantasy: The Ideological Construction of Male Lust." In *Male Lust: Power, Pleasure, and Transformation,* Kerwin Kay et al., eds. New York: Haworth. pp. 267–273.

Kinsey, Alfred, Wardell Pomeroy, and Clyde E. Martin. 1948. *Sexual Behavior in the Human Male.* Philadelphia, PA: W.B. Saunders Company.

Lane, Frederick S. 2000. *Obscene Profits: The Entrepreneurs of Pornography in the Cyber Age.* New York: Routledge.

Lasch, Christopher. 1979. *Haven in a Heartless World: The Family Besieged.* New York: Basic Books.

Learmonth, Michael. 1999. "Siliporn Valley." *San Jose Metro,* November 17, 15(37): 20–29.

Lefler, Julie. 1999. "Shining the Spotlight on Johns: Moving Toward Equal Treatment of Male Customers and Female Prostitutes." *Hastings Women's Law Journal* 10(1): 11–37.

Leidner, Robin. 1993. *Fast Food, Fast Talk: Service Work and the Routinization of Everyday Life.* Berkeley, CA: University of California Press.

Leigh, Carol. 1994. "Prostitution in the United States: The Statistics." *Gauntlet: Exploring the Limits of Free Expression* 1: 17–19.

Lever, Janet, and Deanne Dolnick. 2000. "Clients and Call Girls: Seeking Sex and Intimacy." In *Sex for Sale: Prostitution, Pornography, and the Sex Industry,* Ronald Weitzer, ed. New York: Routledge. pp. 85–103.

Lewis, Diane. 1999. "Naming 'Johns': Suicide Raises Ethical Questions About Policy." *FineLine: The Newsletter on Journalism Ethics* 2(6): 3.

Lopez, Steve. 2000. "Hold the Pickles, Please: This Drive-Through Has a New Menu Item." *Time,* October 2: p. 6.

Luker, Kristin. 1984. *Abortion and the Politics of Motherhood.* Berkeley, CA: University of California Press.

Luker, Kristin. 1998. "Sex, Social Hygiene, and Syphilis: The Double-Edged Sword of Social Reform." *Theory and Society 27:* 601–634.

MacDonald, William. 1978. *Victimless Crimes: A Description of Offenders and their Prosecution in the District of Columbia.* Washington, DC: Institute for Law and Social Research.

Mansson, Sven-Axel. 1988. *The Man in Sexual Commerce.* Lund, Sweden: Lund University School of Social Work.

Marinucci, Carla. 1995a. "International Praise for S.F. 'School for Johns." *San Francisco Examiner,* November 14.

Marinucci, Carla. 1995b. "A School for Scandal." *San Francisco Examiner,* April 16.

Marx, Karl. [1844] 1978. "The Economic and Philosophic Manuscripts of 1844." In *The Marx-Engels Reader,* R. Tucker, ed. New York: W Norton, pp. 66–129.

McIntosh, Mary. 1978. "Who Needs Prostitutes: The Ideology of Male Sexual Needs." *Women, Sexuality, and Social Control,* Carol Smart and Barry Smart, eds. London, UK: Routledge. pp. 53–65.

McKeganey, Neil, and Marina Barnard. 1996. *Sex Work on the Streets: Prostitutes and Their Clients.* Buckingham, UK: Open University Press.

Monto, Martin. 2000. "Why Men Seek Out Prostitutes." In *Sex for Sale,* Ron Weitzer, ed. New York: Routledge. pp. 67–85.

"Names of Alleged U.S. Prostitute Client Released." 1999. Reuters, January 13. www.infonautics. com.

Nieves, Evelyn. 1999. "For Patrons of Prostitutes, Remedial Instruction." *The New York Times,* March 18. Al, A20.

O'Connell Davidson, Julia. 1998. *Prostitution, Power, and Freedom.* Cambridge, UK: Polity Press.

Pateman, Carole. 1988. *The Sexual Contract.* Stanford, CA: Stanford University Press. Pheterson, Gail. 1993. "The Whore Stigma: Female Dishonor and Male Unworthiness." *Social Text* 37: 39–65.

Pierre-Pierre, Garry. 1994. "Police Focus on Arresting Prostitutes' Customers." *New York Times,* November 20. p. 51

Prasad, Monica. 1999. "The Morality of Market Exchange: Love, Money, and Contractual Justice." *Sociological Perspectives 42(2):* 181–215.

Prial, Dunstan. 1999. "IPO Outlook: Adult' Web Sites Profit, Though Few are Likely to Offer Shares." *The Wall Street Journal,* March 8. B10.

Prieur, Annick, and Arnhild Taksdal.1993. "Clients of Prostitutes: Sick Deviants or Ordinary Men? A Discussion of the Male Role Concept and Cultural Changes in Masculinity." *NORA 2:* 105–114.

Rosen, Ruth. 1982. *The Lost Sisterhood: Prostitution in America, 1900–1918.* Baltimore, MD: Johns Hopkins University Press.

San Francisco Task Force on Prostitution. 1994. *Interim Report.* Submitted to the Board of Supervisors of the City and County of San Francisco, California.

San Francisco Task Force on Prostitution. 1996. *Final Report.* Submitted to the Board of Supervisors of the City and County of San Francisco, California.

Schlosser, Eric. 1997. "The Business of Pornography." *U.S. News and World Report,* February 10, 43–52.

Seidman, Steven. 1991. *Romantic Longings*. New York: Routledge

"Sex, News, and Statistics: Where Entertainment on the Web Scores." 2000. *The Economist*, October 7. www.economist.com.

Simmel, Georg. [1907] 1971. "Prostitution." In *On Individuality and Social Forms*, Donald N. Levine, ed. Chicago, IL: University of Chicago Press, pp. 121–126.

Sorrentino, Constance. 1990. "The Changing Family in International Perspective." *Monthly Labor Review*, March, 41–58.

"Suburban Detroit Police Release Names of Prostitution Ring's Clients." 1999. *Associated Press Online*, January 15. www.freedomforum.org

Sullivan, Elroy, and William Simon. 1998. "The Client: A Social, Psychological, and Behavioral Look at the Unseen Patron of Prostitution." In *Prostitution: On Whores, Hustlers, and Johns*, James Elias, ed. Amherst, NY: Prometheus Books, pp. 134–155.

Swidler, Ann. 1980. "Love and Adulthood in American Culture." In *Themes of Work and Love In Adulthood*, Neil J. Smelser and E. H. Erikson, eds. Cambridge, MA: Harvard University Press.

Sykes, Gresham, and David Matza. [1957] 1985. "Techniques of Neutralization: A Theory of Delinquency." In *Theories of Deviance*, Stuart Traub and Craig Little, eds. Itasca, IL: F. E. Peacock.

Symbaluk, D. C, and K. M. Jones. 1998. "Prostitution Offender Programs: Canada Finds New Solutions to an Old Problem." *Corrections Compendium* 23(11): 1–2, 8.

Weeks, Jeffrey. [1981] 1997. "Inverts, Perverts, and Mary-Annes." In *The Subcultures Reader*, Ken Gelder and Sarah Thornton, eds. London, UK: Routledge. pp. 268–281.

Weitzer, Ron. 2000a. "Why We Need More Research on Sex Work." In *Sex for Sale*, Ron Weitzer, ed. New York: Routledge. pp. 1–17.

Weitzer,Ron.2000b."The Politics of Prostitution in America." In *Sex for Sale*, Ron Weitzer, ed. New York: Routledge. pp. 159–181.

INTRODUCTION TO: THE NEW SEXUALITY STUDIES

Theoretical Perspectives

JAN CAMPBELL

Steven Seidman asks the reader to determine the relationship between sex and society. He then defines the basis for sexology, describes its key ideas, and discusses the aim of researchers to discover the laws of sexuality. Seidman maintains that these views, while sometimes tedious, have shaped western sexual culture. The basis of who we are and what we incur as natural sexual drive, the acknowledgement that sexuality is the powerful driving force in our behavior, and the understanding that sexual instinct is, by nature, heterosexual are the underlying themes of sexology.

The article then discusses the teachings of Freud and the battle between biology and sociology. To bring into the discussion the concept of normal versus abnormal, one has to disagree with the sexologists. Freud felt if the sexual instinct is flexible in purpose, it is society that shapes our psyches and sexualities. Seidman says our psychological and sexual selves are shaped as we have conflict between the sexual pleasure drive and the social expectations of society to be productive and responsible, which produces the struggle.

Continuing on with theoretical perspectives, Seidman introduces us to feminism, which is driven by gender. He cites the ideas that girls develop a psyche that is relationship oriented. In boys, who identify with their achievement-oriented fathers, the psyche is more goal oriented.

Other researchers see sexuality through the feminist perspective as conflict theory. Some insist that the role of male dominance shapes women's sexuality through sex, which is a means by which men control women.

Sexuality has also been seen as a product of Social Learning Theory. The role of the cultural and behavioral shift that changed during the 1960s and 1970s from sex within marriage as an exclusive form of morality to one in which sex was permitted within the guise of affection also had its place. Sociologists talked of "scripts" and made the case that sexuality is socially learned. This learned response may take the form of stigmatized identity if we are taught to think in terms of what is acceptable and what is not.

THE NEW SEXUALITY STUDIES

Theoretical Perspectives

STEVEN SEIDMAN

W hat is the relationship between sex and society? Beginning with sexologists who propose a view of sex as fundamentally biological, I review various social approaches to understanding sexuality. I take for granted that there is a biological basis for human impulses, drives, and desires. However, it is social forces that fashion a biological reality into "sexuality." Individuals and groups give meaning to bodily sensations and feelings, make erotic acts into sexual identities, and create norms distinguishing between acceptable and unacceptable sexualities.

SEXOLOGY: THE SCIENCE OF SEXUALITY

Why do many of us in America and Europe view sexuality as natural? One reason is the development of a science of sexuality. In the late nineteenth and early twentieth centuries, there developed a science aimed at discovering the laws of sexuality. This science has come to be called sexology.

Who are the sexologists? Among the more famous are Richard von Krafft-Ebing, Havelock Ellis, and Magnus Hirschfeld. While few of us today have heard of these nineteenth century pioneers of sexology, many of us have heard of Alfred Kinsey or of Masters and Johnson. Sexologists have produced a body of knowledge that has influenced the way many of us think about sex, in part because their ideas have been stamped with the imprimatur of science.

What are the key ideas of sexology? First, sexology claims that humans are born with a sexual nature, and that sexuality is part of the biological makeup of all individuals. Second, sexology views sexuality as being at the core of what it means to be human: our sexual drive is no less basic than our need to eat or sleep. Sexuality is said to be basic to who we are. Third, sexuality is viewed as a powerful and driving force in our behavior. It influences all aspects of our lives, from the physical to the psychological. It motivates much of human behavior. Fourth, sexology states that the sexual instinct is, by nature, heterosexual. There is said to be a natural attraction between men and women. While few sexologists today believe that the chief purpose of sexuality is to procreate, they continue to think that heterosexuality is the natural and normal form of sexuality.

Sexologists aim to discover the laws of sexuality. Just as physics and biology distrust inherited ideas and test them in experiments, sexology has championed a vigorously scientific approach. Facts, not beliefs, are to guide this science. The truth of sexuality is to be discovered by means of the "case study" method. Like physicians or psychiatrists, sexologists use intensive interviews and observation to uncover the true nature of sexuality. The details of human sexual desires, fantasies, and practices are recorded for the purpose of revealing the laws of the sexual instinct. Sexologists develop elaborate classifications of sexual types and detail the range of normal and abnormal forms of sexuality.

Sexology has always had a social purpose. In the nineteenth and early twentieth centuries, some sexologists sought to expand tolerance for different forms of human sexuality by emphasizing that sexuality is natural. Other sexologists saw their work as a way to contribute to creating a healthy, fit population. Often this meant that sexology was aligned to a belief in racial purity and improvement. Some sexologists even discouraged the sexual intermingling of races.

As racist ideas lost favor during the twentieth century, sexology has often been allied to a mission of strengthening the institutions of marriage and the family. Sexologists have argued that sex is at the core of love and marriage, and that a stable happy marriage requires a mutually satisfying sexual relationship. Individuals should not be burdened by guilt; they must be sexually knowledgeable and skilled. Sexology has aimed to make sexually enlightened and skillful citizens who would marry and stay married, in part because of a mutually satisfying sex life.

While their writings are sometimes technical and often tedious, sexologists have shaped Western sexual culture. Their ideas about the naturalness of sexuality have been popularized by an army of sex advice writers. Many of us believe in the idea of a natural sexuality because of the sexologists.

Alongside sexology, the discipline of psychology has been the source of many of our ideas about sex. In particular, Freud, the founder of psychoanalysis, has been probably the single most influential thinker in shaping Western sexual culture.

Freud aimed to uncover the roots of human psychology in our sex drives. Freud accepted many of the ideas of the sexologists. He believed in the biological basis of sexuality and insisted that sexuality is at the root of many of our feelings and actions. Freud also thought that there is a normal course of sexual development and there are abnormal or perverse forms of sexuality. The defining feature of sexual abnormality was deviation from genital-centered, intercourse-oriented heterosexuality based on love and monogamy.

But Freud also disagreed with the sexologists. Whereas sexologists defined the sexual instinct as reproductive and naturally heterosexual, Freud argued that the sexual instinct is oriented to pleasure. Moreover, humans get pleasure not only from sexual intercourse, but also from kissing, touching, caressing, looking, and sometimes dominating and being dominated. Freud argued that the body has many erotic areas and there are many ways of experiencing sexual satisfaction. Accordingly, he held that nongenital pleasures are not necessarily abnormal. It is normal, for example, to enjoy the range of pleasures that are today called foreplay.

Viewing the sexual instinct as a drive for pleasure blurs the line between normal and abnormal. To most sexologists, any sexual expression that deviated from a heterosexual reproductive aim was abnormal. However, Freud allows for a wide range of normal sexual expression beyond heterosexual reproduction. Pursuing nonprocreative pleasures is not in itself abnormal; sex drives become abnormal only when they are fixated on one specific sex act or pleasure. For example, it is normal for individuals to feel pleasure from looking at someone or from kissing and touching. It is abnormal, though, when these pleasures replace heterosexual intercourse.

Freud was convinced that sex is at the core of the self. It is, he thought, the drive for erotic pleasure that places the individual in conflict with social norms of respectability and self-control. Sexuality is then a major focus of psychological and social conflict. The psychological character of the individual rests on how the sex drive is managed. Too much sexual expression leads to psychological and social instability. Excessive social control results in psychosexual frustration that brings personal unhappiness.

Freud adhered to a much deeper social understanding of sexuality than the sexologists. If the sexual instinct is somewhat flexible in its purpose, it is society that shapes its form and meaning. In particular, the family is the formative social environment shaping our psyches and sexualities. Our psychological and sexual selves take shape as we struggle with the conflict between a drive for sexual pleasure and the social expectation to be productive, responsible citizens.

Feminists point out that all of us step into the world as men or women, regardless of the economic system. Our gender identity is not a superficial part of our lives, but shapes the personal and social aspects of our lives in important ways. Feminists view gender as a social identity and a set of norms that guide behavior. We are not born men or women but acquire these gender identities through a social process of learning and sometimes coercion. Feminists believe that our sexual desires, feelings, and preferences are imprinted by gender.

Feminists say that individuals acquire a sexual nature as they develop a gender identity. What exactly is the relationship between gender and sexuality?

In *The Reproduction of Mothering*, Nancy Chodorow argues that when women do the chief parenting work, gender patterns of sexual and individual development are different. For both boys and girls, the mother is often the primary source of love. However, girls sustain an intimacy with their mothers throughout their maturation; boys separate from their mothers at an early age in order to learn to be men. This difference shapes the psychosexual character of girls and boys.

The extended and intense intimacy between mothers and daughters results in girls developing a psyche that is relationship-oriented. Accordingly, girls tend to connect sex with intimacy and as a means of caring. They often approach sex more as a means of communication and intimacy than as a vehicle of erotic pleasure. Because boys typically break sharply from their mothers at an early age, and identify with their achievement-oriented fathers, they are more performance- and goal-oriented. Boys' sexuality tends to be more performance- and body-oriented. Boys can be intimate, but they will likely express sexual love in terms of the giving and receiving of erotic pleasure.

Chodorow's perspective is important because she holds that the family plays a crucial role in the making of the sexual self. Also, she says that boys and girls develop different sexual values and orientations.

Adrienne Rich also believes that gender dynamics creates sexual differences between men and women. She emphasizes the social creation of heterosexual men and women. In "Compulsive Heterosexuality and Lesbian Existence" she argues that we are all taught and coerced into adopting conventional gender identities. Why? Gender difference, Rich says, reinforces a society organized around the norm of heterosexuality. Shaping individuals into heterosexual men and women is a complex social process. Societies use positive inducements like economic rewards or a culture that romanticizes heterosexuality, but also resorts to ridicule, harassment, and violence to punish gender nonconformists and nonheterosexuals. The belief that heterosexuality is normal and natural plays a key role in creating heterosexual men and women. For example, many Europeans and Americans believe that there is a natural attraction between the sexes, that their bodies and minds "naturally" fit. Heterosexuality is then viewed as an extension of a natural order composed of two complementary sexes.

Catherine MacKinnon insists on the role of male dominance in shaping women's sexuality. She views sexuality as a product of men's power; sex is a means by which men control women. Indeed, it is the very basis of male domination. To the extent that men have the power to define what desires, feelings, and behaviors are sexual, they can define women's sexuality in a way that positions them as subordinate. For example, in male-dominated America, women's sexuality is supposed to be oriented to vaginal intercourse in marriage with the ultimate aim of procreation. This view defines women as heterosexual, or needing men, and as motivated to become wives and mothers, and therefore dependent on men.

Feminists like Rich and MacKinnon claim that the very essence of sexuality expresses men's wish for dominance. Every sexual desire and behavior in male-dominated societies is said to be related to gender dynamics, and either expresses men's dominance or women's resistance. From this perspective, feminists criticize the notion that women's sexual liberation is about claiming the right to pleasure or the freedom to do as one pleases, an approach that expresses men's view of sexual freedom. Instead, women's sexual liberation involves fashioning a sexual life that reflects their own needs, feelings, and desires. The point is not to liberate sexuality from social control, which could lead to more violence or unwanted pregnancy, but to claim the power to define one's own sexual desires and forge sexual-intimate lives.

Some feminists, like the anthropologist Gayle Rubin, have objected to the view that sexuality is a direct expression of gender politics. She argues that this perspective ignores considerable variation within women's and men's sexuality. Rubin believes that sexuality is connected to gender, yet also has its own dynamics.

In "Thinking Sex," Rubin makes the case that sex is fundamentally about erotic desires, fantasies, acts, identities, and politics—none of which are reducible to gender dynamics. She argues that all societies create sexual hierarchies that establish boundaries between good and bad or legitimate and illicit sexualities. Societies value specific desires, acts, and identities as normal, respectable, good, healthy, and moral; other forms of sexuality are classified as unhealthy, abnormal, sinful, and immoral. Society supports and privileges the "normal and good" forms of sexuality and aims to punish the "abnormal and bad" ones through law, violence, ridicule, or stigma. These sexual hierarchies create a series of outsider sexualites. This system of sexual regulation applies to both men and women. American society considers heterosexuality, monogamy, marriage, and reproductive sex to be considered good and normal; S/M (sadomasochism) and multiple-partner sex, commercial and public sex are defined and treated as bad. There are of course many sexualities that fall somewhere in between—for example, promiscuous heterosexuals or gays and lesbians in long-term monogamous relationships. It may be less socially acceptable for a woman to have multiple sex partners or to engage in S/M because of a gender order that associates femininity with purity and maternal feelings: still, these behaviors are disparaged by both men and women. Those who engage in such behaviors, regardless of gender, will be stigmatized and subject to a range of sanctions, from ridicule to criminalization. Rubin's point is simply that gender influences patterns of sexuality, but there is still a great deal about the organization and dynamics of sexuality that cannot be viewed solely through the lens of gender.

GAY AND LESBIAN STUDIES

Paralleling the rise of a gay movement, many advocates argued that some people are just born homosexual. If homosexuals have always existed, it is a natural status and therefore they should not be punished.

However, this view has been challenged by the new gay/lesbian studies. These new scholars assume that homosexual behavior is a natural part of the human condition, but the appearance of a homosexual identity is a rare historical event. When and why did a homosexual identity emerge, and how has the meaning of homosexuality changed historically?

Jonathan Katz argued that, between colonial times and the 1970s, homosexuality in the U.S. changed from indicating a behavior (sodomy), to an abnormal personality (the homosexual), and finally to an affirmative social identity (gay/lesbian). Carroll Smith-Rosenberg showed that Victorian women, whose lives were organized around domestic tasks, often formed close ties with each other that at times blurred the line between friendship and romance. These intimate bonds sometimes developed into romantic relationships that were celebrated as complementary to marriage. These "romantic friendships" were often romantic bonds which lasted a lifetime. Similarly, Lillian Faderman wrote the first history of lesbianism in the United States, in which she documents changes in the meaning of same-sex behavior and in the social organization of lesbianism. Both Smith-Rosenberg and Faderman make the provocative argument that tolerance for intimacy between women diminished in the first decades of the twentieth century. As women started to attend college, work outside the home, and demand equal rights, their close ties to one another were often viewed as threatening. These women were stigmatized as lesbians.

Building on this growing body of historical scholarship on sexuality, John D'Emilio offered the first detailed analysis of the rise of a homosexual identity and community in the United States. He analyzed the social forces that shaped homosexuality into an identity, community, and social movement. For example, D'Emilio argued that the Second World War played a key role in shaping an awareness of homosexuality and homosexual bonds. During the war, many soldiers were, for the first time, exposed to individuals who thought of themselves as homosexual. Moreover, the intense closeness among the men and women in the military encouraged homosexual experimentation. After the war, many of these men and women with homosexual feelings settled in New York, Chicago, San Francisco, and Los Angeles. It was in these cities that the first major gay and lesbian political organizations initially took shape in the 1950s.

Historians have continued to refine their conceptions of the sexual past. One significant revision is in George Chauncey's *Gay New York*. Whereas historians and sociologists had come to believe that the modern homosexual emerged in the early twentieth century and was immediately stuffed into the closet, Chauncey argues that, in working-class New York, individuals were not classified as either homosexual or heterosexual, but as either "normal men" or "fairies." The former were masculine men, while the latter were effeminate. In other words, the homosexual indicated a type of gender deviance. If you were a masculine man who had sex with effeminate men, you were not necessarily considered a homosexual. Gender expression, not sexual preference, defined being a homosexual. Moreover, rather than being isolated and closeted, an open public gay life flourished in bars, taverns, speakeasies, restaurants, ballrooms, and parks.

FOUCAULT: SEXUALITY AS A SYSTEM OF SOCIAL CONTROL

Michel Foucault challenged the idea that sex was biological and natural. He proposed that it was the very idea or, in his terms, the discourse of sexuality that created what we know as sex. We are not born sexual, but learn to be sexual beings; this occurs only in societies that have created the idea of "sexuality."

But when did this idea of sexuality originate, and why? The birth of the science of sexuality in the nineteenth century was crucial. Scientists aimed to discover the hidden truth of human nature by uncovering the secrets of the sexual instinct. Sexologists charted the physiology and behavior of sexual desire, psychiatrists listened to their clients confess to a shadowy world of sexual fantasies, and demographers surveyed human fertility. But these researchers did not discover an uncharted territory of sex; they fashioned human pleasures, excitations, and acts into a new object of knowledge and social regulation: human sexuality. Foucault is not saying that the feelings and behaviors associated with the body were created by these discourses. Rather, these discourses compelled us to view these bodily experiences as expressions of human sexuality. The science of sexuality organized our diverse somatic experiences into a coherent, organized subject called sexuality.

Why did a discourse of sexuality appear and what was its social importance? Foucault thought that the modern state and other social institutions had good reasons to want to control people's sexuality. Between the seventeenth and nineteenth centuries in many European nations there were massive migrations to cities, a growing need for mass literacy and schooling, intense economic competition between nations, and the growing dependence of national power on economic prosperity. These developments created a strong political interest in gaining detailed and useful information about human bodies—how they reproduce, stay healthy, react to different external stimulation, and can be made more productive, efficient, and cooperative. For example, as cities became social and economic centers, governments and other institutions responsible for keeping order and for the care of the indigent sought information about migration patterns, fertility rates, nutrition, and health. This growing need to know and control bodies helped to create the idea of sexuality. To control sex is to exercise great control over the individual and whole populations. Sexuality is at the center of a modern system of social control.

Did Foucault give up the notion of sexual freedom? He wrote during a period of sexual rebellion. Sexual liberationists of all types declared that today we are more enlightened; the present is pregnant with possibilities for sexual freedom. Sexual liberation had two aspects. The first was a negative freedom—freedom from unnecessary control. Liberation also had a positive aspect—the right to express one's true sexual nature and identity.

Foucault agreed that expanding individual choice is a good thing. He supported the fight for gay rights. But gay rights is not liberation. It does not relieve individuals of horrific stigma and social discrimination. Also, the gay rights movement has reinforced a system that forces individuals to declare themselves either straight or gay, and reinforces the deviant status of bisexuality and other nonconventional sexualities. Moreover, a gay movement has its own ideal of how a gay person is supposed to look and act. In other words, the gay movement exercises control over its members, pressuring them to identify exclusively as gay and to act in ways that are recognized as gay.

If sexuality is today a system of social control, then ironically sexual liberation might involve freeing ourselves from the idea of sexuality. This would mean approaching our erotic desires and acts not as expressions of sexuality but as simply feelings and acts that give pleasure, create social ties, or are a source of cultural creativity. Foucault advocates a politics against sexuality—against a society that sexualizes selves, identities, and acts. Why would this be a good thing? By not assigning a moral meaning (either normal or abnormal) to adult, consensual sexual desires and behaviors, individuals would be subject to less social regulation. For example, instead of reversing the stigma of homosexuality by championing a normal gay identity, we could approach homosexuality as a desire and as a source of pleasure, new relationships and cultural expressions. Or, instead of celebrating the sexualization of the human body and all of its feelings and sensations, perhaps it is more liberating to desexualize pleasures, focus on nonsexual pleasures, learn to enjoy a wide range of sensual pleasures, and be free of controls that rely on notions of normality.

SEXUALITY AND SOCIAL LEARNING

Since the early decades of the twentieth century, sociologists have researched the role of religion, gender, class, race, and social values in shaping patterns of premarital, marital, and extramarital sex. In the 1960s and 1970s, Ira Reiss charted cultural and behavioral shifts among American youth as a sexual morality that associated sex exclusively with marriage transformed into one that permitted sex in a context of affection. Reiss believed that this cultural change was related to women's growing economic and social power. In this regard, he observed the decline of a double standard that permitted men to have sex outside of marriage, while labeling women who engaged in the same behavior as "bad girls."

Some sociologists have pressed for a full-blown sociology of sexuality. John Gagnon and William Simon proposed a "script" theory of sexuality. Instead of understanding humans as born sexual, they argued that sexuality is socially learned. In the course of growing up, society teaches us what feelings and desires count as sexual and what the appropriate "scripts" for sexual behavior are. Sexual scripts tell us with whom we're supposed to have sex (based on age, race, or class), where, when, and what it means when we do. Gagnon and Simon were in effect saying that sexuality is not an inborn property, but a product of social labeling.

The British sociologist, Ken Plummer, developed a labeling perspective on sex. In *Sexual Stigma*, he argued that individuals aren't born homosexual, but learn to be homosexual. An individual may feel desire or attraction to people of the same sex, but he or she must learn that these feelings are sexual and that they indicate a homosexual identity. People learn this in the course of interacting with both the straight and gay world. For example, a high-school student hearing derogatory comments about "fags" and "dykes" begins to associate homosexuality with a stigmatized identity. This same individual may eventually be exposed to a gay subculture, which champions a view of homosexuality as natural and good.

One of the pioneers of a sociological approach to sexuality was the British sociologist Jeffrey Weeks. He introduced the ideas of essentialism and constructionism. Essentialism is the notion that sexuality is a basic and essential part of being human. Constructionism states that sexuality is a product of social forces. Weeks proposed a strong view of the social character of sexuality: "First, we can no longer set 'sex' against 'society' as if they were separate domains. Secondly, there is a widespread recognition of the social variability of sexual forms, beliefs, ideologies, and behavior. Sexuality has … many histories. … Thirdly, we must learn to see that sexuality is something which society produces in complex ways. It is a result of diverse social practices that give meaning to human activities, to struggles between those who have power to define and regulate, and those who resist. Sexuality is not given, it is a product of negotiation, and struggle."

CONCLUSION

There has been a revolution in the way scholars think about sexuality. Until recently, scholars believed that humans were born with a sexual nature; the natural order created a series of sexual types: heterosexuals, homosexuals, masochists, pedophiles, and so on. A science of sexuality would reveal the nature of the sexual instinct. The idea of sexual normality would serve as the standard to judge and regulate sexual behavior.

Today, the leading edge of scholarship views sex as fundamentally social. We're born with bodies but it is society that determines which parts of the body and which pleasures and acts are sexual. And, the classification of sex acts into good and bad or acceptable and illicit is a product of social power; the dominant sexual norms express the dominant social groups. If we are supposed to grow up to be heterosexual, and if we are expected to link sex to love and marriage, this is because specific groups impose these social norms. Beliefs that there are natural and normal ways to be sexual are ideological. How we come to have such beliefs, and their personal and social consequences, are important questions for the study of sexuality. Indeed, the question of who gets to define what is sexual and which institutions are responsible for regulating our sexualities are key sociological and political questions in their own right.

DISCUSSION QUESTIONS

1. How would you define sexuality? What is the difference between sexuality and gender?
2. Do you agree that our ideas of sexuality come more from society and culture than biology? What are some commonly held views of sexuality—that is, what does our culture see as "normal" and "abnormal"? Can you trace where these views might come from?

REFERENCES

Butler, Judith, *Gender Trouble: Feminism and the Subversion of Identity* (NewYork: Routledge, 1990).

Chauncey, George, Gay *New York: Gender, Urban Culture, and the Making of the Gay Male World, 1890–1940* (New York: Basic Books, 1994).

Chodorow, Nancy, *The Reproduction of Mothering: Psychoanalysis and the Sociology of Gender* (Berkeley: University of California Press, 1978).

D'Emilio, John, *Sexual Politics, Sexual Communities: The Making of a Homosexual Minority in the United States, 1940–1970* (Chicago: University of Chicago Press. 1983).

Faderman, Lillian, *Odd Girls and Twilight Lovers: A History of Lesbian Life in Twentieth-Century America* (New York: Columbia University Press, 1991).

Foucault, Michel *The History of Sexuality. Vol 1: An Introduction* (New York: Vintage, 1980).

Gagnon, John and Simon, William, *Sexual Conduct: The Social Sources of Human Sexuality* (Chicago: Aldine, 1973).

Ned Katz, Jonathan, Gay, *American History* (New York: Crowell, 1976) and *Gay/Lesbian Almanac* (NewYork: Harper & Row, 1983).

MacKinnon, Catherine, *Towards a Feminist Theory of the State* (Cambridge, Mass.: Harvard University Press, 1989).

Plummer, Ken, *Sexual Stigma: An Interactionist Account* (London: Routledge & Kegan Paul, 1975). Reiss, Ira, *Premarital Sexual Standards in America* fGlencoe, 111.: Free Press, 1960) and The *Social Context o f Premarital Sexual Permissiveness* (NewYork: Holt, Rinehart & Winston, 1967).

Rich, Adrienne, "Compulsory Heterosexuality and Lesbian Existence," *Signs 5* (1980).

Rubin, Gayle, "Thinking Sex: Notes for a Radical Theory of the Politics of Sexuality," in *Pleasure and Danger: Exploring Female Sexuality,* ed. Carole Vance (Boston: Routledge & Kegan Paul, 1984).

Smith-Rosenberg, Carroll, "The Female World of Love and Ritual," *Signs 1* (1975).Weeks, Jeffrey, *Sexuality* (London: Tavistock, 1986), p. 26.

INTRODUCTION TO: THINKING SEX

Notes for a Radical Theory of the Politics of Sexuality

JAN CAMPBELL

G ayle Rubin asks us in her article to think about sex. In fact, she maintains that much of our thinking about sex and the behaviors and attitudes that are associated with it come from nineteenth-century "morality crusades." The recurrent theme recounts many laws and witch hunts over the years that were waged in order to purge the country of various aspects of sex.

Rubin's article cites ideology ranging from "linking non-familial sex and communism" to attacking Alfred Kinsey and his institute during the McCarthy era "for weakening the moral fiber of Americans and rendering them more vulnerable to communist influence." She cites the political campaigns and legislation that has been linked to sexuality, such as the Teen Chastity Program ($15 million federal dollars allocated to encourage teens to refrain from intercourse, discourage them from using contraceptives if they did have intercourse, and discourage them from having abortions if they did get pregnant).

She also cites the fact that even during the bleak periods when sex was vilified, many writings and laws were passed to accommodate choice, and conceptual frameworks were constructed to address the relationships between sex and politics. She describes the negativity of sexuality throughout decades and refers to it as the "fallacy of misplaced scale. " Rubin indicates that medicine and psychiatry "multiplied the categories of sexual misconduct" in the Diagnostic and Statistical Manual of Mental and Physical Disorders (DSM). The DSM III removed homosexuality from the area of mental disorders. The mass media is referred to as nourishing attitudes of relentless propaganda by holding onto what Rubin calls "the system of erotic stigma" and in continuing to support ideas that erotic variety is "dangerous, unhealthy, depraved and a menace to everything from small children to national security."

THINKING SEX

Notes for a Radical Theory of the Politics of Sexuality

GAYLE RUBIN

THE SEX WARS

> Asked his advice, Dr. J. Guerin affirmed that, after all other treatments had
> failed, he had succeeded in curing young girls affected by the vice of onanism
> by burning the clitoris with a hot iron. … I apply the hot point three times to
> each of the large labia and another on the clitoris. … After the first operation,
> from forty to fifty times a day, the number of voluptuous spasms was reduced
> to three or four. … We believe, then, that in cases similar to those submitted to
> your consideration, one should not hesitate to resort to the hot iron, and at an
> early hour, in order to combat clitoral and vaginal onanism in the little girls.
> —(Zambaco, 1981, pp. 31, 36)

The time has come to think about sex. To some, sexuality may seem to be an unimportant topic, a frivolous diversion from the more critical problems of poverty, war, disease, racism, famine, or nuclear annihilation. But it is precisely at times such as these, when we live with the possibility of unthinkable destruction, that people are likely to become dangerously crazy about sexuality. Contemporary conflicts over sexual values and erotic conduct have much in common with the religious disputes of earlier centuries. They acquire immense symbolic weight. Disputes over sexual behavior often become the vehicles for displacing social anxieties, and discharging their attendant emotional intensity. Consequently, sexuality should be treated with special respect in times of great social stress.

The realm of sexuality also has its own internal politics, inequities, and modes of oppression. As with other aspects of human behavior, the concrete institutional forms of sexuality at any given time and place are products of human activity. They are imbued with conflicts of interest and political maneuver, both deliberate and incidental. In that sense, sex is always political. But there are also historical periods in which sexuality is more sharply contested and more overtly politicized. In such periods, the domain of erotic life is, in effect, renegotiated.

In England and the United States, the late nineteenth century was one such era. During that time, powerful social movements focused on 'vices' of all sorts. There were educational and political campaigns to encourage chastity, to eliminate prostitution, and to discourage masturbation, especially among the young. Morality crusaders attacked obscene literature, nude paintings, music halls, abortion, birth-control information, and public dancing (see Gordon and Dubois, 1983; Marcus, 1974; Ryan, 1979; Walkowitz, 1980, 1982; Weeks, 1981). The consolidation of Victorian morality, and its apparatus of social, medical, and legal enforcement, was the outcome of a long period of struggle whose results have been bitterly contested ever since.

The consequences of these great nineteenth-century moral paroxysms are still with us. They have left a deep imprint on attitudes about sex, medical practice, child-rearing, parental anxieties, police conduct, and sex law.

The idea that masturbation is an unhealthy practice is part of that heritage. During the nineteenth century, it was commonly thought that 'premature' interest in sex, sexual excitement, and, above all, sexual release, would impair the health and maturation of a child. Theorists differed on the actual consequences of sexual precocity. Some thought it led to insanity, while others merely predicted stunted growth. To protect the young from premature arousal, parents tied children down at night so they would not touch themselves; doctors excised the clitorises of onanistic little girls (see Barker-Benfield, 1976; Marcus, 1974; Weeks, 1981; Zambaco, 1981). Although the more gruesome techniques have been abandoned, the attitudes that produced them persist. The notion that sex per se is harmful to the young has been chiseled into extensive social and legal structures designed to insulate minors from sexual knowledge and experience.

Much of the sex law currently on the books also dates from the nineteenth-century morality crusades. The first federal anti-obscenity law in the United States was passed in 1873. The Comstock Act named for Anthony Comstock—an ancestral anti-porn activist and the founder of the New York Society for the Suppression of Vice—made it a federal crime to make, advertise, sell, possess, send through the mails, or import books or pictures deemed obscene. The law also banned contraceptive or abortifacient drugs and devices and information about them (Beserra, Franklin and Clevenger, 1977). In the wake of the federal statute, most states passed their own anti-obscenity laws.

The Supreme Court began to whittle down both federal and state Comstock laws during the 1950s. By 1975, the prohibition of materials used for, and information about, contraception and abortion had been ruled unconstitutional. However, although the obscenity provisions have been modified, their fundamental constitutionality has been upheld. Thus it remains a crime to make, sell, mail, or import material which has no purpose other than sexual arousal (Beserra, Franklin and Clevenger, 1977).

Although sodomy statutes date from older strata of the law, when elements of canon law were adopted into civil codes, most of the laws used to arrest homosexuals and prostitutes come out of the Victorian campaigns against 'white slavery'. These campaigns produced the myriad prohibitions against solicitation, lewd behavior, loitering for immoral purposes, age offences, and brothels and bawdy houses.

In her discussion of the British 'white slave' scare, historian Judith Walkowitz observes that: 'Recent research delineates the vast discrepancy between lurid journalistic accounts and the reality of prostitution. Evidence of widespread entrapment of British girls in London and abroad is slim' (Walkowitz, 1980, p. 83)[1]. However, public furor over this ostensible problem forced the passage of the Criminal Law Amendment Act of 1885, a particularly nasty and pernicious piece of omnibus legislation. The 1885 Act raised the age of consent for girls from 13 to 16, but it also gave police far greater summary jurisdiction over poor working-class women and children … it contained a clause making indecent acts between consenting male adults a crime, thus forming the basis of legal prosecution of male homosexuals in Britain until 1967 … the clauses of the new bill were mainly enforced against working-class women, and regulated adult rather than youthful sexual behavior. (Walkowitz, 1982, p. 85)

In the United States, the Mann Act, also known as the White Slave Traffic Act, was passed in 1910. Subsequently, every state in the union passed anti-prostitution legislation (Beserra, Franklin and Clevenger, 1977).

In the 1950s, in the United States, major shifts in the organization of sexuality took place. Instead of focusing on prostitution or masturbation, the anxieties of the 1950s condensed most specifically around the image of the 'homosexual menace' and the dubious specter of the 'sex offender'. Just before and after World War II, the 'sex offender' became an object of public fear and scrutiny. Many states and cities, including Massachusetts, New Hampshire, New Jersey, New York State, New York City, and Michigan, launched investigations to gather information about this menace to public safety (Commonwealth of Massachusetts, 1947; State of New Hampshire, 1949; City of New York, 1939; State of New York, 1950; Hartwell, 1950; State of Michigan, 1951). The term 'sex offender' sometimes applied to rapists, sometimes to 'child molesters', and eventually functioned as a code for homosexuals. In its bureaucratic, medical, and popular versions, the sex offender discourse tended to blur distinctions between violent sexual assault and illegal but consensual acts such as sodomy. The criminal justice system incorporated these concepts when an epidemic of sexual psychopath laws swept through state legislatures (Freedman, 1983). These laws gave the psychological professions increased police powers over homosexuals and other sexual 'deviants'.

From the late 1940s until the early 1960s, erotic communities whose activities did not fit the postwar American dream drew intense persecution. Homosexuals were, along with communists, the objects of federal witch hunts and purges. Congressional investigations, executive orders, and sensational exposes in the media aimed to root out homosexuals employed by the government. Thousands lost their jobs, and restrictions on federal employment of homosexuals persist to this day (Berube, 1981a, 1981b; D'Emilio, 1983; Katz, 1976). The FBI began systematic surveillance and harassment of homosexuals, which lasted at least into the 1970s (D'Emilio, 1983; Berube, personal communication).

Many states and large cities conducted their own investigations, and the federal witch hunts were reflected in a variety of local crackdowns. In Boise, Idaho, in 1955, a schoolteacher sat down to breakfast with his morning paper and read that the vice-president of the Idaho First National Bank had been arrested on felony sodomy charges; the local prosecutor said that he intended to eliminate all homosexuality from the community. The teacher never finished his breakfast. 'He jumped up from his seat, pulled out his suitcases, packed as fast as he could, got into his car, and drove straight to San Francisco … The cold eggs, coffee, and toast remained on his table for two days before someone from his school came by to see what had happened' (Gerassi, 1968, p. 14).[2]

In San Francisco, police and media waged war on homosexuals throughout the 1950s. Police raided bars, patrolled cruising areas, conducted street sweeps, and trumpeted their intention of driving the queers out of San Francisco (Berube, personal communication; D'Emilio, 1981, 1983). Crackdowns against gay individuals, bars, and social areas occurred throughout the country. Although anti-homosexual crusades are the best-documented examples of erotic repression in the 1950s, future research should reveal similar patterns of increased harassment against pornographic materials, prostitutes, and erotic deviants of all sorts. Research is needed to determine the full scope of both police persecution and regulatory reform.[3]

The current period bears some uncomfortable similarities to the 1880s and the 1950s. The 1977 campaign to repeal the Dade County, Florida, gay rights ordinance inaugurated a new wave of violence, state persecution, and legal initiatives directed against minority sexual populations and the commercial sex industry. For the last six years, the United States and Canada have undergone an extensive sexual repression in the political, not the psychological, sense. In the spring of 1977, a few weeks before the Dade County vote, the news media were suddenly full of reports of raids on gay cruising areas, arrests for prostitution, and investigations into the manufacture and distribution of pornographic materials. Since then, police activity against the gay community has increased exponentially. The gay press has documented hundreds of arrests, from the libraries of Boston to the streets of Houston and the beaches of San Francisco. Even the large, organized, and relatively powerful urban gay communities have been unable to stop these depredations.

Gay bars and bath houses have been busted with alarming frequency, and police have gotten bolder. In one especially dramatic incident, police in Toronto raided all four of the city's gay baths. They broke into cubicles with crowbars and hauled almost 300 men out into the winter streets, clad in their bath towels. Even 'liberated' San Francisco has not been immune. There have been proceedings against several bars, countless arrests in the parks, and, in the fall of 1981, police arrested over 400 people in a series of sweeps of Polk Street, one of the thoroughfares of local gay nightlife. Queerbashing has become a significant recreational activity for young urban males. They come into gay neighborhoods armed with baseball bats and looking for trouble, knowing that the adults in their lives either secretly approve or will look the other way.

The police crackdown has not been limited to homosexuals. Since 1977, enforcement of existing laws against prostitution and obscenity has been stepped up. Moreover, states and municipalities have been passing new and tighter regulations on commercial sex. Restrictive ordinances have been passed, zoning laws altered, licensing and safety codes amended, sentences increased, and evidentiary requirements relaxed. This subtle legal codification of more stringent controls over adult sexual behavior has gone largely unnoticed outside of the gay press.

For over a century, no tactic for stirring up erotic hysteria has been as reliable as the appeal to protect children. The current wave of erotic terror has reached deepest into those areas bordered in some way, if only symbolically, by the sexuality of the young. The motto of the Dade County repeal campaign was 'Save Our Children' from alleged homosexual recruitment. In February 1977, shortly before the Dade County vote, a sudden concern with 'child pornography' swept the national media. In May, the Chicago Tribune ran a lurid four-day series with three-inch headlines, which claimed to expose a national vice ring organized to lure young boys into prostitution and pornography.[4] Newspapers across the country ran similar stories, most of them worthy of the National Enquirer. By the end of May, a congressional investigation was underway. Within weeks, the federal government had enacted a sweeping bill against 'child pornography' and many of the states followed with bills of their own. These laws have reestablished restrictions on sexual materials that had been relaxed by some of the important Supreme Court decisions. For instance, the Court ruled that neither nudity nor sexual activity per se was obscene. But the child pornography laws define as obscene any depiction of minors who are nude or engaged in sexual activity. This means that photographs of naked children in anthropology textbooks and many of the ethnographic movies shown in college classes are technically illegal in several states. In fact, the instructors are liable to an additional felony charge for showing such images to each student under the age of 18. Although the Supreme Court has also ruled that it is a constitutional right to possess obscene material for private use, some child pornography laws prohibit even the private possession of any sexual material involving minors.

The laws produced by the child-porn panic are ill-conceived and misdirected. They represent far-reaching alterations in the regulation of sexual behavior and abrogate important sexual civil liberties. But hardly anyone noticed as they swept through Congress and state legislatures. With the exception of the North American Man/Boy Love Association and American Civil Liberties Union, no one raised a peep of protest.[5]

A new and even tougher federal child-pornography bill has just reached House-Senate conference. It removes any requirement that prosecutors must prove that alleged child pornography was distributed for commercial sale. Once this bill becomes law, a person merely possessing a nude snapshot of a 17-year-old lover or friend may go to jail for fifteen years, and be fined $100,000. This bill passed the House 400 to 1.[6]

The experiences of art photographer Jacqueline Livingston exemplify the climate created by the child-porn panic. An assistant professor of photography at Cornell University, Livingston was fired in 1978 after exhibiting pictures of male nudes that included photographs of her seven-year-old son masturbating. *Ms. Magazine*, *Chrysalis*, and *Art News* all refused to run ads for Livingston's posters of male nudes. At one point, Kodak confiscated some of her film, and for several months Livingston lived with the threat of prosecution under the child-pornography laws. The Tompkins Country Department of Social Services investigated her fitness as a parent. Livingston's posters have been collected by the Museum of Modern Art, the Metropolitan, and other major museums. But she has paid a high cost in harassment and anxiety for her efforts to capture on film the uncensored male body at different ages (Stambolian, 1980, 1983).

It is easy to see someone like Livingston as a victim of the child-porn wars. It is harder for most people to sympathize with actual boy-lovers. Like communists and homosexuals in the 1950s, boy-lovers are so stigmatized that it is difficult to find defenders for their civil liberties, let alone for their erotic orientation. Consequently, the police have feasted on them. Local police, the FBI, and watchdog postal inspectors have joined to build a huge apparatus whose sole aim is to wipe out the community of men who love underaged youth. In twenty years or so, when some of the smoke has cleared, it will be much easier to show that these men have been the victims of a savage and undeserved witch hunt. A lot of people will be embarrassed by their collaboration with this persecution, but it will be too late to do much good for those men who have spent their lives in prison.

While the misery of boy-lovers affects very few, the other long-term legacy of the Dade County repeal affects almost everyone. The success of the anti-gay campaign ignited long-simmering passions of the American right, and sparked an extensive movement to compress the boundaries of acceptable sexual behavior.

Right-wing ideology linking non-familial sex with communism and political weakness is nothing new. During the McCarthy period, Alfred Kinsey and his Institute for Sex Research were attacked for weakening the moral fiber of Americans and rendering them more vulnerable to communist influence. After congressional investigations and bad publicity, Kinsey's Rockefeller grant was terminated in 1954 (Gebhard, 1976).

Around 1969, the extreme right discovered the Sex Information and Education Council of the United States (SIECUS). In books and pamphlets, such as *The Sex Education Racket: Pornography in the Schools* and *SIECUS: Corrupter of Youth*, the right attacked SIECUS and sex education as communist plots to destroy the family and sap the national will (Courtney, 1969; Drake, 1969). Another pamphlet, *Pavlov's Children (They May Be Yours)* (n.a., 1969), claims that the United Nations Educational, Scientific and Cultural Organization (UNESCO) is in cahoots with SIECUS to undermine religious taboos, to promote the acceptance of abnormal sexual relations, to downgrade absolute moral standards, and to 'destroy racial cohesion', by exposing white people (especially white women) to the alleged 'lower' sexual standards of black people.

New Right and neo-conservative ideology has updated these themes, and leans heavily on linking 'immoral' sexual behavior to putative declines in American power. In 1977, Norman Podhoretz wrote an essay blaming homosexuals for the alleged inability of the United States to stand up to the Russians (Podhoretz, 1977). He thus neatly linked 'the anti-gay fight in the domestic arena and the anti-Communist battles in foreign policy' (Wolfe and Sanders, 1979).

Right-wing opposition to sex education, homosexuality, pornography, abortion, and pre-marital sex moved from the extreme fringes to the political centre-stage after 1977, when right-wing strategists and fundamentalist religious crusaders discovered that these issues had mass appeal. Sexual reaction played a significant role in the right's electoral success in 1980 (Breslin, 1981; Gordon and Hunter, 1977–78; Gregory-Lewis, 1977a, 1977b, 1977c; Kopkind, 1977; Petchesky 1981). Organizations such as the Moral Majority and Citizens for Decency have acquired mass followings, immense financial resources, and unanticipated clout. The Equal Rights Amendment has been defeated, legislation has been passed that mandates new restrictions on abortion, and funding for programs such as Planned Parenthood and sex education has been slashed. Laws and regulations making it more difficult for teenage girls to obtain contraceptives or abortions have been promulgated. Sexual backlash was exploited in successful attacks on the Women's Studies Program at California State University at Long Beach.

The most ambitious right-wing legislative initiative has been the Family Protection Act (FPA), introduced in Congress in 1979. The Family Protection Act is a broad assault on feminism, homosexuals, non-traditional families, and teenage sexual privacy (Brown, 1981). The Family Protection Act has not and probably will not pass, but conservative members of Congress continue to pursue its agenda in a more piecemeal fashion. Perhaps the most glaring sign of the times is the Adolescent Family Life Program. Also known as the Teen Chastity Program, it gets some 15 million federal dollars to encourage teenagers to refrain from sexual intercourse, and to discourage them from using contraceptives if they do have sex, and from having abortions if they get pregnant. In the last few years, there have been countless local confrontations over gay rights, sex education, abortion rights, adult bookstores, and public school curricula. It is unlikely that the anti-sex backlash is over, or that it has even peaked. Unless something changes dramatically, it is likely that the next few years will bring more of the same.

Periods such as the 1880s in England, and the 1950s in the United States, recodify the relations of sexuality. The struggles that were fought leave a residue in the form of laws, social practices, and ideologies which then affect the way in which sexuality is experienced long after the immediate conflicts have faded. All the signs indicate that the present era is another of those watersheds in the politics of sex. The settlements that emerge from the 1980s will have an impact far into the future. It is therefore imperative to understand what is going on and what is at stake in order to make informed decisions about what policies to support and oppose.

It is difficult to make such decisions in the absence of a coherent and intelligent body of radical thought about sex. Unfortunately, progressive political analysis of sexuality is relatively underdeveloped. Much of what is available from the feminist movement has simply added to the mystification that shrouds the subject. There is an urgent need to develop radical perspectives on sexuality.

Paradoxically, an explosion of exciting scholarship and political writing about sex has been generated in these bleak years. In the 1950s, the early gay rights movement began and prospered while the bars were being raided and anti-gay laws were being passed. In the last six years, new erotic communities, political alliances, and analyses have been developed in the midst of the repression. In this essay, I will propose elements of a descriptive and conceptual framework for thinking about sex and its politics. I hope to contribute to the pressing task of creating an accurate, humane, and genuinely liberatory body of thought about sexuality.

SEXUAL THOUGHTS

> 'You see, Tim', Phillip said suddenly, 'your argument isn't reasonable. Suppose I granted your first point that homosexuality is justifiable in certain instances and under certain controls. Then there is the catch: where does justification end and degeneracy begin? Society must condemn to protect. Permit even the intellectual homosexual a place of respect and the first bar is down. Then comes the next and the next until the sadist, the flagellist, the criminally insane demand their places, and society ceases to exist. So I ask again: where is the line drawn? Where does degeneracy begin if not at the beginning of individual freedom in such matters?'
>
> —[Fragment from a discussion between two gay men trying to decide if they may love each other (Barr, 1950, p. 310)]

A radical theory of sex must identify, describe, explain, and denounce erotic injustice and sexual oppression. Such a theory needs refined conceptual tools which can grasp the subject and hold it in view. It must build rich descriptions of sexuality as it exists in society and history. It requires a convincing critical language that can convey the barbarity of sexual persecution.

Several persistent features of thought about sex inhibit the development of such a theory. These assumptions are so pervasive in Western culture that they are rarely questioned. Thus, they tend to reappear in different political contexts, acquiring new rhetorical expressions but reproducing fundamental axioms.

One such axiom is sexual essentialism—the idea that sex is a natural force that exists prior to social life and shapes institutions. Sexual essentialism is embedded in the folk wisdoms of Western societies, which consider sex to be eternally unchanging, asocial, and transhistorical. Dominated for over a century by medicine, psychiatry, and psychology, the academic study of sex has reproduced essentialism. These fields classify sex as a property of individuals. It may reside in their hormones or their psyches. It may be construed as physiological or psychological. But within these ethnoscientific categories, sexuality has no history and no significant social determinants.

During the last five years, a sophisticated historical and theoretical scholarship has challenged sexual essentialism both explicitly and implicitly. Gay history, particularly the work of Jeffrey Weeks, has led this assault by showing that homosexuality as we know it is a relatively modern institutional complex.[7] Many historians have come to see the contemporary institutional forms of heterosexuality as an even more recent development (Hansen, 1979). An important contributor to the new scholarship is Judith Walkowitz, whose research has demonstrated the extent to which prostitution was transformed around the turn of the century. She provides meticulous descriptions of how the interplay of social forces such as ideology, fear, political agitation, legal reform, and medical practice can change the structure of sexual behavior and alter its consequences (Walkowitz, 1980, 1982).

Michel Foucault's *The History of Sexuality* (1978) has been the most influential and emblematic text of the new scholarship on sex. Foucault criticizes the traditional understanding of sexuality as a natural libido yearning to break free of social constraint. He argues that desires are not pre-existing biological entities, but rather that they are constituted in the course of historically specific social practices. He emphasizes the generative aspects of the social organization of sex rather than its repressive elements by pointing out that new sexualities are constantly produced. And he points to a major discontinuity between kinship-based systems of sexuality and more modern forms.

The new scholarship on sexual behavior has given sex a history and created a constructivist alternative to sexual essentialism. Underlying this body of work is an assumption that sexuality is constituted in society and history, not biologically ordained[8]. This does not mean the biological capacities are not prerequisites for human sexuality. It does mean that human sexuality is not comprehensible in purely biological terms. Human organisms with human brains are necessary for human cultures, but no examination of the body or its parts can explain the nature and variety of human social systems. The belly's hunger gives no clues as to the complexities of cuisine. The body, the brain, the genitalia, and the capacity for language are necessary for human sexuality. But they do not determine its content, its experiences, or its institutional forms. Moreover, we never encounter the body unmediated by the meanings that cultures give to it. To paraphrase Levi-Strauss, my position on the relationship between biology and sexuality is a 'Kantianism without a transcendental libido'.[9]

It is impossible to think with any clarity about the politics of race or gender as long as these are thought of as biological entities rather than as social constructs. Similarly, sexuality is impervious to political analysis as long as it is primarily conceived as a biological phenomenon or an aspect of individual psychology. Sexuality is as much a human product as are diets, methods of transportation, systems of etiquette, forms of labor, types of entertainment, processes of production, and modes of oppression. Once sex is understood in terms of social analysis and historical understanding, a more realistic politics of sex becomes possible. One may then think of sexual politics in terms of such phenomena as populations, neighbourhood, settlement patterns, migration, urban conflict, epidemiology, and police technology. These are more fruitful categories of thought than the more traditional ones of sin, disease, neurosis, pathology, decadence, pollution, or the decline and fall of empires.

By detailing the relationships between stigmatized erotic populations and the social forces that regulate them, work such as that of Allan Berube, John D'Emilio, Jeffrey Weeks, and Judith Walkowitz contains implicit categories of political analysis and criticism. Nevertheless, the constructivist perspective has displayed some political weaknesses. This has been most evident in misconstructions of Foucault's position.

Because of his emphasis on the ways that sexuality is produced, Foucault has been vulnerable to interpretations that deny or minimize the reality of sexual repression in the more political sense. Foucault makes it abundantly clear that he is not denying the existence of sexual repression so much as inscribing it within a large dynamic (Foucault, 1978, p. 11). Sexuality in Western societies has been structured within an extremely punitive social framework, and has been subjected to very real formal and informal controls. It is necessary to recognize repressive phenomena without resorting to the essentialist assumptions of the language of libido. It is important to hold repressive sexual practices in focus, even while situating them within a different totality and a more refined terminology (Weeks, 1981, p. 9).

Most radical thought about sex has been embedded within a model of the instincts and their restraints. Concepts of sexual oppression have been lodged within that more biological understanding of sexuality. It is often easier to fall back on the notion of a natural libido subjected to inhumane repression than to reformulate concepts of sexual injustice within a more constructivist framework. But it is essential that we do so. We need a radical critique of sexual arrangements that has the conceptual elegance of Foucault and the evocative passion of Reich.

The new scholarship on sex has brought a welcome insistence that sexual terms be restricted to their proper historical and social contexts, and a cautionary skepticism towards sweeping generalizations. But it is important to be able to indicate groupings of erotic behavior and general trends within erotic discourse. In addition to sexual essentialism, there are at least five other ideological formations whose grip on sexual thought is so strong that to fail to discuss them is to remain enmeshed within them. These are sex negativity, the fallacy of misplaced scale, the hierarchical valuation of sex acts, the domino theory of sexual peril, and the lack of a concept of benign sexual variation.

Of these five, the most important is sex negativity. Western cultures generally consider sex to be a dangerous, destructive, negative force (Weeks, 1981, p. 22). Most Christian tradition, following Paul, holds that sex is inherently sinful. It may be redeemed if performed within marriage for procreative purposes and if the pleasurable aspects are not enjoyed too much. In turn, this idea rests on the assumption that the genitalia are an intrinsically inferior part of the body, much lower and less holy than the mind, the 'soul', the 'heart', or even the upper part of the digestive system (the status of the excretory organs is close to that of the genitalia).[10] Such notions have by now acquired a life of their own and no longer depend solely on religion for their perseverance.

This culture always treats sex with suspicion. It construes and judges almost any sexual practice in terms of its worst possible expression. Sex is presumed guilty until proven innocent. Virtually all erotic behavior is considered bad unless a specific reason to exempt it has been established. The most acceptable excuses are marriage, reproduction, and love. Sometimes scientific curiosity, aesthetic experience, or a long-term intimate relationship may serve. But the exercise of erotic capacity, intelligence, curiosity, or creativity all require pretexts that are unnecessary for other pleasures, such as the enjoyment of food, fiction, or astronomy.

What I call the fallacy of misplaced scale is a corollary of sex negativity. Susan Sontag once commented that since Christianity focused 'on sexual behavior as the root of virtue, everything pertaining to sex has been a "special case" in our culture' (Sontag, 1969, p. 46). Sex law has incorporated the religious attitude that heretical sex is an especially heinous sin that deserves the harshest punishments. Throughout much of European and American history, a single act of consensual anal penetration was grounds for execution. In some states, sodomy still carries twenty-year prison sentences. Outside the law, sex is also a marked category. Small differences in value or behavior are often experienced as cosmic threats. Although people can be intolerant, silly, or pushy about what constitutes proper diet, differences in menu rarely provoke the kinds of rage, anxiety, and sheer terror that routinely accompany differences in erotic taste. Sexual acts are burdened with an excess of significance.

Modern Western societies appraise sex acts according to a hierarchical system of sexual value. Marital, reproductive heterosexuals are alone at the top erotic pyramid. Clamoring below are unmarried monogamous heterosexuals in couples, followed by most other heterosexuals. Solitary sex floats ambiguously. The powerful nineteenth-century stigma on masturbation lingers in less potent, modified forms, such as the idea that masturbation is an inferior substitute for partnered encounters. Stable, long-term lesbian and gay male couples are verging on respectability, but bar dykes and promiscuous gay men are hovering just above the groups at the very bottom of the pyramid. The most despised sexual castes currently include transsexuals, transvestites, fetishists, sadomasochists, sex workers such as prostitutes and porn models, and the lowliest of all, those whose eroticism transgresses generational boundaries.

Individuals whose behavior stands high in this hierarchy are rewarded with certified mental health, respectability, legality, social and physical mobility, institutional support, and material benefits. As sexual behaviors or occupations fall lower on the scale, the individuals who practice them are subjected to a presumption of mental illness, disreputability, criminality, restricted social and physical mobility, loss of institutional support, and economic sanctions.

Extreme and punitive stigma maintains some sexual behaviors as low status and is an effective sanction against those who engage in them. The intensity of this stigma is rooted in Western religious traditions. But most of its contemporary content derives from medical and psychiatric opprobrium.

The old religious taboos were primarily based on kinship forms of social organization. They were meant to deter inappropriate unions and to provide proper kin. Sex laws derived from Biblical pronouncements were aimed at preventing the acquisition of the wrong kinds of affinal partners: consanguineous kin (incest), the same gender (homosexuality), or the wrong species (bestiality). When medicine and psychiatry acquired extensive powers over sexuality, they were less concerned with unsuitable mates than with unfit forms of desire. If taboos against incest best characterized kinship systems of sexual organization, then the shift to an emphasis on taboos against masturbation was more apposite to the newer systems organized around qualities of erotic experience (Foucault, 1978, pp. 106–7).

Medicine and psychiatry multiplied the categories of sexual misconduct. The section on psychosexual disorders in the *Diagnostic and Statistical Manual of Mental and Physical Disorders (DSM)* of the American Psychiatric Association (APA) is a fairly reliable map of the current moral hierarchy of sexual activities. The APA list is much more elaborate than the traditional condemnations of whoring, sodomy, and adultery. The most recent edition, *DSMIII*, removed homosexuality from the roster of mental disorders after a long political struggle. But fetishism, sadism, masochism, transsexuality, transvestism, exhibitionism, voyeurism, and pedophilia are quite firmly entrenched as psychological malfunctions (American Psychiatric Association, 1980). Books are still being written about the genesis, aetiology, treatment, and cure of these assorted 'pathologies.'

Psychiatric condemnation of sexual behaviors invokes concepts of mental and emotional inferiority rather than categories of sexual sin. Low-status sex practices are vilified as mental diseases or symptoms of defective personality integration. In addition, psychological terms conflate difficulties of psycho-dynamic functioning with modes of erotic conduct. They equate sexual masochism with self-destructive personality patterns, sexual sadism with emotional aggression, and homoeroticism with immaturity. These terminological muddles have become powerful stereotypes that are indiscriminately applied to individuals on the basis of their sexual orientations.

Popular culture is permeated with ideas that erotic variety is dangerous, unhealthy, depraved, and a menace to everything from small children to national security. Popular sexual ideology is a noxious stew made up of ideas of sexual sin, concepts of psychological inferiority, anti-communism, mob hysteria, accusations of witchcraft, and xenophobia. The mass media nourish these attitudes with relendess propaganda. I would call this system

Figure 3-1. *The Sex Hierarchy: the Charmed Circle vs. the Outer Limits.*

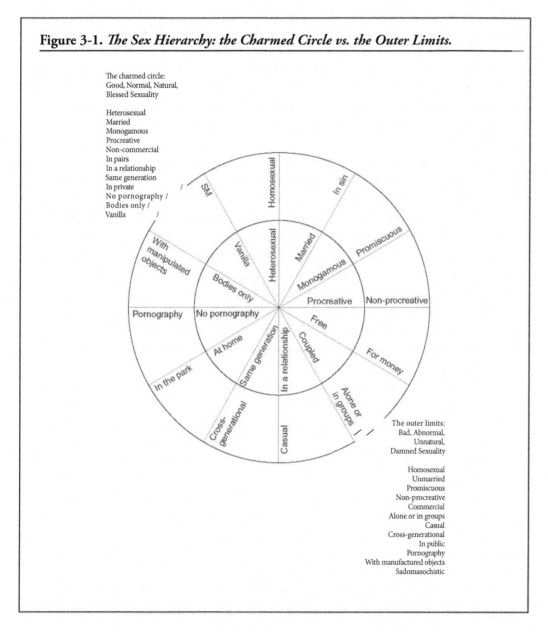

The charmed circle:
Good, Normal, Natural,
Blessed Sexuality

Heterosexual
Married
Monogamous
Procreative
Non-commercial
In pairs
In a relationship
Same generation
In private
No pornography
Bodies only
Vanilla

The outer limits:
Bad, Abnormal,
Unnatural,
Damned Sexuality

Homosexual
Unmarried
Promiscuous
Non-procreative
Commercial
Alone or in groups
Casual
Cross-generational
In public
Pornography
With manufactured objects
Sadomasochistic

of erotic stigma the last socially respectable form of prejudice if the old forms did not show such obstinate vitality, and new ones did not continually become apparent.

All these hierarchies of sexual value—religious, psychiatric, and popular—function in much the same ways as do ideological systems of racism, ethnocentrism, and religious chauvinism. They rationalize the well-being of the sexually privileged and the adversity of the sexual rabble.

Figure 3-1 diagrams a general version of the sexual value system. According to this system, sexuality that is 'good', 'normal', and 'natural' should ideally be heterosexual, marital, monogamous, reproductive, and non-commercial. It should be coupled, relational, within the same generation, and occur at home. It should not involve pornography, fetish objects, sex toys of any sort, or roles other than male and female. Any sex that violates these rules is 'bad', 'abnormal', or 'unnatural'. Bad sex may be homosexual, unmarried, promiscuous, non-procreative, or commercial. It may be masturbatory or take place at orgies, may be casual, may cross generational lines, and may take place in 'public', or at least in the bushes or the baths. It may involve the use of pornography, fetish objects, sex toys, or unusual roles (see Figure 3-1).

Figure 3-2 diagrams another aspect of the sexual hierarchy: the need to draw and maintain an imaginary line between good and bad sex. Most of the discourses on sex, be they religious, psychiatric, popular, or political, delimit a very small portion of human sexual capacity as sanctifiable, safe, healthy, mature, legal, or politically correct. The 'line' distinguishes these from all other erotic behaviors, which are understood to be the work of the devil, dangerous, psychopathological, infantile, or politically reprehensible. Arguments are then conducted over 'where to draw the line', and to determine what other activities, if any, may be permitted to cross over into acceptability.

All these models assume a domino theory of sexual peril. The line appears to stand between sexual order and chaos. It expresses the fear that if anything is permitted to cross this erotic DMZ, the barrier against scary sex will crumble and something unspeakable will skitter across.

Most systems of sexual judgment—religious, psychological, feminist, or socialist— attempt to determine on which side of the line a particular act falls. Only sex acts on the good side of the line are accorded moral complexity. For instance, heterosexual encounters may be sublime or disgusting, free or forced, healing or destructive, romantic or mercenary. As long as it does not violate other rules, heterosexuality is acknowledged to exhibit the full range of human experience. In contrast, all sex acts on the bad side of the line are considered utterly repulsive and devoid of all emotional nuance. The further from the line a sex act is, the more it is depicted as a uniformly bad experience.

As a result of the sex conflicts of the last decade, some behavior near the border is inching across it. Unmarried couples living together, masturbation, and some forms of homosexuality are moving in the direction of respectability (see Figure 3-2). Most homosexuality is still on the bad side of the line. But if it is coupled and monogamous, the society is beginning to recognize that it includes the full range of human interaction. Promiscuous

Figure 3.2. *The Sex Hierarchy: The Struggle Over Where to Draw the Line*

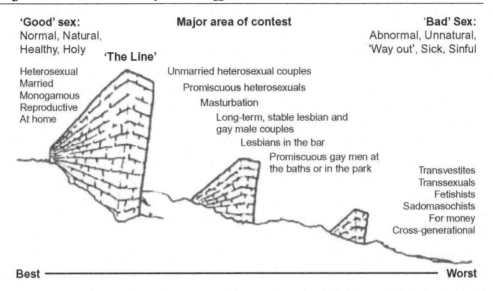

homosexuality, sadomasochism, fetishism, transsexuality, and cross-generational encounters are still viewed as unmodulated horrors incapable of involving affection, love, free choice, kindness, or transcendence.

This kind of sexual morality has more in common with ideologies of racism than with true ethics. It grants virtue to the dominant groups, and relegates vice to the underprivileged. A democratic morality should judge sexual acts by the way partners treat one another, the level of mutual consideration, the presence or absence of coercion, and quantity and quality of the pleasures they provide. Whether sex acts are gay or straight, coupled or in groups, naked or in underwear, commercial or free, with or without video, should not be ethical concerns.

It is difficult to develop a pluralistic sexual ethics without a concept of benign sexual variation. Variation is a fundamental property of all life, from the simplest biological organisms to the most complex human social formations. Yet sexuality is supposed to conform to a single standard. One of the most tenacious ideas about sex is that there is one best way to do it, and that everyone should do it that way.

Most people find it difficult to grasp that whatever they like to do sexually will be thoroughly repulsive to someone else, and that whatever repels them sexually will be the most treasured delight of someone, somewhere. One need not like or perform a particular sex act in order to recognize that someone else will, and that this difference does not indicate a lack of good taste, mental health, or intelligence in either party. Most people mistake their sexual preferences for a universal system that will or should work for everyone.

This notion of a single ideal sexuality characterizes most systems of thought about sex. For religion, the ideal is procreative marriage. For psychology, it is mature heterosexuality.

Although its content varies, the format of a single sexual standard is continually reconstituted within other rhetorical frameworks, including feminism and socialism. It is just as objectionable to insist that everyone should be lesbian, non-monogamous, or kinky, as to believe that everyone should be heterosexual, married, or vanilla—though the latter set of opinions are backed by considerably more coercive power than the former.

Progressives who would be ashamed to display cultural chauvinism in other areas routinely exhibit it towards sexual differences. We have learned to cherish different cultures as unique expressions of human inventiveness rather than as the inferior or disgusting habits of savages. We need a similarly anthropological understanding of different sexual cultures.

Empirical sex research is the one field that does incorporate a positive concept of sexual variation. Alfred Kinsey approached the study of sex with the same uninhibited curiosity he had previously applied to examining a species of wasp. His scientific detachment gave his work a refreshing neutrality that enraged moralists and caused immense controversy (Kinsey et ai, 1948, 1953). Among Kinsey's successors, John Gagnon and William Simon have pioneered the application of sociological understandings to erotic variety (Gagnon and Simon, 1967, 1970; Gagnon, 1977). Even some of the older sexology is useful. Although his work is imbued with unappetizing eugenic beliefs, Havelock Ellis was an acute and sympathetic observer. His monumental *Studies in the Psychology of Sex* is resplendent with detail (Ellis, 1936).

Much political writing on sexuality reveals complete ignorance of both classical sexology and modern sex research. Perhaps this is because so few colleges and universities bother to teach human sexuality, and because so much stigma adheres even to scholarly investigation of sex. Neither sexology nor sex research has been immune to the prevailing sexual value system. Both contain assumptions and information which should not be accepted uncritically. But sexology and sex research provide abundant detail, a welcome posture of calm, and a well-developed ability to treat sexual variety as something that exists rather than as something to be exterminated. These fields can provide an empirical grounding for a radical theory of sexuality more useful than the combination of psychoanalysis and feminist first principles to which so many texts resort.

SEXUAL TRANSFORMATION

As defined by the ancient civil or canonical codes, sodomy was a category of forbidden acts; their perpetrator was nothing more than the juridical subject of them. The nineteenth-century homosexual became a personage, a past, a case history, and a childhood, in addition to being a type of life, a life form, and a morphology, with an indiscreet anatomy and possibly a mysterious physiology ... The sodomite had been a temporary aberration; the homosexual was now a species (Foucault, 1978, p. 43).

In spite of many continuities with ancestral forms, modern sexual arrangements have a distinctive character which sets them apart from preexisting systems. In Western Europe and the United States, industrialization and urbanization reshaped the traditional rural and peasant populations into a new urban industrial and service workforce. It generated new forms of state apparatus, reorganized family relations, altered gender roles, made possible new forms of identity, produced new varieties of social inequality, and created new formats for political and ideological conflict. It also gave rise to a new sexual system characterized by distinct types of sexual persons, populations, stratification, and political conflict.

The writings of nineteenth-century sexology suggest the appearance of a kind of erotic speciation. However outlandish their explanations, the early sexologists were witnessing the emergence of new kinds of erotic individuals and their aggregation into rudimentary communities. The modern sexual system contains sets of these sexual populations, stratified by the operation of an ideological and social hierarchy. Differences in social value create friction among these groups, who engage in political contest to alter or maintain their place in the ranking. Contemporary sexual politics should be reconceptualized in terms of the emergence and on-going development of this system, its social relations, the ideologies that interpret it, and its characteristic modes of conflict.

Homosexuality is the best example of this process of erotic speciation. Homosexual behavior is always present among humans. But in different societies and epochs it may be rewarded or punished, required or forbidden, a temporary experience or a life-long vocation. In some New Guinea societies, for example, homosexual activities are obligatory for all males. Homosexual acts are considered utterly masculine, roles are based on age, and partners are determined by kinship status (Baal, 1966; Herdt, 1981; Kelly, 1976; Rubin, 1974, 1982; Williams, 1936). Although these men engage in extensive homosexual and pedophile behavior, they are neither homosexuals nor pederasts.

Nor was the sixteenth-century sodomite a homosexual. In 1631, Mervyn Touchet, Earl of Castlehaven, was tried and executed for sodomy. It is clear from the proceedings that the Earl was not understood by himself or anyone else to be a particular kind of sexual individual. 'While from the twentieth-century viewpoint Lord Casdehaven obviously suffered from psychosexual problems requiring the services of an analyst, from the seventeenth-century viewpoint he had deliberately broken the Law of God and the Laws of England, and required the simpler services of an executioner' (Bingham, 1971, p. 465). The Earl did not slip into his tightest doublet and waltz down to the nearest gay tavern to mingle with his fellow sodomists. He stayed in his manor house and buggered his servants. Gay self-awareness, gay pubs, the sense of group commonality, and even the term homosexual were not part of the Earl's universe.

The New Guinea bachelor and the sodomite nobleman are only tangentially related to a modern gay man, who may migrate from rural Colorado to San Francisco in order to live in a gay neighborhood, work in a gay business, and participate in an elaborate experience that includes a self-conscious identity, group solidarity, a literature, a press, and a high level of political activity. In modern, Western, industrial societies, homosexuality has acquired much of the institutional structure of an ethnic group (Murray, 1979).

The relocation of homoeroticism into these quasi-ethnic, nucleated, sexually constituted communities is to some extent a consequence of the transfers of population brought by industrialization. As laborers migrated to work in cities, there were increased opportunities for voluntary communities to form. Homosexually inclined women and men, who would have been vulnerable and isolated in most pre-industrial villages, began to congregate in small corners of the big cities. Most large nineteenth-century cities in Western Europe and North America had areas where men could cruise for other men. Lesbian communities seem to have coalesced more slowly and on a smaller scale. Nevertheless, by the 1890s, there were several cafes in Paris near the Place Pigalle that catered to a lesbian clientele, and it is likely that there were similar places in the other major capitals of Western Europe.

Areas like these acquired bad reputations, which alerted other interested individuals of their existence and location. In the United States, lesbian and gay male territories were well established in New York, Chicago, San Francisco, and Los Angeles in the 1950s. Sexually motivated migration to places such as Greenwich Village had become a sizable sociological phenomenon. By the late 1970s, sexual migration was occurring on a scale so significant that it began to have a recognizable impact on urban politics in the United States, with San Francisco being the most notable and notorious example.[11]

Prostitution has undergone a similar metamorphosis. Prostitution began to change from a temporary job to a more permanent occupation as a result of nineteenth-century agitation, legal reform, and police persecution. Prostitutes, who had been part of the general working-class population, became increasingly isolated as members of an outcast group (Walkowitz, 1980). Prostitutes and other sex workers differ from homosexuals and other sexual minorities. Sex work is an occupation, while sexual deviation is an erotic preference. Nevertheless, they share some common features of social organization. Like homosexuals, prostitutes are a criminal sexual population stigmatized on the basis of sexual activity. Prostitutes and male homosexuals are the primary prey of vice police everywhere.[12] Like gay men, prostitutes occupy well-demarcated urban territories and battle with police to defend and maintain those territories. The legal persecution of both populations is justified by an elaborate ideology that classifies them as dangerous and inferior undesirables who are not entitled to be left in peace.

Besides organizing homosexuals and prostitutes into localized populations, the 'modernization of sex' has generated a system of continual sexual ethnogenesis. Other populations of erotic dissidents—commonly known as the 'perversions' or the 'paraphilias'—also began to coalesce. Sexualities keep marching out of the *Diagnostic and Statistical Manual* and on to the pages of social history. At present, several other groups are trying to emulate the successes of homosexuals. Bisexuals, sadomasochists, individuals who prefer cross-generational encounters, transsexuals, and transvestites are all in various states of community formation and identity acquisition. The perversions are not proliferating as much as they are attempting to acquire social space, small businesses, political resources, and a measure of relief from the penalties for sexual heresy.

An entire sub-race was born, different—despite certain kinship ties—from the libertines of the past. From the end of the eighteenth century to our own, they circulated through the pores of society; they were always hounded, but not always by laws; were often locked up, but not always in prisons; were sick perhaps, but scandalous, dangerous victims, prey to a strange evil that also bore the name of vice and sometimes crime. They were children wise beyond their years, precocious little girls, ambiguous schoolboys, dubious servants and educators, cruel or maniacal husbands, solitary collectors, ramblers with bizarre impulses; they haunted the houses of correction, the penal colonies, the tribunals, and the asylums; they carried their infamy to the doctors and their sickness to the judges. This was the numberless family of perverts who were on friendly terms with delinquents and akin to madmen. (Foucault, 1978, p. 40)

The industrial transformation of Western Europe and North America brought about new forms of social stratification. The resultant inequalities of class are well known and have been explored in detail by a century of scholarship. The construction of modern systems of racism and ethnic injustice has been well documented and critically assessed. Feminist thought has analyzed the prevailing organization of gender oppression. But although specific erotic groups, such as militant homosexuals and sex workers, have agitated against their own mistreatment, there has been no equivalent attempt to locate particular varieties of sexual persecution within a more general system of sexual stratification. Nevertheless, such a system exists, and in its contemporary form it is a consequence of Western industrialization.

Sex law is the most adamantine instrument of sexual stratification and erotic persecution. The state routinely intervenes in sexual behavior at a level that would not be tolerated in other areas of social life. Most people are unaware of the extent of sex law, the quantity and qualities of illegal sexual behavior, and the punitive character of legal sanctions. Although federal agencies may be involved in obscenity and prostitution cases, most sex laws are enacted at the state and municipal level, and enforcement is largely in the hands of local police. Thus, there is a tremendous amount of variation in the laws applicable to any given locale. Moreover, enforcement of sex laws varies dramatically with the local political climate. In spite of this legal thicket, one can make some tentative and qualified generalizations. My discussion of sex law does not apply to laws against sexual coercion, sexual assault, or rape. It does pertain to the myriad prohibitions on consensual sex and the 'status' offences such as statutory rape.

Sex law is harsh. The penalties for violating sex statutes are universally out of proportion to any social or individual harm. A single act of consensual but illicit sex, such as placing one's lips upon the genitalia of an enthusiastic partner, is punished in many states with more severity than rape, battery, or murder. Each such genital kiss, each lewd caress, is a separate crime. It is therefore painfully easy to commit multiple felonies in the course of a single evening of illegal passion. Once someone is convicted of a sex violation, a second performance of the same act is grounds for prosecution as a repeat offender, in which case penalties will be even more severe. In some states, individuals have become repeat felons for having engaged in homosexual love-making on two separate occasions. Once an erotic activity has been proscribed by sex law, the full power of the state enforces conformity to the values embodied in those laws. Sex laws are notoriously easy to pass, as legislators are loath to be soft on vice. Once on the books, they are extremely difficult to dislodge.

Sex law is not a perfect reflection of the prevailing moral evaluations of sexual conduct. Sexual variation perse is more specifically policed by the mental-health professions, popular ideology, and extra-legal social practice. Some of the most detested erotic behaviors, such as fetishism and sadomasochism, are not as closely or completely regulated by the criminal justice system as somewhat less stigmatized practices, such as homosexuality. Areas of sexual behavior come under the purview of the law when they become objects of social concern and political uproar. Each sex scare or morality campaign deposits new regulations as a kind of fossil record of its passage. The legal sediment is thickest—and sex law has its greatest potency—in areas involving obscenity, money, minors, and homosexuality.

Obscenity laws enforce a powerful taboo against direct representation of erotic activities. Current emphasis on the ways in which sexuality has become a focus of social attention should not be misused to undermine a critique of this prohibition. It is one thing to create sexual discourse in the form of psychoanalysis, or in the course of a morality crusade. It is quite another to depict sex acts or genitalia graphically. The first is socially permissible in a way the second is not. Sexual speech is forced into reticence, euphemism, and indirection. Freedom of speech about sex is a glaring exception to the protections of the First Amendment, which is not even considered applicable to purely sexual statements.

The anti-obscenity laws also form part of a group of statutes that make almost all sexual commerce illegal. Sex law incorporates a very strong prohibition against mixing sex and money, except via marriage. In addition to the obscenity statutes, other laws impinging on sexual commerce include anti-prostitution laws, alcoholic-beverage regulations, and ordinances governing the location and operation of 'adult' businesses. The sex industry and the gay economy have both managed to circumvent some of this legislation, but that process has not been easy or simple. The underlying criminality of sex-oriented business keeps it marginal, underdeveloped, and distorted. Sex businesses can only operate in legal loopholes. This tends to keep investment down and to divert commercial activity towards the goal of staying out of jail rather than delivery of goods and services. It also renders sex workers more vulnerable to exploitation and bad working conditions. If sex commerce were legal, sex workers would be more able to organize and agitate for higher pay, better conditions, greater control, and less stigma.

Whatever one thinks of the limitations of capitalist commerce, such an extreme exclusion from the market process would hardly be socially acceptable in other areas of activity. Imagine, for example, that the exchange of money for medical care, pharmacological advice, or psychological counseling were illegal. Medical practice would take place in a much less satisfactory fashion if doctors, nurses, druggists, and therapists could be hauled off to jail at the whim of the local 'health squad'. But that is essentially the situation of prostitutes, sex workers, and sex entrepreneurs.

Marx himself considered the capitalist market a revolutionary, if limited, force. He argued that capitalism was progressive in its dissolution of pre-capitalist superstition, prejudice, and the bonds of traditional modes of life. 'Hence the great civilizing influence of capital, its production of a state of society compared with which all earlier stages appear to be merely local progress and idolatry of nature' (Marx, 1971, p. 94). Keeping sex from realizing the positive effects of the market economy hardly makes it socialist.

The law is especially ferocious in maintaining the boundary between childhood 'innocence' and 'adult' sexuality. Rather than recognizing the sexuality of the young, and attempting to provide for it in a caring and responsible manner, our culture denies and punishes erotic interest and activity by anyone under the local age of consent. The amount of law devoted to protecting young people from premature exposure to sexuality is breathtaking.

The primary mechanism for insuring the separation of sexual generations is age of consent laws. These laws make no distinction between the most brutal rape and the most gentle romance. A 20-year-old convicted of sexual contact with a 17-year-old will face a severe sentence in virtually every state, regardless of the nature of the relationship (Norton, 1981).[13] Nor are minors permitted access to 'adult' sexuality in other forms. They are forbidden to see books, movies, or television in which sexuality is 'too' graphically portrayed. It is legal for young people to see hideous depictions of violence, but not to see explicit pictures of genitalia. Sexually active young people are frequently incarcerated in juvenile homes, or otherwise punished for their 'precocity'.

Adults who deviate too much from conventional standards of sexual conduct are often denied contact with the young, even their own. Custody laws permit the state to steal the children of anyone whose erotic activities appear questionable to a judge presiding over family court matters. Countless lesbians, gay men, prostitutes, swingers, sex workers, and 'promiscuous' women have been declared unfit parents under such provisions. Members of the teaching professions are closely monitored for signs of sexual misconduct. In most states, certification laws require that teachers arrested for sex offences lose their jobs and credentials. In some cases, a teacher may be fired merely because an unconventional lifestyle becomes known to school officials. Moral turpitude is one of the few legal grounds for revoking academic tenure (Beserra, Franklin and Clevenger, 1977, pp. 165–7). The more influence one has over the next generation, the less latitude one is permitted in behavior and opinion. The coercive power of the law ensures the transmission of conservative sexual values with these kinds of controls over parenting and teaching.

The only adult sexual behavior that is legal in every state is the placement of the penis in the vagina in wedlock. Consenting adults statutes ameliorate this situation in fewer than half the states. Most states impose severe criminal penalties on consensual sodomy, homosexual contact short of sodomy, adultery, seduction, and adult incest. Sodomy laws vary a great deal. In some states, they apply equally to homosexual and heterosexual partners and regardless of marital status. Some state courts have ruled that married couples have the right to commit sodomy in private. Only homosexual sodomy is illegal in some states. Some sodomy statutes prohibit both anal sex and oral-genital contact. In other states, sodomy applies only to anal penetration, and oral sex is covered under separate statutes (Beserra etai, 1973, pp. 163–8).[14]

Laws like these criminalize sexual behavior that is freely chosen and avidly sought. The ideology embodied in them reflects the value hierarchies discussed above. That is, some sex acts are considered to be so intrinsically vile that no one should be allowed under any circumstance to perform them. The fact that individuals consent to or even prefer them is taken to be additional evidence of depravity. This system of sex law is similar to legalized racism. State prohibition of same-sex contact, anal penetration, and oral sex make homosexuals a criminal group denied the privileges of full citizenship. With such laws, prosecution is persecution. Even when the laws are not strictly enforced, as is usually the case, the members of criminalized sexual communities remain vulnerable to the possibility of arbitrary arrest, or to periods in which they become the objects of social panic. When those occur, the laws are in place and police action is swift. Even sporadic enforcement serves to remind individuals that they are members of a subject population. The occasional arrest for sodomy, lewd behavior, solicitation, or oral sex keeps everyone else afraid, nervous, and circumspect.

The state also upholds the sexual hierarchy through bureaucratic regulation. Immigration policy still prohibits the admission of homosexuals (and other sexual 'deviates') into the United States. Military regulations bar homosexuals from serving in the armed forces. The fact that gay people cannot legally marry means that they cannot enjoy the same legal rights as heterosexuals in many matters, including inheritance, taxation, protection from testimony in court, and the acquisition of citizenship for foreign partners. These are but a few of the ways that the state reflects and maintains the social relations of sexuality. The law buttresses structures of power, codes of behavior, and forms of prejudice. At their worst, sex law and sex regulation are simply sexual apartheid.

Although the legal apparatus of sex is staggering, most everyday social control is extra-legal. Less formal, but very effective social sanctions are imposed on members of 'inferior' sexual populations.

In her marvelous ethnographic study of gay life in the 1960s, Esther Newton observed that the homosexual population was divided into what she called the 'overts' and 'coverts'. "The overts live their entire working lives within the context of the [gay] community; the coverts live their entire nonworking lives within it' (Newton, 1972, p. 21, emphasis in the original). At the time of Newton's study, the gay community provided far fewer jobs than it does now, and the non-gay work world was almost completely intolerant of homosexuality. There were some fortunate individuals who could be openly gay and earn decent salaries. But the vast majority of homosexuals had to choose between honest poverty and the strain of maintaining a false identity.

Though this situation has changed a great deal, discrimination against gay people is still rampant. For the bulk of the gay population, being out on the job is still impossible. Generally, the more important and higher paid the job, the less the society will tolerate overt erotic deviance. If it is difficult for gay people to find employment where they do not have to pretend, it is doubly and triply so for more exotically sexed individuals. Sadomasochists leave their fetish clothes at home, and know that they must be especially careful to conceal their real identities. An exposed pedophile would probably be stoned out of the office. Having to maintain such absolute secrecy is a considerable burden. Even those who are content to be secretive may be exposed by some accidental event. Individuals who are erotically unconventional risk being unemployable or unable to pursue their chosen careers.

Public officials and anyone who occupies a position of social consequence are especially vulnerable. A sex scandal is the surest method for hounding someone out of office or destroying a political career. The fact that important people are expected to conform to the strictest standards of erotic conduct discourages sex perverts of all kinds from seeking such positions. Instead, erotic dissidents are channeled into positions that have less impact on the mainstream of social activity and opinion.

The expansion of the gay economy in the last decade has provided some employment alternatives and some relief from job discrimination against homosexuals. But most of the jobs provided by the gay economy are low-status and low-paying. Bartenders, bathhouse attendants, and disc jockeys are not bank officers or corporate executives. Many of the sexual migrants who flock to places like San Francisco are downwardly mobile. They face intense competition for choice positions. The influx of sexual migrants provides a pool of cheap and exploitable labor for many of the city's businesses, both gay and straight.

Families play a crucial role in enforcing sexual conformity. Much social pressure is brought to bear to deny erotic dissidents the comforts and resources that families provide. Popular ideology holds that families are not supposed to produce or harbor erotic nonconformity. Many families respond by trying to reform, punish, or exile sexually offending members. Many sexual migrants have been thrown out by their families, and many others are fleeing from the threat of institutionalization. Any random collection of homosexuals, sex workers, or miscellaneous perverts can provide heartstopping stories of rejection and mistreatment by horrified families. Christmas is the great family holiday in the United States and consequently it is a time of considerable tension in the gay community. Half the inhabitants go off to their families of origin; many of those who remain in the gay ghettos cannot do so, and relive their anger and grief.

In addition to economic penalties and strain on family relations, the stigma of erotic dissidence creates friction at all other levels of everyday life. The general public helps to penalize erotic non-conformity when, according to the values they have been taught, landlords refuse housing, neighbors call in the police, and hoodlums commit sanctioned battery. The ideologies of erotic inferiority and sexual danger decrease the power of sex perverts and sex workers in social encounters of all kinds. They have less protection from unscrupulous or criminal behavior, less access to police protection, and less recourse to the courts. Dealings with institutions and bureaucracies—hospital, police coroners, banks, public officials—are more difficult.

Sex is a vector of oppression. The system of sexual oppression cuts across other modes of social inequality, sorting out individuals and groups according to its own intrinsic dynamics. It is not reducible to, or understandable in terms of, class, race, ethnicity, or gender. Wealth, white skin, male gender, and ethnic privileges can mitigate the effects of sexual stratification. A rich, white male pervert will generally be less affected than a poor, black, female pervert. But even the most privileged are not immune to sexual oppression. Some of the consequences of the system of sexual hierarchy are mere nuisances. Others are quite grave. In its most serious manifestations, the sexual system is a Kafkaesque nightmare in which unlucky victims become herds of human cattle whose identification, surveillance, apprehension, treatment, incarceration, and punishment produce jobs and self-satisfaction for thousands of vice police, prison officials, psychiatrists, and social workers.[15]

SEXUAL CONFLICTS

The moral panic crystallizes widespread fears and anxieties, and often deals with them not by seeking the real causes of the problems and conditions which they demonstrate but by displacing them on to 'Folk Devils' in an identified social group (often the 'immoral' or 'degenerate'). Sexuality has had a peculiar centrality in such panics, and sexual 'deviants' have been omnipresent scapegoats (Weeks, 1981, p. 14).

The sexual system is not a monolithic, omnipotent structure. There are continuous battles over the definitions, evaluations, arrangements, privileges, and costs of sexual behavior. Political struggle over sex assumes characteristic forms.

Sexual ideology plays a crucial role in sexual experience. Consequently, definitions and evaluations of sexual conduct are objects of bitter contest. The confrontations between early gay liberation and the psychiatric establishment are the best example of this kind of fight, but there are constant skirmishes. Recurrent battles take place between the primary producers of sexual ideology—the churches, the family, the shrinks, and the media—and the groups whose experience they name, distort, and endanger.

The legal regulation of sexual conduct is another battleground. Lysander Spooner dissected the system of state-sanctioned moral coercion over a century ago in a text inspired primarily by the temperance campaigns. In *Vices Are Not Crimes: A Vindication of Moral Liberty*, Spooner argued that government should protect its citizens against crime, but that it is foolish, unjust, and tyrannical to legislate against vice. He discusses rationalizations still heard today in defense of legalized moralism—that 'vices' (Spooner is referring to drink, but homosexuality, prostitution, or recreational drug use may be substituted) lead to crimes, and should therefore be prevented; that those who practice 'vice' are *non compos mentis* and should therefore be protected from their self-destruction by state-accomplished ruin; and that children must be protected from supposedly harmful knowledge (Spooner, 1977). The discourse on victimless crimes has not changed much. Legal struggle over sex law will continue until basic freedoms of sexual action and expression are guaranteed. This requires the repeal of all sex laws except those few that deal with actual, not statutory, coercion; and it entails the abolition of vice squads, whose job it is to enforce legislated morality.

In addition to the definitional and legal wars, there are less obvious forms of sexual political conflict which I call the territorial and border wars. The processes by which erotic minorities form communities and the forces that seek to inhibit them lead to struggles over the nature and boundaries of sexual zones.

Dissident sexuality is rarer and more closely monitored in small towns and rural areas. Consequently, metropolitan life continually beckons to young perverts. Sexual migration creates concentrated pools of potential partners, friends, and associates. It enables individuals to create adult, kin-like networks in which to live. But there are many barriers which sexual migrants have to overcome.

According to the mainstream media and popular prejudice, the marginal sexual worlds are bleak and dangerous. They are portrayed as impoverished, ugly, and inhabited by psychopaths and criminals. New migrants must be sufficiently motivated to resist the impact of such discouraging images. Attempts to counter negative propaganda with more realistic information generally meet with censorship, and there are continuous ideological struggles over which representations of sexual communities make it into the popular media.

Information on how to find, occupy, and live in the marginal sexual worlds is also suppressed. Navigational guides are scarce and inaccurate. In the past, fragments of rumor, distorted gossip, and bad publicity were the most available clues to the location of underground erotic communities. During the late 1960s and early 1970s, better information became available. Now groups like the Moral Majority want to rebuild the ideological walls around the sexual undergrounds and make transit in and out of them as difficult as possible.

Migration is expensive. Transportation costs, moving expenses, and the necessity of finding new jobs and housing are economic difficulties that sexual migrants must overcome. These are especially imposing barriers to the young, who are often the most desperate to move. There are, however, routes into the erotic communities that mark trails through the propaganda thicket and provide some economic shelter along the way. Higher education can be a route for young people from affluent backgrounds. In spite of serious limitations, the information on sexual behavior at most colleges and universities is better than elsewhere, and most colleges and universities shelter small erotic networks of all sorts.

For poorer kids, the military is often the easiest way to get the hell out of wherever they are. Military prohibitions against homosexuality make this a perilous route. Although young queers continually attempt to use the armed forces to get out of intolerable hometown situations and closer to functional gay communities, they face the hazards of exposure, court martial, and dishonorable discharge.

Once in the cities, erotic populations tend to nucleate and to occupy some regular, visible territory. Churches and other anti-vice forces constantly put pressure on local authorities to contain such areas, reduce their visibility, or to drive their inhabitants out of town. There are periodic crackdowns in which local vice squads are unleashed on the populations they control. Gay men, prostitutes, and sometimes transvestites are sufficiently territorial and numerous to engage in intense battles with the cops over particular streets, parks, and alleys. Such border wars are usually inconclusive, but they result in many casualties.

For most of this century, the sexual underworlds have been marginal and impoverished, their residents subjected to stress and exploitation. The spectacular success of gay entrepreneurs in creating a variegated gay economy has altered the quality of life within the gay ghetto. The level of material comfort and social elaboration achieved by the gay community in the last fifteen years is unprecedented. But it is important to recall what happened to similar miracles. The growth of the black population in New York in the early part of the twentieth century led to the Harlem Renaissance, but that period of creativity was doused by the Depression. The relative prosperity and cultural florescence of the ghetto may be equally fragile. Like blacks who fled the South for the metropolitan North, homosexuals may have merely traded rural problems for urban ones.

Gay pioneers occupied neighborhoods that were centrally located but run down. Consequently, they border poor neighborhoods. Gays, especially low-income gays, end up competing with other low-income groups for the limited supply of cheap and moderate housing. In San Francisco, competition for low-cost housing has exacerbated both racism and homophobia, and is one source of the epidemic of street violence against homosexuals. Instead of being isolated and invisible in rural settings, city gays are now numerous and obvious targets for urban frustrations.

In San Francisco, unbridled construction of downtown skyscrapers and high-cost condominiums is causing affordable housing to evaporate. Megabuck construction is creating pressure on all city residents. Poor gay renters are visible in low-income neighborhoods; multimillionaire contractors are not. The specter of the 'homosexual invasion' is a convenient scapegoat, which deflects attention from the banks, the planning commission, the political establishment, and the big developers. In San Francisco, the well-being of the gay community has become embroiled in the high-stakes politics of urban real estate.

Downtown expansion affects all the territorial erotic underworlds. In both San Francisco and New York, high investment construction and urban renewal have intruded on the main areas of prostitution, pornography, and leather bars. Developers are salivating over Times Square, the Tenderloin, what is left of North Beach, and South of Market. Anti-sex ideology, obscenity law, prostitution regulations, and the alcoholic beverage codes are all being used to dislodge seedy adult business, sex workers, and leathermen. Within ten years, most of these areas will have been bulldozed and made safe for convention centers, international hotels, corporate headquarters, and housing for the rich.

The most important and consequential kind of sex conflict is what Jeffrey Weeks has termed the 'moral panic'. Moral panics are the 'political moment' of sex, in which diffuse attitudes are channeled into political action and from there into social change.[16] The white-slavery hysteria of the 1880s, the anti-homosexual campaigns of the 1950s, and the child pornography panic of the late 1970s were typical moral panics.

Because sexuality in Western societies is so mystified, the wars over it are often fought at oblique angles, aimed at phony targets, conducted with misplaced passions, and are highly, intensely symbolic. Sexual activities often function as signifiers for personal and social apprehensions to which they have no intrinsic connection. During a moral panic such fears attach to some unfortunate sexual activity or population. The media become ablaze with indignation, the public behaves like a rabid mob, the police are activated, and the state enacts new laws and regulations. When the furor has passed, some innocent erotic group has been decimated, and the state has extended its power into new areas of erotic behavior.

The system of sexual stratification provides easy victims who lack the power to defend themselves, and a preexisting apparatus for controlling their movements and curtailing their freedoms. The stigma against sexual dissidents renders them morally defenseless. Every moral panic has consequences on two levels. The target population suffers most, but everyone is affected by the social and legal changes.

Moral panics rarely alleviate any real problem, because they are aimed at chimeras and signifiers. They draw on the pre-existing discursive structure which invents victims in order to justify treating 'vices' as crimes. The criminalization of innocuous behaviors such as homosexuality, prostitution, obscenity, or recreational drug use, is rationalized by portraying them as menaces to health and safety, women and children, national security, the family, or civilization itself. Even when an activity is acknowledged to be harmless, it may be banned because it is alleged to 'lead' to something ostensibly worse (another mani-festation of the domino theory).[17] Great and mighty edifices have been built on the basis of such phantasms. Generally, the outbreak of a moral panic is preceded by an intensification of such scapegoating.

It is always risky to prophesy. But it does not take much prescience to detect potential moral panics in two current developments: the attacks on sadomasochists by a segment of the feminist movement, and the right's increasing use of AIDS to incite virulent homophobia.

Feminist anti-pornography ideology has always contained an implied, and sometimes overt, indictment of sadomasochism. The pictures of sucking and fucking that comprise the bulk of pornography may be unnerving to those who are not familiar with them. But it is hard to make a convincing case that such images are violent. All of the early anti-porn slide shows used a highly selective sample of S/M imagery to sell a very flimsy analysis. Taken out of context, such images are often shocking. This shock value was mercilessly exploited to scare audiences into accepting the anti-porn perspective.

A great deal of anti-porn propaganda implies sadomasochism is the underlying and essential 'truth' towards which all pornography tends. Porn is thought to lead to S/M porn which in turn is alleged to lead to rape. This is a just-so story that revitalizes the notion that sex perverts commit sex crimes, not normal people. There is no evidence that the readers of S/M erotica or practicing sadomasochists commit a disproportionate number of sex crimes. Anti-porn literature scapegoats an unpopular sexual minority and its reading material for social problems they do not create.

The use of S/M imagery in anti-porn discourse is inflammatory. It implies that the way to make the world safe for women is to get rid of sadomasochism. The use of S/M images in the movie *Not a Love Story* was on a moral par with the use of depictions of black men raping white women, or of drooling old Jews pawing young Aryan girls, to incite racist or anti-Semitic frenzy.

Feminist rhetoric has a distressing tendency to reappear in reactionary contexts. For example, in 1980 and 1981, Pope John Paul II delivered a series of pronouncements reaffirming his commitment to the most conservative and Pauline understandings of human sexuality. In condemning divorce, abortion, trial marriage, pornography, prostitution, birth control, unbridled hedonism, and lust, the pope employed a great deal of feminist rhetoric about sexual objectification. Sounding like lesbian feminist polemicist Julia Penelope, His Holiness explained that 'considering anyone in a lustful way makes that person a sexual object rather than a human being worthy of dignity'.[18]

The right wing opposes pornography and has already adopted elements of feminist anti-porn rhetoric. The anti-S/M discourse developed in the women's movement could easily become a vehicle for a moral witch hunt. It provides a ready-made defenseless target population. It provides a rationale for the recriminalization of sexual materials that have escaped the reach of current obscenity laws. It would be especially easy to pass laws against S/M erotica resembling the child pornography laws. The ostensible purpose of such laws would be to reduce violence by banning so-called violent porn. A focused campaign against the leather menace might also result in the passage of laws to criminalize S/M behavior that is not currently illegal. The ultimate result of such a moral panic would be the legalized violation of a community of harmless perverts. It is dubious that such a sexual witch hunt would make any appreciable contribution towards reducing violence against women.

An AIDS panic is even more probable. When fears of incurable disease mingle with sexual terror, the resulting brew is extremely volatile. A century ago, attempts to control syphilis led to the passage of the Contagious Diseases Acts in England. The Acts were based on erroneous medical theories and did nothing to halt the spread of the disease. But they did make life miserable for the hundreds of women who were incarcerated, subjected to forcible vaginal examination, and stigmatized for life as prostitutes (Walkowitz, 1980; Weeks, 1981).

Whatever happens, AIDS will have far-reaching consequences on sex in general, and on homosexuality in particular. The disease will have a significant impact on the choices gay people make. Fewer will migrate to the gay meccas out of fear of the disease. Those who already reside in the ghettos will avoid situations they fear will expose them. The gay economy, and political apparatus it supports, may prove to be evanescent. Fear of AIDS has already affected sexual ideology. Just when homosexuals have had some success in throwing off the taint of mental disease, gay people find themselves metaphorically welded to an image of lethal physical deterioration. The syndrome, its peculiar qualities, and its transmissibility are being used to reinforce old fears that sexual activity, homosexuality, and promiscuity led to disease and death.

AIDS is both a personal tragedy for those who contract the syndrome and a calamity for the gay community. Homophobes have gleefully hastened to turn this tragedy against its victims. One columnist has suggested that AIDS has always existed, that the Biblical prohibitions on sodomy were designed to protect people from AIDS, and that AIDS is therefore an appropriate punishment for violating the Levitical codes. Using fear of infection as a rationale, local right-wingers attempted to ban the gay rodeo from Reno, Nevada. A recent issue of the *Moral Majority Report* featured a picture of a 'typical' white family of four wearing surgical masks. The headline read: 'AIDS: HOMOSEXUAL DISEASES THREATEN AMERICAN FAMILIES'.[19] Phyllis Schlaflyhas recently issued a pamphlet arguing that passage of the Equal Rights Amendment would make it impossible to 'legally protect ourselves against AIDS and other diseases carried by homosexuals' (cited in Bush, 1983, p. 60). Current right-wing literature calls for shutting down the gay baths, for a legal ban on homosexual employment in food-handling occupations, and for state-mandated prohibitions on blood donations by gay people. Such policies would require the government to identify all homosexuals and impose easily recognizable legal and social markers on them.

It is bad enough that the gay community must deal with the medical misfortune of having been the population in which a deadly disease first became widespread and visible. It is worse to have to deal with the social consequences as well. Even before the AIDS scare, Greece passed a law that enables police to arrest suspected homosexuals and force them to submit to an examination for venereal disease. It is likely that until AIDS and its methods of transmission are understood, there will be all sorts of proposals to control it by punishing the gay community and by attacking its institutions. When the cause of Legionnaires' Disease was unknown, there were no calls to quarantine members of the American Legion or to shut down their meeting halls. The Contagious Diseases Acts in England did little to control syphilis, but they caused a great deal of suffering for the women who came under their purview. The history of panic that has accompanied new epidemics, and of the casualties incurred by their scapegoats, should make everyone pause and consider with extreme skepticism any attempts to justify anti-gay policy initiatives on the basis of AIDS.

THE LIMITS OF FEMINISM

We know that in an overwhelmingly large number of cases, sex crime is associated with pornography. We know that sex criminals read it, are clearly influenced by it. I believe that, if we can eliminate the distribution of such items among impressionable children, we shall greatly reduce our frightening sex-crime rate.

(J. Edgar Hoover, cited in Hyde, 1965, p. 31)

In the absence of a more articulated radical theory of sex, most progressives have turned to feminism for guidance. But the relationship between feminism and sex is complex. Because sexuality is a nexus of relationships between genders, much of the oppression of women is borne by, mediated through, and constituted within, sexuality. Feminism has always been vitally interested in sex. But there have been two strains of feminist thought on the subject. One tendency has criticized the restrictions on women's sexual behavior and denounced the high costs imposed on women for being sexually active. This tradition of feminist sexual thought has called for a sexual liberation that would work for women as well as for men. The second tendency has considered sexual liberalization to be inherently a mere extension of male privilege. This tradition resonates with conservative, anti-sexual discourse. With the advent of the anti-pornography movement, it achieved temporary hegemony over feminist analysis.

The anti-pornography movement and its texts have been the most extensive expression of this discourse.[20] In addition, proponents of this viewpoint have condemned virtually every variant of sexual expression as anti-feminist. Within this framework, monogamous lesbianism that occurs within long-term, intimate relationships and which does not involve playing with polarized roles, has replaced married, procreative heterosexuality at the top of the value hierarchy. Heterosexuality has been demoted to somewhere in the middle. Apart from this change, everything else looks more or less familiar. The lower depths are occupied by the usual groups and behaviors: prostitution, transsexuality, sadomasochism, and cross-generational activities (Barry, 1979,1982; Linden etai, 1982; Raymond, 1979; Rush, 1980). Most gay male conduct, all casual sex, promiscuity, and lesbian behavior that does involve roles or kink or non-monogamy are also censured.[21] Even sexual fantasy during masturbation is denounced as a phallocentric holdover (Penelope, 1980).

This discourse on sexuality is less a sexology than a demonology. It presents most sexual behavior in the worst possible light. Its descriptions of erotic conduct always use the worst available example as if it were representative. It presents the most disgusting pornography, the most exploited forms of prostitution, and the least palatable or most shocking manifestations of sexual variation. This rhetorical tactic consistently misrepresents human sexuality in all its forms. The picture of human sexuality that emerges from this literature is unremittingly ugly.

In addition, this anti-porn rhetoric is a massive exercise in scapegoating. It criticizes non-routine acts of love rather than routine acts of oppression, exploitation, or violence. This demon sexology directs legitimate anger at women's lack of personal safety against innocent individuals, practices, and communities. Anti-porn propaganda often implies that sexism originates within the commercial sex industry and subsequently infects the rest of society. This is sociologically nonsensical. The sex industry is hardly a feminist Utopia. It reflects the sexism that exists in the society as a whole. We need to analyze and oppose the manifestations of gender inequality specific to the sex industry. But this is not the same as attempting to wipe out commercial sex.

Similarly, erotic minorities such as sadomasochists and transsexuals are as likely to exhibit sexist attitudes or behavior as any other politically random social grouping. But to claim that they are inherently anti-feminist is sheer fantasy. A good deal of current feminist literature attributes the oppression of women to graphic representations of sex, prostitution, sex education, sadomasochism, male homosexuality, and transsexualism. Whatever happened to the family, religion, education, child-rearing practices, the media, the state, psychiatry, job discrimination, and unequal pay?

Finally, this so-called feminist discourse recreates a very conservative sexual morality. For over a century, battles have been waged over just how much shame, distress, and punishment should be incurred by sexual activity. The conservative tradition has promoted opposition to pornography, prostitution, homosexuality, all erotic variation, sex education, sex research, abortion, and contraception. The opposing, pro-sex tradition has included individuals such as Havelock Ellis, Magnus Hirschfeld, Alfred Kinsey, and Victoria Woodhull, as well as the sex-education movement, organizations of militant prostitutes and homosexuals, the reproductive rights movement, and organizations such as the Sexual Reform League of the 1960s. This motley collection of sex reformers, sex educators, and sexual militants has mixed records on both sexual and feminist issues. But surely they are closer to the spirit of modern feminism than are moral crusaders, the social purity movement, and anti-vice organizations. Nevertheless, the current feminist sexual demonology generally elevates the anti-vice crusaders to positions of ancestral honor, while condemning the more liberatory tradition as anti-feminist. In an essay that exemplifies some of these trends, Sheila Jeffreys blames Havelock Ellis, Edward Carpenter, Alexandra Kollantai, 'believers in the joy of sex of every possible political persuasion', and the 1929 congress of the World League for Sex Reform for making 'a great contribution to the defeat of militant feminism' (Jeffreys, 1981, p. 26).[22]

The anti-pornography movement and its avatars have claimed to speak for all feminism. Fortunately, they do not. Sexual liberation has been and continues to be a feminist goal. The women's movement may have produced some of the most retrogressive sexual thinking this side of the Vatican. But it has also produced an exciting, innovative, and articulate defense of sexual pleasure and erotic justice. This 'pro-sex' feminism has been spearheaded by lesbians whose sexuality does not conform to movement standards of purity (primarily lesbian sadomasochists and butch/femme dykes), by unapologetic heterosexuals, and by women who adhere to classic radical feminism rather than to the revisionist celebrations of femininity that have become so common.[23] Although the anti-porn forces have attempted to weed anyone who disagrees with them out of the movement, the fact remains that feminist thought about sex is profoundly polarized (Orlando, 1982b; Willis, 1982).

Whenever there is polarization, there is an unhappy tendency to think the truth lies somewhere in between. Ellen Willis has commented sarcastically that 'the feminist bias is that women are equal to men and the male chauvinist bias is that women are inferior. The unbiased view is that the truth lies somewhere in between' (Willis, 1982, p. 146).[24] The most recent development in the feminist sex wars is the emergence of a 'middle' that seeks to evade the dangers of anti-porn fascism, on the one hand, and a supposed 'anything goes' libertarianism, on the other.[25] Although it is hard to criticize a position that is not yet fully formed, I want to draw attention to some incipient problems.

The emergent middle is based on a false characterization of the poles of debate, construing both sides as equally extremist. According to B. Ruby Rich, 'the desire for a language of sexuality has led feminists into locations (pornography, sadomasochism) too narrow or overdetermined for a fruitful discussion. Debate has collapsed into a rumble' (Rich, 1983, p. 76). True, the fights between Women Against Pornography (WAP) and lesbian sadomasochists have resembled gang warfare. But the responsibility for this lies primarily with the anti-porn movement, and its refusal to engage in principled discussion. S/M lesbians have been forced into a struggle to maintain their membership in the movement, and to defend themselves against slander. No major spokeswoman for lesbian S/M has argued for any kind of S/M supremacy, or advocated that everyone should be a sadomasochist. In addition to self-defense, S/M lesbians have called for appreciation for erotic diversity and more open discussion of sexuality (Samois, 1979, 1982; Califia, 1980e, 1981a). Trying to find a middle course between WAP and Samois is a bit like saying that the truth about homosexuality lies somewhere between the positions of the Moral Majority and those of the gay movement.

In political life, it is all too easy to marginalize radicals, and to attempt to buy acceptance for a moderate position by portraying others as extremists. Liberals have done this for years to communists. Sexual radicals have opened up the sex debates. It is shameful to deny their contribution, misrepresent their positions, and further their stigmatization.

In contrast to cultural feminists, who simply want to purge sexual dissidents, the sexual moderates are willing to defend the rights of erotic non-conformists to political participation. Yet this defense of political rights is linked to an implicit system of ideological condescension. The argument has two major parts. The first is an accusation that sexual dissidents have not paid close enough attention to the meaning, sources, or historical construction of their sexuality. This emphasis on meaning appears to function in much the same way that the question of aetiology has functioned in discussions of homosexuality. That is, homosexuality, sadomasochism, prostitution, or boy-love are taken to be mysterious and problematic in some way that more respectable sexualities are not. The search for a cause is a search for something that could change so that these 'problematic' eroticisms would simply not occur. Sexual militants have replied to such exercises that although the question of aetiology or cause is of intellectual interest, it is not high on the political agenda and that, moreover, the privileging of such questions is itself a regressive political choice.

The second part of the 'moderate' position focuses on questions of consent. Sexual radicals of all varieties have demanded the legal and social legitimation of consenting sexual behavior. Feminists have criticized them for ostensibly finessing questions about 'the limits of consent' and 'structural constraints' on consent (Orlando, 1983; Wilson, 1983, especially pp. 35–41). Although there are deep problems with the political discourse of consent, and although there are certainly structural constraints on sexual choice, this criticism has been consistently misapplied in the sex debates. It does not take into account the very specific semantic content that consent has in sex law and sex practice.

As I mentioned earlier, a great deal of sex law does not distinguish between consensual and coercive behavior. Only rape law contains such a distinction. Rape law is based on the assumption, correct in my view, that heterosexual activity may be freely chosen or forcibly coerced. One has the legal right to engage in heterosexual behavior as long as it does not fall under the purview of other statutes and as long as it is agreeable to both parties.

This is not the case for most other sexual acts. Sodomy laws, as I mentioned above, are based on the assumption that the forbidden acts are an 'abominable and detestable crime against nature'. Criminality is intrinsic to the acts themselves, no matter what the desires of the participants. 'Unlike rape, sodomy or an unnatural or perverted sexual act may be committed between two persons both of whom consent, and, regardless of which is the aggressor, both may be prosecuted.'[26] Before the consenting adults statute was passed in California in 1976, lesbian lovers could have been prosecuted for committing oral copulation. If both participants were capable of consent, both were equally guilty (Beserra et al., 1973, pp. 163–5).[27]

Adult incest statutes operate in a similar fashion. Contrary to popular mythology, the incest statutes have little to do with protecting children from rape by close relatives. The incest statutes themselves prohibit marriage or sexual intercourse between adults who are closely related. Prosecutions are rare, but two were reported recently. In 1979, a 19-year-old Marine met his 42-year-old mother, from whom he had been separated at birth. The two fell in love and got married. They were charged and found guilty of incest, which under Virginia law carries a maximum ten-year sentence. During their trial, the Marine testified, 'I love her very much. I feel that two people who love each other should be able to live together.'[28] In another case, a brother and sister who had been raised separately met and decided to get married. They were arrested and pleaded guilty to felony incest in return for probation. A condition of probation was that they not live together as husband and wife. Had they not accepted, they would have faced twenty years in prison (Norton, 1981, p. 18). In a famous S/M case, a man was convicted of aggravated assault for a whipping administered in an S/M scene. There was no complaining victim. The session had been filmed and he was prosecuted on the basis of the film. The man appealed his conviction by arguing that he had been involved in a consensual sexual encounter and had assaulted no one. In rejecting his appeal, the court ruled that one may not consent to an assault or battery 'except in a situation involving ordinary physical contact or blows incident to sports such as football, boxing, or wrestling'.[29] The court went on to note that the 'consent of a person without legal capacity to give consent, such as a child or insane person, is ineffective', and that 'It is a matter of common knowledge that a normal person in full possession of his mental faculties does not freely consent to the use, upon himself, of force likely to produce great bodily injury'.[30] Therefore, anyone who would consent to a whipping would be presumed *non compos mentis* and legally incapable of consenting. S/M sex generally involves a much lower level of force than the average football game, and results in far fewer injuries than most sports. But the court ruled that football players are sane, whereas masochists are not.

Sodomy laws, adult incest laws, and legal interpretations such as the one above clearly interfere with consensual behavior and impose criminal penalties on it. Within the law, consent is a privilege enjoyed only by those who engage in the highest-status sexual behavior. Those who enjoy low-status sexual behavior do not have the legal right to engage in it. In addition, economic sanctions, family pressures, erotic stigma, social discrimination, negative ideology, and the paucity of information about erotic behavior, all serve to make it difficult for people to make unconventional sexual choices. There certainly are structural constraints that impede free sexual choice, but they hardly operate to coerce anyone into being a pervert. On the contrary, they operate to coerce everyone towards normality.

The 'brainwash theory' explains erotic diversity by assuming that some sexual acts are so disgusting that no one would willingly perform them. Therefore, the reasoning goes, anyone who does so must have been forced or fooled. Even constructivist sexual theory has been pressed into the service of explaining away why otherwise rational individuals might engage in variant sexual behavior. Another position that is not yet fully formed uses the ideas of Foucault and Weeks to imply that the 'perversions' are an especially unsavoury or problematic aspect of the construction of modern sexuality (Valverde, 1980; Wilson, 1983, p. 38). This is yet another version of the notion that sexual dissidents are victims of the subtle machinations of the social system. Weeks and Foucault would not accept such an interpretation, since they consider all sexuality to be constructed, the conventional no less than the deviant.

Psychology is the last resort of those who refuse to acknowledge that sexual dissidents are as conscious and free as any other group of sexual actors. If deviants are not responding to the manipulations of the social system, then perhaps the source of their incomprehensible choices can be found in a bad childhood, unsuccessful socialization, or inadequate identity formation. In her essay on erotic domination, Jessica Benjamin draws upon psychoanalysis and philosophy to explain why what she calls 'sadomasochism' is alienated, distorted, unsatisfactory, numb, purposeless, and an attempt to 'relieve an original effort at differentiation that failed' (Benjamin, 1983, p. 292).[31] This essay substitutes a psycho-philosophical inferiority for the more usual means of devaluing dissident eroticism. One reviewer has already construed Benjamin's argument as showing that sadomasochism is merely an 'obsessive replay of the infant power struggle' (Ehrenreich, 1983, p. 247).

The position which defends the political rights of perverts but which seeks to understand their 'alienated' sexuality is certainly preferable to the WAP-style blood-baths. But for the most part, the sexual moderates have not confronted their discomfort with erotic choices that differ from their own. Erotic chauvinism cannot be redeemed by tarting it up in Marxist drag, sophisticated constructivist theory, or retro-psychobabble.

Whichever feminist position on sexuality—right, left, or centre—eventually attains dominance, the existence of such a rich discussion is evidence that the feminist movement will always be a source of interesting thought about sex. Nevertheless, I want to challenge the assumption that feminism is or should be the privileged site of a theory of sexuality. Feminism is the theory of gender oppression. To assume automatically that this makes it the theory of sexual oppression is to fail to distinguish between gender, on the one hand, and erotic desire, on the other.

In the English language, the word 'sex' has two very different meanings. It means gender and gender identity, as in 'the female sex' or 'the male sex'. But sex also refers to sexual activity, lust, intercourse, and arousal, as in 'to have sex'. This semantic merging reflects a cultural assumption that sexuality is reducible to sexual intercourse and that it is a function of the relations between women and men. The cultural fusion of gender with sexuality has given rise to the idea that a theory of sexuality may be derived directly out of a theory of gender.

In an earlier essay, 'The Traffic in Women', I used the concept of sex/gender system, defined as a 'set of arrangements by which a society transforms biological sexuality into products of human activity' (Rubin, 1975, p. 159). I went on to argue that 'Sex as we know it—gender identity, sexual desire and fantasy, concepts of childhood—is itself a social product' (1975, p. 66). In that essay, I did not distinguish between lust and gender, treating both as modalities of the same underlying social process.

'The Traffic in Women' was inspired by the literature on kin-based systems of social organization. It appeared to me at the time that gender and desire were systematically intertwined in such social formations. This may or may not be an accurate assessment of the relationship between sex and gender in tribal organizations. But it is surely not an adequate formulation for sexuality in Western industrial societies. As Foucault has pointed out, a system of sexuality has emerged out of earlier kinship forms and has acquired significant autonomy.

Particularly from the eighteenth century onward, Western societies created and deployed a new apparatus which was superimposed on the previous one, and which, without completely supplanting the latter, helped to reduce its importance. I am speaking of the deployment of sexuality. ... For the first [kinship], what is pertinent is the link between partners and definite statutes; the second [sexuality] is concerned with the sensations of the body, the quality of pleasures, and the nature of impressions (Foucault, 1978, p. 106).

The development of this sexual system has taken place in the context of gender relations. Part of the modern ideology of sex is that lust is the province of men, purity that of women. It is no accident that pornography and perversions have been considered part of the male domain. In the sex industry, women have been excluded from most production and consumption, and allowed to participate primarily as workers. In order to participate in the 'perversions', women have had to overcome serious limitations on their social mobility, their economic resources, and their sexual freedoms. Gender affects the operation of the sexual system, and the sexual system has had gender-specific manifestations. But although sex and gender are related, they are not the same thing, and they form the basis of two distinct arenas of social practice.

In contrast to my perspective in 'The Traffic in Women', I am now arguing that it is essential to separate gender and sexuality analytically to reflect more accurately their separate social existence. This goes against the grain of much contemporary feminist thought, which treats sexuality as a derivation of gender. For instance, lesbian feminist ideology has mostly analyzed the oppression of lesbians in terms of the oppression of women. However, lesbians are also oppressed as queers and perverts, by the operation of sexual, not gender, stratification. Although it pains many lesbians to think about it, the fact is that lesbians have shared many of the sociological features and suffered from many of the same social penalties as have gay men, sadomasochists, transvestites, and prostitutes.

Catherine MacKinnon has made the most explicit theoretical attempt to subsume sexuality under feminist thought. According to MacKinnon, 'Sexuality is to feminism what work is to Marxism … the molding, direction, and expression of sexuality organizes society into two sexes, women and men' (MacKinnon, 1982, pp. 5–16). This analytic strategy in turn rests on a decision to 'use sex and gender relatively interchangeably' (MacKinnon, 1983, p. 635). It is this definitional fusion that I want to challenge.

There is an instructive analogy in the history of the differentiation of contemporary feminist thought from Marxism. Marxism is probably the most supple and powerful conceptual system extant for analyzing social inequality. But attempts to make Marxism the sole explanatory system for all social inequalities have been dismal exercises. Marxism is most successful in the areas of social life for which it was originally developed—class relations under capitalism.

In the early days of the contemporary women's movement, a theoretical conflict took place over the applicability of Marxism to gender stratification. Since Marxist theory is relatively powerful, it does in fact detect important and interesting aspects of gender oppression. It works best for those issues of gender most closely related to issues of class and the organization of labor. The issues more specific to the social structure of gender were not amenable to Marxist analysis.

The relationship between feminism and a radical theory of sexual oppression is similar. Feminist conceptual tools were developed to detect and analyze gender-based hierarchies. To the extent that these overlap with erotic stratifications, feminist theory has some explanatory power. But as issues become less those of gender and more those of sexuality, feminist analysis becomes misleading and often irrelevant. Feminist thought simply lacks angles of vision that can fully encompass the social organization of sexuality. The criteria of relevance in feminist thought do not allow it to see or assess critical power relations in the area of sexuality.

In the long run, feminism's critique of gender hierarchy must be incorporated into a radical theory of sex, and the critique of sexual oppression should enrich feminism. But an autonomous theory and politics specific to sexuality must be developed.

It is a mistake to substitute feminism for Marxism as the last word in social theory. Feminism is no more capable than Marxism of being the ultimate and complete account of all social inequality. Nor is feminism the residual theory which can take care of everything to which Marx did not attend. These critical tools were fashioned to handle very specific areas of social activity. Other areas of social life, their forms of power, and their characteristic modes of oppression, need their own conceptual implements. In this essay, I have argued for theoretical as well as sexual pluralism.

CONCLUSION

... these pleasures which we lightly call physical ...
(Colette, 1982, p. 72)

Like gender, sexuality is political. It is organized into systems of power, which reward and encourage some individuals and activities, while punishing and suppressing others. Like the capitalist organization of labor and its distribution of rewards and powers, the modern sexual system has been the object of political struggle since it emerged and as it has evolved. But if the disputes between labor and capital are mystified, sexual conflicts are completely camouflaged.

The legislative restructuring that took place at the end of the nineteenth century and in the early decades of the twentieth was a refracted response to the emergence of the modern erotic system. During that period, new erotic communities formed. It became possible to be a male homosexual or a lesbian in a way it had not been previously. Mass-produced erotica became available, and the possibilities for sexual commerce expanded. The first homosexual rights organizations were formed, and the first analyses of sexual oppression were articulated (Lauritsen and Thorstad, 197A).

The repression of the 1950s was in part a backlash to the expansion of sexual communities and possibilities which took place during World War Two (Berube, 1981a, 1981b; D'Emilio, 1983). During the 1950s, gay rights organizations were established, the Kinsey reports were published, and lesbian literature flourished. The 1950s were a formative as well as a repressive era.

The current right-wing sexual counter-offensive is in part a reaction to the sexual liberalization of the 1960s and early 1970s. Moreover, it has brought about a unified and self-conscious coalition of sexual radicals. In one sense, what is now occurring is the emergence of a new sexual movement, aware of new issues and seeking a new theoretical basis. The sex wars out on the streets have been partly responsible for provoking a new intellectual focus on sexuality. The sexual system is shifting once again, and we are seeing many symptoms of its change.

In Western culture, sex is taken all too seriously. A person is not considered immoral, is not sent to prison, and is not expelled from her or his family, for enjoying spicy cuisine. But an individual may go through all this and more for enjoying shoe leather. Ultimately, of what possible social significance is it if a person likes to masturbate over a shoe? It may even be non-consensual, but since we do not ask permission of our shoes to wear them, it hardly seems necessary to obtain dispensation to come on them.

If sex is taken too seriously, sexual persecution is not taken seriously enough. There is systematic mistreatment of individuals and communities on the basis of erotic taste or behavior. There are serious penalties for belonging to the various sexual occupational castes. The sexuality of the young is denied, adult sexuality is often treated like a variety of nuclear waste, and the graphic representation of sex takes place in a mire of legal and social circumlocution. Specific populations bear the brunt of the current system of erotic power, but their persecution upholds a system that affects everyone.

The 1980s have already been a time of great sexual suffering. They have also been a time of ferment and new possibility. It is up to all of us to try to prevent more barbarism and to encourage erotic creativity. Those who consider themselves progressive need to examine their preconceptions, update their sexual educations, and acquaint themselves with the existence and operation of sexual hierarchy. It is time to recognize the political dimensions of erotic life.

A NOTE ON DEFINITIONS

Throughout this essay, I use terms such as homosexual, sex worker, and pervert. I use 'homosexual' to refer to both women and men. If I want to be more specific, I use terms such as 'lesbian' or 'gay male'. 'Sex worker' is intended to be more inclusive than 'prostitute', in order to encompass the many jobs of the sex industry. Sex worker includes erotic dancers, strippers, porn models, nude women who will talk to a customer via telephone hookup and can be seen but not touched, phone partners, and the various other employees of sex businesses such as receptionists, janitors, and barkers. Obviously, it also includes prostitutes, hustlers, and 'male models'. I use the term 'pervert' as a shorthand for all the stigmatized sexual orientations. It is used to cover male and female homosexuality as well but as these become less disreputable, the term has increasingly referred to the other 'deviations'. Terms such as 'pervert' and 'deviant' have, in general use, a connotation of disapproval, disgust, and dislike. I am using these terms in a denotative fashion, and do not intend them to convey any disapproval on my part.

DISCUSSION QUESTIONS

1. Although written nearly twenty five years ago, this landmark essay by Gayle Rubin provides a historical perspective on the relationship between politics, cultural processes, and sexuality in the United States that remains remarkably relevant to our society today. Which of her main points are surprisingly valid and pertinent for American society today?

2. Writing in 1983, Gayle Rubin feared the onset of a "moral panic" engineered by political conservatives in the United States, using the fear of the spread of AIDS to incite "virulent homophobia." Did this "moral panic" materialize in your view? If not, what factors might have contributed to a shift in public opinion?

NOTES

1. Walkowitz's entire discussion of the *Maiden Tribute of Modern Babylon* and its aftermath (1982, pp. 83–5) is illuminating.

2. I am indebted to Allan Berube for calling my attention to this incident.

3. The following examples suggest avenues for additional research. A local crackdown at the University of Michigan is documented in Tsang (1977a, 1977b). At the University of Michigan, the number of faculty dismissed for alleged homosexuality appears to rival the number fired for alleged communist tendencies. It would be interesting to have figures comparing the number of professors who lost their positions during this period due to sexual and political offences. On regulatory reform, many states passed laws during this period prohibiting the sale of alcoholic beverages to 'known sex perverts' or providing that bars that catered to 'sex perverts' be closed. Such a law was passed in California in 1955, and declared unconstitutional by the state Supreme Court in 1959 (Allan Berube, personal communication). It would be of great interest to know exactly which states passed such statutes, the dates of their enactment, the discussion that preceded them, and how many are still on the books. On the persecution of other erotic populations, evidence indicates that John Willie and Irving Klaw, the two premier producers and distributors of bondage erotica in the United States from the late 1940s through the early 1960s, encountered frequent police harassment and that Klaw, at least, was affected by a congressional investigation conducted by the Kefauver Committee. I am indebted to personal communication from J.B. Rund for information on the careers of Willie and Klaw. Published sources are scarce, but see Willie (1974); Rund (1977, 1978, 1979). It would be useful to have more systematic information on legal shifts and police activity affecting non-gay erotic dissidence.

4. 'Chicago is center of national child porno ring: the child predators', 'Child sex: square in new town tells it all', 'U.S. orders hearings on child pornography: Rodino calls sex racket an "outrage"', 'Hunt six men, twenty boys in crackdown', *Chicago Tribune*,

16 May 1977; 'Dentist seized in child sex raid: Carey to open probe', 'How ruses lure victims to child pornographers', *Chicago Tribune*, 1977; 'Child pornographers thrive on legal confusion', 'U.S. raids hit porn sellers', *Chicago Tribune*, 1977.

5. For more information on the 'Kiddie porn panic' see Califia (1980c, 1980d); Mitzel (1980); Rubin (1981). On the issue of cross-generational relationships, see also Moody (1980), O'Carroll (1980),Tsang (1981), and Wilson (1981).

6. 'House passes tough bill on child porn', *San Francisco Chronicle*, 15 November 1983, p. 14.

7. This insight was first articulated by Mary McIntosh (1968); the idea has been developed in Jeffrey Weeks (1977, 1981); see also D'Emilio (1983) and Rubin (1979).

8. A very useful discussion of these issues can be found in Robert Padgug (1979).

9. Levi-Strauss (1970). In this conversation, Levi-Strauss calls his position 'a Kantianism without a transcendental subject'.

10. See, for example, 'Pope praises couples for self-control', *San Francisco Chronicle*, 13 October 1980; 'Pope says sexual arousal isn't a sin if it's ethical', *San Francisco Chronicle*, 6 November 1980; 'Pope condemns "carnal lust" as abuse of human freedom', *San Francisco Chronicle*, 15 January 1981; 'Pope again hits abortion, birth control', *San Francisco Chronicle*, 16 January 1981; and 'Sexuality, not sex in heaven', *San Francisco Chronicle*, 3 December 1981. See also footnote 18 below.

11. For further elaboration of these processes, see: Berube (1981a); D'Emilio (1981, 1983); Foucault (1978); Katz (1976); Weeks (1977, 1981).

12. Vice cops also harass all sex businesses, be these gay bars, gay baths, adult book stores, the producers and distribution of commercial erotica, or swing clubs.

13. This article (Norton, 1981) is a superb summary of much current sex law and should be required reading for anyone interested in sex.

14. This earlier edition of the Sex Code of California preceded the 1976 consenting adults statute and consequently gives a better overview of sodomy laws.

15. D'Emilio (1983, pp. 40–53) has an excellent discussion of gay oppression in the 1950s, which covers many of the areas I have mentioned. The dynamics he describes, however, are operative in modified forms for other erotic populations, and in other periods. The specific model of gay oppression needs to be generalized to apply, with appropriate modifications, to other sexual groups.

16. I have adopted this terminology from the very useful discussion in Weeks, 1981, pp. 14–15.

17. See Spooner, 1977, pp. 25–9. Feminist anti-porn discourse fits right into the tradition of justifying attempts at moral control by claiming that such action will protect women and children from violence.

18. 'Pope's talk on sexual spontaneity', *San Francisco Chronicle*, 13 November 1980, p. 8; see also footnote 10 above. Julia Penelope argues that 'we do not need anything that labels

itself purely sexual' and that 'fantasy, as an aspect of sexuality, may be a phallocentric "need" from which we are not yet free ... ' in Penelope, 1980, p. 103.

19. *Moral Majority Report,* July 1983. I am indebted to Allan Berube for calling my attention to this image.

20. See for example Lederer (1980); Dworkin (1981). The *Newspage* of San Francisco's Women Against Violence in Pornography and Media and the *Newsreport* of New York Women Against Pornography are excellent sources.

21. Gearhart (1979); Rich (1979, p. 225). (On the other hand, there is homosexual patriarchal culture, a culture created by homosexual men, reflecting such male stereotypes as dominance and submission as modes of relationship, and separation of sex from emotional involvement—a culture tainted by profound hatred for women. The male 'gay' culture has offered lesbians the imitation role-stereotypes of 'butch' and 'femme', 'active' and 'passive', cruising, sadomasochism, and the violent, self-destructive world of 'gay bars': Pasternack, 1983; Rich, 1983.)

22. A further elaboration of this tendency can be found in Pasternack, 1983.

23. Califia (1980a, 1980b, 1980c, 1980d, 1980e, 1981b, 1982a, 1982b, 1983a, 1983b, 1983c); English, Hollibaugh, and Rubin (1981a, 1981b); Hollibaugh (1983); Holz (1983); O'Dair (1983); Orlando (1982a); Russ (1982); Samois (1979, 1982); Sundhal (1983); Wechsler (1981a, 1981b); Willis (1981). For an excellent overview of the history of the ideological shifts in feminism that have affected the sex debates, see Echols (1983).

24. I am indebted to Jeanne Bergman for calling my attention to this quote.

25. See for example, Benjamin (1983, p. 297) and Rich (1983).

26. *Taylor v. State*, 214 Md. 156, 165, 133 A. 2d 414, 418. This quote is from a dissenting opinion, but it is a statement of prevailing law.

27. See note 14 above.

28. 'Marine and Mom Guilty of Incest', *San Francisco Chronicle,* 16 November 1979, p. 16.

29. *People v. Samuels*, 250 Cal. App. 2d 501, 513, 58 Cal. Rptr. 439, *AAl* (1967).

30. *People v. Samuels*, 250 Cal. App. 2d at 513–14, 58 Cal. Rptr. at *AAl.*

31. But see also pp. 286, 291–7.

REFERENCES

[N.A.], (1969) *Pavlov's Children (They May Be Yours),* Los Angeles: Impact Publishers.

Alderfer, H., Jaker, B. and Nelson, M. (1982) *Diary of a Conference on Sexuality,* New York: Faculty Press.

American Psychiatric Association (1980) *Diagnostic and Statistical Manual of Mental and Physical Disorders,* Third Edition, Washington, DC: American Psychiatric Association.

Baal, J.V. (1966) *Dema,* Tne Hague: Nijhoff.

Barker-Benfield, G.J. (1976) *The Horrors of the Half-Known Life,* New York: Harper Colophon.

Barr, J. (1950) *Quatrefoil,* New York: Greenberg.

Barry, K. (1979) *Female Sexual Slavery,* Englewood Cliffs, NJ: Prentice-Hall.

(1982) 'Sadomasochism: the new backlash to feminism', *Trivia,* 1, fall, [n.p.n.].

Benjamin, J. (1983) 'Master and slave: the fantasy of erotic domination', in Sni-Tow, A., Stansell, C. and Thompson, S. (eds) *Powers of Desire,* New York: Monthly Review Press.

Berube, A. (1981a) 'Behind the specter of San Francisco', *Body Politic,* April, [n.p.n.].

(1981b) 'Marching to a different drummer', *Advocate,* 15 October, [n.p.n.].

Beserra, S.S., Franklin, S.G. and Clevenger, N. (eds) (1977) *Sex Code of California,* Sacramento: Planned Parenthood Affiliates of California., Jewel, N.M., Matthews, M.W. and Gatov, E.R. (eds) (1973) *Sex Code of California,* Public Education and Research Committee of California.

Bingham, C. (1971) 'Seventeenth-century attitudes toward deviant sex", *Journal of Interdisciplinary History,* spring, pp. 447–68.

Breslin, J. (1981) 'The moral majority in your motel room', *San Francisco Chronicle,* 22 January, p. 41. Brown, R. (1981) 'Blueprint for a moral America, *Nation,* 23 May, [n.p.n.].

Bush, L. (1983) 'Capitol report', *Advocate,* 8 December, [n.p.n.].

Califia, P. (1980a) Among us, against us—the new puritans', *Advocate,* 17 April, [n.p.n.].

(1980b) 'Feminism vs. sex: a new conservative wave', *Advocate,* 21 February, [n.p.n.].

(1980c) 'The great kiddy porn scare of'77 and its aftermath', *Advocate,* 16 October, [n.p.n.].

(1980d) A thorny issue splits a movement', *Advocate,* 30 October, [n.p.n.].

(1980e) *Sapphistry,* Tallahassee: Naiad.

(1981a) 'Feminism and sadomasochism', *Co-Evolution Quarterly,* 33, spring, [n.p.n.].

(1981b) 'What is gay liberation?', *Advocate,* 25 June, [n.p.n.].

(1982a) 'Public sex', *Advocate,* 30 September, [n.p.n.].

(1982b) 'Response to Dorchen Leidholdt', *New Women's Times,* October, [n.p.n.].

(1983a) 'Doing it together: gay men, lesbians and sex', *Advocate,* 7 July, [n.p.n.].

(1983b) 'Gender-bending', *Advocate,* 15 September, [n.p.n.].

(1983c) "The sex industry', *Advocate,* 13 October, [n.p.n.].

City Of New York (1939) *Report of the Mayor's Committee for the Study of Sex Offenses.*

Colette, S.G. (1982) *The Ripening Seed,* translated and cited in Alderfer, H., Jaker, B. and Nelson, M., *Diary of a Conference on Sexuality,* New York: Faculty Press.

Commonwealth Of Massachusetts (1947) *Preliminary Report of the Special Commission Investigating the Prevalence of Sex Crimes.*

Courtney, P. (1969) *The Sex Education Racket: Pornography in the Schools (An Expose),* New Orleans: Free Men Speak.

D'Emilio, J. (1981) 'Gay politics, gay community: San Francisco's experience', *Socialist Review,* 55, pp. 77–104.

(1983) *Sexual Politics, Sexual Communities: The Making of the Homosexual Minority in the United States, 1940–1970,* Chicago: University of Chicago Press.

Drake, G.V. (1969) *SIECUS: Corrupter of Youth,* Tulsa, OK: Christian Crusade Publications.

Dworkin, A. (1981) *Pornography,* New York: Perigee.

Echols, A. (1983) 'Cultural feminism: feminist capitalism and the anti-pornography movement', *Social Text, 7,* spring/summer, pp. 34–53.

Ehrenreich, B. (1983) 'What is this thing called sex?', *Nation, 24* September, p. 247.

Ellis, H. (1936) *Studies in the Psychology of Sex,* 2 vols, New York: Random House.

English, D., Hollibaugh, A. and Rubin, G. (1981a) 'Talking sex', *Socialist Review,* July–August, [n.p.n.].

(1981b) 'Sex issue', *Heresies,* 12, [n.p.n.].

Foucault, M. (1978) *The History of Sexuality, Volume 1: An Introduction,* New York: Pantheon.

Freedman, E.B. (1983) '"Uncontrolled desire": the threat of the sexual psychopath in America, 1935–60', paper presented at the Annual Meeting of the American Historical Association, San Francisco, December.

Gagnon, J. (1977) *Human Sexualities,* Glenview: Scott, Foresman.

and Simon, W (eds) (1967) *Sexual Deviance,* New York: Harper & Row.

(1970) *The Sexual Scene,* Chicago: Transaction Books, Aldine.

Gearhart, S. (1979) An open letter to the voters in district 5 and San Francisco's gay community' [no publication details available].

Gebhard, PH. (1976) 'The institute,' in Weinberg, M.S. (ed.) *Sex Research: Studies From the Kinsey Institute,* New York: Oxford University Press.

Gerassi, J. (1968) *The Boys of Boise,* New York: Collier.

Gordon, L. and Dubois, E. (1983) 'Seeking ecstasy on the battlefield: danger and pleasure in nineteenth century feminist sexual thought', *Feminist Studies,* 9, pp. 7–26.

and Hunter, A. (1977–78) 'Sex, family, and the new right', *Radical America,* [no issue no.], pp. 9–26.

Gregory-Lewis, S. (1977a) 'Right wing finds new organizing tactic', *Advocate,* 23 June, [n.p.n.].

(1977b) 'The neo-right political apparatus', *Advocate,* 8 February, [n.p.n.].

(1977c) 'Unraveling the anti-gay network', *Advocate, 7* September, [n.p.n.].

Hansen, B. (1979) 'The historical construction of homosexuality', *Radical History Review,* 20, pp. 66–73.

Hartwell, S. (1950) A Citizen's Handbook *of Sexual Abnormalities and the Mental Hygiene Approach to Their Prevention,* State of Michigan.

Herdt, G. (1981) *Guardians of the Flutes,* New York: McGraw-Hill.

Hollibaugh, A. (1983) 'The erotophobic voice of women: building a movement for the nineteenth century', *New York Native,* 26 September-9 October, [n.p.n.].

Holz, M. (1983) 'Porn: turn on or put down, some thoughts on sexuality', *Processed World, 7,* spring, [n.p.n.].

Hyde, H.M. (1965) *A History of Pornography,* New York: Dell.

Jeffreys, S. (1981) 'The spinster and her enemies: sexuality and the last wave of feminism', *Scarlet Woman*, 13, July, [n.p.n.].

Katz, J. (1976) *Gay American History*, New York: Thomas Y. Crowell.

Kelly, R. (1976) 'Witchcraft and sexual relations', in Brown, P. and Buchbind-Er, G. (eds) *Man and Woman in the New Guinea Highlands*, Washington, DC: American Anthropological Association.

Kinsey, A., Pomeroy, W and Martin, C. (1948) *Sexual Behavior in the Human Male*, Philadelphia, PA: WB. Saunders.

Kinsey, A., Pomeroy, W, Martin, C. and Gebhard, P. (1953) *Sexual Behavior in the Human Female*, Philadelphia, PA: WB. Saunders.

Kopkind, A. (1977) 'America's new right', *New Times*, 30 September, [n.p.n.].

Lauritsen, J. andTHORSTAD, D. (1974) *The Early Homosexual Rights Movement in Germany*, New York: Times Change Press.

Lederer, L. (ed.) (1980) *Take Back the Night*, New York: William Morrow.

Lévi-Strauss, C. (1970) 'A confrontation', *New Left Review*, 62, July-August, [n.p.n.].

Linden, R.R., Pagano, D.R., Russell, D.E.H. and Starr, S.L. (eds) (1982) *Against Sadomasochism*, East Palo Alto, CA: Frog in the Well.

Mcintosh, M. (1968) 'The homosexual role', *Social Problems*, 16, pp. 182–92.

Mackinnon, C. (1982) 'Feminism, marxism, method and the state: an agenda for theory', *SignsJ*, pp. 515–44.

(1983) 'Feminism, marxism, method and the state: toward feminist jurispru dence', *Signs*, 8(4), pp. 635–58.

Marcus, S. (1974) *The Other Victorians*, New York: New American Library.

Marx, K. (1971) *The Grundrisse*, New York: Harper Torchbooks.

Mitzel (1980) *The Boston Sex Scandal*, Boston, MA: Glad Day Books.

Moody, R (1980) *Indecent Assault*, London: Word Is Out Press.

Moral Majority (1983) *Moral Majority Report*, July, [no publication details available].

Murray, S.O. (1979) 'The institutional elaboration of a quasi-ethnic community', *International Review of Modern Sociology*, 9(2), pp. 165–78.

Newton, E. (1972) *Mother Camp: Female Impersonators in America*, Englewood Cliffs, NJ: Prentice Hall.

Norton, C. (1981) 'Sex in America', *Inquiry*, 5 October, [n.p.n.].

O'Carroll, T (1980) *Paedophilia: The Radical Case*, London: Peter Owen.

O'Dair, B. (1983) 'Sex, love and desire: feminists struggle over the portrayal of sex', *Alternative Media*, spring, [n.p.n.].

Orlando, L. (1982a) 'Bad girls and "good" polities', *Village Voice*, Literary Supple ment, December, [n.p.n.]. (1982b) 'Lust at last! Spandex invades the academy, *Gay Community News*, 15 May, [n.p.n.]. (1983) 'Power plays: coming to terms with lesbian S/M', *Village Voice*, 26 July, [n.p.n.].

Padgug, R (1979) 'Sexual matters: on conceptualizing sexuality in history', *Radical History Review*, 20, pp. 3–23.

Pasternack, J. (1983) 'The strangest bedfellows: lesbian feminism and the sexual revolution', *WomanNews*, October, [n.p.n.].

Penelope, J. (1980) 'And now for the really hard questions', *Sinister Wisdom*, 15, fall, [n.p.n.].

Petchesky, R.P. (1981) 'Anti-abortion, anti-feminism, and the rise of the new right', *Feminist Studies*, 7(2), pp. 206–46.

Podhoretz, N. (1977) 'The culture of appeasement', *Harper's*, October, [n.p.n.]. Raymond, J. (1979) *The Transsexual Empire*, Boston, MA: Beacon.

Rich, A. (1979) *On Lies, Secrets, and Silence*, New York: WW Norton.

(1983) 'Compulsory heterosexuality and lesbian existence', in Snitow, A., Stansell, C. and Thompson, S. (eds) Powers of Desire: The Politics of Sexuality, New York: Monthly Review Press.

Rich, B.R (1983) 'Review of Powers of Desire', *In These Times*, 16–22 November.

Rubin, G. (1974) 'Coconuts: aspects of male/female relationships in New Guinea', unpublished manuscript.

(1975) 'The traffic in women: notes on the political economy of sex', in Reiter, R (ed.) *Toward an Anthropology of Women*, New York: Monthly Review Press.

(1979) 'Introduction', in Vivien, R., *A Woman Appeared to Me*, Weatherby Lake: Naiad Press.

(1981) 'Sexual politics, the new right and the sexual fringe', in Tsang, D. (ed.) *The Age Taboo*, Boston, MA: Alyson.

(1982) 'Guardians of the Flutes', *Advocate*, 23 December, [n.p.n.].

Rund, J.B. (1977) 'Preface', *Bizarre Commix*, vol. 8, New York: Belier Press.

(1978) 'Preface', *Bizarre Fotos*, vol. 1, New York: Belier Press.

(1979) 'Preface', *Bizarre Katalogs*, New York: Belier Press.

Rush, F. (1980) *The Best Kept Secret*, New York: McGraw-Hill.

Russ, J. (1982) 'Being against pornography', *Thirteenth Moon*, 6(1–2), [n.p.n.].

Ryan, M. (1979) 'The power of women's networks: a case study of female moral reform in America', *Feminist Studies*, 5(1), pp. 66–85.

Samois (1979) *What Color Is Your Handkerchief*, Berkeley, CA: Samois.

(1982) *Coming to Power*, Boston, MA: Alyson.

Sontag, S. (1969) *Styles of Radical Will*, New York: Farrar, Straus, & Giroux. SPOONER, L. (1977) *Vices Are Not Crimes: A Vindication of Moral Liberty*, Cupertino, CA: Tanstaafl Press.

Stambolian, G. (1980) 'Creating the new man: a conversation with Jacqueline Livingston', *Christopher Street*, May, [n.p.n.].

(1983) 'Jacqueline Livingston', *Clothed With the Sun*, 3(1), May, [n.p.n.].

State Of Michigan (1951) *Report of the Governor's Study Commission on the Deviated Criminal Sex Offender.*

State Of New Hampshire (1949) *Report of the Interim Commission of The State of New Hampshire to Study the Cause and Prevention of Serious Sex Crimes.*

State Of New York (1950) *Report to the Governor on a Study of 102 Sex Offenders at Sing Sing Prison.*

Sundhal, D. (1983) 'Stripping for a living', *Advocate*, 13 October, [n.p.n.].

Tsang, D. (1977a) 'Gay Ann Arbor purges', *Midwest Gay Academic Journal*, 1(1), [n.p.n.].

(1977b) Ann Arbor purges, part 2', *Midwest Gay Academic Journal*, 1(2), [n.p.n.].

(ed.) (1981) *The Age Taboo*, Boston, MA: Alyson Publications.

Valverde, M. (1980) 'Feminism meets fist-fucking: getting lost in lesbian S & M', *Body Politic*, February, [n.p.n.].

Walkowitz, J.R. (1980) *Prostitution and Victorian Society*, Cambridge: Cambridge University Press.

(1982) 'Male vice and feminist virtue: feminism and the politics of prostitution in nineteenth-century Britain', *History Workshop Journal*, 13, spring, pp. 77–93

Wechsler, N. (1981a) 'Interview with Pat Califia and Gayle Rubin, part I', *Gay Community News*, 18 July, [n.p.n.].

(1981b) 'Interview with Pat Califia and Gayle Rubin, part IF, *Gay Community News*, 15 August, [n.p.n.].

Weeks, J. (1977) *Coming Out: Homosexual Politics in Britain from the Nineteenth Century to the Present*, New York: Quartet.

(1981) *Sex, Politics and Society: The Regulation of Sexuality since 1800*, New York: Longman.

Williams, F.E. (1936) *Papuans of the Trans-Fly*, Oxford: Clarendon.

Willie, J. (1974) *The Adventures of Sweet Gwendoline*, New York: Belier Press.

Willis, E. (1981) *Beginning to See the Light*, New York: Knopf.

(1982) 'Who is feminist? An open letter to Robin Morgan', *Village Voice*, Liter ary Supplement, December, [n.p.n.].

Wilson, E. (1983) 'The context of "between pleasure and danger": The Barnard Conference on Sexuality', *Feminist Review*, 13, spring, pp. 35–41.

Wilson, P. (1981) *The Man They Called A Monster*, New South Wales: Cassell Australia.

Wolfe, A., and Sanders, J. (1979) 'Resurgent cold war ideology: the case of the Committee on the Present Danger', in Fagen, R (ed.) *Capitalism and the State in US-Latin American Relations*, Stanford, CA: Stanford University Press.

Zambaco, D. (1981) 'Onanism and nervous disorders in two girls', in Peraldi, F. (ed.) *Poly sexuality, Semiotext(e)*, 4(1), [n.p.n.].

INTRODUCTION TO: PERSPECTIVES ON SEXUALITY IN THE U.S.

1900–2010

JAN CAMPBELL

T he events that influenced sexuality in the U.S. between 1900–2010 are identified and discussed in this article. The chronology, showing contributing factors that shaped current views and behaviors, gives the reader a perspective of
contemporary thinking in the sexuality arena.

Each decade has produced a focus on how sexuality was viewed. Beginning in the 1900s
with the ideas that sex was for the right reason, with the right person and in the right position, until this decade, in which legalities of who can marry whom are challenged, we can
see a progression of contributing factors that have created varied views of the discipline.

The world wars, the industrial revolution, developing medicine and pharmaceuticals,
greater geographic mobility, the baby boom and baby bust, the sexual revolution, hippies
"turning on, tuning in, and dropping out," the movements of the 1960s and 1970s like
Civil Rights, Women's Movement, Chicano Movement, and the "pill," have all contributed
to influence our ways of life and our sexuality. These events along with cultural diversity
seem to create us anew, as an entire nation, each decade or so.

PERSPECTIVES ON SEXUALITY IN THE U.S.

1900–2010

JAN CAMPBELL

Human sexuality is the integral characteristic that allows us to bond with one another in ways other than for erotic pleasure or mating. In fact, human sexuality is a lifelong process of connectedness with other humans. We never stop needing human touch, we relate to one another in various ways (depending on our connections), and everything we do affects our sexuality. In fact, sexuality also affects everything we do—from establishing gender roles and finding a mate to child rearing and growing old.

Contributing factors that have affected human sexuality behavior and health over the years have been numerous. Progress in medicine and pharmaceuticals has provided Americans with longer and better lives. We have been able to witness events made possible through the technologies of satellites and high-resolution television. Since the advent of these technologies, we view our world in a much more cosmopolitan way. We have seen the Eiffel Tower and witnessed war occurring on the front lines, all from our living rooms. We have been exposed to labor-saving devices that have given us more leisure time. Childhood and infectious diseases have been curtailed so we can live well into later years. Because of the addition of immigrants since our country's inception, we are culturally more diverse and have a richer human landscape in our food, language, clothing, and art. The cultural, technological, social, environmental, and political impacts in the last one hundred ten years have given us a perspective on how our sexuality has been affected—in both positive and negative ways.

Until now, each generation has been able to do better economically than the one previous. Education gives us prosperity and an ability to live longer. These are only a few of the contributing factors that have sped our lives, made them easier, allowed us to live longer, and, in the process, altered the way we see each other. Human sexuality is based on how we view ourselves and interact with each other. Since our world has had such change since 1900, we would expect our sexuality to change in reflection to the world around us. Anatomy, of course, has not changed much. Knowledge about physiology has changed a great deal. But sexuality is much more than that. It is the bond that allows us to connect with each other and provide our future generations with this connectedness.

With these and other contributing factors, our population has witnessed changes in how we raise offspring, what values and beliefs our population prizes, and how modern life has been shaped. With all of the advantages and vast successes in the areas of medicine, technology, and social and sexual diversity, we have also seen adversity. Before 1900, and until public health agencies created better and cleaner water, sanitary conditions in the U.S. were poor and mortality was high, presumably due to infectious diseases (Cutler and Miller, 2005). The advent of modern ways of disposing of sewage allowed individuals to stave off debilitating and often fatal illnesses like cholera and typhoid fever. After the two major world wars, numerous hospitals were erected under the Hill-Burton Act to care for the sick and train physicians (Thomas, 2006). New occupations had to be developed to effect changes in the enormous boom in medicine and the pharmaceutical industries. Women went into the work force en masse, although women of color and poor immigrant women had always worked outside the home (or inside the home for someone else). Diseases of civilization and crowding began to occur. Today, we deal with more chronic illnesses, but we have also seen the AIDS pandemic decimate populations around the world and new microscopic superbugs develop.

When we look at human behavior, we see that accelerated social, economic, and political changes occur in many areas; these changes affect human sexuality, too. With prosperity came trains and planes and automobiles so that bergs and communities that to some degree had been isolated were now seeing newcomers. The gene pools of those small bergs became less isolated. The farms and small stores of the new frontiers soon gave way to small cities, and in large cities the Industrial Revolution began mass production of goods and services that had once been part of a bartering or trading system.

The American family, whose sustainability had been dependent on being a microcosm of society (a small unit characterized by an extended kinship within which each person has a function, produces a good or service, and sells, trades or barters that product), was now finding that moving to a city to find work in factories was a better way to make a living. It was less expensive for the nuclear family to move to the jobs, leaving the extended family behind. This created a new way of viewing the jobs within the family. Children were employed in factories for pennies a day. Sometimes tragedies happened that resulted in laws to ensure health and safety. Upton Sinclair wrote, in *The Jungle* (1906), of the atrocities in the meat-packing industry: accidents involving children workers who slipped on animal parts or had fingers amputated that ended up in the sausage grinder. Accidents like these necessitated child-labor laws, and later, laws were added detailing how long women could work each day in industries. Institutions were established to educate children in public schools while parents went to work. Religious institutions picked up more of the task of preparing youth for spiritual education. Government began to develop more programs to help with Americans' growing concerns with laws to keep the peace (especially on the frontier), economic stability, and social problems.

Looking at the decades since 1900, it is clear that each one provided much to our view of human sexuality, especially roles, behaviors, and family.

The 1900s

The decade beginning in 1901 was, for most Americans, a period of new frontiers on the western front and prim and proper etiquette in the cities. Many western and eastern Europeans were immigrating, and with them came new ideas, dress, languages, and foods. The tenor of the times was primarily dictated by what was happening socially in England. Queen Victoria was enthroned, and while she was not viewed in later biographies as quite as prudish as once thought, most of social America followed the lead of her reign. Women wore high collars and floor-length dresses with lots of crinoline slips. Even table legs, which in Victorian style represented the feet of animals, were covered to the floor—so as not to show too much leg. Bathing suits were similar to long Johns for men, and women wore ruffled bloomers and a hat and carried a parasol (umbrella) to the beach. Women were modest; men were "knowers and doers" of all. They were supposed to fix things and oversee situations. Men were not supposed to fail—at anything! This idea created a role for men—they were stoic and nonemotional.

Sexuality was not discussed, except euphemistically, and women were taught to "grin and bear it," as their duty was to sexually please their spouse. Since marital rape exemption laws were in effect and were expected, the idea of refusing was not an option. In fact, the idea of the times was that people were supposed to be sexual with the right person, which was the spouse, in the right position, which was missionary, and for the right reason, which was procreation. Activity, in anything other than those conditions, was considered deviant. Of course, missionary style of intercourse, with male on top, was the way missionaries and clergy around the world had introduced civilized behavior to native persons in their own lands. It wasn't until the anthropologists Franz Boas and Dr. Margaret Mead (Lutkehaus, N. 2008) spoke of being "cultural relative" about behaviors seen as "different" in a new culture that the idea of anything other than being sexually civilized was questioned. We should not judge behaviors or cultural ideas differently than those we've been exposed to but merely see them as different.

In addition to the ways in which people were to consider sex, another curious behavior was taking place. Young men, upon reaching a milestone birthday, maybe around sixteen years old, might be introduced to the world of prostitution. In major cities, young men would be taken to brothels by their male kin and taught about sex. This is because women were mostly thought of as either women you married or women you learned about sex with. In the early part of the century, a song by Harry Von Tilzer called "I Want a Girl

Just Like the Girl That Married Dear Old Dad" (DapperDan-Field Notebook, n.d.) was popular. The implication was that the women suitable for marriage to young men were pure, chaste, and prepared for marriage—just like Mom. Of course, since slavery had been a large part of the early years in the newly discovered West, the idea of marriage had not always been part of African-American heritage. Slaves were sold and were moved from plantation to plantation, and families were often separated (Martin, M. and Tera Hunter, 2010).

As the decade progressed, the "war to end all wars," World War I, broke out in Europe. Many young men were picked up and transported far across the European landscape to help the allies. Many of these men had never left their farms, their cities of birth. It was apparent to them that Europe was quite different. First, the men were cold, frightened, and away from home. They were given cigarettes by the military to calm their nerves and to help keep them warm. The idea of taking rest and recreation in Paris during the 1920s allowed these young soldiers to see burlesque shows and the can-can, in which women lifted their skirts and showed their legs. The idea of variety and vaudeville shows then spread to the new frontiers of America. The new freedoms changed these men, and songs like "How Ya Gonna Keep 'Em Down on the Farm After They've Seen Paree" again reflected the new ways of life.

When these troops returned to America, they not only smoked but now they didn't see the ideas of sexuality behavior quite the same as before they had embarked on their European tour of duty. Cars, trains, and new ways of transportation also allowed for more geographic freedom, and with more travel came the recognition that villages, cities, and communities had many different cultural ideas. The Little Italy and Chinatown populations, the South Boston Irish, the Ukrainian population in Upstate New York, and many of the Scandinavians living in the Upper Midwest all had specific cultures that were somewhat different from those of the early English settlers. The Wild West initiated the pony express and rail travel, which opened up the frontier areas as new towns began.

The 1920s and 1930s

The "Roaring 20s" and the depression years of the 1930s changed behaviors dramatically. The antithesis of the Victorian Era brought with it women flappers, who danced with their breasts taped down to flatten them and wore fringed dresses that seemed animated during risqué dances like the Charleston. These were certainly not the ways of the 1900s.

Prohibition and bathtub gin ushered in an era of corruption and crimes that were accentuated by gangsters like Pretty Boy Floyd, Al Capone, Machine Gun Kelly, and others. The FBI sought to restore order, and newspapers reported on the latest villain to be taken down. The 1967 movie, *Bonnie and Clyde*, portrayed the era as being about bank robbers who terrorized Americans during the Great Depression of the 1930s with the tag line, "They're young, they're in love, they rob banks!" It even had a young Gene

Hackman leaping over the teller's cage, which was something routinely done by John Dillinger (Internet Movie Database, n.d.).

It was a push-pull era. People were rebelling against the staunch, repressed Victorian times. The Industrial Revolution had pulled people into new lives with better living conditions. Women were able to vote with the passage of the Nineteenth Amendment on August 26, 1920 (Lewis, n.d.).

As the economy began to collapse with the run on the banks in 1929, the Great Depression was born. The term "handicapped," first used in the 1600s from a lottery game (hand in cap), was then applied to crippled children in about 1915. The term evolved into "to humbly seek a favor" (Rogers, n.d.) and was associated in the depression years erroneously with hand-in-cap, someone asking or begging for money.

John Steinbeck wrote of the Depression in his novel, *The Grapes of Wrath*. The plot discussed the dust bowl in Texas and followed the travels of the Joad family, who migrated west out of desperation after drought threatened their existence. Again, songs like Jay Gorney's 1931 composition, "Buddy Can You Spare a Dime" (Songs of the Great Depression, n.d.), reflected the tenor of the time.

The 1940s

Early in the 1940s, the U.S. was further thrust into World War II, which had been raging in Europe after Japan entered the war, attacked Pearl Harbor, and wiped out most of the western fleet of ships. The mobilization that followed involved a mass enlistment of servicemen and servicewomen into the armed forces. Since many ships were lost, the shipbuilding industry needed to replace America's lost fleet. This meant that aircraft, ships, K-rations (preserved food) for service personnel serving overseas, and clothing had to be fabricated at home. For the first time, women entered the work force en masse to produce the "war machine" at home. As stated previously, women of color and poor women had always worked outside the home, but this was not the norm for most American women. The gender roles were specific for women before the war, and being a homemaker, raising children, and keeping the home fires burning was expected of women. Even though women and children had worked in factories before, it hadn't been seen to this extent. Billboards and propaganda ad campaigns portrayed pictures of women in jumpsuits engaged in pipe fitting jobs (Rosie the Riveter) or in aircraft factories or shipyards, doing the labor that had once been done by men (www.adcouncil.org).

The people who were left to provide these services and keep farms producing crops were women, children, elders, and those who couldn't serve because of disabilities or hardship. Many more women began to smoke cigarettes during that time. Lung cancer rates rose for men who had smoked since the first world war, and the lung cancer rates for women were about twenty years behind those of men. In the 1980s, lung cancer became the most lethal type of cancer for both men and women (Medical News Today, 2006).

When the war ended and service personnel returned, family life became the new theme. The baby boom began in 1946 and ended in 1964; the largest year for producing babies was 1957. War Department films warning of the perils of V.D. (venereal disease) or sexually transmitted diseases and infections were widely shown as newsreels in theaters and, ultimately, in schools. Certain aspects of family life also ventured out of the traditional molds of the Victorian Era or the Roaring Twenties, when anything sexually was permissive as long as it was within the guise of marriage. The missionary position was now merely a position rather than the position of choice during intercourse. The first cases of genital herpes were seen in the 1940s, even though oral herpes (herpes simplex virus I) had been around for centuries (it wasn't known to be a virus). The expanded idea of sexuality allowed for more experimentation, like oral genital sex, which most likely added to the development of the new strain of herpes simplex II, or genital herpes.

During this time, the government awarded those who served in the military a form of compensation called the G.I. Bill, which could be used after the war for education to become trained in new careers. For the first time, people other than the elite of the society could go to trade school or college. America needed to train doctors, hospitals had to be built, and new communities had to be constructed with larger homes for growing families. As prosperity began again, it opened up new opportunities for people to experience life—and especially their sexuality—in a different way.

The 1960s/1970s

Since 1900, each new generation of parents has expected their offspring to do better economically than they themselves did in their lifetimes. The 1960s was an experiential and experimental time that brought new ideas, turbulence, and openness that hadn't been seen before. The children of veterans, who took advantage of the G.I. Bill after WWII, were now able to send their children to schools of higher learning. "The suburbs" was a phrase coined to describe new neighborhoods that sprung up outside the center cities. The existence of suburbs necessitated either automobiles or mass transit to shuttle people to their jobs and back to their residences. Working in the cities while living in the "burbs" contributed to urban blight. People moved out of the apartments and into single-family dwellings, leaving the cities to be occupied by new immigrants, sometimes two or three families in one tenement. This crowding led to disease, and because new immigrants didn't always have skills needed to earn a living wage, many center cities became areas of squalor and were victimized by high rates of crime.

The 1960s spawned unrest because of a number of social, political, and economic situations. First, unrest occurred because of a conflict in Southeast Asia, in Vietnam, due to an incident in the Bay of Tonkin. The U.S. entered the conflict under the policy of saving the South Vietnamese people from the perils of Communism at the hands of the North Vietnamese and their leader, Ho Chi Min. This produced a division at home: The "hawks" were those who saw the conflict as a necessary evil to curtail the Communist expansion from Russia, and the "doves" were pacifists who felt it was not our place to intervene. The "dove" division largely involved the college population, who were protesting against the war (conflict). At the same time, college students protested on their campuses about curricular issues and whether they should have a say in their own education. This first occurred in 1963 at the University of California, Berkeley, under the direction of Mario Savio, and came to be known as the Student Free Speech Movement (Free Speech Movement Archives). The first time the word "sit-in" was used was when these students occupied the administration building on that campus for three days. With the war in turmoil politically and the education system also in turmoil, an educator at Harvard, Dr. Timothy Leary, espoused the ideas of using drugs to change minds. He proposed that people use LSD (acid) to expand their minds. His mantra was "Turn On, Tune in, and Drop Out" (Leary, BrainyQuote.com). Students and others in Haight Ashbury, a district in downtown San Francisco, took the cue to drop out of society and formed the flower children or Hippie movement, which was about love, sex, drugs, and rock and roll. So turbulent was this movement that on May 4, 1970, at Kent State University in Ohio, a female student was killed by National Guard Troops who had been summoned to the campus to quell the protests (Lewis and Hensley, 1998).

Adding to the turbulence was the fact that the so-called Cold War with the Soviet Union had escalated when Khrushchev, the Russian Premier, in 1962, "conceived of an idea of placing nuclear missiles in Cuban waters to restore the balance of power in the Cold War" (library.thinkquest.org, n.d.). The idea of a nuclear showdown culminated in a standoff between the Premier and President Kennedy. The U.S. was concerned about how this would play out politically. Socially, the youth and the baby boomers engaged in behaviors that created a live-for-today attitude. Hence, the Sexual Revolution was born.

The gender role issues had their resurgence in the 1960s, when women's issues came to the forefront as a reaction to their roles in society. Young men were burning their government-issued draft cards in protest of the war effort. Women began to burn bras to protest their roles in society, mostly because they earned less money when working outside of the home than men did for the same job. Women felt that their roles as homemakers and mothers were being demeaned on the home front. The movements began with the Women's Liberation Movement under the tutelage of Ms. Gloria Steinem, a feminist activist and founder of both *New York Magazine* and *Ms. Magazine* (www.feminist.com/gloriasteinem). The other feminist writer to gain a following related to her writings on women's issues was Germaine Greer, who wrote *The Female Eunuch* (Miller, 1999). What is now the Feminist Movement began as conflict over the subjugation of women. Pronouns in books were revised from the word "him" or "his," which referred to all of mankind, to the more inclusive "he/she" or "him/her." Politically correct language changed words like manhole cover, stewardess, and fireman. One now may file for "worker's compensation," rather than "workman's compensation," as it was then. Women, after marriage, had a choice to adopt the name of their husband, hyphenate it with their maiden name, or keep their maiden name instead. Pink Collar Jobs (secretary, schoolteacher, and nurse) were now open to males and females. More males became nurses because many had worked as medics during the Vietnam war. Likewise, previously male occupations were not so quick to be occupied by females. Today, female physicians represent about 45 percent of exiting medical school graduates, but in 1974 it was only 22.4 percent (Looking back over women in medicine, n.d.). There aren't high representations of women in engineering, aeronautics, or construction work, although recently women have gained more seats in Congress and in governorships. These days, men have been able to become stay-at-home dads and care for their children while women work outside the home.

Other groups also had their consciousness-awakening era. The Civil Rights Movement's time had come. Rosa Parks had refused to give up her seat to a white person on a public bus in 1955 (Rosa and Raymond Parks Institute, N.D.). But it wasn't until Dr. Martin Luther King, Jr. talked in 1963 of having a dream, telegraphing the idea that all people could be treated equally, that the movement actually took shape (Martin Luther King Speeches online). Voter registration began in the South to ensure that African-American voters had a voice. The Anti-miscegenation Laws were finally repealed beginning in 1948 and ending in all states in 1967 with the *Loving v. Virginia case* (Anti-miscegenation Laws, no author), allowing interracial marriages. Before the 1960s, Blacks and Caucasians had separate drinking fountains, restrooms, and even lunch counters in parts of the South (Civil Rights Timeline, n.d). In 1963, James Meredith, attempting to enter the University of Mississippi (Ole Miss), had to be escorted into the previously all-white campus by police as he entered as the first African American at that school (www.jfklibrary.org). We saw the Pan Indian Movement cite the plight of Native Americans who had been sequestered on reservations, unable to vote or buy alcohol, well into the 20th century. Also in the 1960s, the Braceros, a group of migrant farm workers under the direction of Cesar Chavez, became the United Farm Workers after an attempt to be paid a decent wage for picking grapes in California (Martin, 2006).

In medicine, oral contraceptives ("the pill") was marketed in 1960 in the U.S. after experimental trials with Puerto Rican women on the isolated "natural laboratory" island of Puerto Rico. This pill freed women to decide if and/or when they might reproduce. The idea of marrying and having no good reliable birth control was now a thing of the past. The pill had a low failure rate, and it allowed for family planning. Even Catholic women who wished to adhere to the doctrines of the church regarding natural family planning began taking Enovid for so-called menstrual regulation because the label indicated it would also prevent ovulation. By 1959, a half million women were using this drug for "off-label" use (PBS American Experience-The Pill, n.d.).

This decade, with political ado, social upheaval, and a new type of birth control, which revolutionized family planning, was one of the most turbulent times in history. It changed human sexuality so that many issues, topics, behaviors, and values were forever questioned.

Perhaps one of the most influential and most controversial decisions about sexuality, in the 1970s, occurred in 1973 regarding the *Roe vs. Wade* decision. This Supreme Court ruling, legalizing abortion, was written by Justice Harry Blackmun, in a 5 to 4 decision, and it paved the way for women to have a choice when it came to abortion. This ruling determined that abortions were legal, in the first trimester, when a woman, along with her physician, made that choice. Abortions were legal in the second trimester, up to the "age of viability," (which was determined to be when a fetus could potentially survive outside the womb on its own) or 24 weeks LMP (from the first day of the woman's last menstrual period). This second trimester abortion was only to be performed if the physical or psychological health of the mother would be endangered by the pregnancy, and it was to be determined by her physician. While the first trimester abortions could take place in clinics, the second trimester (13–24 weeks LMP) abortions had to be performed in a hospital setting.

While many applauded this change, others were stunned. For much of the 1970s, legislators, theologians, academicians, and other reputable groups were trying to decide the issue of when life begins. When it couldn't be absolutely verified as to the beginning of life, there were efforts to pose end runs around the Constitutionality of abortion. The Hatch Amendment which stated that abortion deprives the fetus the right to life, it didn't pass Congress. But, in 1980, the Hyde Amendment (Congressman Henry Hyde of Illinois) was passed that determined how the government's role in paying for poor women's abortions would take shape. It eventually became a state's rights issue, with regard to Medicaid (Medi-Cal in California), and the federal government was not responsible for matched funds payment with the states. Since that time, many legal issues have been raised, and states have determined their own protocols for the legality of abortion, or not. The Congress did pass the Partial Birth Abortion Ban several decades later, which is an emotionally charged attempt to ban late second trimester abortions by first dismembering the fetus. The American College of Obstetricians and Gynecologists indicate that this is not a common medical practice, and may be a term used to incite the public about abortion.

The 1980s/1990s

By the end of the 1970s and early 1980s, Marital Rape Exemption Laws were beginning to be repealed in a number of states, making it unlawful to have sex with a spouse coercively. However, even twenty years later, in 1993, North Carolina had a law that stated "a person may not be prosecuted under this article if the victim is the person's legal spouse at the time of the commission of the alleged rape or sexual offense unless the parties are living separate and apart" (National Center for Victims of Crime, para 1). Even though it is a crime to rape one's spouse in all fifty states, some states, such as California, may punish an offender with probation (NCVC, n.d.).

The 1970s had been a decade involving a baby bust, and the conflict in Southeast Asia was still continuing. A president had resigned in disgrace as a result of the Watergate break-in and the subsequent cover-up. By 1980, the dot-com industry was beginning and, for the first time, individuals had personal computers. This new age in technology ushered in opportunities for making big money quickly. In many areas, the blight of the inner cities was replaced with urban renewal. The decade was about status symbols, lavish lifestyles, and living big. The decade was what author Tom Wolfe called the "Me Decade" (Rose, 2008). Acquiring goods and spending lavishly was for those Americans who had this instant wealth. Women were beginning to gain acceptance in the major industries as part of management, and it seemed the glass ceiling and glass walls were finally being penetrated (Clark, 2006). The Internet was born, and with it came endless new opportunities for education, leisure, convenience, and connection with the rest of the world in a whole new way. It caused online etiquette to be established as well as surveillance of more sinister intentions by some users.

We saw changes in marriage; divorce increased and cohabitation increased. Babies born to single mothers accounted for about one in four births, in contrast to today's rate of 40 percent (Stein, R. and Donna St. George, 2009).

The drug scene somewhat changed from the downer types of drugs seen during early part of the sexual revolution. The era of the 1980s was about being active, and stimulants such as cocaine, crank, and speed quickly became the drugs of choice. While alcohol and marijuana have always been the most predominant drugs for initial adolescent use, the upper society and the nouveau riche in America were getting high on expensive products like cocaine (Grabowski, J. 1984). The sexual revolution had left its mark, though, and sexually transmitted infections and disorders began to flourish. The pill had freed couples of the fear of unintended pregnancy, but it hadn't accounted for the fact that transmission of disease was not being addressed. Chlamydia became the number one bacterial STD (sexually transmitted disease). Genital warts were quickly becoming prominent, with gonorrhea, herpes simplex virus, pelvic inflammatory disease, and syphilis still high in incidence (CDC & P, 2010). When human immunodeficiency virus (HIV) and acquired immune deficiency syndrome (AIDS) were first seen in the U.S. in 1981, there were five cases. By 1982, there were 250 cases. Of course, it wasn't known then that AIDS was a virus. In fact, it was termed GRID (Gay Related Immunodeficiency) until identified as a virus in 1984 by Robert Gallo at the U.S. National Institutes of Health and at the Luc Montainer Clinic in Paris. Today, 1.1 million Americans are infected, with an estimated 56,000 people becoming infected in the U.S. in 2006 alone (CDC & P, 2010).

The 2000s

We began the decade with the fear that Y2K would shut down the computer industry, which was essentially tied to everything else the modern world enjoyed. The fear was short-lived, but the high-tech jobs that had been created in preparation for this potential event were lost just after the turn of the century (Durmeyer, n.d.).

With the World Trade Center bombing and the downing of aircraft at the Pentagon and in Pennsylvania in September 2001, an awakening of sorts shook Americans to the core. The world had changed—it was no longer "the world as we knew it." In the horror of the event, Americans saw the complexities and juxtaposition of both the strength of the human spirit and the potential darkness of human behavior. The complacency of life, love, and day-to-day activities was replaced by Americans' recognition of our vulnerability to the unpredictability and quickness of change, just like other nations who deal with terrorism have experienced.

In 2003, the Supreme Court of Massachusetts ruled that barring same-sex couples the right to marriage was unconstitutional. This followed the 1993 Supreme Court ruling in Hawaii stating that denying same-sex couples from civil unions violated their constitutional equal protection unless the state could show a compelling reason for it. But by 1998, the ruling had been overturned. Since that time, states like Vermont, California (until 2008), and Iowa have passed laws granting same-sex unions (National Conference of State Legislatures, 2010). On July 15, 2010, Argentina legalized same-sex marriage (Warren, M., The Sacramento Bee, 2010).

Our fast-paced lives produced a new concern. Just as money was to the 1980s and time was to the 1990s, sleep became a buzzword of the new millennium. People worked longer and played longer; days became shorter. Programs in colleges and universities were specifically developed in recreation planning because it was thought that Americans needed help planning their expanded leisure time, since their work week would be shorter. If the idea of spending leisure time because computers would spare us the extra workload was entertained, it was brief. The computer era had produced more work, not less, and the 2000s were about not enough time or sleep. Our day seemed to shrink and abbreviations and acronyms became the mode of communicating. Cell phone calls, made at any time or place, became the norm. Many professional and public places had to enact policies and protocols for people using cell phones. Instant messaging was new and trendy and configured a new form of communication. Text messaging, Facebook, and MySpace were hits for adolescents but soon infiltrated the older population as a form of connecting. Young and old were starting to abbreviate language with acronyms and shortened phrases. There seemed to be no downtime. The days of long, hand-written letters, poetry, and leisurely talks were replaced by such shortened communication that it almost became gibberish. Add to that the language of the youth in America, and one needed a Dictionary of American Slang to understand "brb", "lol," and "ping"—common Internet slang terms (Spears, Richard, Dictionary of American Slang, 4th edition).

The Internet was not without its dark side, however; pornography found its way into the computer and scored big with revenue for online books, movies, chat rooms, and, ultimately, real-time cybersex. Mary Anne Layden, co-director of the Sexual Trauma and Psychopathology Program at the University of Pennsylvania's Center for Cognitive Therapy, called porn the "most concerning thing to psychological health that I know of existing today." She continued, "The Internet is a perfect drug delivery system because you are anonymous, aroused and have role models for these behaviors. To have drug pumped into your house 24/7, free, and children know how to use it better than grownups know how to use it—it's a perfect delivery system if we want to have a whole generation of young addicts who will never have the drug out of their mind." (Singel, 2004, para 3,4).

Television capitalized on the reality venue after twenty-four-hour webcams on the Internet posed the idea of voyeuristic engagement into the life of someone on screen. Programming has become a venue for addressing social, political, economic, and ecological issues in serious and compelling ways through documentaries, by imbedding journalists into areas of conflict and by showing live real-time photos of events as they unfold (Gulf of Mexico British Petroleum oil spill) and the effects these events will have on our lives and our relationships (msnbc.com-live stream coverage of Disaster in the Gulf, July 15, 2010). It is now not a question of whether the earth can support seven billion people, but whether or not seven billion people can support the earth!

Even though all the saturation with technology altered our communication style, the 1990s and 2000s did become eras in which the population reached out to those in need. We began to view poverty, famine, and the HIV/AIDS pandemic as social atrocities, and that led to financial aid and social awareness. In another area, the idea of young girls being victimized by female genital mutilation, which occurs in about forty areas of the world, reminded us of Margaret Mead's words about cultural relativism. Were these problems human rights issues, or were they cultural norms that just didn't jibe with the rest of the industrialized world?

However, here at home, we had a boom and a bubble before the economic bust of the decade. The downfall of pillars of Wall Street, the housing industry, and lost jobs all contributed to an uncertainty in people's economic lives today. As a result of those uncertainties, relationships have been impacted and divorce has increased. Suicides have risen nearly 20 percent in 45–54-year-olds in the years 1999 to 2004 (Cohen, 2008).

It remains to be seen what kinds of perspectives we will have as far as the 2010–2020 decade is concerned. It is fair to say that we have created a faster-paced society with more social change than at any time in history. Some futurists are already calling it the Virtual Decade. Our relationships to one another are continually dynamic and there is still much to be learned about caring for one another, no matter what decade we are living in.

REFERENCES

Ad Council: Women in War Jobs—Rosie the Riveter (1942–1945) (N.A.). Retrieved from www. adcouncil.org/default.aspx?id=128. July 12, 2010. Anti-miscegenation laws. (N.A.). Retrieved from en.wikipedia.org/wiki/Anti- miscegenationjaws July 15, 2010.

Civil Rights Timeline (n.a.). Africanaonline, n.d. Retrieved from africanaonline.com/civil_rights_ timeline.htm.

Clark, Hannah (2006). Are women happy under the glass ceiling? Forbes. March 3rd. Retrieved from www.forbes.com/2006/03/07/glass-ceiling-opportunities—cx he 0308 glass.html

Cohen, Patricia (2008). Researchers puzzled by rise in midlife suicide in U.S. *New York Times.* January 19.

Cutler, David and Grant Miller (2005). The role of Public Health improvements in Health Advances: The Twentieth-Century United States *Demography,* Vol. 42, No. 1 February, pp. 1–22 Published by: Population /Association of America Stable URL: http://www.jstor.org/stable/1515174

DapperDan-Field Notebook, (n.d.) "I Want a Girl, Just Like the Girl that Married Dear Old Dad"- lyrics of Harry Von Tilzer. Retrieved from www.auntieweasel.com/victrola/dadderdan.html

Department of Health and Human Services. The Centers for Disease Control and Prevention (2010). Basic information about HIV/AIDS. Retrieved from www.CDC.gov . July 13, 2010.

Department of Health and Human Services. The Centers for Disease Control and Prevention (2010). Reportable STDs in young people 15–24 years of age, by State, 2007, 2008. Modified February 3. Retrieved from www.CDC.gov., July 14,2010.

Durmeyer, Randy (n.d.). Trends and events from 2000–2009. About.com Guide. Retrieved from www.about.com July 15, 2010.

Free Speech Movement Official Web site. Retrieved atwww.fsm-a.org/, July 15, 2010.

Gloria Steinem's New, Official Web site, www/feminist.com. (n.d.). Retrieved from www.feminist.com/gloriasteinem. July 12, 2010.

Grabowski, John (1984). Cocaine: Pharmacology, effects, and treatment of abuse. NIDA Research Monograph 50. Department of Health and Human Services, Public Health Services, Alcohol, Drug Abuse, and Mental Health Administration. National Institute on Drug Abuse. Retrieved from National Institute on Drug Abuse www.archives.drugabuse.gov/pdf/monographs/50.pdf.

Internet Database (n.d.,). *Bonnie and Clyde* film, 1967. Retrieved from Internet Database at www.imdb.com on July 16, 2010.

Jfklibrary.org (n.d.). Integrating Ole Miss: Who was James Meredith? Retrieved from www.jfklibrary.org/meredith/jm.html.

King Jr., Martin Luther (1963). Martin Luther King Speeches—I Have a Dream-Address at March on Washington. August 28. Retrieved from www.mlkonline.net/dream.html on July 14, 2010.

Leary, Timothy (N.D.). Turn on, Tune In, Drop Out. Retrieved from http://www.brainyquote.com/quotes/quotes/t/timothylea380739.html on July 2, 2010.

Lewis, Jane Johnson (n.d.). The day the Suffrage battle was won. About.com: Women's History. Retrieved from www.women's history.about.com/od/suffrage1900/a/august_26_wed.htm

Lewis, Jerry and Thonas R. Hensley (1998). May 4 shootings at Kent State University: the search for historial accuracy. Published in revised form by the Ohio Council For The Social Studies Review. Vol. 34, No. 1, PP. 19–21.

Library.thinkquest.org. (n.d.). Nikita Khruschev. Background on the Soviet leader from a Web site on the Cuban Missile Crisis. Retrieved from www.librarv.thinkquest.org/11046/people/khruschev.html on July 15, 2010. Para 3. Looking back over the history of women in medicine (N.A.). Retrieved from www.mommd.com/lookingback.shtml. July 15, 2010.

Lutkehaus, Nancy C. (2008). Margaret Mead: The Making of an American Icon.

Princeton. Martin, Michel (2010). Host. Slave Marriages Were Often Shattered by Auction Block: NPR (National Public Radio) Broadcast interview with Professor Tera Hunter. February 11.9 minutes, 9 seconds. Retrieved from www.npr.org/templates/story/

Story. php?storyid-123608207. Martin, Philip (2006). The Bracero Program: Was it a failure? History News Network. Retrieved from www.hnn.us/articles/27336.html Medical News Today (2006). Women catching up to men in lung cancer deaths.

Medical News Today. November 12. Retrieved from www.medicalnewstoday.com July 16, 2010.

Miller, Laura (1999). Germain Greer. Retrieved from www.salon.com/people/bc/1999/06/22/greer on July 15, 2010.

MSNBC.com (July 15, 2010). Live coverage of "Disaster in the Gulf."

National Center for Victims of Crime (n.d.). Spousal rape laws: 20 years later. Retrieved fro www.ncvc.org/ncvc/main.aspx?dbName=DocumentViewer&DocumentID=32701 on July 14, 2010.

National Conference of State Legislatures (2010). Same sex marriage, civil unions, and Domestic partnership. Same sex marriage overview. April 10. Retrieved from www.ncsl.org. on July 16, 2010.

Public Broadcasting System (n.d.). American Experience Film: *The Pill.*

Rogers, Gene (n.d.). Handicapped vs. disabled. DBTAC Southwest ADA Center. Retrieved from www.bcm.edu. July 16, 2010.

Rosa and Raymond Parks Institute for Self Development (N.D.) Rosa Louise Parks Biography. Retrieved from www.rosaparks.org/bio.html on March, 2010. Para 1.

Rose, Charlie (2008). A Conversation with author Tom Wolfe. June 11.

Sinclair, Upton (1906). The Jungle. Retrieved from www.online-literature.com/upton_sinclair/ July 12, 2010.

Singel, Ryan (2004). Internet Porn: Worse than Crack? Wired. November, 19. Para 3,4. Retrieved from www.wired.com/science/discoveries/news/2004/11/65772.

Songs of the Great Depression, (n.d.). Retrieved from www.library.csi.cunv.edu/dept/historv/lavender;/cherries.html July 15, 2010.

Spears, Richard (n.d.). McGraw-Hill's Dictionary of American Slang and Colloquial Expressions. McGraw-Hill Publishing. 4th ed.

Stein, Rob and Donna St. George (2009). Number of unwed mothers has risen sharply In the U.S. The Washington Post online. Retrieved from www.washingtonpost.com/wp-dvn/content/article/2009/05/13/AR200905 July 15, 2010.

Steinbeck, John (1939). The Grapes of Wrath. Viking Press (1939); Penguin Books, (2002).

Thomas, Karen Kruse (2006). The Hill-Burton Act and civil rights expanding; hospital care for black southerners: 1939–1960. The Journal of Southern History. November

Warren, Michael (2010). Argentina legalizes same-sex marriage. Associated Press. In *The Sacramento Bee*. July 16, 2010.

INTRODUCTION TO: SCHOOLS AND THE SOCIAL CONTROL OF SEXUALITY

JAN CAMPBELL

T his article by Melinda S. Miceli proposes the idea that public schools teach many lessons about sexuality: the definition of normalcy, the historical lack of discussions about alternative lifestyles, and the promotion of an ideal family. The debate has raged for years about whether sexuality should be taught in American public schools, and the contrast with how sexuality education is taught in other countries, namely, Western European countries, is also noted.

Miceli makes the case that all aspects of the negatives of early sexual experience, such as STDs, STIs, unwanted teen pregnancy, abortion, and AIDS, are lower in Western Europe than in the United States. The power struggle over sex education curricula keeps both the school systems and the public, who often encourages a broader curriculum, at bay with political policies. Comprehensive sex education programs have much public support (89%), but abstinence-only programs are government funded, and the religious right has had a loud voice in this arena.

SCHOOLS AND THE SOCIAL CONTROL OF SEXUALITY

MELINDA S. MICELI

The question of whether or not schools should teach students about sexuality has been one of heated debate since the early twentieth century. The simple fact remains that schools do teach students countless lessons about sexuality, in a variety of ways, every single day. As social institutions through which every citizen passes, schools have an enormous amount of power to influence the beliefs and values of young people. In this chapter, I analyze some of the ways that public schools shape America's sexual culture by looking at their informal and formal curriculum, culture, and their sex education policies. My chief claim is that schools have tried to promote what is considered a "normal" and "respectable" sexuality, that is, heterosexuality, conventionally gendered norms governing sexual behavior, and an ideal of marriage and family.

Michel Foucault argued persuasively "Western societies simultaneously repress and obsess over sexuality. Sexual speech is both amplified and silenced. The patterns of what about sex is spoken about and what is silenced is not random, but rather both are part of the weave of power relations and social control." According to Foucault, it is a mistake to conclude that, as Western cultures increased the amount of sexual speech and the number of arenas where sex is discussed, the less sexuality is repressed and controlled. Conversely, it is incorrect to conclude that, in spaces where sexual speech is forbidden or regulated, it is successfully repressed or absent.

Foucault argued that a concerted effort to control the sexuality of youth began in the eighteenth century, with schools being a logical target of rules and regulations. However, he argued:

> It would be less than exact to say that the pedagogical institution has imposed a ponderous silence on the sex of children and adolescents. On the contrary since the eighteenth century it has multiplied the forms of discourse on the subject; it has established various points of implantation for sex; it has coded contents and qualified speakers. Speaking about children's sex, inducing educators, physicians, administrators, and parents to speak of it, or speaking to them about it, causing children themselves to talk about it, and enclosing them in a web of discourses which sometimes address them, sometimes speak about them, or impose canonical bits of knowledge about them, or use them as a basis for constructing a science that is beyond their grasp—all this together enables us to link an intensification of the interventions of power to a multiplication of discourse. The sex of children and adolescents has become, since the eighteenth century, an important area of contention around which innumerable institutional devices and institutional strategies have been deployed. (Foucault 1976: 29–30)

Sex education classes introduce direct and purposeful sexual discourse into the regulated space of the school. Janice Irvine (2002) argues that "[s]ince the sixties, as openness about sexuality in popular culture has intensified, U.S. communities have fought over whether to allow discussions about sexual topics in the classroom. At stake is what is in the best interest of young people. The history of sex education in America is part of long-standing efforts to regulate sexual morality through the control of sexual speech" (2002: 4). In her book, *Talk About Sex: the Battle over Sex Education in the United States*, Irvine provides a detailed historical account and a sophisticated sociological analysis of these battles and how they fit into larger power struggles to control cultural norms, beliefs, and values.

The idea of formal sexual education classes in schools was first proposed in the early twentieth-century by a collection of moral reformers, which included suffragists, clergy, temperance workers, and physicians dedicated to eliminating venereal disease. From the beginning there was disagreement about the specific content and aim of sex education classes, and yet agreement that accurate information about sexuality needed to be taught for the good of public health. This group also felt that the restrictive measures of the Comstock laws that sought state restriction of virtually all public discussion of sexuality, including sex education and contraception information, had to be combated (Irvine 2002). Contemporary conflicts between advocates of abstinence-only and proponents of comprehensive sex education are situated in this long-standing tension between those who feel that the public is best served by limiting children's access to information about sexuality and those groups who feel that public health problems are caused by a lack of such information.

Comprehensive sexuality education stresses abstinence for youth, and it also provides information on contraception and abortion. The Sex Information and Education Council of the United States (SIECUS) was founded in 1964, and has become the leading advocate of comprehensive sexuality education programs being integrated into schools at all levels. SIECUS and its supporters argue that students should receive age-appropriate information on subjects like human reproduction, anatomy, physiology, sexually transmitted diseases, masturbation, and homosexuality, and engage in discussion of sexual values. "Advocates of comprehensive sex education endorse what they consider to be the therapeutic potential of open and informative sexual discussion in the classroom. They believe that silence has fostered ignorance, shame and social problems like teen pregnancy and sexually transmitted diseases. They view sexuality as positive and healthy and they generally support gender equality and acceptance of sexual diversity" (Irvine 2002).

Opponents criticize SIECUS's model of sexual education as irresponsible and misinformed. These groups argue that providing students with information about sexual practices, such as the use of contraceptives, has contributed to rising levels of adolescent sexual activity, sexually transmitted diseases, and teenage pregnancy. Since the 1960s conservative Catholics and Christian fundamentalists have founded a variety of political organizations in order to fight for regulation of sex education. These groups are affiliated with the religious right, and opposition to sex education has bolstered their social movement to restore traditional sexual and gender values and norms to American culture (Irvine 2002). One of many strategies for achieving this goal is restricting the sexual discourses to which young people are exposed. Carefully controlling or eliminating sexual discussion from school, they argue, is essential to efforts to protect children and adolescents from the "dangers" of sexuality and to reinstating sexual morality to the culture (Irvine 2002).

All schools promote what Bourdieu and others (e.g. Sears 1992; Giroux and McLaren 1989) have called a hegemonic curriculum, a curriculum which simultaneously legitimizes the dominant culture and marginalizes or rejects other cultures and forms of knowledge. The concept of the hegemonic curriculum, and the closely related concept of the hidden curriculum, have been well documented in research into educational institutions and practices since the 1960s. Early studies examined the ways in which upper- and middle-class, white and male culture, history, morals, behaviors, norms and values are taught and enforced in schools through the power of a hegemonic process where they are also naturalized, neutralized, and made invisible. Over the past decade and a half several studies of school culture have included an examination of a hidden sexuality curriculum in schools (Sears 1992; Epstein 1994; Miceli 1998; Best 2000; Irvine 2002; Kehily 2002). Michelle Fine (1988) and others have argued that the struggles over sex education are not only about broadly whether "talk about sex" in schools is appropriate or not, but also, through what is said and what is unsaid, to specifically define appropriate sexuality for males and females. Fine's (1988) investigation into the content of the prevalent sex education programs in the United States concluded that "within today's standard sex education curricula and many public school classrooms, we find:

1. the authorized suppression of a discourse of female sexual desire;
2. the promotion of a discourse of female sexual victimization; and
3. the explicit privileging of married heterosexuality over other practices of sexuality. (1988:30)

The sex education programs to which Fine refers emerged in the early 1980s as a result of the Adolescent Family Life Act (AFLA), the first federal law specifically passed to fund sex education. The AFLA, which is still in use and has become increasingly funded and expanded since, was written by conservative Republican senators with the goal of ending premarital teen sex and therefore teen pregnancy and teen abortion (Levine 2002). Because it is girls who get pregnant and have abortions, they became the target of the abstinence education programs. These programs, Fine (1988) and others have argued, teach girls to fear their own sexuality, to view sex as dangerous and harmful, and to guard themselves from becoming the victims of their own or males' uncontrolled sexuality. In this discourse of abstinence education, young women are held responsible not only for controlling their own sexuality but also for preventing their own victimization.

This approach to sex education in the United States contrasts sharply with that taken by many other countries. In countries like Sweden, France, Germany, and The Netherlands the approach is to educate students about sexuality in all of its aspects so that they can develop healthy and responsible sexual attitudes and behavior. Judith Levine argues that studies of sex education in other countries prove that their more comprehensive approach has been successful.

> In many European countries, where teens have as much sex as in America, sex ed starts in the earliest grades. It is informed by a no-nonsense, even enthusiastic, attitude toward the sexual; it is explicit and doesn't teach abstinence. Rates of unwanted teen pregnancy, abortion, and AIDS in every "Western European country are a fraction of our own; the average age of first intercourse is about the same as in the United States. (Levine 2002: 98)

Interestingly, surveys on public opinion about sex education constantly find that the majority of Americans support a more comprehensive model. "In fact, the degree of consensus reported in national surveys about sex education is striking. A 1998 national survey found that 87 percent of Americans favor sex education and of those 89 percent believe that, along with abstinence, young people should also have information about contraception and STD prevention" (Irvine 2002). Despite public opinion, the issue of expanding current sex education curricula more often than not sparks intense local controversies and makes national headlines. In addition, despite the opinion polls, the federal government has continued to increase its funding of abstinence-only programs and the religious right has continued to have a loud voice in the discourse of sexuality.

In 1997, the U.S. Congress committed a quarter billion dollars over five years to finance more education in ... abstinence. As part of the omnibus "welfare reform bill," the government's Maternal and Child Health Bureau extended grants to the states for programs whose exclusive purpose is teaching the social, psychological, and health gains to be realized by abstaining from sexual activity In a country where only one in ten school-children receives more than forty hours of sex ed in any year, the regulations prohibit funded organizations from instructing kids about contraception or condoms except in terms of their failures. In a country where 90 percent of adults have sex before marriage and as many as 10 percent are gay or lesbian, the law underwrites one message and one message only: that "a mutually faithful monogamous relationship in the context of marriage is the expected standard of human sexual activity." Non-marital sex, educators are required to tell children, "is likely to have harmful psychological effects." (Levine 2002: 91)

These debates over sex education curricula are a prime example of the efforts to regulate sexual discourse, knowledge, and behavior, and of the fact that schools are central arenas in this power struggle. The amount of energy, resources, and passion expended by all sides to control what schools teach about sexuality indicates the impact schools have on the broader social control of sexuality.

DISCUSSION QUESTIONS

1. Do you think it is appropriate for a sexual education classes to promote abstinence for teenagers or young adults? Why or why not?
2. Do you think it is appropriate for a sexual education classes to promote particular kinds of sexual practices and relationships as "healthy"? Why or why not?
3. Who are the interest groups standing behind abstinence-only sex education programs and why do they support these programs?
4. Why is it that the typical sexual education curriculum singles out girls and their sexual behavior as problematic and in need of control more so than boys and their sexual behavior?

REFERENCES

Best, Amy L. 2000. *Prom Night: Youth Schools and Popular Culture.* New York: Routledge. 2005. "The Production of Heterosexuality at the High School Prom", in Chrys Ingraham (ed.), *Thinking Straight: The Power, the Promise, and the Paradox of Heterosexuality.* New York: Routledge.

Epstein, Debbie (ed.). 1994. *Challenging Lesbian and Gay Inequalities in Education.* Buckingham, UK: Open University Press.

Fine, Michelle. 1988. "Sexuality, Schooling, and Adolescent Females: The Missing Discourse of Desire." *Harvard Educational Review 58:* 29–53.

Foucault, Michel 1990. *The History of Sexuality: An Introduction, Volume 1.* New York: Vintage Books.

Giroux, Henry A. and Peter McClaren. 1989. *Critical Pedagogy: The State and Culture Struggle.* Albany: SUNY Press.

GLSEN. 2003. The 2003 National School Climate Survey. New York: GLSEN. Irvine, Janice M. 2002. *Talk About Sex: The Battles over Sex Education in the United States.* Berkeley, CA: University of California Press.

Kehily, Mary Jane. 2002. *Sexuality, Gender and Schooling: Shifting Agendas in Social Learning.* New York: Routledge.

Levine, Judith. 2002. *Harmful to Minors.* Minneapolis: University of Minnesota Press.

Miceli, Melinda S. 2005. *Standing Out, Standing Together: The Social and Political Impact of Gay-Straight Alliances.* New York: Routledge.

Pascoe, C. J. 2007. *Dude, You 're a Fag: Masculinity and Sexuality in High School.* Berkeley, CA: University of California Press.

Sears, James T. 1992. *Sexuality and the Curriculum: The Politics and Practices of Sex Education.* New York: Teachers College Press.

INTRODUCTION TO: HOW AIDS CHANGED AMERICA

JAN CAMPBELL

David Jefferson provides an apt description of how AIDS changed America by introducing a time line of events for the almost-thirty-year history of the pandemic. He shows us in various examples and events how we have matured in our understanding of this killer that has taken more than 25 million lives since first being identified in 1981.

Through these examples, we can see how vulgar jokes, denial, and prejudice were somewhat replaced with compassion, activism, research, and grace throughout the history of AIDS. While far from wiping out the scourge, the softening of attitudes is now seen as something of a unifier in the quest to bring about an understanding of this disease—first to the gay community and ultimately to all who have endured it. This is a compelling article and one that is integral to our recognition of what fear can do to a population. Education and changes in attitude have occurred because we have seen what a hands-on approach, support, and activism can do.

HOW AIDS CHANGED AMERICA

DAVID JEFFERSON

The plague years: It brought out the worst in us at first, but ultimately it brought out the best, and transformed the nation. The story of a disease that left an indelible mark on our history, our culture and our souls.

May 15, 2006 issue—Jeanne White-Ginder sits at home, assembling a scrapbook about her son, Ryan. She pastes in newspaper stories about his fight to return to the Indiana middle school that barred him in 1985 for having AIDS. She sorts through photos of Ryan with Elton John, Greg Louganis, and others who championed his cause. She organizes mementos from his PBS special, "I Have AIDS: A Teenager's Story." "I just got done with his funeral. Eight pages. That was very hard," says White-Ginder, who buried her 18-year-old son in 1990, seven years after he was diagnosed with the disease, which he contracted through a blood product used to treat hemophiliacs. The scrapbook, along with Ryan's bedroom, the way his mother left it when he died, will be part of an exhibit at the Children's Museum of Indianapolis on three children who changed history: Anne Frank. Ruby Bridges. And Ryan White. "He put a face to the epidemic, so people could care about people with AIDS," his mother says.

At a time when the mere threat of avian flu or SARS can set off a coast-to-coast panic—and prompt the federal government to draw up contingency plans and stockpile medicines—it's hard to imagine that the national response to the emergence of AIDS ranged from indifference to hostility. But that's exactly what happened when gay men in 1981 began dying of a strange array of opportunistic infections. President Ronald Reagan didn't discuss AIDS in a public forum until a press conference four years into the epidemic, by which time more than 12,000 Americans had already died. (He didn't publicly utter the term "AIDS" until 1987.) People with the disease were routinely evicted from their homes, fired from jobs, and denied health insurance. Gays were demonized by the extreme right wing: Reagan adviser Pat Buchanan editorialized in 1983, "The poor homosexuals—they have declared war against nature, and now nature is exacting an awful retribution." In much of the rest of the culture, AIDS was simply treated as the punch line to a tasteless joke: "I just heard the Statue of Liberty has AIDS," Bob Hope quipped during the rededication ceremony of the statue in 1986. "Nobody knows if she got it from the mouth of the Hudson or the Staten Island Fairy." Across the river in Manhattan, a generation of young adults was attending more funerals than weddings.

As AIDS made its death march across the nation, killing more Americans than every conflict from World War II through Iraq, it left an indelible mark on our history and culture. It changed so many things in so many ways, from how the media portray homosexuality to how cancer patients deal with their disease. At the same time, AIDS itself changed, from a disease that killed gay men and drug addicts to a global scourge that has decimated the African continent, cut a large swath through black America, and infected almost as many women as men worldwide. The death toll to date: 25 million and counting. Through the crucible of AIDS, America was forced to face its fears and prejudices—fears that denied Ryan White a seat in school for a year and a half, prejudices that had customers boycotting restaurants with gay chefs. "At first, a ton of people said that whoever gets AIDS deserves to have AIDS, deserves to literally suffer all the physical pain that the virus carries with it," says Tom Hanks, who won an Oscar for playing a gay lawyer dying of the disease in 1993's *Philadelphia*. "But that didn't hold." Watching a generation of gay men wither and die, the nation came to acknowledge the humanity of a community it had mostly ignored and reviled. "AIDS was the great unifier," says Craig Thompson, executive director of AIDS Project Los Angeles and HIV-positive for 25 years.

Without AIDS, and the activism and consciousness-raising that accompanied it, would gay marriage even be up for debate today? Would we be welcoming *Will & Grace* into our living rooms or weeping over *Brokeback Mountain*? Without red ribbons, first worn in 1991 to promote AIDS awareness, would we be donning rubber yellow bracelets to show our support for cancer research? And without the experience of battling AIDS, would scientists have the strategies and technologies to develop the antiviral drugs we'll need to battle microbial killers yet to emerge?

AIDS, of course, did happen. "Don't you dare tell me there's any good news in this," says Larry Kramer, who has been raging against the disease—and those who let it spread unchecked—since it was first identified in 1981. "We should be having a national day of mourning!" True. But as we try to comprehend the carnage, it's impossible not to acknowledge the displays of strength, compassion and, yes, love, that were a direct result of all that pain and loss. Without AIDS, we wouldn't have the degree of patient activism we see today among people with breast cancer, lymphoma, ALS and other life-threatening diseases. It was Kramer, after all, who organized 10,000 frustrated AIDS patients into ACT UP, a street army chanting "Silence equals death" that marched on the White House and shut down Wall Street, demanding more government funding for research and quicker access to drugs that might save lives. "The only thing that makes people fight is fear. That's what we discovered about AIDS activism," Kramer says.

Fear can mobilize, but it can also paralyze—which is what AIDS did when it first appeared. And no one—not the government, not the media, not the gay community itself—reacted fast enough to head off disaster. In the fiscally and socially conservative climate of Reagan's America, politicians were loath to fund research into a new pathogen that was killing mostly gay men and intravenous drug users. "In the first years of AIDS, I imagine we felt like the folks on the rooftops during Katrina, waiting for help," says Dr. Michael Gottlieb, the Los Angeles immunologist credited as the first doctor to recognize the looming epidemic. When epidemiologist Donald Francis of the federal Centers for Disease Control in Atlanta tried to get $30 million in funding for an AIDS-prevention campaign, "it went up to Washington and they said f— off," says Francis, who quit the CDC soon after, defeated.

"Gay Cancer," as it was referred to at the time, wasn't a story the press wanted to cover—especially since it required a discussion of gay sex. While the media had a field day with Legionnaire's disease, toxic shock syndrome and the Tylenol scare, few outlets paid much attention to the new syndrome, even after scores of people had died. *The New York Times* ran fewer than a dozen stories about the new killer in 1981 and 1982, almost all of them buried inside the paper. (*Newsweek*, for that matter, didn't run its first cover story on what "may be the public-health threat of the century" until April 1983.) The *Wall Street Journal* first reported on the disease only after it had spread to heterosexuals: NEW, OFTEN-FATAL ILLNESS IN HOMOSEXUALS TURNS UP IN WOMEN, HETEROSEXUAL MALES, read the February 1982 headline. Even the gay press missed the story at first: afraid of alarming the community and inflaming antigay forces, editors at the *New York Native* slapped the headline DISEASE RUMORS LARGELY UNFOUNDED atop the very first press report about the syndrome, which ran May 18, 1981. There were a few notable exceptions, particularly the work of the late Randy Shilts, an openly gay journalist who convinced his editors at the *San Francisco Chronicle* to let him cover AIDS as a full-time beat: that reporting led to the landmark 1987 book *And the Band Played On*, a detailed account of how the nation's failure to take AIDS seriously allowed the disease to spread exponentially in the early '80s.

Many gay men were slow to recognize the time bomb in their midst, even as people around them were being hospitalized with strange, purplish skin cancers and life-threatening pneumonia. Kramer and his friends tried to raise money for research during the 1981 Labor Day weekend in The Pines, a popular gay vacation spot on New York's Fire Island. "When we opened the collection boxes, we could not believe how truly awful the results were," says Kramer. The total? $769.55. "People thought we were a bunch of creeps with our GIVE TO GAY CANCER signs, raining on the parade of Pines' holiday festivities." The denial in some corners of the gay community would continue for years. Many were reluctant to give up the sexual liberation they believed they'd earned: as late as 1984, the community was bitterly debating whether to close San Francisco's gay bathhouses, where men were having unprotected sex with any number of partners in a single night.

With death a constant companion, the gay community sobered up from the party that was the '70s and rose to meet the unprecedented challenge of AIDS. There was no other choice, really: they had been abandoned by the nation, left to fend for themselves. "It's important to remember that there was a time when people did not want to use the same bathroom as a person with AIDS, when cabdrivers didn't want to pick up patients who had the disease, when hospitals put signs on patients' doors that said WARNING. DO NOT ENTER," recalls Marjorie Hill, executive director of Gay Men's Health Crisis in New York. Organizations like GMHC sprang up around the country to provide HIV patients with everything from medical care to counseling to food and housing. "Out of whole cloth, and without experience, we built a healthcare system that was affordable, effective and humane," says Darrel Cummings, chief of staff of the Los Angeles Gay & Lesbian Center. "I can't believe our community did what it did while so many people were dying." Patients took a hands-on approach to managing their disease, learning the intricacies of T-cell counts and grilling their doctors about treatment options. And they shared what they learned with one another. "There's something that a person with a disease can only get from another person with that disease. It's support and information and inspiration," says Sean Strub, who founded the magazine *Poz* for HIV-positive readers.

It took a movie star to get the rest of the nation's attention. In the summer of 1985, the world learned that Rock Hudson—the romantic leading man who'd been a symbol of American virility—was not only gay, but had full-blown AIDS. "It was a bombshell event," says Gottlieb, who remembers standing on the helipad at UCLA Medical Center, waiting for his celebrity patient to arrive, as news helicopters circled overhead. "For many Americans, it was their first awareness at all of AIDS. This prominent man had been diagnosed, and the image of him looking as sick as he did really stuck." Six years later, basketball legend Magic Johnson announced he was HIV-positive, and the shock waves were even bigger. A straight, healthy-looking superstar athlete had contracted the "gay" disease. "It can happen to anybody, even me, Magic Johnson," the 32-year-old announced to a stunned nation, as he urged Americans to practice safe sex.

Given the tremendous stigma, most well-known public figures with AIDS tried to keep their condition a secret. Actor Brad Davis, the star of "Midnight Express," kept his diagnosis hidden for six years, until he died in 1991. "He assumed, and I think rightly so, that he wouldn't be able to find work," says his widow, Susan Bluestein, a Hollywood casting director. After Davis died, rumors flew that he must have been secretly gay. "That part of the gossip mill was the most hurtful to me and my daughter," says Bluestein, who acknowledges in her book "After Midnight" that her husband was a drug addict and unfaithful—but not gay.

With the disease afflicting so many of their own, celebrities were quick to lend support and raise money. Elizabeth Taylor was among the first, taking her friend Rock Hudson's hand in public, before the TV cameras and the world, to dispel the notion that AIDS was something you could catch through casual contact. Her gesture seems quaint today, but in 1985—when the tabloids were awash with speculation that Hudson could have infected actress Linda Evans by simply kissing her during a love scene in "Dynasty"—Taylor's gesture was revolutionary. She became the celebrity face of the American Foundation for AIDS Research. "I've lost so many friends," Taylor says. "I have so many friends who are HIV-positive and you just wonder how long it's going to be. And it breaks your heart."

Behind the scenes, Hollywood wasn't nearly as progressive as it likes to appear. John Erman recalls the uphill battle getting the 1985 AIDS drama, "An Early Frost," on TV. "The meetings we had with NBC's Standards and Practices [the network's censors] were absolutely medieval," says Erman. One of the censors' demands: that the boyfriend of the main character be portrayed as "a bad guy" for infecting him: "They did not want to show a positive gay relationship," Erman recalls. Ultimately, with the support of the late NBC Entertainment president Brandon Tartikoff, Erman got to make the picture he wanted—though major advertisers refused to buy commercial time during the broadcast. Within a decade, AIDS had changed the face of television. In 1991, "thirty something" featured a gay character who'd contracted the disease. And in 1994, on MTV's "The Real World," 23-year-old Pedro Zamora, who died later that same year, taught a generation of young people what it meant to be HIV-positive.

If TV was slow to deal with AIDS, cinema was downright glacial. "Longtime Companion," the first feature film about the disease, didn't make it to the screen until 1990, nine years into the epidemic. "There was a lot of talk before the movie came out about how this was going to hurt my career, the same way there was talk about Heath Ledger in 'Brokeback Mountain'," says Bruce Davison, who received an Oscar nomination for his role. As for "Philadelphia," Hanks is the first to admit "it was late to the game."

Broadway was the major exception when it came to taking on AIDS as subject matter—in part because so many early casualties came from the world of theater. "I remember in 1982 sitting in a restaurant with seven friends of mine. All were gay men either working or looking to work in the theater, and we were talking about AIDS," recalls Tom Viola, executive director of Broadway Cares/Equity Fights AIDS. "Of those eight guys, four are dead, and two, including myself, are HIV-positive." By the time Tony Kushner's Pulitzer Prize-winning "Angels In America" made its Broadway debut in 1993, some 60 plays about the disease had opened in New York. Producer Jeffrey Seller remembers how he was told he "could never do a show on Broadway that's about, quote unquote, AIDS, homosexuality and drug addiction." He's talking about "Rent," which a decade later still draws capacity crowds.

The world of "Rent" is something of an artifact now. Just before it hit Broadway in 1996, scientists introduced the antiretroviral drug cocktails that have gone on to extend the lives of millions of patients with HIV. Since then, the urgency that once surrounded the AIDS fight in the United States has ebbed, as HIV has come to be seen as a chronic, rather than fatal, condition. But the drugs aren't a panacea—despite the fact that many people too young to remember the funerals of the '80s think the new medications have made it safe to be unsafe. "Everywhere I go, I'm meeting young people who've just found out they've been infected, many with drug-resistant strains of the virus," says Cleve Jones, who two decades ago decided to start stitching a quilt to honor a friend who had died of AIDS. That quilt grew to become an iconic patchwork of more than 40,000 panels, each one the size of a grave, handmade by loved ones to honor their dead. Ever-expanding, it was displayed several times in Washington, transforming the National Mall into what Jones had always intended: a colorful cemetery that would force the country to acknowledge the toll of AIDS. "If I'd have known 20 years ago that in 2006 I'd be watching a whole new generation facing this tragedy, I don't think I would have had the strength to continue," says Jones, whose own HIV infection has grown resistant to treatment.

Inner strength is what has allowed people living with HIV to persevere. "They think I'm going to die. You know what, they better not hold their breath," Ryan White once told his mother. Though given six months to live when he was diagnosed with HIV, Ryan lived five and a half years, long enough to prod a nation into joining the fight against AIDS. When he died in 1990 at the age of 18, Congress named a new comprehensive AIDS funding act after him. But the real tribute to Ryan has been the ongoing efforts of his mother. "I think the hostility around the epidemic is still there. And because of religious and moral issues, it's been really hard to educate people about this disease and be explicit," says White-Ginder, who continues to give speeches about watching her son live and die of AIDS. "We should not still be facing this disease." Sadly, we are.

With Ramin Setoodeh
Correction: The original version of this report incorrectly stated that Ryan White's funeral took place in 1991. In fact, it was in 1990, © 2006 Newsweek, Inc.

INTRODUCTION TO: AMERICAN COLLEGE HEALTH ASSOCIATION ANNUAL PAP TEST AND SEXUALLY TRANSMITTED INFECTION SURVEY

2006

JAN CAMPBELL

Smith and Roberts looked at annual sexually transmitted infection (STI) testing patterns conducted by the American College Health Association regarding the sexually transmitted infection rates of college students at 128 self-selected college health centers. This sample represented 2 million college students. In their article, the authors disclosed that college student data on the prevalence of these infections had not been previously collected at the government level.

A survey was taken at the college health centers to determine enrollment in health center use, screening practices for PAP (Papanicolau test for cervical cancer) and STI tests, and the test result data.

Included in the article were the results for STI prevalence and test results for cytologic results of PAP tests regarding HPV (Human Papilloma Virus). The article also indicates that HIV testing is widely available at college health centers.

This article is a contemporary look at a historical problem of STI transmission among an age group that has a high prevalence of sexually transmitted infections. The authors confirmed that the STI data collected was consistent with national trends.

Additionally, this article provides college students with direct information about how health centers on campus are conducting tests and the relevance of testing and prevention.

AMERICAN COLLEGE HEALTH ASSOCIATION ANNUAL PAP TEST AND SEXUALLY TRANSMITTED INFECTION SURVEY

2006

DAVIS P. SMITH, MD; CRAIG M. ROBERTS, PA-C, MS

ABSTRACT OBJECTIVE

The authors describe the cervical cytology and sexually transmitted infection (STI) testing patterns of US college health centers. Participants and Methods: A total of 128 self-selected US college health centers—representing more than 2 million college students—completed an online survey during February and March 2007. Results: Almost 13% of cervical cytology results were abnormal; most of these were atypical squamous cells of undetermined significance and low-grade squamous intraepithelial lesions. In women, 2.9% of chlamydia tests and 0.4% of gonorrhea tests were positive. Human immunodeficiency virus (HIV) and syphilis tests were positive in 0.1% and 0.3% of students tested, respectively. Herpes simplex virus type 1 (HSV-1) accounted for 59.9% of genital herpes infections. Conclusions: College health centers are important sources for Pap and STI test data. Pap tests frequently yield low-grade abnormalities, and screening tests for chlamydia and especially gonorrhea are infrequently positive. Rates of HIV and syphilis in this population are low, raising concerns about positive predictive value when screening low-risk students. A majority of genital herpes infections are caused by HSV-1.

Keywords: cervical cytology, chlamydia, college health, herpes, sexually transmitted infections.

Davis P. Smith and Craig M. Roberts, "American College Health Association Annual Pap Test Sexually Transmitted Infection Survey: 2006," *Journal of American College Health*, vol. 57, issue 4. Copyright © 2009 by Taylor & Francis Group LLC. Reprinted with permission.

For the past 17 years, the American College Health Association (ACHA) has conducted an annual survey of college and university health centers to track Pap smear and sexually transmitted infection (STI) test data in this population. Originally developed to better understand the link between human papillomavirus (HPV) infection and cervical cytopathology, the survey has evolved into a more general assessment of screening practices and STI incidence. Survey results have become an important source of benchmark data for many college health centers. Although the STIs of interest are reportable in most states, college student status is not routinely collected in these reports. As a result, there is no comprehensive source of data at the government level about the prevalence of these infections in college health centers or college student populations.

Researchers assessing the prevalence of STIs in college populations have usually focused on a single college or university. In an early study of HIV prevalence in a national sample of students, Gayle et al used residual blood specimens and found that 0.2% were positive for the HIV antibody. Recently, investigators assessing chlamydia incidence in college students found a wide variation in positivity depending on the population studied. Roberts et al demonstrated that herpes simplex virus type 1 (HSV-1) is a common cause of genital herpes infections in college students, but this study was limited to a single institution.

There are approximately 4,100 degree-granting institutions of higher education in the United States, enrolling more than 17 million students. These institutions comprise a mix of public and private institutions, technical schools, community colleges, 4-year colleges, and large research universities. The total number of schools that have a designated health center or in some way provide health care services to their students is unknown, and there is no accessible database with this information. At the time the survey was distributed, ACHA had a membership of 963 institutions and 3,350 individuals, with another 200 to 300 non-member schools included in their mailing lists (R. Ward, e-mail communication, October 6, 2008).

METHODS

In January 2007, ACHA invited individuals representing approximately 1,100 US colleges and universities to participate in the annual ACHA Pap Test and STI Survey via e-mail. The mailing list included all current ACHA institutional and individual members, previous survey participants, and several nonmember institutions included in ACHA's database. We also posted information about the survey on the national student health service listserv. Invitations included explanatory information and a link to the survey form. The survey was hosted online at a commercial survey site (Web Surveyor; Vovici, Inc, Dulles, VA). Respondents were able to complete surveys in multiple sittings between February 1, 2007, and March 23, 2007. We permitted only 1 response per institution.

As members of the ACHA STI committee, we developed the survey instrument, which included questions related to institutional enrollment and health center use, screening practices for Pap and STI tests, and Pap and STI test result data. All data pertained to the period January 1, 2006, through December 31, 2006 (i.e., calendar year 2006). Most questions were identical to those in previous versions of the survey.

We excluded incomplete responses from the analysis when computing positivity rates and the distribution of results for Pap and STI testing. To assess the internal consistency of reported data for these items, we compared the sum of positive and negative results for a given test type with the reported total number of tests done. If the sum varied by more than 5% from the total, we did not include the data for that item in the analysis reported here. We used SPSS version 15 (SPSS Inc, Chicago, IL) for statistical analysis.

RESULTS

Survey respondents represented 128 institutions, with a combined enrollment of 2,178,086 students (range = 840–51,200 students; M = 17,016, SD = 12,207). Table 1 shows the variety of respondents' institutional characteristics. In 2006, staff at these student health centers conducted 2.9 million medical visits (M = 23,969, SD = 22,487), of which 62% were from female students; 413,583 visits (23% of all female visits) were characterized as women's health visits. Of the women's health visits, 65% were conducted by an advance practice nurse, 18% by nongynecologist physicians, 7% by nurses, 5% by gynecologists, and 4% by physician assistants.

Cervical Cytology

Several survey questions addressed current practices related to cervical cytology screening done in the health center, including the recommended age for initiation of Pap testing in their student population. About half $(n = 62)$ of these health centers recommended a first Pap at 3 years after first intercourse; 25 schools (19.8%) recommend it at onset of sexual activity, 16 schools (12.8%) recommend it at age 21, 8 schools (6.4%) recommended it at age 18, and the remaining 11.9% of schools had no uniform practice. Most (75.4%) respondents' practice was to routinely document a patient's age at first intercourse.

With regard to modalities offered for Pap testing and follow-up (we allowed multiple responses), 109 schools (85.2%) offered liquid-based cytology with reflex HPV testing, 64 schools (50.0%) offered liquid-based without reflex HPV testing, and 45 schools (35.4%) used conventional slide cytology (Pap smear). Follow-up procedures for management of abnormal cytology were less likely to be available on-site: 32.3% of respondents provided colposcopy, 23.6% offered cryotherapy, and 7.1% performed loop electrosurgical excision procedure (LEEP) in house.

Two-thirds of student health centers tracked cervical cytology results with logbooks: 43.3% by use of a tickler file, 34.6% by laboratory-generated reminders, 26.0% by

TABLE 1. Characteristics of Respondent	
Institutions	
Characteristic	%
ACHA member	93.0
Institutional control	
Public	72.2
Private	27.8
Community size	
Urban > 1 million	13.3
Urban < 1 million	35.9
Urban < 100,000	21.1
Suburban	14.1
Rural	14.8
Other	0.8
Note. ACHA = American College Health Association.	

computerized tracking programs, and 16.5% by electronic medical record systems. Only a single respondent indicated that his or her center had no formal tracking system in place.

Cervical Cytology Test Results

In all, 104 respondents provided data on the number and outcome of Pap or cytology tests. After applying our inclusion criteria as specified previously, we included 123,249 tests in the analysis. Of these, 106,078 tests (86.1%) were normal. We defined abnormal results (12.9%) as those reported as atypical squamous cells of undetermined significance (ASC-US), atypical squamous cells—cannot exclude high-grade lesion (ASC-H), atypical glandular cells (AGC), low-grade squamous intraepithelial lesion (LSIL), high-grade squamous intraepithelial lesion (HSIL), unsatisfactory, or other. We categorized most abnormal findings as ASC-US (5.8%) or LSIL (5.1%; see Figure 1).

The usual practice for managing a first ASC-US Pap test showed some variation: 66.9% of schools routinely performed HPV DNA testing, and 23.1% recommend repeating the Pap test in 4 to 6 months. One respondent reported that his or her school referred or performed immediate colposcopy. The practice is not standard and varied by provider for 9.1% of respondents.

Respondents reported follow-up testing results for 6,917 ASC-US Pap tests: 4,224 (61.1%) conducted HPV DNA testing, of which 2,065 (48.9%) were positive for high-risk types of HPV (HR HPV); 1,148 patients (16.6%) had repeat cytology at 4 to 6 months, of which 614 (53.5%) were abnormal; and 869 patients (12.6%) underwent colposcopy. For 569 (8.2%) tests, follow-up test results were unknown, and 107 (1.5%) were worked up through an unspecified strategy.

Respondents provided additional data regarding colposcopy results for 4,767 patients. On the survey, respondents documented colposcopic results for each of 4 indications for colposcopy (initial ASC-US, HR HPV identified, abnormal follow-up Pap test, or other indication). Unfortunately, for half of these patients no outcome data was available (see Table 2).

Sexually Transmitted Infection Testing

Nearly all schools (93.8%) offered some type of routine STI screening for asymptomatic women, and 83.6% offered routine screening for asymptomatic men. Of schools offering STI screening, 96.9% provided chlamydia tests and 94.5% provided gonorrhea tests. Slightly fewer schools offered screening for HIV (84.4%), syphilis (87.5%), hepatitis B (66.4%), trichomoniasis (55.5%), and herpes (52.3%).

Specimen collection methods for chlamydia testing were fairly uniform. In female patients, 77.9% of schools collected tests using a cervical swab as the preferred specimen. A

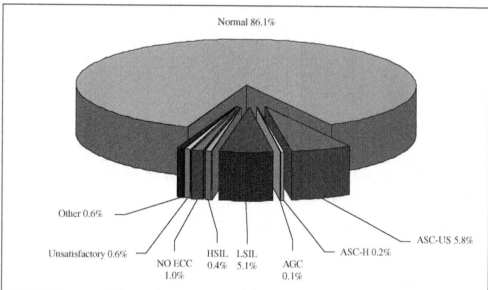

FIGURE 1. Pap test results for calendar year 2006 (*n* = 123, 249 pap tests from 104 institutions). ASC-US = atypical squamous cells of undetermined significance; ASC-H = atypical squamous cells—cannot exclude high-grade lesion; AGC = atypical glandular cells; ECC = endocervical curretage; LSIL = low-grade squamous intraepithelial lesion; HSIL = high-grade squamous intraepithelial lesion.

minority (5.7%) used urine specimens, and 15.6% indicated that the specimen varied by practitioner or that there was no preference. For male patients, 71.1% of schools reported that urine was the standard specimen used for chlamydia tests, 15.7% favored a urethral swab, and 11.6% indicated that it varied or that there was no preference.

Most survey respondents provided numerator (number of positive tests) and denominator (number of tests done) data for chlamydia tests and gonorrhea tests conducted at their health center, allowing us to calculate test positivity. We excluded incomplete or inconsistent data from this analysis using the same methodology we used for cervical cytology tests. Separate questions asked for totals of all persons tested (undifferentiated by sex) and test results grouped by sex (see Table 3).

The survey results indicate that HIV testing is widely available in college health centers. Among 108 (84.4%) schools responding to this question, 35% offered confidential and anonymous testing for HIV, 58% offered confidential tests only, and 2% offered anonymous testing only. With regard to HIV test type, 83.6% of respondents offered conventional serum antibody tests, 19.5% offered oral fluid testing, 14.1% offered rapid testing of blood specimens, and 13.3% offered rapid oral fluid testing (categories not exclusive). Also, 104 respondents reported HIV test result data, totaling 39,655 tests. Of these, 51 tests (0.13%) were positive. We did not ascertain whether this included only confirmed (Western blot) results versus screening (ELISA) results.

TABLE 2. Colposcopy Results, by Indication (%)

Indication	n	Normal	CIN1	CIN 2 or 3	Unknown
First ASC-US High-	754	45.2	6.8	3.4	44.6
risk HPV positive	1,309	24.8	19.3	4.4	51.5
Abnormal second pap	1,659	27.6	15.1	6.1	51.1
Unspecified	1,045	15.6	29.2	6.1	51.1

Note. ASC-US = atypical squamous cells of undetermined significance; CIN = cervical dysplasia; HPV = human papillomavirus.

TABLE 3. Results of Chlamydia and Gonorrhea Testing		
Group	Tests (n)	% positive
Chlamydia		
All	133,108	3.6
Women	82,427	2.9
Men	18,669	6.3
Gonorrhea		
All	107,456	0.6
Women	60,788	0.4
Men	16,173	1.4
Note. Not all respondents reported gender-specific test data.		

Ninety-eight respondents submitted syphilis testing data, totaling 25,491 tests. Of these, 75 (0.29%) were positive. In addition, 66 schools reported a total of 508 cases of trichomoniasis. We did not ascertain the overall number of trichomoniasis tests conducted.

Respondents reported multiple testing modalities for genital herpes diagnosis testing. Most (80.3%) schools used viral culture; 20.5% used polymerase chain reaction (PCR), 9.4% used antigen tests, and 3.1% used Tzanck smears (multiple responses permitted). In addition, 66.9% of respondents reported that type-specific serology was available for diagnostic testing or screening. Genital herpes diagnosis test result data were available from 98 schools, and 76 schools provided type-specific results. This group reported 965 positive tests (by viral culture or PCR), and HSV-1 caused most (59.9%) of these infections. Respondents reported an additional 621 positive tests results as type unknown.

COMMENT

The ACHA Pap Test and STI Survey provides useful information regarding abnormal cervical cytology and STIs seen at college and university health centers. One current area of interest is the recommended age for initiation of Pap testing. The trend away from initiating Pap testing at onset of sexual activity and toward doing so 3 years after first intercourse or age 21—whichever comes first—continues (as per current guidelines). The uptake of these recommendations is a minor marker of evidence-based focus in college health; our results show that this has now become a norm among responding schools. Of note, the framing of the question in the survey used 3 years after first intercourse and age 21 as 2 separate response items. We plan to modify the question in future surveys to better reflect the language of current recommendations.

Incorporating new guidelines for Pap testing and management may result in changes to the way health centers provide STI testing to female patients as well. One of the potential outcomes of wider adoption of these guidelines in young women is that it may eliminate the need for the annual gynecological exam. This presents potential challenges—fewer women being screened for STIs—and opportunities—many women may find screening with urine tests, rather than cervical swabs, more acceptable. Some health center staff already promote sexual health counseling and testing visits during which they use urine-based nucleic acid amplification testing (NAAT) for women who do not yet meet criteria for Pap testing. Our data show an increasing use of urine-based chlamydia testing in college students, particularly in men but for women as well. Health center visits for the HPV vaccine may also become the opportunity to deliver these important services.

Also significant in this survey is the trend toward increased use of liquid-based cervical cytology screening technology with reflex HPV testing. Commensurate with this is the steady erosion in use of conventional Pap smear slides. In 2006, only 35.4% of health centers still used a conventional slide compared with 63.4% of centers in the 2003 survey.[8]

The overall abnormal rate for Pap tests in this survey was 12.9%. The large majority of abnormal results comprised ASC-US or LSIL at rates that are typical (as evidenced by previous surveys) and serve as useful benchmarks. The most common choice for standard management of a first ASC-US Pap test among our respondents is HPV DNA testing, a relatively new option for providers. Half of those patients who underwent DNA tests were positive for high-risk HPV. The next most common choice was to repeat the Pap smear in 4 to 6 months, but this is becoming a less frequently advised choice for young college women. Similar to HPV DNA testing, about half of these repeated Pap tests were abnormal. Over the past 3 years, use of HPV DNA testing has become increasingly the test of choice for college health providers in managing ASC-US results. New guidelines with an emphasis on prolongation of observation in young women will likely lead to further decreases in the number of follow-up Pap smears.

Interpretation of the survey data regarding colposcopic evaluation of ASC-US Pap tests is limited because nearly half of responses had unknown or incomplete data for this group of patients. This includes abnormal Pap tests that did not fall neatly into the survey period, patients who had been referred out for evaluation, or data that was otherwise not subject to easy extraction from records.

These data appear to reinforce the findings from other studies that, especially in this age group, persistence of HPV infection and histologically higher-grade lesions are infrequent (consistently in the range of 5%). Knowing that a fair proportion of moderate-dysplasia (CENT 2) or severe-dysplasia (CIN 3) lesions are likely to regress in healthy young adults, more observation and less intervention, with its attendant morbidities, is the most evidence-based course of action at this time.

The STI data are consistent with national trends. Chlamydia and gonorrhea tests are the most common STI tests conducted, offered by nearly all schools surveyed. Although gonorrhea infection is much less common than is chlamydia, most laboratories run both tests simultaneously. Consistent with published guidelines, nearly all health centers stated that they routinely screen sexually active women for chlamydia. Chlamydia was the most common bacterial STI identified in this population, with an overall positivity rate of 3.6%. Men had higher positivity rates of chlamydia and gonorrhea than did women, but this likely reflects more selective testing in men; the survey did not distinguish between tests done for screening versus those done for diagnosis. For chlamydia and gonorrhea, respondents reported 4 times as many test results for women as men.

Although most college health centers now use highly sensitive and specific NAATs for chlamydia and gonorrhea, there are still concerns about the positive predictive value for these tests when used in low-risk populations with a low prevalence of disease. This is particularly the case for gonorrhea, for which even a test specificity of 99.5% still accompanies a positive predictive value in college women of less than 50%. Thus, many positive gonorrhea results may in fact be false positives. Many health centers may benefit from applying selective screening criteria, rather than providing universal screening for gonorrhea. However, this is an area of research that is data-poor, as ideal gonorrhea-screening criteria have not been developed for this population.

HIV testing is widely available, and rapid testing is increasingly an option for many students. The overall positivity rate in surveyed health centers was extremely low at 0.13% (1 in 769 tests). As with gonorrhea, a concern about the positive predictive value of a positive test is again relevant. Using survey data as the estimate of prevalence (0.13%), we calculated the positive predictive value for a screening HIV antibody test (specificity = 99.9%) to be only 56% in this population. Health centers that conduct a lot of HIV antibody testing in lower-risk students are likely to find more false positive tests than true positives.

Although viral culture remains the most common diagnostic test for herpes infection in the surveyed health centers, more schools are beginning to use PCR, which offers a much improved test sensitivity but is not available in all settings. In students tested for herpes with either PCR or a culture from a genital site (presumably for evaluation of symptoms), 22.1% were positive. Although many schools could not provide type-specific data, most (60%) of the subsample of positive test results with a known type were caused by HSV-1. This finding is consistent with other published studies showing that HSV-1 has become the most common cause of genital herpes in college students.

Limitations

First, participating schools were self-selected and are not necessarily representative of all college health centers. There is likely a strong bias toward participation from schools with better data systems and the means to track and report the data requested by the survey. Furthermore, respondents may have entered data incorrectly or had nothing to report for certain questions. We excluded data from certain analyses from up to 19% of respondent schools because of incomplete or missing data for Pap or STI test results. The detail requested in some of the questions may have strained the ability of many centers to report their own data. Fortunately, many centers have integrated newer data-tracking mechanisms with the implementation of clinical information systems in recent years. Last, reporting of test positivity in our analysis should not be interpreted as being equivalent to incidence. In this survey, we did not assess an institution's complete ascertainment of either numerator or denominator data for STIs, and the true incidence of these infections in college populations may vary from data reported here.

Conclusions

Overall, the results of this 2006 ACHA Pap Test and STI Survey provide a valuable compendium of usual practices for sexual health testing, benchmark values for the tests analyzed, and recent trends among practices and test results. We are eager to promote and contribute to further study of these important conditions in this population.

ACKNOWLEDGMENT

The American College Health Association funded this survey project. The authors thank the staff of ACHA for assistance with data collection and survey design and thank all the survey participants and their patients for providing the data.

REFERENCES

Gayle H.D., Keeling R.P., Garcia-Tunon M., et al. Prevalence of the human immunodeficiency virus among university students. N Eng J Med. 1990;323:1538–1541.

James A., Simpson T., Chamberlain W. Chlamydia Prevalence Among University Freshman and Implications for Improved STI Reduction Programs on Campuses. Poster presented at: 2006 National STD Prevention Conference; May 8–11, 2006; Jacksonville, FL.

Roberts C. Genital herpes in young adults: changing sexual behaviours, epidemiology and management. *Herpes*. 2005;12:10–14.

Roberts C.M., Pfister J.R., Spear S.J. Increasing proportion of herpes simplex virus type 1 as a cause of genital herpes infection in college students. *Sex Transm Dis*. 2003;30:797–800.

Sipkin D.L., Gillam A., Grady L.B. Risk factors for chlamydia trachomatis infection in a California collegiate population. *J Am Coll Health*. 2003;52:65–71.

Smith D,, Wiesmeier E. ACHA annual Pap Test and STI Survey for calendar year 2003. ACHA Action Newsletter. 2004;44:l,7.

Smith P.D., Roberts C.M. ACHA annual Pap Test and STI Survey for calendar year 2005. ACHA Action Newsletter. 2006;46:l,10.

Snyder T.D., Tan A.G., Hoffman C.M.; National Center for Education Statistics. *Digest of Education Statistics*, 2005. Washington, DC: U.S. Department of Education; 2006. NCES 2006–030.

U.S. Preventive Services Task Force. Screening for cervical cancer: recommendations and rationale. *Am Fam Physician*. 2003;67:1759–1766.

U.S. Preventive Services Task Force. Screening for chlamydial infection: US Preventive Services Task Force recommendation statement. *Ann Intern Med*. 2007;147:128–134.

INTRODUCTION TO: PROMISCUOUS PLAGUE

JAN CAMPBELL

Karen Testerman brings into focus the magnitude of the problem with sexually transmitted infections among youth in the U.S. She clarifies the fact that this plague of a multitude of infections and an alarming number of new strains of previously known infections is rampant in 15–19-year-olds and also 20–24-year-olds.

The article is intent on identifying causes that have contributed to the vast increase in these infections among youth. She cites as the main culprit in the epidemic the promotion of sex in society through magazines, movies, and catalogs, which influence youth into thinking that sex is a way to be cool. She instills the facts that while teen pregnancy is an overwhelming issue regarding poverty, lack of education, and increased risk of crimes committed by children born to single mothers, the risk of acquiring a sexually transmitted infection is even more serious, as a young woman is four times more likely to contract an STI/STD than she is to become pregnant.

This is a vital article for recognizing how dangerous the numbers of sex partners are. She cites numerous resources supporting the idea that the exchange of body fluids is not the only way STI/STDs can be transmitted. We have to be cautious of skin-to-skin contact as well. In cases of life-threatening diseases, we may not recognize the effects of an unprotected encounter for up to thirty years. Other latent health concerns involve infertility and infections like Pelvic Inflammatory Disease.

PROMISCUOUS PLAGUE

KAREN TESTERMAN

S exually transmitted diseases (STDs) are the single greatest health threat affecting our youth. A girl is four times more likely to contract an STD than she is to become pregnant, and a young mother has had an average of 2.3 STDs.

We are facing a plague of massive proportions, a plague made more sinister because it attacks not only adults but our youth. What is this crisis? It is a pandemic of sexually transmitted diseases (STDs) that is encouraged by a message of "safe sex" and an adult population that acts as if self-control and traditional morality are outdated and without value.

Society focuses on out-of-wedlock and teen births. Meanwhile STDs tear through our youth and adult population at alarming and deadly rates. They are "not your father's" STDs, which were few and easily cured with penicillin (see sidebar).

In the 1960s, syphilis and gonorrhea were the two most prevalent STDs; today, there are more than 20 and some have as many as 80–100 strains. Despite the fitting publicity that the deadly epidemic of human immunodeficiency virus/acquired immune disorder syndrome (HIV/AIDS) commands, according to research at the University of New Mexico, human papilloma virus (HPV), not HIV, is the most common STD transmitted today.

What is the magnitude of the problem? According to recent testimony before the House Committee on Energy and Commerce, "Three to four million STDs are contracted yearly by 15- to 19-year-olds, and another five to six million STDs are contracted annually by 20- to 24-year-olds."

Karen Testerman, "Promiscuous Plague," *The World & I*, vol. 19, issue 3, pp. 26-33. Copyright © 2004 by The World & I Online. Reprinted with permission.

Perhaps the most tragic aspect of this plague is the role adults play in it. Failures by grown-ups are the primary cause of the pandemic among our youth. Adults are failing our children by promoting a fatal message about sex: both in education and in actions. Youth are allowed to believe that there is such a thing as safe sex outside of marriage and that any sexual practice is acceptable as long as the participants are smiling.

MARKETING SEX

Billboards, TV, magazines, movies, and catalogs promote the message that sex is the way to be cool, to fit in, to solve life's challenges. Today, the initial onset of sexual activity is occurring at younger ages, while couples delay the decision to marry or prefer cohabitation. Dr. Meg Meeker, a pediatrician and author of *Epidemic: How Teen Sex Is Killing Our Kids*, reports that half of all students in the ninth through twelfth grades have had sexual intercourse. Additionally, the average age for the onset of puberty in girls has dropped from 12 to 10.

There are physical and emotional consequences of engaging in sexual activity outside of marriage. Unwed childbearing costs American taxpayers $29 billion a year in social services and lost tax revenue, and results in delinquency and poverty among teenage parents. These teens will enter adulthood disadvantaged and will convey this disadvantage to their children.

In 1960, 15 percent of teen births in the United States were out-of-wedlock. More recently, despite the reduction in teen pregnancy, the out-of-wedlock birthrate was 78 percent among teens, according to the National Center for Health Statistics (2000).

Meanwhile, a primary indicator of poverty in our nation is single-parent households among 15- to 19-year-olds. Ninety percent of these young people will never attend college. Eighty percent of women who choose to parent while they are teens will live at the poverty level for 10 years or more.

Linda Waite, professor of urban sociology at the University of Chicago, and Maggie Gallagher, affiliate scholar at the Institute for American Values, have found that children born to unmarried mothers are more likely to die in infancy. Boys raised in single-parent homes are twice as likely to commit a crime that leads to incarceration by their early thirties.

Adolescents raised by single parents or stepfamilies are more likely to engage in sexual intercourse and to be sexually active at an earlier age, according to Dawn M. Upchurch, professor at the UCLA School of Public Health. None of this takes into account the impact of post-abortive trauma or the emotional trauma of making tough decisions to allow adoption so that the child will have better opportunities.

A girl is four times more likely to contract an STD than she is to become pregnant. Today, a young mother has had on average 2.3 STDs. Syphilis, gonorrhea, herpes, chlamydia, hepatitis A and B, HIV, and HPV are the most common. Many of the viral STDs have multiple strains.

SEXUAL RUSSIAN ROULETTE

A leading risk factor is the number of sexual partners. Vital health statistics directly link this factor to the early onset of sexual activity. Consider the infected teen who has sex with 6 people, each of whom has 6 partners. According to Dr. Meeker, this means that 36 people have been exposed to disease.

Marcel T. Saghir, coauthor of Male and Female Homosexuality: A Comprehensive Investigation, cites the magnification of this problem in the homosexual community, even among those who define themselves as monogamous. The average such relationship among homosexual males lasts less than three years. Despite attempts to portray their choice for living as normal and healthy, homosexuals are in the highest risk group for several of the most serious STDs.

Evidence from the National Cancer Institute that smoking shortens a person's life by 7–10 years led to a multibillion-dollar lawsuit by state governments. However, despite numerous studies that reveal homosexual relationships can reduce male or female lives by 10–30 years, tolerance and political correctness reign.

As even homosexual supporters and the media admit, the increasing pressure to accept homosexual practices as mainstream is dramatically affecting our society. According to the New York Blade News Reports, gay men are in the highest-risk group for several of the most serious diseases, including STDs.

Instability and promiscuity are characteristic of homosexual relationships. Even the Gay Lesbian Medical Association agrees with mainstream reports that, despite decades of intensive efforts to educate, HIV/AIDS continues to increase among the homosexual community.

According to another homosexual newspaper, the Washington Blade, HPV is "almost universal" among homosexuals. HPV, often asymptomatic, is believed to be the causative vector of cervical cancer in women. It can also lead to anal cancer in men.

Add to this the confusion about what constitutes sexual activity. Is it just penile penetration of the vagina? Does oral sex count? Is heavy petting to be included? What about practices of homosexuals? Conventional wisdom seems to promote the idea that these questions are irrelevant, as a condom can prevent the passing of bodily fluids, and thus STDs.

Sadly, this misconception leads to even more danger, as the passing of body fluids is not the only way to contract these diseases. Even a properly used and defect-free latex condom will not completely protect against all STDs. Any genital contact can cause an infection. Genital warts are the common name for HPV. The most common and contagious of STDs, HPV is passed by skin-to-skin contact. It is the leading cause of cervical cancer and in its cancerous form does not exhibit any symptoms.

Alas, most of our sexually active, infected youth do not know they have a disease. Some viruses can lie dormant in the body for up to 30 years before symptoms develop. Ninety percent of those infected with chlamydia exhibit no symptoms and receive no treatment.

According to abstinence speaker Pam Stenzel, the statistics of this disaster are staggering, especially among our youth. Every day in America, 12,000 teenagers contract a sexually transmitted disease.

The American Medical Association recommends that sexually active girls be tested for chlamydia every six months. Why just girls? Aren't boys infected as well? Yes, men carry the infection, but as is often the case, girls endure most of the consequences. Stenzel points out that the female reproductive system is open; scar tissue builds up on the cervix, fallopian tubes, and ovaries as a result of pelvic inflammatory disease (PID) from the chlamydia infection

With a single chlamydia infection, there is a 25 percent chance of sterility. With a second infection there is a 50 percent chance of sterility. If there is a third infection, it is almost certain that the girl will be sterile—all due to PID.

This is why, some people reason, we should promote a dual message and sell teens on abstinence with "safe sex" as a backup. The dual message approach says that abstinence is best, but if you choose to engage in genital contact, use some form of contraception, usually condoms. This comprehensive message indicates that our youth are no more than bundles of uncontrollable hormones—that they are no more than mere animals. Many public school sexuality education programs instruct youth in the proper use of condoms and contraception. The information given is that condoms significantly reduce the chance of STD infection.

In reality, even if a condom is used 100 percent of the time, a sexually active young person is at risk to contract STDs including gonorrhea, chlamydia, and trichomoniasis. Even when used, a condom fails to prevent pregnancy 12 percent of the time, according to the Maryland Center for Mental and Child Health. Despite faithful use of the condom, the person who engages in genital contact is not immune from contracting an STD that spreads through skin-to-skin contact.

It is time that adults clean up their act and encourage youth to aspire to achieve the goal of being responsible, thinking people. Young people need adults who will trust them enough to give them the information they need to make good choices.

Young people need to know that sex without boundaries is deadly. There are consequences when engaging in genital contact outside the bonds of marriage. Young people need to know that both parties should wait until they make a lifelong commitment to one another in marriage to have sex. Within marriage, they have a better chance to be healthier, to attain a higher level of education, to be financially secure, to be happier and enjoy sex more, but only if that sex is with their marital partner.

The only way to protect against STDs that can have lifelong, physically and emotionally painful consequences is to abstain from genital contact outside of marriage. According to the University of Chicago research in Sex in America, researchers report that when a marriage is intact, the couple almost never have sex outside their marital relationship.

Promiscuous sexual practices, whether heterosexual or homosexual, are highly costly to Americans. The health of present and future generations is in jeopardy. Simply avoiding pregnancy or homosexual behavior is not enough. This attitude completely ignores the possibility and consequences of exposure to STDs. Add to this the disease of substance abuse and emotional trauma due to abortion, depression, anxiety, and subsequent problems, and it is clear that one should avoid promiscuity at all costs.

Despite the rhetoric, everyone is not doing it. Over 50 percent of our youth are not engaging in genital contact with one another. Given the information, our young people are capable of making informed decisions. Once we realize this, we can give them (and society) a future without this plague.

The promiscuous plague has many facets. Messages in the media, peer pressure, alcohol, and drugs all influence teen sexual behavior. The biggest influences, of course, are parents. The actions of young people reflect what adults transmit. This is done through how adults behave and what is communicated as acceptable. By allowing the media to undermine morality, the plague is fostered. By engaging in dangerous sexual practices, the plague is encouraged.

More important, by abdicating parental responsibility, the plague is promoted. A recent survey of teens conducted by L.B. Whitbeck, professor of sociology at the University of Nebraska, found that parents have the strongest effect on a teen's decision whether to have sex. Parents influence the attitude of their teens by their own marital status, their attitudes, the amount of supervision they provide, and how involved they are with their children

Ultimately, the most effective inoculation against this plague is effective parenting. Certainly parenting would be made easier if the entertainment media reduced their hard sell of "anything goes" sex and schools truly taught nonmarital abstinence and credited our youth with the ability to use good sense. If given the opportunity, teens can and will make good choices. Our next generation needs to know it is okay to say no!

- There are physical and emotional consequences of engaging in sexual activity outside of marriage.
- Unwed childbearing costs American taxpayers $29 billion a year in social services, lost tax revenue, and the consequences of delinquency and poverty among the teenage parents.
- In 1960, 15 percent of teen births in the United States were out-of-wedlock.
- More recently, despite the reduction in teen pregnancy, the out-of-wedlock birthrate was 78 percent.
- Adolescents raised by single parents or stepfamilies are more likely to engage in sexual intercourse and to be sexually active at an earlier age.
- Most sexually active, infected youth do not know they have a disease (Homosexuality and Health).

Little is heard today about the devastating health effects of homosexual promiscuity. A panoply of diseases—not only the well-publicized AIDS but lesser-known scourges such as hepatitis A, B, and C; herpes; cytomegalovirus; gay bowel syndrome; amoebiasis; anal warts and anal cancer; shigellosis; chlamydia; gonorrhea; and syphilis-serve to truncate the average gays life expectancy to roughly 50 years. And these pestilences not only shorten lives but sharply erode quality of life.

Behavioral disorders and mental illnesses also are far more prevalent among homosexuals than their heterosexual counterparts. High rates of alcoholism, drug addiction, "spousal" abuse, depression, and suicide all militate against living to old age.

Gay sex is of particular concern because among homosexuals, promiscuity is more the rule than the exception. For example, the December 1989 Archives of Internal Medicine refers to a Los Angeles report's finding that gay males averaged over 20 sex partners annually. Some studies show that those in supposedly "steady" relationships are even more promiscuous, engaging in dozens of trysts a year outside the relationship.

A 1998 study that appeared in Psychological Reports used four databases to investigate the life spans of gays versus heterosexuals. It concluded that the homosexual lifestyle sliced 20 to 30 years from practitioners' life expectancy. Supporting this was a 1994 obituary investigation, which determined that the median age of death for gay males was 42 and for lesbians 49. It ran in the Omega Journal of Death and Dying.

Medical statistics show the gay community to be virtually awash in pathogens:

- Over 50 percent of all homosexual men are carriers of the human papilloma virus, which produces anal warts and can often lead to anal cancer, according to Stephen Goldstone, assistant clinical professor of surgery at Mount Sinai Medical Center, speaking at a 1999 Gay Men's Health Summit in Boulder, Colorado.
- Male homosexuals are about 1,000 times more likely to acquire AIDS than the general population (National Center for Infectious Diseases, 1992).

- A survey of more than 2,300 gays in New York and three other cities found that 37 percent of the men and 14 percent of the women reported having a non-HIV sexually transmitted infection (Washington Blade, October 9, 1998). Ten years earlier, male homosexuals (less than 1 percent of the population) accounted for 50 percent of U.S. syphilis cases (Atlantic Monthly, January 1988).
- Hepatitis B is about five times more prevalent among homosexuals than among heterosexual men, according to the National Health and Nutrition Examination Surveys, 1976–1994 (American Journal of Public Health).
- A young gay man has about a 50 percent chance of acquiring the AIDS virus by middle age, and the incidence of gonorrhea rose 74 percent among homosexuals from 1993–1996 (New York Times, November 23, 1997).
- Behavioral and mental disorders are likewise widespread in the gay community. Among the evidence is the following:
- A 1992 Boston study found that of 262 gay male subjects, 49 percent used drugs with sex, 9 percent weekly; 57 percent used alcohol with sex, 9 percent weekly (AIDS).
- Forty-six percent of homosexual and bisexual youths in a 1997 study of Massachusetts high-school students had attempted suicide in the preceding year (Newsweek).
- Forty percent of male homosexual subjects had a history of major depressive disorder (Archives of General Psychiatry, February 1991; Comprehensive Psychiatry, May/June 1993).

STDS: YESTERDAY AND TODAY

The basic types of organisms responsible for STDs are bacteria, parasites, and viruses. Bacterial diseases are treatable with antibiotics such as penicillin, but the organism often develops a resistance to the antibiotic, complicating treatment. Most parasitic diseases are treatable, but viruses often remain in the host for life. Many produce symptoms with a secondary impact to the host—a reduced immune system, stress, or another infection There are no known cures for viruses, and many hosts infected with them exhibit no symptoms.

In 1960 there were 5 primary STDs: gonorrhea, syphilis, granuloma inguinale, chancroid, and lymphogranuloma venereum. Today there are over 20. Unless otherwise noted, the following figures refer to the United States.

Herpes simplex virus (HSV) Types I and II—Genital herpes results from viral infection transmitted through intimate contact with the moist mucous lining of the genitals. Once in the body it remains, and there is no cure. A rash or liberations may be exhibited. Genital herpes can be transmitted without the host experiencing symptoms. Only 80 percent of those infected will test positive for the virus.

Human papilloma virus (HPV)—HPV is the most commonly transmitted STD. There are between 80 and 100 strains of the virus. Some cause genital warts, but the strains that cause cervical cancer and were recently linked to anal cancer do not produce symptoms in the host. HPV is spread through skin-to-skin contact.

Gonorrhea—A bacterial infection, gonorrhea is one of the oldest STDs. Estimates are that over 1 million women are infected with gonorrhea-causing bacteria, which infect the vagina, cervix, urethra, throat, and rectum. The disease is treatable.

Syphilis—A chronic disease, syphilis is caused by a bacterial spirochete that bores into the mucous membranes of the mouth or genitals. It is treatable but in the secondary stage is highly contagious, with a rash on the hands that can be transmitted through casual contact.

Chlamydia—A bacterial infection, first reported in 1984, chlamydia affects an estimated 3–5 million women annually. It infects the cervix, urethra, throat, and rectum While treatable, it is highly destructive to the fallopian tubes and can cause infertility or ectopic pregnancies.

Human herpes virus 8 (HHV8)—HHV8 is a virus associated with Kaposi's sarcoma, an unusual skin tumor usually found in HIV-infected men. While the virus has been found in the semen of HIV-infected men, its impact is yet to be determined.

Trichomoniasis—Caused by Trichomonas vaginalis, a sexually transmitted parasite, trichomoniasis affects approximately 5 million people annually.

HIV/AIDS—Acquired immune deficiency syndrome is caused by the human immunodeficiency virus. An HIV infection weakens the body's immune system and increases the body's vulnerability to many infections as well as the development of certain cancers. AIDS is one of the most frightening of the STDs because it is the most uniformly fatal of the group.

Hepatitis A, B, C (*), D (*)—These viruses cause inflammation of the liver and can lead to cirrhosis, liver failure, and liver cancer. The B virus form is transmitted through sexual intimacy in about 30 percent of the cases. The C form is spread mainly through blood contact, although it has been spread through semen

Chancroid—One of the older bacterial STDs, chancroid is usually diagnosed through a culture of the ulcer. It must be distinguished from syphilis or herpes. All partners should be treated whether or not the ulcer was present at the time of exposure.

Lymphogranuloma venereum—Caused by a type of chlamydia, this disease affects the genitals, anus, or rectum Another strain of the bacteria affects the urethra and can coexist with the former. Both are treatable with an oral antibiotic.

Donovanosis (granuloma inguinale)—A chronic bacterial infection of the genitals that is found in tropical areas, donovanosis can cause severe complications if left untreated.

Molluscum contagiosum—A common noncancerous skin growth, molluscum is caused by a viral infection in the top layers of the skin The growths are similar to warts but are caused by a different virus. The virus and growths are easily spread by skin contact.

Ureaplasma urealyticum—A bacterial infection, generally asymptomatic in nature, ureaplasma is sexually transmitted between partners. The bacteria can survive undetected in the reproductive tract for many years, until a patient is specifically tested for the infection. Although generally asymptomatic, ureaplasma can lead to fertility problems including tubal disease, recurrent miscarriages, decreased sperm motility and count.

Shigellosis (*) and salmonellosis (*)—These bacterial infections cause diarrhea and are spread through contamination from the stool or soiled fingers of one person to the mouth of another. These are STDs common among men having sex with men.

Cytomegalovirus (*)—An asymptomatic disease, cytomegalovirus is caused by a virus that usually remains dormant in the body for life. Severe impairment of the immune system by medication or disease reactivates it. Infectious CMV may be shed in the bodily fluids of any infected person and thus may be found in urine, saliva, blood, tears, semen, and breast milk.

Giardiasis (*)—A diarrheal illness, giardiasis is caused by a one-celled, microscopic parasite that lives in the intestines of people and animals and is passed in the stool. The parasite is protected by an outer shell that allows it to survive outside the body for long periods. Giardiasis is more common at present among homosexuals, as it may be spread through oral-anal sexual contact.

Amoebiasis (*)—Caused by a one-celled parasite, amoebiasis is most commonly found in Mexico, South America, India, and South and West Africa. The parasite is harbored in the human intestinal tract and is passed along by contamination of food and water or by anal or anal/oral sex.

Bacterial vaginosis (*)—The condition is caused by excessive bacteria that may normally be present in the vagina. It is not clear whether it is sexually transmitted, but it is associated with other sexually transmitted diseases. Bacterial vaginosis is more common in women with multiple sexual partners, and it often develops soon after intercourse with a new partner. The disorder is relatively common among women with female partners, where the condition may be triggered by shared objects used in sexual acts.

(*) Sexual transmission occurs but is not the primary mode of transmission.

INTRODUCTION TO: BEYOND BAD GIRLS

Meanness, Violence, and Gender

JAN CAMPBELL

This article exposes the fact that we have always had "bad" girls. Yet it seems there has been more violence in the twenty-first century, with these girls becoming more menacing. Chesney-Lind and Irwin describe the various bad girl images during the years 1960–1990 and then discuss the types of jolting, violent images of girls today. Are these new images of girls, or are we seeing violent patterns in inner cities and elsewhere? The authors suggest the fact girls are mean to other girls, and this is not a new, Hollywood theme, as portrayed in the movie *Mean Girls* and in some publications.

The publications of many books and articles in the past two decades have increased the notion that girls are meaner than ever and have elevated levels of aggression. The authors cite researchers' works that tend to blame television viewing, video games, abuse, and even girls' sports participation as evidence of this aggression, but attempt to debunk some of the findings.

BEYOND BAD GIRLS

Meanness, Violence, and Gender

MEDA CHESNEY-LIND AND KATE IRWIN

CONSTRUCTING MEAN AND VIOLENT GIRLS

It seems like the news about girls is increasingly grim, at least if you rely on the mass media. While we've always known about "bad" girls, during the past decade we've been jolted by ever more violent media images of girlhood. Take the girl gang members of the nineties seen as every bit as menacing as their male counterparts, often portrayed peering at the world over the barrel of a gun. As we entered the 21st century, popular culture discovered "mean" girls, backstabbing their way to popularity, and now, only a few years later, it seems as though our mean girls have also turned violent. After endless viewings of the "cheerleader beating" in 2008 and the 2003 Glenbrook High girl fight, do we now need to worry about girls causing "savagery in the suburbs" as a headline in *Newsweek* warned? (Meadows and Johnson, 2003).

It is important to place these media stories about and popular constructions of aggressive girls in an historic context. We have always had "bad" girls and a collection of media eager to showcase their dangerousness. A quick glance of media reports during the past 50 years reveals this trend. In the sixties and seventies, we had female revolutionary figures such as Patti Hearst, Friederike Krabbe, and Angela Davis who carried guns and fought alongside male revolutionaries. The eighties and nineties ushered in news reports featuring female gang members who, like their male counterparts, carried guns, killed people, and practiced brutal initiation rituals. The turn of the century saw mean girls take center stage in media messages about wayward young females. Most recently, the story about relationally aggressive girls took a violent turn as books and news stories argued that there was a connection between relational and physical aggression among girls.

At the same time that the media were warning us that bad girls were dangerous to society, a small collection of journalists and researchers argued that society was dangerous for girls. Piqued by Pipher's *Reviving Ophelia* (1994), adults in the nineties became concerned with the toxic and sexist culture that encouraged girls to fall behind boys in a number of ways. According to researchers, girls, more than boys, lost self esteem during adolescence, monitored and felt badly about their looks and their bodies, and were sexually harassed at school. The popular idea that society polluted girlhood has been lost in this century. Now it is girls, and not society, who are to blame for poisoning girlhood with their meanness, gossip, and violent outbursts. Instead of pathologically falling behind boys, girls are said to be catching up with boys in dangerous new ways. But are today's girls really seeking equality with boys in crime and violence the same way they have with soccer? The notion has a clear intuitive appeal. It seems obvious to many that as girls seek "equality" with boys, they run the risk of picking up the downsides of masculinity, including aggression and violence.

While mean girls appear to be quite different than girl gang members or female revolutionaries, what is common among these many bad girl constructions is that they usually do not reflect the complexity of girls' and young women's behaviors. Often they imply that girls' violence is simply a by product of girls becoming more like boys and implying that this "masculinization" is an unfortunate outcome of girls and women seeking equality with boys and men. Similarly, in many ways the "discovery" of girls' meanness is simply a revisiting of a centuries old pattern of stressing women's duplicitous nature—appearing superficially "innocent" and "nice" while actually being manipulative, devious, and occasionally evil. As a result, these constructions tend to distort and misrepresent the context of girls' aggression and violence, and more importantly, ignore girls' and women's place in a larger social structure, particularly their relative powerlessness compared with boys and men.

Here, we will briefly explore the popular culture "bad" and "mean" and "violent" girl hype of the last few decades, and we also critically review the evidence for widely accepted notions that girls' violence is increasing. Finally, we consider the impact these constructions have had on real girls' lives, with a focus on the ways these girl images and their consequences are racialized.

POPULAR CONSTRUCTIONS OF BAD GIRLS

In her bestselling book, *Backlash,* Susan Faludi (1991) documented some of the ways in which the detractors of feminism used the media to attack and dismiss a wide array of feminist goals. Faludi (1991: 80) specifically chronicled journalism's efforts to frame "female trends" of the eighties as a litany of female shortcomings including "the failure to get husbands, get pregnant, or properly bond with their children." In the context of that discussion, Faludi noted that "NBC, for instance, devoted an entire evening news special to the pseudo trend of 'bad girls' yet ignored the real trends of bad boys: the crime rate among boys was climbing twice as fast as for girls."

By focusing, even briefly, on the media love affair with "bad girls," Faludi hit on a historic trend in the representation of female criminals. At its core, the "bad girl" hypothesis is that the women's movement has a "dark" side, encouraging girls and women to seek equality in the illicit world of crime as well as licit labor. Freda Adler, for example, wrote in her book, *Sisters in Crime* (1975) that "the movement for full equality has a darker side which has been slighted even by the scientific community. … In the same way that women are demanding equal opportunity in the fields of legitimate endeavor, a similar number of determined women are forcing their way into the world of major crimes." (Adler, 1975: 3).

While the argument that women and girls seek criminal equality with men and boys sounds relatively recent, it is actually about a century old. Ever since the first wave of feminism, there has been no shortage of scholars and political commentators issuing dire warnings that women's demand for equality would result in a dramatic change in the character and frequency of women's crime. The central hypothesis underlying concerns about emancipated, criminal women is what is called the "masculinization" theory. The theory is that as women and girls break free from the constraints of their gender, they will become increasingly masculine. Implicit in this "masculinization" theory of women's crime is the companion notion that contemporary theories of violence (and crime more broadly) need not attend to gender, but can simply "add women and stir." Moreover, the masculinization framework lays the foundation for simplistic notions of "good" and "bad" femininity, standards that will permit the demonization of some girls and women if they stray from the path of "true" (passive) womanhood.

Media treatments of girls' violence during the past few decades routinely stress the equity or masculinization hypothesis; girls are increasingly behaving like boys, we are told. They are carrying guns, joining gangs, and engaging in violence as often as boys are. For example, on August 2, 1993, a *Newsweek* feature spread on teen violence included a box entitled "Girls will be Girls" and claimed that "some girls now carry guns. Others hide razor blades in their mouths" (Leslie et al., 1993, p. 44). Explaining this trend, the article noted that "The plague of teen violence is an equal-opportunity scourge. Crime by girls is on the rise, or so various jurisdictions report" (Leslie et al., 1993, p. 44).

Years later, the theme was still quite popular. On November 5, 1997, ABC *Primetime Live* aired two segments on Chicanas involved in gangs, also called "Girls in the Hood" (ABC 1997) that followed two young women around their barrio for four months. The series opened with Sam Donaldson announcing that "There are over six hundred thousand gang members in the United States. What might surprise you is that many of them are young women." Warning viewers that "some of the scenes you may see are quite graphic and violent," the segment featured dramatic shots of young women with large tattoos on their stomachs, girls carrying weapons and making gang signs, young women selling dope and talking about being violent, and distant shots of the covered bodies of victims of drive-by shootings.

And the pattern continues through most of the nineties, although in later years it moved from a specific concern about the "girl gangsta" to a more general moral panic about girls' violence. As an example, the *Boston Globe Magazine* ran an article that proclaimed on its cover, over huge red letters that said BAD GIRLS, "Girls are moving into the world of violence that once belonged to boys" (Ford 1998). From the *San Jose Mercury* (Guido 1998) came a story titled "In a new twist on equality, girls' crime resembles boys'" and featured an opening paragraph that argues:

> Juvenile crime experts have spotted a disturbing nationwide pattern of teenage girls becoming more sophisticated and independent criminals. In the past, girls would almost always commit crimes with boys or men. But now, more than ever, they're calling the shots (Guido 1998, IB).

In virtually all the print stories on this topic, the issue is framed in a similar fashion. Generally, a specific and egregious example of female violence is described, usually with considerable, graphic detail about the injury suffered by the victim. In the *Mercury* article, for example, the reader learns how a seventeen year old girl, Linna Adams "lured" the victim into a car where her boyfriend "pointed a .357 magnum revolver at him, and the gun went off" (Guido 1998, IB). These details are then followed by a quick review of the Federal Bureau of Investigation's arrest statistics showing what appear to be large increases in the number of girls arrested for violent offenses. Finally, there are quotes from "experts," usually police officers, teachers, or other social service workers, but occasionally criminologists, interpreting the events.

GIRLS, GANGS, GUNS, AND EMANCIPATION?

The media hype of the 1990s about girls and gangs primarily focused on gender and crime. Interestingly, media constructions also told a story about race, class, and crime as well. The imagery of the gun toting, tattooed, African American boy heavily clad in gold jewelry and gang colors was eventually followed by an African American girl or Latina who was also tattooed, dressed in gang colors, and sported firearms. With this parallel imagery of the violent boys and girls came an explanatory parallel as well. The media was correct in noting that the problem of soaring youth homicide rates was primarily located in poor, inner city neighborhoods and seemed to affect black and Latino youths more often than white juveniles. On the surface, the media imagery suggested that the forces driving African American boys and Latinos to be violent were also driving girls' violence. The pro-violence forces, therefore, seemed to dissolve the gender gap in crime for particular communities.

What these constructions ignored was that violent ways of life in inner-city America are not gender blind. In the violent milieu of distressed urban areas, girls do not find equal opportunities. As urban ethnographers looking at underground economies illustrate, men who are left with few legitimate means to establish masculine identities often use partner abuse and rape to establish powerful personas. Gang researchers consistently reveal that girls have very limited power vis à vis male gang members, and, although they are more violent than girls who are not in gangs, they are less violent than male gang members. Gang research also reveals that male gang members sometimes used rape or the threat of rape to control female gang members. Drug researchers also consistently note that drug markets, even the exploding crack market with seemingly limited sales opportunities in the eighties and early nineties, tended to be male dominated domains in which women had a difficult time gaining an equal footing. Thus, although the media portrayed an image of the liberated female gang banger, research showed a different image in which girls and women have a very tenacious foothold in street cultures, gangs, and underground drug markets.

Thus, the world of crime and especially the underground crack markets, were far from being locations in which women and girls achieved emancipation. In fact, as gang and drug researchers often indicated, large-scale social problems such as the migration of jobs out of and a lack of services within inner-cities in the 1980s and early 1990s, left many men of color without jobs or legitimate avenues for success. These changes left men of color scrambling for ways to achieve positive identities in many U.S. urban centers. Alternately the hyper-masculine norms established as a response to the lack of jobs and legitimate avenues for respect and status, placed women of color in difficult positions as well as they often became the targets for men's efforts to take control and earn respect through violence.

GIRL BULLIES?

By the mid-nineties, gang violence stories slipped out of the public spotlight, as national youth homicide rates began to decline. Attention to the subject of youth violence, however, did not abate. A collection of sensationalized and horrific school shootings, the most notorious being the Columbine High School massacre in April of 1999, caught the media's attention. The gangs, guns, and drugs story of the late eighties and early nineties was replaced with images of white suburban teens seeking revenge against their classmates. While virtually all school shooters were boys and the media repeatedly neglected that theme, in favor of framing the issue as "kids killing kids" (Garvey, 1999). Then, when research conducted by the U.S. Secret Service appeared suggesting that many school shooters had been the victims of bullying (Vossekuil, 2002) policy makers, in particular, took notice. Several states, including Colorado, passed laws mandating that schools implement violence prevention programs, many of which promised to increase school safety by changing the social dynamics in school. Specifically, bullying prevention programs began to emerge, without much media fanfare, until the popular discovery of girls' relational aggression.

One of the staples of bullying prevention programming is the notion that both boys and girls "bully." These claims are loosely based on the psychological literature on adolescent aggression. Specifically, psychologists define aggression as behaviors that intentionally harm others. Crick (1996), among others, argued that indirect and or relationship "aggression" is more typical of girls' aggression while boys tended to specialize in direct aggression (including violence).

The discovery of girls' aggression in the psychological literature was popularized in such bestsellers as *Odd Girl Out*, which suggested that mean girls destroyed their victims' self esteem and made going to school a painful event for many girls. These claims came, in part, as a backlash against years of feminist research arguing that women are more nurturing, caring, and relationship-oriented than men.

Virtually all popular treatments of the new girl bully open with the personal experiences of the authors. *Odd Girl Out*, as an example, opens with Rachel Simmons telling us that when she was eight, a "popular" friend whispered to Rachel's "best" friend that they should run away from Rachel and they did, on the way to dance class at a local community theater. Simmons spent much of that year trying to make sense of their desertion. As she put it: "The sorrow is overwhelming." She concludes that it is time to tell this story and expose the "… hidden culture of girls' aggression in which bullying is epidemic, distinctive, and destructive" (Simmons, 2002: 3).

Television and print news media further diffused the images of mean girls found in popular books on girls' aggression. Rosalind Wiseman, author of *Queenbees and Wannabees*, made a guest appearance on *Oprah*, Rachel Simmons' work became the focus of a *Dateline* story titled "Fighting with Friends." In addition, the mean girl story was told in a series of newspaper and magazine articles with titles such as "Girls Just Want to Be Mean" (Talbot, 2002), "Girl Bullies Don't Leave Black Eyes, Just Agony" (Elizabeth, 2002), "She Devils" (Metcalf, 2002), and "Just Between Us Girls: Not Enough Sugar, Too Much Spite" (*Pittsburgh Post-Gazette*, 2002). The central idea communicated in these news stories was that girls are socially competitive creatures and that, in their efforts to be popular and powerful, they inflict lifelong damages on their female victims.

In addition, the connection between girls' mean and manipulative natures was often linked in these reports to the larger social problem of bullying. In an article titled "Outcast no More," reporter Slayer notes that "up to 20 percent of American students are chronic targets of bullying at school. Six out of 10 teenagers witness bullying at least once a day." Kiristi, a once popular, blonde haired middle school girl, provided the human interest example of the extent of bullying problems in school. According to the reports "a group of girls at North Lake Middle School who had once been her friends suddenly turned against her."

In 2004, Rosalind Wiseman's *Queen Bees and Wannabes* was adapted for the big screen; the result was the Hollywood block buster *Mean Girls,* which offered a comic portrayal of girls' incivility to other girls. The theme of girls' bullying also made it to the stage in Joan MacLeod's play *The Shape of a Girl,* which has toured through Canada and received the Betty Mitchell Award for Outstanding Original Script. Even at the height of the youth violence epidemic, the story of girl gangsters did not make it to best selling popular books, profitable Hollywood films, or acclaimed plays. Relatively speaking, girl gangsters who were demonized, masculinized, and denounced were more physically threatening and dangerous than mean girls. Why then, would the mean girls become a best selling topic?

The answer is because the mean girl story is a new twist on a very old and damaging construction of women. As we noted earlier, traditionally women have been viewed as nice on the outside, but venomous and manipulative on the inside. That girls are mean to other girls is not a new popular or Hollywood theme in the slightest. In fact, films have consistently portrayed girls as mean to one another. *Jawbreakers* (1999), *Heathers* (1989), *Carrie* (1976), *Peyton Place* (1957), *All About Eve* (1950), *Mildred Pierce* (1945), and *Rebecca* (1940) depict vivid and often deadly images of women's incivility to other women. So the popular culture discovery of relationally aggressive girls was really not a new discovery at all. It was rooted in historic messages about girls' and women's subversive and even evil natures.

Are Mean Girls Becoming Violent?

What happens when cliques' relationship violence becomes physical? An incident at Glenbrook High School on May 4, 2003 gave a new spin to the mean girl hype. On May 4, 2003, the annual powder puff football game began as a regular hazing ritual with senior girls smearing muck all over a band of girls from the junior class. According to witness Nick Babb, quoted in the newspaper Glenview Announcements (Leavitt, 2003, p. 2), the event turned violent when "a few individuals in the senior class decided they hated some of the juniors. Certain people decided they wanted to turn this whole thing into something personal." The violence reported included placing buckets over the heads of girls and beating the buckets with bats as well as pushing and kicking. Girls were seen smearing feces, pig guts, fish guts, paint, and coffee grounds on girls. A collection of students, including boys, looked on, cheered, and drank beer. After the event, five girls required medical attention, one had a concussion, one had a broken ankle, and another needed stitches on a head wound.

When the videotape revealing the mayhem was aired, the incident received national attention and became another example of "girls gone bad." Except this time, the bad girls used violence against their victims rather than simply ostracism, rumors, and manipulation, thus, illustrating that under the right circumstances (alcohol, hazing traditions, lack of adult supervision), girls can be physically violent. And, as noted earlier, the notion that even white girls were becoming more aggressive and violent was later solidified in *Newsweek's* article on this widely viewed fight was entitled "Girl Fight: Savagery in the Suburbs" which breathlessly reported the details of the incident.

"Savagery in the Suburbs?"

The idea that these newly discovered aggressive girls could move to violence came with the publication of two mass market books contending that girls' aggression is now becoming increasingly violent. Harvard professor Deborah Prothrow-Stith and pediatrician Howard Spivak's published *Sugar and Spice and No Longer Nice: How We Can Stop Girls' Violence in 2005, and a year later, psychologist James Garbarino published See Jane Hit: Why Girls are Growing More Violent and What We Can Do About It.* Somewhat predictably, the publication of these books, prompted yet another round of articles including *Newsweek's* "Bad Girls Go Wild," which noted that "a rise in girl on girl violence is making headlines nationwide and prompting scientists to ask why (Scelfo, 2005). *Time* followed suit with "Taming Wild Girls" (which opened with "never mind the gentler gender. Girls, too can be brawlers") (Kluger, 2006: 54).

Both these books, unlike earlier depictions of violent girls, feature Caucasian girls looking somewhat menacing on their covers. They both also rely heavily on arrest statistics to support their contention that girls are becoming more violent. Prothrow-Stith and Spivak note that self-report data do not confirm their contention, which they justify ignoring "considering the numerous stories we have been told for over a decade" (Prothrow-Stith and Spivak, 2005: 51). Apparently, anecdotal evidence trumps data in this instance. In Garbarino's case there's even evidence that he misstates the arrest data. In a critical review of this book, Males comments: "Twenty-five years ago, almost ten boys were arrested for assault for every one girl," Garbarino writes, misstating numbers from Prothrow-Stith. "Now, the ratio is four to one." Wrong. FBI figures show that 25 years ago, five boys were arrested for assault per girl, not 10." (Males, 2006: 34). Garbarino certainly shops carefully among even the arrest data (sometimes stopping well short of the most up to date statistics); he has for example an entire chapter on girls who kill despite the fact that girls' arrests for lethal violence actually declined by 36.9 percent between 1995–2004 (FBI, 2006: 285).

These newest books on girls' aggression and violence showcase scary arrest statistics about girls' violence, supply lots of powerful anecdotes and media accounts of girls' "brawls," and then proceed to round up the usual suspects (as well as a few unusual ones) to blame. Both books hit the media, particularly "the feminization of the superhero" (Prothrow-Stith and Spivak, 2005: 80), television viewing, video games, abuse, and the "intensity" of girls' meanness. In Gabarino's (2006: 113) case, feminism ("female liberation and equalization is nearly complete when it comes to aggression"), and girls' sports participation are added to the list of problems, along with a "toxic" culture. Sports, he contends, which he argues produce girls getting more "physical" and "assertive" also produces "elevated levels of aggression." In this instance, Garbarino is specifically accessing the "masculization hypothesis."

Significantly, both books spend a considerable amount of time with advice to parents and others who work with girls to address girls' "new" problems, again stressing the relevance of "bullying" prevention programs and other efforts to make both gender prevention and intervention programs more girl relevant. Given both books' focus on white girls, the emphasis on programming, as opposed to justice responses, is significant and noteworthy, suggesting that since youth violence is now the province of white girls, we should seek to prevent rather than punish.

Trends in Girls' Violence: Is the Gender Gap Closing?

Why the media fascination with youth violence and particularly girls' violence? To put this in perspective, it is important to review the crime trends that drew media attention to youth violence in general. Although the U.S. had experienced relatively stable crime rates from the early 1980s to the mid 1990s, violent crime rates for juveniles soared during this period. By the mid-nineties, the grim statistics regarding adolescent violence gained national attention. Among the more sobering statistics was an approximately 70 percent increase in youth arrest rates for violent offenses and a nearly 300 percent growth in youth homicide arrest rates from 1983 to 1994 (Snyder and Sickmund, 1999). Soon the attention of the media was drawn to what some were calling an "epidemic of youth violence."

Criminologists explained that the epidemic was caused by a combination of the introduction of new crack markets to inner-cities, increased distribution of guns among juveniles, and the involvement of gangs in the crack and underground gun markets (all far more relevant to boys' but not girls' violence) (Blumstein, 1995). Initially, the media chronicled this trend with alarmist messages about the savage nature of the coming generation of boys—often called "super-predators." But the boy "super-predator" failed to appear, and by 1994, the violence epidemic among boys, according to most accounts, began to abate as youth homicide rates dropped steadily. Instead of reporting the end of epidemic of violence—a mostly male phenomenon—the media and the public latched onto the fact that girls' were making up a larger percentage of juvenile arrests since the 1980s, and that many of these new arrests of girls were for violent offenses.

Indeed, a review often year juvenile arrest trends revealed rising rates of girls' arrests. Between 1985 and 1996, boys' arrests increased by 24.4 percent, while girls' rates increased 50.1 percent (FBI 1995) and from 1991 to 2000 boys' arrests declined (by 3.2 percent), while girls' arrests climbed by 25.5 percent. Eventually, girls' arrest rates also began to decline. Despite these declines, the fact that girls were outpacing boys in arrest rates meant that girls were making up a larger portion of juvenile arrests. In 1991 girls made up 23 percent of all juvenile arrestees and by 2004 they made up 30.5 percent (FBI, 1997: 215; FBI, 2005: 285).

What makes this surge most noteworthy is that girls are increasingly being arrested for violent offenses, not traditional status offenses (non-criminal offenses like running away from home). Over the last two decades, increases in girls' arrests rates for a number of violent offenses have clearly outpaced boys' arrest rates. Between 1980 and 2000, for example, girls' arrests for aggravated assault, simple assault, and weapons law violations increased by 121 percent, 257 percent, and 134 percent (respectively). Boys' arrests also increased in these categories, but by far less (28 percent, 109 percent, and 20 percent). And the trend continues; between 1995 and 2004, girls' arrests for simple assault increased by 31.4 percent while boys' arrests decreased by 1.4 percent. Arrests of girls for aggravated assault did drop (by 2.9 percent), but compare that to the 27.6 percent drop in boys' arrests for this offense (FBI, 2006: 285).

These data certainly caught the attention of media already focused on "youth violence" and, as we've documented, the first media explanation was that girls were changing. They were becoming increasingly like boys and, thus, were being arrested for violations that were historically viewed as boys' domain. Despite the intuitive popularity of the claims that girls were achieving a violent brand of equality, there are good reasons to be skeptical.

The first indication that something more complex was occurring came when several self report data (that is, survey data drawn from young people about their behavior, including delinquency) failed to corroborate this supposed "surge" in girls' violence. In fact, self report studies often found that girls were becoming less violent throughout the 1990s. In the Centers for Disease Control and Prevention's biennial Youth Risk Behavior Survey, girls' self reported involvement in physical fights decreased. In 1991, 34.2 percent of girls reported being in a fight versus 26.5 percent of girls in 2007. Boys' self reported violence during the same time also decreased, from 50.2 percent to 44.4 percent (Centers for Disease Control and Prevention, 1992–2008). A meta-analysis of data collected from 1991 to 1997 showed that while both male and female violence rates declined, girls' rates declined more dramatically (Brener et al., 1999, p. 444).

Comparing multiple data sources over several consecutive years, Steffensmeier et al. (2005) found that the dramatic increases in girls' arrest rates for violent offenses were significantly out of step with victim reports (the NCVSO) and two different self report data (the Monitoring the Future study and the Youth Risk Behavior Survey). And in a matched sample of "high risk" youth surveyed in the 1997 National Youth Survey and the 1989 Denver Youth Survey, Huizinga (1997) found significant decreases in girls' involvement in felony and minor assaults.

Finally, there are the trends in girls' lethal violence. While girls' arrests for all forms of assault have been skyrocketed, girls' arrests for murder dropped by 36.9 percent between 1995 and 2004 and girls' arrests for robbery also dropped by 37.2 percent. If girls were in fact closing the gap between their behavior and that of boys, would not one expect to see the same effect across all the violent offenses (including the most violent offense)? That simply is not happening.

Table 1. *Trends in Self-Reported Delinquency: Percentage of High School Students Reporting*

GIRLS	1991	1993	1995	1997	1999	2001	2003	2005	2007
In a Physical Fight	34.2	31.7	30.6	26.0	27.3	23.9	25.1	28.1	26.5
Carried a Weapon	10.9	9.2	8.3	7.0	6.0	6.2	6.7	7.1	7.5
Carried a Gun		1.8	2.5	1.4	.8	1.3	1.6	.09	1.2
BOYS	1991	1993	1995	1997	1999	2001	2003	2005	2007
In a Physical Fight	50.2	51.2	46.1	45.5	44.0	43.1	40.5	43.4	44.4
Carried a Weapon	40.6	34.3	31.1	27.7	28.6	29.3	26.9	29.8	28.5
Carried a Gun		13.7	12.3	9.6	9.0	10.3	10.2	9.9	9.0

Source-Youth Risk Surveillance data (CDC, 1992, 1994, 1998, 2000, 2002, 2004, 2006, 2008).

Regional data also cast doubt on the "surge" in girls' violence. Males and Shorter's (2001) analyses of vital statistics maintained by health officials (rather than arrest data) conclude that there has been a 63 percent drop in San Francisco teen-girl fatalities between the 1960s and the 1990s, and they also report that hospital injury data show that girls are dramatically under-represented among those reporting injury (including assaults) (girls are 3.7 percent of the population but were only 0.9 percent of those seeking treatment for violent injuries) (Males and Shorter, 2001, p. 1–2). They conclude: "Compared to her counterpart of the Baby Boom generation growing up in the 1960s and 1970s, a San Francisco teenage girl today is 50 percent less likely to be murdered, … 45 percent less likely to die by guns, … and 60 percent less likely to commit murder …" (Males and Shorter 2001, p. 1). If girls were becoming more violent, in San Francisco and elsewhere, one would expect other systems (like hospitals and health departments) to also be noting this trend, but that was not seen.

Data from Canada, which has also seen a barrage of media coverage of girls' violence, also indicate that violent female delinquency is rare, even among incarcerated girls. A report on delinquent girls incarcerated in British Columbia notes that "despite isolated incidents of violence, the majority of offending by female youth in custody is relatively minor" (Corrado, Odgers, and Cohen, 2000, p. 189). Surprisingly, a recent study of girls tried and convicted as adults in the U.S. also found the majority of the girls had committed relatively minor offenses (Gaarder and Belknap, 2002).

If girls' violence was not increasing, then what accounts for their increasing arrest rates during the past two decades? A collection of researchers have offered an alternative to the masculinization or parity hypothesis by arguing that the surge in girls' violent arrests reflects an intensified policing, or "hyper-policing" of youthful misbehaviors, rather than a dramatic change in girls' behaviors. The reason that girls' violence arrest rates are increasing faster than boys' rates is three-fold. First, the policing of youth has become especially vigilant in intimate settings (home and peer groups at school)—the contexts in which girls are likely to offend (although most of their offenses are minor). Second, girls have been particularly denounced in popular venues, which has led to increased scrutiny of them, and increased the likelihood that their misbehaviors will be treated seriously. And third, as a result of national concerns about youth violence and school safety in the post-Columbine years, there has been a widespread re-crafting of definitions of violence to include behaviors that would have never been considered violent decades ago (think zero tolerance).

Youth Violence, Bad Girl Hype, and Real Consequences

The new century has opened with numerous news stories warning of increasing violence among girls; this on the heels of several decades of negative stories showcasing various "bad" girl epidemics. A close look at arrest data, however, fails to support this notion (particularly if you consider lethal or predatory violence like murder or robbery). If the media is correct, other data sources (like self report and victimization studies) should show increases in girls' violence, but they have not. There is very little corroborating evidence to suggest that girls are closing the gender gap in violence.

Despite the fact that multiple data sources tell us that girls are not becoming more violent, popular constructions of violent and aggressive girls are alarming, and in fact, are complicating the trend in girls' arrests. Clearly, the rise in girls' violence arrest rates began before the popular press ran the first stories of gang banging girls. After all it was girls' arrest statistics that piqued the media interest and lent credibility to the violent girl story. Therefore, media constructions certainly did not, at first, cause increases in girls' arrests, but they have probably complicated the problem. In some cases, the media constructions have helped justify the high rates of girls' arrests after the fact. And, in other cases, the media hype has persuaded those who have traditionally controlled girlhood to increase the policing of girls in ways that seriously disadvantage all girls and most particularly girls of color.

The differences between the way that violent girls and youth of color are constructed and treated can be clearly seen when examining two different publicized episodes of youth violence. In the Glenbrook High School hazing incident on May 4, 2003, 32 students were suspended and 12 girls and three boys confronted misdemeanor battery charges. If they were found guilty, these youths could have confronted 364 days in jail and $2,000 in fines. The students, however, secured lawyers and fought these charges. Two students even filed a federal lawsuit to lift their suspensions and recover monetary damages from the school, though this was later denied. The parents, who provided the resources for these lawyers stood by their children and claimed repeatedly to reporters that their daughters or sons were good kids and had been only marginally involved in the event. In the end, the school offered the students the chance to graduate on time if they agreed in writing to forgo movie, book, and television deals.

Contrast this case with similar high profile set of suspensions in a Decatur, Illinois neighborhood. There a seventeen second fight between seven boys attending a high school football game resulted in the boys being expelled from school for two years—despite the fact that the fight involved no weapons and injured no one. Until the intervention of Jesse Jackson, none of these youths was allowed counsel and the two seniors, with less than four credits to go to graduation, would have lost the chance to graduate (Wing and Keleher, 2000:1). While zero tolerance for violence policies in the Decatur school kept students from returning to school, Jackson coaxed the school district into allowing two of the boys to transfer to a reform school in the area and graduate on time.

These two cases clearly highlight the ways that class and race privilege can blunt the force of the official intervention into the "youth violence" problem. Despite the intense media focus on the Glenbrook case, the relatively serious nature of the girls' violence was over shadowed by the "girls gone wild" media construction, and the parents' quick insistence on re-labeling the incident as "hazing." The Decatur incident initially failed to receive the same fanfare and only made it into the national press when Jackson became involved. Without Jackson's celebrity status, a group of African Americans threatened with expulsion as a result of a short scuffle, would not have been newsworthy.

The media driven "gangsta girl" hype of the eighties and nineties, the millennium mean girl, and "bad girls go wild" story of the new century, have all served to justify increased formal control of girlhood. Girls' increased arrests came, we argue, not because they were becoming more like boys, but instead because girls would bear the brunt of an intensified system of social control. In short, girls who were "acting out" in the home, in their peer groups, or in the school, are now being punished formally, and often labeled as violent criminals in the process.

It appears that while public fear of the "super-predator" male youth has waned, the public is still very concerned about its female version—the new bad girl, largely because of an unrelenting media hype showcasing images of mean, bad, and violent girls. We are very concerned about the consequences of this hype for girls, particularly girls of color (whose families and communities do not necessarily have the resources to challenge the increasing control of minor forms of youthful misbehavior). Toxic media constructions of girls' "badness" "meanness" and "wildness," un-tethered from reality, have resulted in the increased surveillance and policing of girlhood.

Certainly, when we review trends in the juvenile justice system, we see ample evidence of the serious consequences of social control on girls. Girls' arrests, detentions and incarcerations are soaring, and the trend is clearly related to girls' arrests for "assault." During the period between 1991–2003, the nation saw a 98 percent increase in the detentions of girls (compared to a 29 percent increase in boys' detentions), a 92 percent increase in girls' referrals to juvenile courts (compared to 29 percent among boys), and finally an 88 percent increase in girls' commitments (compared to only 23 percent increase in boys' commitments). Most significantly, more girls in court populations were there for "person" or violent offenses than boys (Snyder and Sickmund, 2006). The role of race is clear in these patterns as well; take girls' detentions where African American girls comprised nearly half of those in juvenile jails, despite being only 15 percent of those in the youth population (American Bar Association, 2001: 21).

Controlling girlhood in the new century includes expanding the formal control of girls through the juvenile justice system while also increasing the scrutiny of girls in their peer groups, family relationships, and school lives. The beginning of this century has been marked by a peculiar pattern, we contend. We have expanded ways to punish and constrain girls while at the same time blaming them for their own problems. A much better approach to girls' problems would be to document the multiple ways that society routinely disempowers girls and to work with girls to give them the tools to undo the damage.

DISCUSSION QUESTIONS

1. Why, according to the authors, are the media so fascinated with mean girls?
2. Are girls getting more violent?
3. What is the "masculinization hypothesis?"
4. What accounts for the increasing number of girls getting arrested for assault?

REFERENCES

ABC, "Girls in the hood," *Primetime Live,* November 5, 1997.

Adler, E., *Sisters in Crime: The Rise of the New Female Criminal,* New York: McGraw-Hill, 1975.

American Bar Association and the National Bar Association, *Justice by Gender: The Lack of Appropriate Prevention, Diversion and Treatment Alternatives for Girls in the Justice System,* 2001.

Blumstein, A., "Youth violence, guns, and the illicit-drug industry," *The Journal of Criminal Law and Criminology,* 86, 10–34, 1995.

Brener, N. D., Simon, T. R., Krug E. G., and Lowry, R., "Recent trends in violence-related behaviors among high school students in the United States," *Journal of the American Medical Association,* 282: 5, 330–446, 1999.

Centers for Disease Control and Prevention, "Youth Risk Behavior Surveillance—United States. CDC Surveillance Summaries." U.S. Department of Health and Human Services. Atlanta: Centers for Disease Control. 1992–2008.

Corrado, R., Odgers, C, and Cohen, I. M., "The incarceration of female young offenders: Protection for whom?" *Canadian Journal of Criminology, 2:* 189—207, 2000.

Crick, N. R., "The role of overt aggression, relational aggression, and prosocial behavior in the prediction of children's future social adjustment," *Childhood Development,* 67: 2317—2327, 1996.

Elizabeth, J., "Girl Bullies Don't Leave Black Eyes, Just Agony," *Pittsburgh Post-Gazette,* April 10: Al, 2002.

Faludi, S., *Backlash: The Undeclared War against American Women,* New York: Crown, 1991.

Federal Bureau of Investigation, *Crime in the United States 1994.* Washington, D.C.: Government Printing Office, 1995.

Federal Bureau of Investigation, *Crime in the United States 1996.* Washington, D.C.: Government Printing Office, 1997.

Federal Bureau of Investigation, *Crime in the United States 2004.* Washington, D.C.: Government Printing Office, 2005.

Federal Bureau of Investigation, *Crime in the United States 2005.* Washington, D.C.: Government Printing Office, 2006.

Ford, R., The razor's edge, *Boston Globe Magazine,* May 24: 13, 22–28, 1998.

Gaarder, E. and Belknap J., "Tenuous borders: Girls transferred to adult court," *Criminology,* 40: 481—518, 2002.

Garbarino, J., *See Jane Hit: Why Girls are Growing More Violent and What We Can Do About Lt,* New York: Penguin Press, 2006.

Garvey J., "Kids killing kids: Does Columbine tell us anything?" *Commonwealth,* June 4, 1999.

Guido, M., "In a new twist on equality, girls' crimes resemble boys'," *San Jose Mercury,* June 4: IB—4B, 1998.

Huizinga, D., Over-time changes in delinquency and drug use: The 1970s to the 1990s. Washington, D.C.: Office of Juvenile Justice and Delinquency Prevention. 1997.

Kluger, J., Taming wild girls, *Time Magazine,* May 1: 54, 2006.

Leslie, C, Biddle, N., Rosenberg, D., and Joe Wayne, J., Girls will be girls, *Newsweek,* August 2: *44,* 1993.

Males, M., *The Scapegoat Generation: America's War on Adolescents,* Monroe, ME: Common Courage Press, 1996.

Males, M. and Shorter, A., *To Cage and Serve,* unpublished manuscript, 2001.

Males, M., And now … superpredatrixes? More fact-bending hype about the spike in girl violence, *Youth Today,* 5: 34, May, 2006.

Meadows, S. and Johnson, D., Girl fight: Savagery in the Chicago suburbs, *Newsweek,* May 19: 37, 2003.

Metcalf, F., She devils, *Courier Mail,* June 22: L 06, 2002.

Pipher, M., *Reviving Ophelia: Saving The Selves of Adolescent Girls,* New York: Ballantine, 1994.

Pittsburgh Post-Gazette, Just between us girls: Not enough sugar, too much spite, June 5: 3–5, 2002.

Prothrow-Stith, D. and Spivak, H. R., *Sugar and Spice and No Longer Nice: How We Can Stop Girls' Violence,* San Francisco: Jossey-Bass, 2005.

Scelfo, J., Bad girls go wild, *Newsweek,* June 13: 66, 2005.

Simmons, R., *Odd Girl Out: The Hidden Culture of Aggression in Girls,* New York: Harcourt, 2002.

Slayer, S., Outcast no More, *HeraldNet* May 19, 2003. www.heraldnet.com/stories/03/5/19/16964394. cfm. retrieved June 9, 2003.

Snyder, H. N. and Sickmund, M., *Juvenile Offenders and Victims: 1999 National Report.* Office of Juvenile Justice and Delinquency Prevention: National Center for Juvenile Justice, 1999.

Snyder, H. N., & Sickmund, M., *Juvenile Offenders and Victims: 2006 National Report* (NCJ 178257), Washington, D.C.: U.S. Department of Justice, Office of Justice Programs, Office of Juvenile Justice and Delinquency Prevention, 2006.

Steffensmeier, D. et al., An assessment of recent trends in girls' violence using diverse longitudinal sources: Is the gender gap closing? *Criminology,* 43: 355—406, 2005.

Talbot, M., Girls just want to be mean, *The New York Times Magazine,* February 24: 24–64, 2002.

Vossekuil, B. et al., The Final Report and Findings of the Safe School Initiative: Implications for the Prevention of School Attacks in the United States. United States Secret Service and United States Department of Education, Washington, D.C., 2002.

Wing, B. and Keleher, T., Zero tolerance: An interview with Jesse Jackson on race and school discipline, *Colorlines,* 3(1): 1–3, 2000.

Wiseman, R., *Queenbees and Wannabees: Helping Your Daughter Survive Cliques, Gossip, Boy fiends and Other Realities of Adolescence,* New York: Crown, 2002.

INTRODUCTION TO: WHO WILL MAKE ROOM FOR THE INTERSEXED?

JAN CAMPBELL

Children born with ambiguous genitalia have recently been able to discuss their issue as more people are gaining an understanding about this topic. Intersexuality was something that was kept hidden for decades, and now more information has enabled us to talk about it. Kate Haas presents the intricacies of how intersexual anatomy occurs and how parents can make decisions, along with the physician, as to how their child can best function. The children, as they grow to the age of consent, can often choose the sex and gender that will ultimately define them.

This article explains how intersex children may feel more confused about their gender if they are raised without an explanation about their condition. Legal questions are posed about whether laws should be in place to protect children who have had genital reconstruction surgery before the age of consent. Laws established in other countries are discussed, as well as the history of how ambiguous genitalia have been medically and social treated over time and cross-culturally.

WHO WILL MAKE ROOM FOR THE INTERSEXED?

KATE HAAS

INTRODUCTION

B etween 1.7 and 4% of the world population is born with intersex conditions, having primary and secondary sexual characteristics that are neither clearly male nor female[1]. The current recommended treatment for an infant born with an intersex condition is genital reconstruction surgery to render the child as clearly sexed either male or female.[2] Every day in the United States, five children are subjected to genital reconstruction surgery that may leave them with permanent physical and emotional scars.[3] Despite efforts by intersexed people to educate the medical community about their rejection of infant genital reconstruction surgery, the American medical community has not yet accepted the fact that differences in genital size and shape do not necessarily require surgical correction.[4]

Genital reconstruction surgery may involve removing part or all of the penis and scrotum or clitoris and labia of a child, remodeling a penis or creating a vaginal opening.[5] While the initial surgery is typically performed in the first month of a child's life, genital reconstruction surgery is not only performed on infants.[6] Older children may be subjected to multiple operations to construct "functional" vaginas, to repair "damaged" penises, and to remove internal sex organs.[7] Personal accounts written by intersexed adults indicate that some children have been subjected to unwanted surgery throughout their childhood and teenage years without a truthful explanation of their condition.[8]

Genital reconstruction is rarely medically necessary.[9] Physicians perform the surgeries so that intersexed children will not be psychologically harmed when they realize that they are different from their peers.[10] Physicians remove external signs that children are intersexed, believing that this will prevent the child and the child's family from questioning the child's gender.[11] However, intersexed children may very well feel more confused about their gender if they are raised without any explanation about their intersex condition or input into their future treatment options.[12] The medical community's current practice focuses solely on genital appearance, discounting the fact that chromosomes also affect individuals' gender identities and personalities.[13]

Operating on children out of a belief that it is crucial for children to have genitals that conform to male/female norms ignores the fact that even the best reconstruction surgery is never perfect.[14] Genital reconstruction surgery may result in scarred genitals, an inability to achieve orgasm, or an inability to reproduce naturally or through artificial insemination.[15] The community-held belief that an individual's ability to engage in intercourse is essential, even without orgasm or reproductive capability, seems to govern the decision to perform genital surgery on many otherwise healthy, intersexed children.[16]

Despite the intersex community's rejection of genital reconstruction surgery, no U.S. court has examined the legality of performing these operations without the individual child's consent.[17] By contrast, Colombian courts have heard three such cases and have created a new standard for evaluating a parent's right to consent to genital reconstruction surgery for their minor children.[18] In response to the Colombian rulings and pressure from intersex activists, the American Bar Association recently proposed a resolution recommending that physicians adopt the heightened informed consent procedures required by the Colombian Constitutional Court decisions.[19]

This Article questions whether genital reconstruction surgery is necessary in the Twenty-first Century. Part II discusses the history and current preferred "treatment" for intersex conditions. Part III explains the groundbreaking Colombian Appellate Court decisions prohibiting parental consent for genital reconstruction on children over the age of five, and establishing a heightened informed consent doctrine for younger children. Part IV analyzes the protection that current U.S. law could provide to intersexed children. Part V explores how international law may influence decisions regarding the treatment of intersexed children.

II. A HISTORY OF COLLUSION: DESTROYING EVIDENCE OF AMBIGUOUS GENITALS

The term "intersex" is used to describe a variety of conditions in which a fetus develops differently than a typical XX female or XY male.[20] Some intersexed children are born with "normal" male or female external genitals that do not correspond to their hormones.[21] Others are born with a noticeable combination of male and female external features, and still others have visually male or female external characteristics that correspond to their chromosomes but do not correspond to their internal gonads.[22] Individuals who are considered intersexed may also be born with matching male chromosomes, gonads, and genitals but suffer childhood disease or accident that results in full or partial loss of their penis.[23] The loss of a penis may lead physicians to recommend that a boy be sexually reassigned as female.[24] Although the conditions differ, the commonality of intersexed people is that their gonads, chromosomes, and external genitalia do not coincide to form a typical male or female[25] The current American medical treatment of intersexuals is to alter the individual's internal and external gonads to sex them as either clearly male or clearly female.[26]

Medical "treatment" of intersexuals has only been practiced in the United States since the 1930s.[27] During that period, the medical community determined that intersexed people were truly male or female but had not fully developed in the womb.[28] Hormone treatments and surgical interventions were meant to complete the formation of an intersexed adult into a "normal" man or woman.[29] By the 1950s, physicians were able to identify most intersex conditions at birth and began operating immediately on intersexed children to eliminate any physical differences.[30]

Prior to the treatment of intersexuality in the United States, intersexed Americans were treated as either male or female according to their dominant physical characteristics.[31] This strict male/female delineation is not used in all countries though. Other cultures have treated intersexuals differently, either as a third sex, neither male nor female, or as natural sexual variations of the male or female sex.[32] Alternatively, some societies still accept intersexed people without clearly defining their sex at birth.[33]

For instance, within small communities in the Dominican Republic and Papua New Guinea, there is a hereditary intersex condition known as 5-alpha reductase deficiency that occurs with a relatively high frequency.[34] This condition causes male children to be born with very small or unrecognizable penises.[35] During puberty, the children's male hormones cause their penises to grow and other secondary male sexual characteristics to develop.[36] Most of these children are raised as girls and begin living as men when they reach puberty.[37] These communities have accepted these intersexuals without genital reconstruction surgery.[38] In the United States, however, a child with the same condition would likely be surgically altered at birth, raised as a girl and treated with hormones to prevent the onset of male physical development.[39]

Genital reconstruction surgery became standard practice in the United States through the efforts of John Money, a John Hopkins University professor.[40] Money introduced the theory that children are not born with a gender identity, but rather form an understanding of gender through their social upbringing.[41] He based this theory on early research done with intersexed children who were surgically altered at birth and raised as either male or female.[42] Money's research found that children who were born with exactly the same genetic makeup and physical appearance fared equally well when raised as either females or males. He concluded that chromosomes did not make any difference in gender differentiation, and that children could be successfully reared as either sex irrespective of their anatomy or chromosomal make-up.[43] Money attempted to prove his theory by demonstrating that a "normal" male child could be successfully raised as a female with Bruce Reimer.[44]

In 1972, Money made public his experimental sex reassignment surgery on a twenty-two-month-old male child named Bruce Reimer who had been accidentally castrated during a routine circumcision.[45] The doctor who examined Reimer shortly after the accident believed that he would be unable to live a normal sexual life as an adolescent and would grow up feeling incomplete and physically defective.[46] Money's solution was to perform a sex change operation on baby Bruce and to have his parents raise him as a girl named Brenda. During Brenda's childhood, Money removed all of "his" internal reproductive organs. As Brenda approached puberty "she" was given female hormones to trigger breast development and other female secondary characteristics.[47] By removing Brenda's gonads, Money destroyed Brenda's reproductive capability. However, Money believed that by changing Brenda's sex, he would make it possible for her to engage in intercourse and marry.[48]

Early reports of Money's experiment claimed that the operation was successful and that Brenda was a happy, healthy girl.[49] Money's research was published throughout the world, convincing doctors that gender was a societal construct, and therefore intersexed children could be raised unconditionally as either male or female.[50] He believed that the only way to ensure that both the family and the child would accept the child's gender was if the child's genitals looked clearly male or female. Based on this theory, babies born with ambiguous genitals or small penises and baby boys who were accidentally castrated were surgically altered and raised as females.[51] Similarly, children born with mixed genitalia, gonads, and chromosomes were surgically altered to fit the definition of a "normal" male or female.[52] Following U.S. lead, other countries also began to practice routine genital reconstruction surgery on intersexed infants.[53]

Despite the widespread use of genital reconstruction surgery, there is no research showing that intersexuals benefit psychologically from the surgery performed on them as infants and toddlers.[54] No follow-up studies were ever done on adult intersexuals who underwent genital reconstruction surgery as children.[55] In the late 1980s, researchers attempting to disprove Money's gender identity theory began searching for Brenda, the subject of Money's highly publicized research.[56] The boy who was raised as a girl was now living as a man and had changed his name to David.[57] In 1997, Milton Diamond and Keith Sigmundson published an article rebutting the results of Money's famous gender research.[58] The publicity caused by Diamond and Sigmundson's article led to a biography of Reimer by John Colapinto. When Colapinto interviewed Reimer in 1997, Reimer admitted that he had always been certain that he was not a girl, despite being deceived by his doctor and his family.[59]

Reimer suffered emotional duress at all stages of his development, despite the corrective surgery that was meant to make him "normal." In his biography of Reimer, Colapinto describes the painful experiences that Reimer suffered throughout his childhood and teenage years.[60] During her childhood, Brenda did not fit in with her peers and felt isolated and confused.[61] As early as kindergarten, other children teased Brenda about her masculinity and failure to adopt "girl's play."[62] Although her kindergarten teacher was not initially told of her sex change, the teacher reported realizing that Brenda was very different from other girls.[63]

In addition to her failure to fit in socially, Brenda was constantly reminded that she was different by her parents and Dr. Money. During her visits to John Hopkins, Money would often force her to engage in sexual role-play with her twin brother in order to enforce that she was a girl and he was a boy.[64] Her genitals were scarred and painful as a child and she hated to look at them.[65] She became suspicious that something terrible had been done to her, primarily due to the frequent doctor's visits with John Money. During these visits, Dr. Money and his associates questioned Brenda about her genitals and her gender identity.[66] Rather than enforcing her gender identity, the medical intervention compounded the trauma caused by her medical condition.

One particularly traumatic procedure inflicted on intersexed children was not discussed in the biography of David Reimer. Intersexed children who have artificially created vaginas must undergo vaginal dilation procedures throughout their early childhood.[67] In order to ensure that the newly created vaginal opening does not close up, the child's parents must insert an object into the child's vagina on a daily basis.[68] This procedure has sexual implications that may be emotionally traumatic for many children.

As a teenager, Reimer rejected his assigned sex and refused to take his female hormones. He reported engaging in typically male behavior throughout his teens. He dressed as a male, chose a trade school for mechanics, and even began urinating standing up.[69] When Reimer's parents finally told him that he was born male, he immediately chose to adopt a male identity and changed his name to David.[70] He had a penis constructed and implanted, and underwent breast reduction surgery to rid himself of the breasts developed through estrogen therapy.[71] There is no procedure that can replace the gonads that were removed as part of Reimer's sex reassignment surgery. There is also no cure for the deception that he experienced upon learning that his parents and doctors had lied to him about many aspects of his life.[72] The trauma of learning about his condition caused David to attempt suicide on several occasions.[73]

David is now married and has adopted his wife's children.[74] His story reads as a happy ending to many people. However, David could have avoided the gender dysphoria, loss of reproductive capability, and many years of therapy that resulted from genital reconstruction surgery. These experiences are not atypical in the intersexed community. According to many intersexed activists, the comfort of being raised in a clear gender role does not outweigh the pain of deception or the physical side effects associated with the surgery.[75]

Despite the emotional and physical scars that people like David Reimer face from genital reconstruction surgery, the majority of American physicians continue to encourage early childhood surgery.[76] In some cases, physicians have insisted on performing genital reconstruction surgery on teenagers without their consent.[77]

In 1993, an intersexed activist named Cheryl Chase began a support and advocacy group for intersexed adults called the Intersex Society of North America ("ISNA").[78]

Chase was born with a large clitoris, which was removed when she was an infant.[79] When she was eight years old, her internal gonads were removed without her knowledge or consent.[80] Because of the surgery, she is no longer capable of having her own children or obtaining orgasm.[81] Today, Chase and other advocates are vocal about their hope for a moratorium on the invasive treatment of intersexed children.[82]

ISNA members have contributed significantly to the debate over genital reconstruction surgery by providing personal insight into the effects of surgery on intersexed adults. As of the late 1990s, more than 400 intersexed individuals from around the world contacted ISNA and recounted stories similar to Ms. Chase's.[83] According to ISNA, sex change operations and genital normalizing surgeries should not be performed on children until the child has the ability to consent personally to the operation.[84]

At this point, there is insufficient proof that intersexed adults who are not operated on fair any worse than intersexed adults who have had genital reconstruction surgery as children.[85] The only research that has been done on intersexed adults who have not been surgically altered also comes from John Money. In the 1940s, prior to his well-known study on Reimer, Money interviewed many intersexed adults about their gender identity and upbringing.[86] To his surprise, he found that intersexed adults who had not undergone genital reconstruction surgery had a gender identity comparable to other adult males and females.[87] Unfortunately this research was done as part of Money's doctoral thesis and was never published.[88]

I. THE COLOMBIAN CONSTITUTIONAL COURT'S RULING

Public authorities, the medical community and the citizens in general must make room for these people who have been silenced until now.[89] In 1995, Colombia's highest court, the Constitutional Court, addressed the legality of performing gender reconstruction surgery on children.[90] The Constitutional Court has issued three decisions on the constitutionality of genital reconstruction surgery, and, as of the publication date of this Article, it is the only court in the world to have rendered an opinion on this issue.[91] The first case that the court considered was brought by a teenage boy who had been raised as a girl under circumstances very much like David Reimer's.[92] Several years after this first case, the court decided two other cases involving children born with intersex conditions.[93] These three cases have limited parents' rights to choose genital reconstruction surgery for their children in Colombia.

The first case, Sentencia No. T-477/95 [hereinafter Gonzalez, involved a male infant who was accidentally castrated during circumcision and was subsequently subjected to a sex change operation.[94] His physicians performed the sex change operation so that his genitals would conform to societal norms and he would be capable of sexual intercourse as an adult.[95] As a teenager, Gonzalez learned of the operation and sued the doctors and hospital that allowed the operation to be performed without his consent.[96] The Colombian Constitutional Court heard Gonzalez's appeal and found that this operation violated the boy's fundamental right to human dignity and gender identity.[97] The court based its decisions on the Colombian Constitution and the international covenant on human rights guaranteed by the Inter-American Court of Human Rights.[98] The court ruled that doctors could not alter the gender of a patient, regardless of the patient's age, without the patient's own informed consent.[99]

Several years after Gonzalez, the parents of two children born with intersex conditions brought their cases to court seeking the authority to consent to surgery on behalf of their minor children.[100] In both cases, the children's physicians had recommended genital reconstruction surgery, but refused to perform the surgery without each child's consent.[101] For the first time in the world, a court addressed the issue of whether parents should be allowed to consent to genital reconstruction surgery on their intersexed children. Although these cases were not identical to Gonzalez, the hospital feared that if it performed genital reconstruction surgery on any child without the child's consent, it could be held liable under Gonzalez.[102] The Colombian Constitutional Court heard both cases on appeal.[103]

In Sentencia No. SU-337/99 [hereinafter Ramos, the Colombian Constitutional Court considered the case of an eight-year-old intersexed child raised as a girl and diagnosed with male pseudo-hermaphroditism.[104] Ramos was born with XY (male) chromosomes but due to her inability to process male hormones, her external genitalia did not fully develop.[105] Ramos had a small penis (three centimeters), folds of skin that did not contain testicles, male gonads, and a urinal opening at the base of her perineum.[106]

According to the documents received at the trial court level, Ramos' doctors were not aware that she was intersexed until she was three years old.[107] Until that point, Ramos' mother had raised her as a girl without questioning whether she might not have female chromosomes. When Ramos' pediatrician became aware that the child was intersexed, the doctor recommended that she receive genital reconstruction surgery to remove her small penis and gonads and to construct a vagina.[108] The doctor recommended the sex change operation because although Ramos had a small penis, it would never grow to the size of a typical penis, and it would never function properly.[109] Additionally, Ramos had been raised as a girl thus far, had a female name, wore feminine clothing, and identified with the social role of Colombian women.[110]

Ramos' mother brought this action to force the hospital to accept her consent on behalf of Ramos so that the doctors could proceed with the surgery.[111] Ramos' mother alleged that if the hospital waited to perform surgery until Ramos could consent for herself, the child would be psychologically harmed because she would grow up without a clear gender identity. [112]

However despite being raised female, the trial court found that Ramos' gender was ambiguous because "in some aspects she behaves like a woman and in some aspects like a man."[113] It also concluded that every person should have the right to develop his or her own gender identity as a part of the development of his or her personality.[114] The trial court stated that nobody could determine what the gender identity of this child would be except for the child herself, denying Ramos' mother the right to consent to surgery.[115] Ramos' mother appealed the case to the Constitutional Court.

By the time the case was heard on appeal, Ramos was eight years old.[116] After considering medical information and briefs from experts around the world, the Constitutional Court upheld the trial court's decision denying Ramos' mother the right to consent to genital reconstruction surgery for her child.[117] In its decision, the court referred extensively to the Colombian Constitution, as well as international laws and norms.[118] The court considered the gravity of the procedure and the negative effects it could have on the child if she were to reject her assigned sex, and found that substitute judgment should not be allowed. The Constitutional Court quoted the trial court's opinion, noting that it would be wrong for anyone to consent to a sex change operation other than the child herself.[119] In reaching its conclusion, the court discussed the lack of evidence of any psychological harm to children that are not operated on, and the existence of actual evidence of psychological harm to children that have had such operations.[120]

The Ramos decision did not seem to rely on the individual facts of the case, but rather on the overreaching harm of the surgery as compared to the unproven benefits. However in its next case, the Constitutional Court seems to have made its decision based on the individual facts of the case, primarily that the surgery had already been performed with no major problems. [121]

In the Constitutional Court's next decision, Sentencia No. T-551/99 [hereinafter Cruz,[122] the court relied heavily on the information provided in Ramos.[123] However, the decision in Cruz was substantially weaker than both of the previous decisions, limiting its prior holdings to children over the age of five.[124] Cruz was born with XX (female) chromosomes and male external genitalia.[125] Her parents were seeking to have her clitoris/penis removed or reduced in size so that she would look more female.[126] At the age of two, Cruz was already aware that her genitals were different from those of her family members.[127] However since Cruz was much younger then Ramos, the trial court did not rely on facts regarding Cruz's own gender identity. After hearing the case, the trial court held that Cruz's parents could consent to genital reconstruction surgery on her behalf if their consent was "informed."[128] Cruz was only three years old when the case was brought to the attention of the Constitutional Court and had already undergone genital reconstruction surgery.[129] The Constitutional Court decided to hear the case in order to set a standard for the lower courts to follow in the future.[130] The court found that Cruz's parents did not really understand the implications of the operation on their child's life. Believing that their child would be "normalized" by the procedure, the parents were given the impression that surgery was their only option.[131] Since the parents were not properly informed about the procedure or provided alternative options, the court held that Cruz's rights had been violated despite her young age.[132] Although it was too late to make any changes in the decision that was already made for Cruz, the court ordered that an interdisciplinary team be put together to support the child and her family in the future.[133]

In this decision, the court could have followed its reasoning in Ramos to ban parental consent to genital reconstruction surgeries on all children.[134] However, instead of following its own precedent, the court decided that parents should be allowed to consent to surgery on children under age five.[135] The court explained that Cruz was too young to have formed a gender identity.[136] By prohibiting parental consent for the surgery, the court stated that it would be intruding into the realm of family privacy.[137] The court also stated that prohibiting this surgery altogether would be like a social experiment in which children were the subjects.[138] Had it decided to prohibit the surgery on young children, the intersexed children following this case would be the first children in the country to be prohibited from obtaining sex assignment/reconstruction surgery.[139]

While deciding not to make room for the intersexed, the court made clear that it did not intend to leave the decision whether to operate at the full discretion of the parents either. It reasoned that parents might be fearful of intersex conditions and discriminate against their children, consenting to operations not truly in the child's best interest.[140] Finally, the court concluded that the medical community should establish a protocol allowing parents to consent to genital reconstruction surgery only after they establish that it is truly in their child's best interest, creating a new form of "qualified and persistent, informed consent.[141]

The court in Cruz gave Colombian parents the right to substitute judgment for infants and young children who have already achieved consciousness of their bodies; however, parents can only give consent after fully understanding the consequences of the surgery for their child. In Cruz, the court clarified that its decision to withhold parental consent in Ramos was based on the fact that Ramos was eight years old when her case was decided.[142] Cruz narrowed the individual consent doctrine to apply to children over the age of five, holding that intersexed children over the age of five must give their informed consent before undergoing genital reconstruction surgery.[143]

In Cruz, the court determined that in order for parental consent to genital reconstruction surgery to be valid for children under the age of five, three criteria must be met: (i) detailed information must be provided, and the parent must be informed of the pros and cons that have sparked the current debate; (ii) the consent must be in writing, to formalize the decision and to ensure its seriousness; and (iii) the authorization must be given in stages.[144] This last qualification is intended to permit the parents the time to bond with their child the way that he or she is, and not to make a prejudicial decision based on shock at the baby's appearance.[145] The court stated that it would be up to the medical community and the legislature to determine the specific details for the consent procedure.[146]

Doctors generally recommend surgery for intersexed children at birth.[147] Ramos' mother was forced to wait until Ramos was eight years old only because the trial court originally denied permission for her to give consent for the operation.[148] However important the investigation and dicta was in Ramos, most intersexed children will not benefit from it. Most often, surgery will be performed when the child is still an infant and only the heightened informed consent will be directly applicable to them.[149] By limiting the holding of Ramos in Cruz to children over the age of five, the court diminished the significance of Ramos.

All three of the Colombian Court's decisions could have fundamentally altered the individual rights of intersexed children in Colombia. Instead, they have only given the parents of intersexed children the right to more information before they consent to genital reconstruction surgery. Perhaps some parents will obtain enough information to decide to decline these operations. However, in the end, it is still the parent and not the child who will be able to determine what gender the child will be, whether the child will be able to reproduce, and who the child will be allowed to marry. Given the opportunity to make a huge difference in the lives of intersexed people around the world, the Colombian Court's decision did not adequately protect this "marginalized and forgotten minority."[150]

Despite the Colombian Court's reticence about banning infant genital reconstruction surgery, Colombian law still provides far more protection for intersex children then current American law. The Colombian Court's decisions have increased the world's awareness of the problems with genital reconstruction surgery and reopened the medical debate regarding genital reconstruction surgery in the United States.

II. MAKING ROOM FOR INTERSEXUALS IN THE UNITED STATES

The United States does not currently provide any procedural protection for intersexed children. In the United States, doctors are not required to receive the consent of intersexed children before performing genital reconstruction surgery.[151] Neither are parents routinely given sufficient information to make an informed decision on their child's behalf.[152] Currently, the United States lacks even the standard for informed consent instituted after the Colombian Court's final decision in Cruz.[153]

Thus far, there has been no legal challenge brought on behalf of intersexed children in the United States. Intersexed adults who have inquired about suing their doctors for performing genital reconstruction surgery that altered their gender have met resistance.[154] Intersexed adults have been told that because the doctors followed standard medical practice when they performed the surgery, the doctors are not liable for medical malpractice.[155]

Unlike the Colombian Constitution, the U.S. Constitution does not have specific provisions protecting a child's right to bodily integrity. However, the Constitution has been interpreted to protect privacy rights, including the right to marry and reproduce, and the right to bodily integrity generally.[156] Common law also provides some protection for children when there is no "informed" consent, or when a parent's consent or lack of consent to medical treatment is found to be contrary to the child's best interest.[157] In addition to case law supporting the need for informed consent and the best interest of the child, there are recent federal and state statutes protecting female children from genital mutilation.[158] Thus, while no intersexed Americans have successfully sued a physician or hospital for conducting early genital reconstructive surgery, they may have grounds to sue based on female genital mutilation laws, the constitutional right to privacy and lack of informed consent by their parents.

A. Constitutional Protection for Intersexuals : Leaving Room for an Open Future

The U.S. Constitution protects individuals from overreaching government power through the Fourteenth Amendment, which states "No state shall make or enforce any law which shall abridge the privileges or immunities of citizens of the United States, nor shall any state deprive any person of life, liberty, or property, without due process of law …"[159] The U.S. Supreme Court has interpreted the Fourteenth Amendment as protecting individuals from government action that infringes upon certain "fundamental rights" considered "implicit in the concept of ordered liberty."[160]

The Supreme Court has found that the right to bodily autonomy, the right to choose whether or not to reproduce, the right to marry, and the right to make decisions about how to raise children are all fundamental privacy rights.[161] The government may not violate a person's liberty by infringing any of these rights without first proving in a court of law that there is a compelling state interest that must be served, and that the method that the government is using is narrowly tailored to achieve a compelling governmental interest.[162]

Historically, children have not been accorded the same constitutional rights as adults. A child's parents and the government are allowed to restrict some rights that would be held fundamental for an adult.[163] The Supreme Court has also recognized a fundamental right to family privacy, according parents a high degree of respect regarding decisions they make about their child's upbringing.[164] This includes the choices parents make regarding their children's medical care.[165] Despite the Fourteenth Amendment right to family privacy, the parents' rights must be weighed against the children's rights to be protected against harm. The doctrine of parens patriae articulates the government's interest in protecting the rights of vulnerable individuals from harm.[166]

The doctrine of parens patriae allows the government to interfere with parents' choices about how to raise their children when the children may be harmed because of the parents' actions or inactions.[167] Generally, the government interferes with parental decisions under laws prohibiting parental abuse or neglect.[168] In the case of intersexed children, the government may have reason to override the parents' decision to perform surgery if the surgery would harm the child.

The Fourteenth Amendment does not prohibit an individual from violating another individual's fundamental rights. Thus, a child cannot generally sue a hospital or a physician for an infringement of his or her constitutional rights. For there to be a constitutional violation, there must be state action.[169] If genital reconstruction surgery is performed at a state hospital, then there is state action allowing the child to sue the hospital directly. If the surgery is conducted at a private hospital, there may not be state action. In that case, in order to implicate the Fourteenth Amendment, an intersexed child who is about to be subjected to genital reconstruction surgery must seek an injunction against the hospital prior to the surgery.[170] If a judge orders the surgery to progress, there is state action, and the child may claim a constitutional violation.[171] If the child successfully claims that the surgery violates a fundamental right, then in order for the court to order the surgery over the objection of the child or his or her court appointed representative, the proponents must prove, by clear and convincing evidence, that the surgery is in the child's best interest.[172] This standard is high, and in order to prevail, the proponent of the surgery must establish that there are no less restrictive means to accomplish the same result.[173] Since there are no studies proving that genital reconstruction surgery psychologically benefits children, and there are testimonial accounts that genital reconstruction surgery causes psychological and physical trauma, it is unlikely that the court would find that there was clear and convincing evidence of best interest.

1. Bodily Integrity: If It Works, Don't Fix It

Included in the Fourteenth Amendment right to privacy is the right to bodily autonomy, which protects individuals from intrusion by the government into their health care decisions.[174] This right includes the right to choose to forego medical treatment, even if foregoing treatment may result in death.[175] For the most part, children are not accorded the right to choose medical treatment or to choose to forego medical treatment without parental consent, despite the fact that it has been found to be a fundamental right.[176] The reason that parents are allowed to consent for children is that a child may not be able to understand fully the consequences of their own consent because of their age or inexperience.[177]

There are several exceptions to the rule requiring parental consent to treatment. The first exception accepted by several states by statute is the "mature minor" exception.[178] Minors who are considered mature enough to make their own medical decisions need not obtain parental consent to medical treatment, and may object to medical treatment that their parents choose for them.[179]

Many states have also provided exceptions to parental consent requirements for children seeking treatment for drug addiction, mental health treatment, and testing and treatment for sexually transmitted diseases.[180] The logic behind these exceptions is that these treatments are very personal, and if required to seek parental consent, many children would forego treatment. If children could not be treated for HIV, drug addiction, or mental illness, they would likely place themselves and others in danger.[181]

These exceptions take into account the fact that parents do not always act in their child's best interest, and a child may suffer abuse or psychological harm if required to seek parental consent to certain treatments. The right to choose whether or not to undergo genital reconstruction surgery should be an exception to the general rule allowing parental consent to treatment of minors. Genital reconstruction surgery is a personal choice that children should be allowed to make on their own in certain circumstances, or, at a minimum, in conjunction with their parents. It is difficult for many children to learn about their intersexuality. However, it is also hard for children to learn to cope with pregnancy, drug addiction, mental illness, or their HIV positive status. In contrast to intersex conditions, all of the above medical conditions are free of parental consent requirements under certain circumstances.

Genital reconstruction surgery is arguably the ultimate infringement of an individual's bodily autonomy. Genital reconstruction surgery can cause a child significant psychological and physical harm.[182] For these reasons, parents should not be allowed to make the decision to alter surgically their child's genitals without the child's consent absent clear and convincing evidence that it is in the child's best interest. If the state participates by allowing the procedure to be performed at a state hospital or by ordering the procedure over the child's objection, then there may be a constitutional violation of the child's right to bodily autonomy under the Fourteenth Amendment.

2. Reproduction: Gonads Cannot Be Replaced

The right to choose whether or not to reproduce is a fundamental right and, accordingly, certain restrictions are placed on the government's right to interfere with decisions bearing on reproduction.[183] For example, all minors regardless of age have the right to seek an abortion without undue burden from the state, though the state may act to ensure that a woman's decision is informed.[184] Therefore, even when state law requires minors to receive parental consent before seeking an abortion, minors are permitted a judicial bypass, allowing them the right to prove to a court that they are mature enough to make the decision to have an abortion without parental consent.[185] Children may also have the right to seek contraception, treatment for pregnancy, and childbirth without parental consent.[186]

Because reproduction is a fundamental right, parents are limited in their ability to consent to sterilization procedures for their children. Generally, sterilization is raised in the context of a parent who wants to sterilize a handicapped child to protect the child from the harm of a dangerous pregnancy. If there is an objection made by the child or an advocate for the child, then a court cannot order the procedure against the child's objections without affording the child due process.[187] The child must be appointed an independent guardian ad litem, and receive a fair trial at which the court must determine by clear and convincing evidence that the operation to remove the child's gonads will be in the child's best interest.[188]

As with all people, some intersexed adults do not have the ability to reproduce even without genital reconstruction surgery.[189] Others will retain their full reproductive capacity even after the surgery is performed.[190] However, some intersexuals have the ability to reproduce either naturally or artificially and are denied that right by the removal of their gonads and other reproductive organs. For those children whose gonads are removed to complete their physical transformation, their fundamental right to reproduce has been violated. For example, a child born with male chromosomes and sexed at birth as female will have her gonads removed, thus, effectively sterilizing her.

Based on the lack of evidence of the effectiveness of genital reconstruction surgery, it would be difficult for a court to determine that this procedure is clearly in the child's best interest. If there are pros and cons to performing the surgery, the court must decide in a manner that will not violate the child's fundamental right to reproduce.[191]

3. Marriage: Determining Gender Determines Sexuality

Genital reconstruction surgery may inhibit or completely interfere with a child's fundamental right to marry. In the United States, there are currently no states in which it is legal to marry someone of the same sex.[192] In 1993, several gay couples challenged the prohibition against same-sex marriages under the Hawaii Constitution.[193] The Hawaii Supreme Court ruled in favor of the plaintiffs and allowed the first gay couples to marry legally.[194] In reaction to the ruling, the Hawaii state legislature immediately amended their own constitution to prohibit same-sex marriages.[195] The federal government reacted to the first gay marriages by passing the Defense of Marriage Act, which allows states to refuse to recognize same-sex marriages that are legally valid in another state.[196] Given that 3% of the world population does not fit into a clearly defined sex and still engage in marriage and child birth, it would be wise to re-think this prohibition.

However, given the laws as they currently stand, genital reconstruction surgically defines an intersexed person as male or female, thus, prohibiting them from marriage to a person of their "same" gender. Intersexuals are in a unique position before they undergo genital reconstruction surgery because they can petition the court to change their legal gender from female to male or male to female without having to undergo a sex change operation. They must prove that they are intersexed, that they have unclear genitals, and that they identify as the opposite sex, and their birth certificate may be altered.[197]

Once an intersexed person has undergone genital reconstruction surgery making his or her genitals clearly male or female, he or she cannot then choose to change his or her birth certificate without having a second round of surgeries performed.[198] For example, if a child born with male chromosomes or mixed chromosomes is surgically assigned a female gender at birth, that individual would be prohibited from marrying a female later in life without first undergoing another sex change operation.[199] In this case, if the initial gender reconstruction surgery had not been performed, this person would be considered a male, not a homosexual female, and thus would have a fundamental right to marry.

By choosing a gender for the child and performing reconstruction surgery at birth, the doctors may be infringing on an individual's ability to marry as an adult. The imposition of additional surgery to change their assigned sex would add such high financial and emotional costs on the individual that it may prohibit some, otherwise qualified, intersexuals from marrying.

B. Taking A First Step: Informing Parents That Their Child is Intersexed

Physicians must receive informed consent from all patients before they treat them for any medical condition.[200] If physicians fail to obtain informed consent from their patients, they may be liable for medical malpractice.[201] Under the informed consent doctrine, a patient may even choose to refuse life saving treatment after weighing their treatment options.[202] The informed consent doctrine originated in the tort doctrine of battery, which includes intentionally touching a person in a way that they find harmful or offensive.[203] The surgical removal of part or all of a child's genitals must only be done after receiving informed consent or it may be considered battery.

Absent a recognized exception allowing children to consent to their own medical treatment, parents will generally be allowed to give or withhold consent for medical treatment on behalf of their children. In the United States, genital reconstruction surgery is not currently a procedure that children are allowed to consent or object to without their parents' participation. For informed consent to be valid, the parents must be informed of the nature and consequence of their child's medical condition, as well as the various treatment options available.

The Colombian standard of informed consent ensures that doctors provide parents with all of the known information about intersex conditions over a prolonged period of time. Doctors must provide surgical and non-surgical options for treatment, and refer parents to support organizations for intersexed individuals.[204] This model ensures that parents are not deceived about their child's prognosis, and that they understand that genital reconstruction surgery is not the only solution for their child.

In the United States, parents of intersexed children are not given enough information to make a truly informed decision about their child's treatment.[205] Some parents are not told that their child is intersexed, but instead that their child is a girl or boy with "unfinished" genitals that the doctor will repair with surgery.[206] Physicians may also tell the parents that their baby will have "normal" genitals after surgery.[207] Surgery may make the child's genitals look more clearly male or female, but it will also leave scarring and possibly diminish sexual functions.[208] Generally, more than one surgery is needed to alter completely the genital appearance, and the average number of surgeries is three or more.[209] Surgery and check-ups will continue through the child's early years and may be extremely stressful for the child and his or her parents.[210]

Additionally, parents must understand that while surgery will make intersexed children look more similar to their peers, it will not change their chromosomes. Even with hormone therapy, many intersexed youth will endure gender dysphoria.[211] They may feel confused about their gender despite having genitals that look clearly male or female. Intersexed adults may decide that their assigned gender is not their gender of choice. This might promp the desire for additional, more complicated surgeries to perform a complete sex change operation.[212] Most of these facts are not presented to the parents of intersexed children at the time that they approve genital reconstruction surgery.[213] If parents are encouraged to consent to surgery without being told of the risks and side effects, their consent is not truly informed.

There are several exceptions to the rule for informed consent. The first exception is when there is a medical emergency and a person's life or health is in immediate danger, the doctors may proceed with a procedure if they have not received instructions to the contrary.[214] Most intersexed infants are not in any immediate danger that would exempt a physician from receiving informed consent to operate.[215] Even when intersexed infants have medical conditions that require surgical intervention on an emergency basis, the emergency aid can be given without removing any part of the child's body that is not immediately harming the child.[216] Physicians have relied upon the emergency doctrine to perform full sex change operations on children.[217] The argument is that if a parent were to learn that their child was intersexed, they might raise their child without a clear gender identity thus causing the child psychological harm.[218]

Additionally, under the guise of an emergency situation, parents are placed under unnecessary time pressure to decide whether or not to consent to surgery. They are encouraged to make a decision about surgery in the first few weeks of their newborn's life. During the first few weeks after giving birth, parents may be stressed and anxious about their newborn's condition. They should be given more time to become accustomed to their child's body before doctors recommend surgery that is not medically necessary. This pressure forces parents to make decisions without seeking outside information to determine if there is a true medical necessity for the surgery.[219] In some cases, children have been operated on even after their parents explicitly refused to give consent.[220]

The emergency doctrine was not meant to prevent hypothetical psychological harm to the patient or their parents, but to prevent death or serious impairment to a patient in an emergency situation.[221] Physicians should not surgically remove or alter any part of an intersexed child's genitals without informed consent absent a true medical emergency.

A doctor may also be exempt from explaining the exact nature of the illness or treatment if it would be unsafe for the patient because it would cause them extreme physical or mental duress that would deteriorate their condition.[222] This exception has also been used by physicians to lie to parents or disguise the truth so that they will raise their child without any doubts as to the child's gender.[223] Reportedly, doctors do not explain intersex conditions to parents because they do not want to shock them.[224] Parents are frequently told that their child must be operated on in order to repair a minor birth defect. Doctors do not always tell the parents the chromosomal make-up of their child, or explain the ramifications of gender reassignment.[225] Although the parents may feel distressed upon learning of the child's condition, the parents' distress is not enough to exempt doctors from fully explaining the whole condition and the treatment options.[226] The emergency exception applies to the patient's condition, not to the parents' reaction to the patient's condition.

Additionally, if parents do not understand that their child was born intersexed, they will not be in a position to understand the issues their child may later develop and his or her potential for gender dysphoria. If the exceptions to informed consent were extended to prevent harmful parental reactions to differences in their child, doctors would have free reign to repair all congenital abnormalities at the parent's cost without informing the parent of the abnormality or obtaining their consent for the surgery. The exceptions to the informed consent doctrine were clearly not meant to extend this far.

C. Genital Mutilation: Equal Protection for Intersexed Children

Intersex children may also have a claim for medical malpractice based on violation of the law prohibiting female genital mutilation.[227] In 1996, Congress passed the Criminalization of Female Genital Mutilation Act.[228] Five states have also individually criminalized female genital mutilation.[229]

The process of removing or altering the genitalia of intersexed children is a form of genital mutilation as defined by the statute.[230] The law prohibits anyone from authorizing or performing an operation on a female child to remove all or part of her genitals for other than health reasons.[231] The statute explicitly covers ritual circumcisions, even if the child herself believes in the religious or cultural significance of the procedure.[232] In section 116(c), the law specifically states that no account shall be taken of the effect of any belief that has led the person or their family to demand the operation.[233] This Act holds the physician liable even if the family believed that the operation would be in the child's best interest and it was standard practice in their ethnic or religious community.[234]

According to the Act, the only way that genital operations can be legally performed on female children in the United States is if the doctor can show that under section 116(b)(l), it is necessary for the health of the person on whom it is performed.[235] As the Colombian Constitutional Court found through its extensive international research, there is no evidence that most surgery performed on intersexed children is done for other than psychological reasons.[236]

When an intersexed child is operated on to normalize his or her genitals, it is also part of a cultural tradition. Parents want their child to look like other children in Western countries, or as close to "normal" as possible.[237] In some Native American cultures, India, the Dominican Republic, and Papua New Guinea, intersexed people are accepted in society and occupy a specific cultural and social position.[238] In those cultures it would not be considered beneficial to the child to alter the child's genitals.

In the United States, intersexed children are operated on in order to make them look like other children who are not intersexed. Although some medical conditions might endanger intersexed children and therefore make the operations beneficial, this is not usually the case.[239] Most doctors who agree with genital operations for intersexed children claim that the surgery is necessary to protect their mental health.[240] However, no studies have been done that support the question of whether or not genital reconstruction and hormones actually protect the mental health of the patient any better then counseling and education.[241]

More than 400 intersexed people internationally have contacted ISNA in support of its opposition to genital reconstruction surgery on children.[242] The Constitutional Court of Colombia noted that doctors could not find any intersexed people willing to speak in support of such surgery on children.[243]

The congressional findings on the practice of female genital mutilation in the United States are particularly relevant to the issue of genital surgery on intersexed children. In particular, Congress found that female genital mutilation harms women both physically and psychologically.[244] They found that the practice violates both federal and state constitutional and statutory laws.[245]

The damaging physical and psychological effects of genital reconstruction surgery are identical to the effects of ritual female circumcision. In both cases, the surgery may result in pain, scarring, and the inability to achieve orgasm.[246] Congressional findings that females should not be subjected to the loss of any part of their genitalia for cultural reasons is directly applicable to intersexed children.

The Act indicates that parents do not have the right to give consent to nonessential genital surgery and doctors do not have the right to perform such surgery even if it will make the children assimilate with their ethnic and religious community.[247] The statute only applies to female children.[248] If taken as such, the statute may violate equal protection.[249] However, the Act does not define "female" by genetic make-up or external characteristics. Arguably, most intersexed children fall under one definition of "female" or another. Thus, intersexed children who have their clitoris reduced or other genital parts removed seem to have a strong claim of assault under the Female Genital Mutilation Act.

III.   SEXUAL DIVERSITY AND THE INTERNATIONAL COMMUNITY

The United States should consider international standards for the treatment of children when considering the legality of genital reconstruction surgery. One of the main standards by which to judge the international consensus on children's rights is the Convention on the Rights of the Child.[250] The United States was one of only two United Nations member countries that did not sign the Convention on the Rights of the Child. [251] Despite the fact that the United States has not signed the Convention, it is an internationally accepted standard that should be considered by U.S. healthcare practitioners.

The Convention recognizes the rights of children independent of their parents by allowing them to veto parents' decisions on issues of health, education, and religious upbringing.[252] The Convention specifically states that a child should have input into all decisions affecting him or her.[253] Because the decision to alter a child's genitals will forever change the course of the child's life, particular care should be taken to involve the child in this decision.

The second international agreement that is relevant to the treatment of intersexuals is the Nuremberg Code, signed by the United States after World War II.[254] The Nuremberg

Code prohibits countries from conducting experimental medical treatments on patients without their express informed consent.[255] Since genital reconstruction surgery has only been in practice during the last thirty years and no studies have been done to prove the procedures effectiveness, critics argue that genital reconstruction surgery is still experimental.[256] If the procedure is an experimental procedure, then the level of consent required should be higher.

Other countries look to the U.S. medical establishment in developing standards of care.[257] It is important for intersexed children around the world that doctors within the United States make a concerted effort to provide parents and children with all available knowledge regarding intersex conditions before making the recommendation to perform genital reconstruction surgery.

IV.   CONCLUSION

Through its research and publication of many of the facts about intersex genital surgery, the Colombian Court has opened up a worldwide medical, ethical, and legal debate.

However, rather than following the Colombian Court's decision, the world should heed the court's advice. Diversity should not be "a factor of violence and exclusion," but rather it should be "an irreplaceable source of social wealth."[258] The court, paraphrasing Johns Hopkins University professor, Dr. William Reiner, challenges the world to listen to intersexuals and to learn to coexist with them.[259]

With those words in mind, future legal decisions in the United States and abroad should prohibit hospitals from performing childhood genital reconstruction surgery when it is not medically necessary. The current insistence on genital "normalizing" surgery can be explained by our society's obsession with physical appearance and our fear of people who are "different."[260] However, as the Americans with Disabilities Act and other anti-discrimination laws integrate more and more people with different physical characteristics and abilities, society will begin to accept physical differences as a natural and positive part of being human. [261] At the point that our society makes room for the intersexed through laws prohibiting gender reassignment surgery and unnecessary genital reconstruction surgery on children, then people will begin to acknowledge the existence of intersexuals. When faced with the fact that 3% of the population has chromosomes, genitals, and sexual characteristics that are different, teachers will need to modify sex education courses. Ideally, children will learn that every individual has unique sexual characteristics that help make up their gender identity and sexual preference. Through open discussions of growth and sexual development, intersexed children will learn that they are not alone, and others will learn that intersexuality is a common condition that may effect someone they know.

dl. Staff Attorney, ChildLaw Services Inc., Princeton, West Virginia; J.D., City University of New York School of Law at Queens College, 2003; B.A., University of California, Santa Barbara, 1996.I would like to thank Professor Ruthann Robson for her guidance on this paper. I would also like to thank Renaldo Wilson for all of his hard work, without which this paper would not have been the same. I am appreciative of Paula Berg, Rosaria Vigorito, Chris Gottlieb, Rocco Robilotto, Bill & Corey Poole, Liz Haas, Julian Rozzell, my parents, and everyone else who supported my efforts to publish this paper.

1. ANNE FAUSTO-STERLING, SEXING THE BODY: GENDER POLITICS AND THE CONSTRUCTION OF SEXUALITY 51 (2000) (reporting that 1.7% of the population may be intersexed); Julie A. Greenberg, Defining Male and Female: Intersexuality and the Collision Between Law and Biology, 41 ARIZ. L. REV. 265, 267 (1999) (reporting that Johns Hopkins sex researcher John Money estimates the number of people born with ambiguous genitals at 4%). Historically, people with intersex conditions were referred to as "hermaphrodites" but this word has been rejected as embodying many of the misperceptions and mistreatment of intersexed people. Raven Kaldera, American Boyz Intersexuality Flyer, at http://www.ambovz.org/intersection/flverprint.html (last visited Mar. 27, 2004).

2. Hazel Glenn Beh & Milton Diamond, An Emerging Ethical and Medical Dilemma: Should Physicians Perform Sex Assignment Surgery on Infants with Ambiguous Genitalia?, 7 MICH. J. GENDER & L. 1, 3 (2000); FAUSTO-STERLING, supra note 1, at 45; see infra note 4.

3. Emi Koyama, Suggested Guidelines for Non-Intersex Individuals Writing About Intersexuality and Intersex People, at http://isna.org/faq/writing-guidelines.html (last visited Mar. 27, 2004). But see Beh & Diamond, supra note 2, at 17 (estimating the number of sex reassignments in the United States at 100 to 200 annually).

4. Kishka-Kamari Ford, "First Do No Harm"–The Fiction of Legal Parental Consent to Genital- Normalizing Surgery onIntersexed Infants, 19 YALE L. & POL'Y REV. 469, 471 (2001).

5. FAUSTO-STERLING, supra note 1, at 61–63.

6. Id. at 45; Ford, supra note 4, at 471; Sentencia No. SU-337/99 (Colom), available at http://www.isna.org/Colombia/casel-partl.html (last visited Mar. 27, 2004) [hereinafter Ramos]. There are currently no published English translations of the three Colombian cases referred to in this Article. E-mail from Cheryl Chase, founding director of Intersex Society of North America ("ISNA") (Mar. 19, 2002) (on file with the author).

7. FAUSTO-STERLING, supra note 1, at 62, 84–85. Id. at 84.

8. Fausto-Sterling recounts the story of a twelve-year-old intersexed girl named Angela 192 Moreno who lost her ability to orgasm after having her enlarged clitoris removed without her consent. She was told that she had ovarian cancer and was going to have a hysterectomy performed. Later she discovered she never had ovaries. Instead, she had testes that were also removed during the procedure. Id.

9. Id. at: 63–65; Ford, supra note 4, at 476–77.

10. FAUSTO-STERLING, supra note 1, at 63–65; Ford, supra note 4, at 476–77. According to Ford, "medical professionals admit that it is the psychosocial problem of intersex that makes it an emergency." Id.

11. FAUSTO-STERLING, supra note 1, at 64–65; Beh & Diamond, supra note 2, at 51.

12. See FAUSTO-STERLING, supra note 1, at 84; Beh & Diamond, supra note 2, at 2; JOHN COLAPINTO, AS NATURE MADE HIM: THE BOY WHO WAS RAISED AS A GIRL 143–50, 212–13 (2000). In his book, Colapinto vividly describes the gender dysphoria and sexual confusion of David Reimer, a boy raised as a girl after his penis was destroyed during a botched circumcision. Id. at 143–50. This biographical account of Reimer's life was written with the cooperation and participation of Reimer himself who sat for more than 100 hours of interviews and allowed the author access to all of his confidential files and medical records. Id. at xvii. Colapinto also discusses other children who have suffered extreme gender dysphoria growing up without being informed of their condition. One fourteen-year-old girl described in the book dropped out of high school and threatened suicide if she could not have reconstructive surgery to make her a boy. Testing revealed that she was intersexed, having male chromosomes and female external genitalia. Id. at 212.

13. COLAPINTO, supra note 12, at 32; FAUSTO-STERLING, supra note 1, at 46. Fausto-Sterling cites Johns Hopkins researcher John Money, "From the sum total of hermaphroditic evidence, the conclusion that emerges is that sexual behavior and orientation as male or female does not have an innate, instinctive basis." Id.

14. FAUSTO-STERLING, supra note 1, at 85–87.

15. Id. at 58, 80, 85–87.

16. Id. at 57–58. Doctors consider a penis adequate if, as a child is able to stand while urinating and, as an adult is able to engage in vaginal intercourse. Id. See also Ford, supra note 4, at 471 (stating the "penis will be deemed 'adequate' at birth if it is no less than 2.5 centimeters long when stretched").

17. Ford, supra note 4, at 474.

18. Julie A. Greenberg & Cheryl Chase, Colombia's Highest Court Restricts Surgery on Intersex Children, at http://www.isna.org/colornbia/background.html (last visited Mar. 27, 2004) (synthesizing in English the three Colombian cases to which this Article will refer).

19. E-mail from Alyson Meiselman, Liaison Representative of NLGLA (Aug. 19, 2002) (on file with author). The American Bar Association ("ABA") resolution was proposed by the International Law and Practice Section regarding surgical alteration of intersexed infants. The memorandum was drafted for the ABA Commission on Women in the Profession Id. The resolution will be voted on by the House of Delegates at the August 2003 ABA meeting in San Francisco, California. E-mail from Alyson Meiselman, Liaison Representative of NLGLA (April 29, 2003) (on file with author). A draft of the proposed resolution is available at http://www.kindredspiritlakeside.homestead.com/P ABA.html (last visited Mar. 27, 2004).

20. FAUSTO-STERLING, supra note 1, at 36–39, 48–54.

21. Id.

22. Id. at 48–54. The most common forms of intersexuality are: Congenital Adrenal Hyperplasia, which affects children with XX chromosomes and is otherwise referred to as "female pseudo-hermaphrodite"; Androgen Insensitivity Syndrome, which affects children with XY chromosomes and is also referred to as "male pseudo-hermaphrodite"; Gonadal Dysgenesis, which predominantly affects children with XX chromosomes; Hypospadias, which affects children with XX chomosomes; Turner Syndrome, which affects children with XO chromosomes and causes these children to lack some feminine characteristics such as breast growth and menstruation; and Klinefelter Syndrome, which affects children with XXY chromosomes and causes these children to lack some external male characteristics. Id.

23. Id. at 66.

24. Beh & Diamond, supra note 2, at 3; see COLAPINTO, supra note 12, at 32.

25. FAUSTO-STERLING, supra note 1, at 51.

26. Id. at 56–63; Beh & Diamond, supra note 2, at 3.

27. FAUSTO-STERLING, supra note 1, at 40.

28. Id.

29. Id.

30. Id. at 44–45.

31. Id. at 40.

32. Id. at 33.

33. Id. at 109. For example, the Dominican Republic and Papua New Guinea acknowledge a "third type of child," however, they still recognize only two gender roles. Id.

34. 193

35. Id.

36. Id.

37. Id.

38. Id.

39. Id.

40. Id.

41. COLAPINTO, supra note 12, at 39. Colopinto quotes Dr. Benjamin Rosenberg, a leading psychologist specialized in sexual identity, as saying, "Money was 'the leader—the front-runner on everything having to do with mixed sex and hermaphrodites …"Id.

42. Id. at 32–35; Ford, supra note 4, at 471.

43. COLAPINTO, supra note 12, at 32.

44. Id. at 32–35.

45. Id. at 50, 67–68, 70.

46. Id. at 65. John Money presented the case at the annual meeting of the American Association for the Advancement of Science on December 28, 1972.

47. Id. at 16.

48. Id. at 131.
49. Id. at 50. Money envisioned Brenda marrying a man and engaging in vaginal intercourse. Id.
50. Id. at 65–71.
51. Id. "The twins case was quickly enshrined in myriad textbooks ranging from the social sciences to pediatric urology and endocrinology." Id. at 70.
52. Ford, supra note 4, at 471–73; Beh & Diamond, supra note 2, at 3.
53. Ford, supra note 4, at 471; Beh & Diamond, supra note 2, at 3.
54. COLAPINTO, supra note 12, at 75.
55. Summary of Sentencia No. SU-337/99 (Colom), at 4 [hereinafter Ramos Summary] (on file with author). The Colombian Court asked for follow-up studies on intersexed children and was not able to obtain any. Id.; COLAPINTO, supra note 12, at 233–35. There have been several cases of genetic males raised as females that were not followed until recently. Id. at 273–75; see also FAUSTO-STERLING, supra note 1, at 80–91 (providing statistics and personal accounts of intersexuals who received surgery during childhood).
56. Ramos Summary, supra note 54, at 4.
57. COLAPINTO, supra note 12, at 208–09. Milton Diamond, an outspoken opponent of John Money put out an advertisement searching for Brenda in the 1980s. With the help of Keith Sigmundson, he tracked down the subject of Money's famous study. Id. at 199, 208–09.
58. Id. at 208.
59. Id. at 214. The article was published in the Archives of Pediatrics and Adolescent Medicine in March 1997. Id.
60. Id. at 216.
61. Id. at 60–63, 145–50.
62. Id.
63. Id. at 60–63.
64. 63. Id. Due to Reimer's negative behavior at school, she was referred to a guidance counselor in the first grade. Brenda's parents then allowed her doctor to speak with her guidance counselor and her teacher about her condition Id. at 63–64.
65. Id. at 87.
66. Id. at 92.
67. Id. at 80.
68. Ramos Summary, supra, note 54, at 9; Kaldera, supra note 1.
69. Kaldera, supra note 1.
70. Colapinto, supra note 12, at 190–95.
71. Id. at 180–85.
72. Id. at 184.

73. Id. at 267. The Reimer family moved after Brenda's sex change operation and her parents created stories about other parts of their family history in order to hide the truth from her. Id. at 100–01, 106, 267.

74. Id. at 188.

75. Id. at 195.

76. Id. at 218–20; Alice Dreger, Why Do We Need ISNA?, ISNA NEWS, May 2001, at http://isna.org /newsletter/may2001/may2001.html. Because of the private nature of the topic many intersexed adults are hesitant about talking of their experiences. Id.; Fausto-Sterling, supra note 1, at 85. The ISNA website provides links to personal accounts written by intersexed adults, press releases, medical information, and other resources.

77. Fausto-Sterling, supra note 1, at 45–50.

78. Id. at 84.

79. Id. at 80; Intersex Society of North America, ISNA News, Feb. 2001, at http://isna.org/ newsletter /feb2001/feb2001.html.

80. Fausto-Sterling, supra note 1, at 80.

81. Id.

82. See id. at 81; ABCNews.com, Intersex Babies: Controversy Over Operating to Change Ambiguous Genitalia, Apr. 19, 2002, at http://abcnews.go.coin/sections/2020/ DairvNews /2020 intersex 020419.html; Colapinto, supra note 12, at 217–18.

83. Colapinto, supra note 12, at 220.

84. Id. at 218.

85. Id. at 220; Intersex Society of North America, ISNA's Anicus Brief on Intersex Genital Surgery, Feb. 7, 1998, available at http://isna.org/colombia/brief.html.

86. Colapinto, supra note 12, at 233–34; Fausto-Sterling, supra note 1, at 94–95.

87. Colapinto, supra note 12, at 233–35.

88. Id. at 234. The study included interviews with ten intersexed adults who had not been operated on as infants. The study found that genital appearance only plays a small part in a person's formation of gender identity.

89. Id.

90. Ramos Summary, supra note 54, at 10.

91. Greenberg& Chase, supra note 18.

92. Id.

93. Id.

94. Id.

95. Id. The first intersex case was heard by the Constitutional Court of Colombia in 1995. This case is available at the Intersex Society of North America website, at http://www. isna.org/colombia/t-477–95.html (last visited Mar. 27, 2004). Although the case has not been officially translated, the original Spanish text of this decision and the two subsequent decisions can be found on the website. E-Mail from Cheryl Chase, founding director of ISNA (March 19, 2002) (on file with author). For purposes of this Article,

I referred to my own translation as well as to summaries of the cases forwarded in an e-mail by Cheryl Chase, written by Sydney Levy, ISNA Board of Directors (March 19, 2002) (on file with author). The names in all three decisions were changed by the Colombian court to maintain the privacy of the individuals involved. Ramos Summary, supra note 54, at 2. The court refers to the cases by number and initials. This Article will refer to each case with a fictitious surname to avoid confusion.

96. Translation of Sentencia No. T-477/95 (Colom), at 11–12 [hereinafter Gonzalez Translation] (on file with author).

97. Id at 7.

98. Id at 14–16.

99. Id. at 4–5, 14–15. Consttucion Politica de Colombia, translated in Constitutions of the World (1998).

100. Gonzalez Translation, supra note 95, at 15; see Greenberg & Chase, supra note 18.

101. Ramos Summary, supra note 54, at 1; Translation of Sentencia No. T-551/99 (Colom), at 1 [hereinafter Cruz Translation] (on file with author).

102. Ramos Summary, supra note 54, at 1; Cruz Translation, supra note 100, at 1.

103. Ramos Summary, supra note 54, at 2.

104. Id. at 1; Cruz Translation, supra note 100, at 1, 6.

105. Ramos, supra note 6. Throughout the case, the court refers to Ramos with female pronouns and so I will also refer to her as female.

106. Ramos Summary, supra note 54, at 1, 3.

107. Id. at 1.

108. Id.

109. Id.

110. Id.

111. Id. at 4.

112. Id. at 1.

113. Id. at 1.

114. Id. at 2. The Constitutional Court quotes directly from the trial court opinion

115. Id.

116. Id.

117. Id. at 9.

118. Id. The court examined the nature and frequency of cases of intersexuality, the various medical procedures considered acceptable by the medical community, the urgency and necessity of the procedures, and the optimal age at which surgery should be performed. Id. at 2. Finally, the court looked at whether there were any studies showing the beneficial or detrimental effects of surgery. Id. The court stated that in response to its request for information it had received numerous documents, most of which concurred. Id. at 3. In the United States, Germany, and Colombia (up until this point), surgery on the external genitalia is performed as soon as possible after the birth of the infant, usually within the first week. Id. at 4. The internal

gonads are generally removed during adolescence. Id. According to medical experts, the surgery is done immediately so that the parents will not raise their child without a clear gender role. Id. Doctors also hope to prevent the child from becoming confused about their gender and deciding to change their assigned sex in the future. Id. When the ambiguity is not discovered at birth, such as in the case of Ramos, the child is usually assigned the gender that the parents have raised him or her with thus far. Id. Proponents of the surgery argue that if the child's genitals do not conform to their social sex, their parents may feel uncomfortable with the child's ambiguity. Id. at 5. In addition, the child may be teased by their peers and develop low self-esteem or other psychological problems. Id. In opposition to the surgery, the court received an amicus brief from ISNA to which it often references in its opinion. Id. See Intersex Society of North America, ISNA's Amicus Brief on Intersex Genital Surgery, Nov. 7, 1998, available at http://isra.ors/colorrMa/brief.hrml. Critiques of the surgery include lack of informed consent by parents, lack of long-term studies, and random choice of sex assignment by doctors and parents. Ramos Summary, supra note 54, at 4. The court was not able to locate any follow-up studies that had been done on the effectiveness of these medical procedures. Id. The court referred to the Nuremberg Code that prohibits research and experimentation on human subjects without the individual's consent. Id. at 6–7.

119. See The International Covenant on Civil and Political Rights, Article 7, G.A. res. 2200A.(XXI), 21 UN GAOR Supp. (No. 16) at 52, UN Doc. A/6316 (1966), 999 U.N.T.S. 171, entered into force Mar. 23, 1976, available at http://www.unm.edu/humanrts/instree/b3ccpr.htm "No one shall be subjected to torture or to cruel, inhuman or degrading treatment or punishment. In particular, no one shall be subjected without his free consent to medical or scientific experimentation." Id. art. 7. In Ramos, the Colombian Constitutional Court explores the legal dilemma created by the doctor's mandate to help the patient in whatever way possible stemming from the benevolence principle in Articles 44 and 49 of the Colombian Constitution; the patient's right to have access to science and technology from Articles 13 and 49 of the Constitution; versus the patient's right to autonomy and physical integrity, from Articles 1, 12, 16 and 44. Ramos Summary, supra note 54, at 6. The court also mentions the advancement of science that is encouraged by allowing doctors to develop new techniques through experimentation without strict judicial control. Id. The court states that these constitutional principles may often be in contradiction. Id. The court's decision is controlled by the principles of autonomy in Article 1, and the preservation of the life and health of the people in Articles 2 and 46. Id. at 7. Thus, the court concludes that people must have more autonomy to consent to procedures that are risky to their life and health. Id.; see also Levy, supra note 94; CONSTITUCION POLITICA DE COLOMBIA, supra note 98, arts. 1, 2, 12, 13, 16, 44, 46, 49.

120. Ramos Summary, supra note 54, at 9.

121. Id.
122. Sentencia No. T-551/99 (Colom), available at http://www.isna.org/colombia/case2. html (last visited Mar. 27, 2004) [hereinafter Cruz].
123. Id. 123. Cruz Translation, supra note 100.
124. Id. at 16, 24; see Levy, supra note 94, at 6.
125. Cruz Translation, supra note 100, at 1–2.
126. Id.
127. Id. at 1; see Levy, supra note 94, at 6.
128. Cruz Translation, supra note 100, at 3.
129. Id. at 1–2, 21.
130. Id. at 18, 22.
131. Id. at 21; see Levy, supra note 94, at 6.
132. Cruz Translation, supra note 100, at 21; see Levy, supra note 94, at 6.
133. Cruz Translation, supra note 100, at 22–23, 26.
134. Id. at 9
135. 135. Id. at 15–16.
136. Id. at 13,15, 23.
137. Id. at 14, 17–18.
138. Id.
139. See id.
140. Id. at 17–18.
141. Id. at 18–20.
142. Id. at 15.
143. Id. at 15–16, 24.
144. Id. at 18.
145. Id. at 19–20.
146. 196
147. Id. at 21, 25.
148. Ramos Summary, supra note 54, at 4.
149. Id. at 9.
150. Id. at 7–8.
151. Cruz Translation, supra note 100, at 23.
152. Beh& Diamond, supra note 2, at 38–39.
153. Ramos Summary, supra note 54, at 4.
154. Glenn M. Burton, General Discussion of Legal Issues Affecting Sexual Assignment of Intersex Infants Born with Ambiguous Genitalia, § IIG, at http://www.isra.org/librarv/burton2002.htnil (last visited Mar. 27, 2004).
155. Beh& Diamond, supra note 2, at 2.
156. See *Helling v. Carey*, 519 P.2d 981, 983 (Wash. 1974). A physician may be negligent even if they follow customary medical practice. Id.; see Burton, supra note 153, § IIA. Burton writes that the American Board of Pediatrics added an addendum

to their 1996 recommendation for early surgical intervention acknowledging the recent debate over infant genital reconstruction surgery. Id.

157. *Loving v. Virginia*, 388 U.S. 1, 12 (1967) (holding that the right to marry is fundamental); *Skinner v. Oklahoma*, 316 U.S. 535, 541 (1942) (holding that the right to reproduce is fundamental); *Rochin v. California*, 342 U.S. 165, 172-73 (1952) (holding that the right to bodily integrity is fundamental).

158. See *Parham v. J.R.*, 442 U.S. 584, 606-07 (1979) (holding that a parent can involuntarily commit a minor child for mental health treatment as long as the treatment is determined to be in the child's best interest by an independent medical determination). The Court stated that there should be an independent examination to determine that parents were not using the hospital as a "dumping ground." Id. at 598. See also I*n re Rosebush*, 491 N.W.2d 633, 640 (1992) (recognizing the best interest standard applies for determining whether life saving treatment should be provided for a minor child against the parent's wishes).

159. E.g., 18 U.S.C. § 116 (2000).

160. U.S. Const, amend. XIV, § 1.

161. *Gideon v. Wainwright*, 372 U.S. 335, 342 (1963).

162. *Washington v. Glucksberg*, 521 U.S. 702, 720 (1997); *Planned Parenthood of Southeastern Pa. v. Casey*, 505 U.S. 833, 851 (1994) ("Our law affords constitutional protection to personal decisions relating to marriage, procreation, contraception, family relationships, child rearing, and education" (citing *Carey v. Population Services International*, 431 U.S. 678 (1977))).

163. Washington, 521 U.S. at 721 ("The 14th Amendment 'forbids the government to infringe ... 'fundamental' interests at all, no matter what process is provided, unless the infringement is narrowly tailored to serve a compelling state interest.'" (quoting *Reno v. Flores*, 507 U.S. 292, 302 (1993))).

164. Casey, 505 U.S. at 899. Although the Court reaffirmed that women have a constitutional right to seek an abortion without undue burden, a state may require minors to seek a parent's consent for an abortion provided that there is an adequate judicial bypass procedure. Id. hi an earlier case, the Supreme Court stated "our cases show that although children generally are protected by the same constitutional guarantees against governmental deprivations as are adults, the State is entitled to adjust its legal system to account for children's vulnerability and their needs for 'concern, ... sympathy, and ... paternal attention'" *Bellotti v. Baird*, 443 U.S. 622. 635 (1979).

165. *Lassiter v. Dep't of Social Services of Durham County* 452 U.S. 18, 39 (1981); see *Wisconsin v. Yoder*, 406 U.S. 205, 232-34 (1972); *Pierce v. Society of Sisters of the Holy Names of Jesus and Mary*, 268 U.S. 510. 534-35(1925); *Meyer v. Nebraska*, 262 U.S. 390. 399 (1923).

166. *Parham v. J.R.*, 442 U.S. 584, 602-04 (1979) ("The fact that a child may balk at hospitalization or complain about a parental refusal to provide cosmetic surgery does not diminish the parents' authority to decide what is best for the child.").

167. Id. "The court is not without constitutional control over parental discretion in dealing with children when their physical or mental health is jeopardized." Id. at 603. "The parent's interests in a child must be balanced against the State's long-recognized interests as parens patriae." *Troxel v. Granville*, 530 U.S. 57, 88 (2000). See also *Prince v. Massachusetts*, 321 U.S. 158 (1944). In Prince, the Supreme Court examines the parents' right to have their child distribute religious material on the street. Id. The Court allowed the state to limit parent's power in this regard stating, "Parents may be free to become martyrs themselves. But it does not follow they are free, in identical circumstances, to make martyrs of their children before they have reached the age of full and legal discretion when they can make that choice for themselves." Id. at 170.

168. Elizabeth J. Sher, Choosing for Children: Adjudicating Medical Care Disputes Between Parents and the State, 58 N.Y.U. L. REV. 157, 169–70, 170 n57 (1983); Jennifer Trahan, Constitutional Law: Parental Denial of a Child's Medical Treatment for Religious Reasons, 1989 ANN. SURV. AM. L. 307, 309 (1990). Trahan has divided the medical neglect cases into three categories: those where the child's death is imminent; those where there is no imminent harm; and those where the child is endangered but death is not imminent. Id. at 314–15. In most cases, courts will interfere when death is imminent and where the child is endangered even where death is not imminent. However, when there is no risk of imminent death, the parent's religious rights and privacy rights are weighed against the state's parens patriae rights. Id. See also hire Richardson, 284 So.2d 185, 187 (1973) (denying parents' request to consent to son's kidney donation for the benefit of his sister where it was not found to be in the son's own best interest).

169. Child Abuse Prevention and Treatment Act of 1996, Pub. L. No. 93–247, 88 Stat. 4 (codified in sections of 42 U.S.C. §§ 5101-5116i (2000)); Adoption and Safe Families Act of 1997, Pub. L. No. 105-89, 111 Stat. 2117 (1997); see Lassiter, 452 U.S. at 34 (citing various statutes in support of decision to uphold a termination of parental rights).

170. U.S. CONST, amend. XIV, § 1 ("No state shall make or enforce any law which shall abridge the privileges or immunities of citizens of the United States; nor shall any state deprive any person of life, liberty, or property without due process of law; nor deny to any person within its jurisdiction the equal protection of the laws."); *Shelley v. Kraemer*, 334 U.S. 1, 13 (1948) ("[A]ction inhibited by the first section of the Fourteenth Amendment is only such action as may fairly be said to be that of the States. That Amendment erects no shield against merely private conduct, however discriminatory or wrongful." (citing the Civil Rights Cases, 109 U.S. 3 (1883))); see also *Moose Lodge No. 107 v. Irvis*, 407 US. 163, 173 (1972).

171. See Shelley, 334 U.S. at 14 .

172. Id. ("That the action of state courts and of judicial officers in their official capacities is to be regarded as action of the State within the meaning of the Fourteenth

Amendment, is a proposition which has long been established by decisions of this Court."); see also *Lugar v. Edmonson Oil Co.*, Inc., 457 U.S. 922. 942 (1982).

173. Estate of CW, 640 A.2d 427 (Pa. Super. Ct. 1994); Matter of Guardianship of Hayes, 608 P.2d 635 (Wash 1980); Elizabeth S. Scott, Sterilization of Mentally Retarded Persons: Reproductive Rights and Family Privacy, 1986 DUKE L.J. 806, 818 (1986).

174. Estate of CW, 640 A.2d at 428; Matter of Guardianship of Hayes, 608 P.2d at 641.

175. *Rochin v. California*, 342 U.S. 165, 172-73 (1952).

176. *Cruzan v. Director, Mo. Dep't of Health*, 497 U.S. 261 (1990).

177. *Parham v. J.R.*, 442 U.S. 584, 603 (1979); Lawrence Schlam & Joseph P. Wood, Informed Consent to the Medical Treatment of Minors: Law & Practice, 10 HEALTH MATRIX 141, 142 (2000); see Andrew Popper, Averting Malpractice by Information: Informed Consent in the Pediatric Treatment Environment, 47 DEPAUL L. REV. 819 (1998).

178. Schlam & Wood, supra note 176, at 147–49.

179. Id. at 151.

180. Id. at 143.

181. Id. at 166–68.

182. Id. at 167.

183. FAUSTO-STERLING, supra note 1, at 81.

184. *Eisenstadt v. Baird*, 405 U.S. 438, 453 (1972). The Court stated that it is the right of the individual to decide "whether to bear or beget children" Id.

185. *Planned Parenthood of Southeastern Pa. v. Casey*, 505 U.S. 833, 899-901 (1994).

186. *Planned Parenthood of Central Mo. v. Danforth*, 428 U.S. 52 (1976); *Bellotti v. Baird*, 443 U.S. 622 (1979).

187. Casey, 505 U.S. at 833 (abortion); *Carey v. Population Serv. Int'l*, 431 U.S. 678 (1977) (contraception); see also Schlam & Wood, supra note 176, at 166.

188. Estate of CW, 640 A.2d 427 (Pa. Super. Ct. 1994).

189. Id.; see *In re Guardianship of Hayes*, 608 P.2d 635 (Wash 1980). In limited circumstances, parents can consent for their incompetent children to be sterilized to protect them from harmful pregnancies. Id. at 638. However, there are strict procedural guidelines that the court follows before allowing parental consent. Id. at 639. The following guidelines must be followed: (1) the child must be represented by a disinterested guardian ad litem; (2) the child must be incapable of making her own decision about sterilization; and (3) the child must be unlikely to develop sufficiently to make an informed judgment about sterilization in the foreseeable future. Id. at 641. Even after the court establishes the listed criteria, the parent or guardian seeking an incompetent's sterilization must prove by clear, cogent, and convincing evidence that there is a need for contraception Id. First the judge must find that the individual is physically capable of procreation Id. Second the judge must find that she is likely to engage in sexual activity at the present or in the near

future under circumstances likely to result in pregnancy. Id. Finally the judge must determine that the nature and extent of the individual's disability, as determined by empirical evidence and not solely on the basis of standardized tests, renders him or her permanently incapable of caring for a child, even with reasonable assistance. Id.

190. Reproductive rights will not be infringed for those intersexed children who are incapable of producing sperm or eggs or who do not have a functional uterus.

191. Reproductive rights will also not be infringed for intersexed children who have clitoral reduction surgery and do not have their gonads or uterus removed.

192. Estate of CW, 640 A.2d at 427.

193. However, in Vermont, same-sex couples may seek a civil union, pursuant to Vt. St. T. 15 § 1201 . These civil unions may not be recognized by other states. See William C. Duncan, Civil Unions in Vermont: Where to Go From Here?, 11 WIDENER J. PUB. L. 361, 373–76 (2002). In addition, the Massachusetts Supreme Judicial Court held in *Goodridge v. Dep't of Public Health,* that barring an individual from the protections, benefits, and obligations of civil marriage solely because that person would marry a person of the same sex violates the Massachusetts Constitution and stayed the judgment for 180 days to permit the Legislature to take action 798 N.E.2d 941 (Mass. 2003).

194. *Baehr v. Lewin*, 852 P.2d 44 (Haw. 1993); *Baehr v. Miike*, No. 91–1394, 1996 WL 694235 (Haw. Cir. Ct. Dec. 3, 1996).

195. Lewin, 852 P.2d at 67.

196. Haw. Const, art. 1, § 23 ; see also *Baehr v. Miike*, No. 91- 1394, 1996 WL 694235 (Cir. Ct. Haw. Dec. 3, 1996) . The Hawaii Constitution was amended by voter referendum shortly before the decision was rendered in *Baehr v. Miike*. David Orgon Coolidge, The Hawai'i Marriage Amendment: Its Origins, Meaning and Fate, 22 U. Haw. L. Rev. 19, 82, 101 (2000).

197. Defense of Marriage Act, 28 U.S.C. § 1738C (1996).

198. Lyrm E. Harris, Born True Hermaphrodite, at http://www.angelfire.com/ca2/ BornHermaphrodite (last visited Mar. 27, 2004). The Superior Court, County of Los Angeles, granted the two-part request of Lynn Elizabeth Harris, Case No. 437625, changing the name and legal sex on her birth certificate from Lynn Elizabeth Harris to Lynn Edward Harris, and from female to male, respectively. Id.

199. See *In re Estate of Gardiner*, 22 P.3d 1086 (Kan Ct. App. 2001). Most court cases discussing the legality of changing birth certificates, names or gender identification only consider chromosomes as one factor in determining a person's legal gender. Id. The main factor that courts consider is the genitalia of the individual requesting a legal change of status. Id. In this case involving a male to female transsexual, the court discusses intersex conditions extensively in explaining the difficulty in determining legal gender. Id.

200. Burton, supra note 153, § IIIC. Burton cites *Littleton v. Prange*, 9 S.W.3d 223 (Tex App. 1999). *In Littleton v. Prange*, a male to female transsexual legally changed her

birth certificate to female and married. 9 S.W.3d at 224–25. However, the court found that she was not a legal spouse because she was born male and thus was unable to sue for the wrongful death of her husband. Id. at 225–26.

201. *Cruzan v. Mo. Dep't of Health*, 497 U.S. 261, 269 (1990). "This notion of bodily integrity has been embodied in the requirement that informed consent is generally required for medical treatment. Justice Cordozo, while on the Court of Appeals of New York, aptly described this doctrine: Every Human being of adult years and sound mind has a right to determine what shall be done with his own body; and a surgeon who performs an operation without his patient's consent commits an assault, for which he is liable in damages." Id.

202. Id.

203. See id. at 279.

204. See *Washington v. Glucksberg*, 521 U.S. 702. 725 (1997).

205. Cruz Translation, supra note 100, at 18–21.

206. Beh & Diamond, supra note 2, at 47–48.

207. FAUSTO-STERLING, supra note 1, at 64–65.

208. Beh & Diamond, supra note 2, at 47; Ford, supra note 4, at 483–84.

209. Ford, supra note 4, at 483.

210. FAUSTO-STERLING, supra note 1, at 86.

211. Ford, supra note 4, at 485.

212. Id. at 484.

213. Id.

214. See Beh & Diamond, supra note 2, at 48–52.

215. Burton, supra note 153, § IF; Ford, supra note 4 , at 475–76; see also *Canterbury v. Spence*, 464 F.2d 772, 788–89(1972).

216. Ford, supra note 4, at 476.

217. Intersex Society of North America, ISNA's Recommendations for Treatment, 1994, at http://isna.org/librarv/recommendations.html (1994). Although not always medical emergencies, some conditions can be painful and require early surgery. Id. Intersex activists opposing genital reconstruction surgery generally do not oppose surgery for these cases which may include "severe second or third degree hypospadias (with extensive exposed mucosal tissue vulnerable to infection), chordee (extensive enough to cause pain), bladder exstrophy, and imperforate anus." Id.

218. Ramos Summary, supra note 54, at 3. See Beh & Diamond, supra note 2, at 44.

219. Beh & Diamond, supra note 2, at 45.

220. See id. at 11–12.

221. FAUSTO-STERLING, supra note 1, at 84.

222. American Medical Association, Code of Medical Ethics § E-8.08, available at http://www.ama- assn.org/ama/pub/category/2503.html (last updated Dec. 22, 2003). The American Medical Association defines informed consent as "a basic social

policy for which exceptions are permitted: (1) where the patient is unconscious or otherwise incapable of consenting and harm from failure to treat is imminent; or (2) when risk disclosure poses such a serious psychological threat of detriment to the patient as to be medically contraindicated. Social policy does not accept the paternalistic view that the physician may remain silent because divulgence might prompt the patient to forego needed therapy. Rational, informed patients should not be expected to act uniformly, even under similar circumstances, in agreeing to or refusing treatment." Id.

223. Beh& Diamond, supra note 2, at 36.
224. See id. at 48.
225. Id. at 47–50.
226. Ramos Summary, supra note 54, at 4. See Beh & Diamond, supra note 2, at 48, 53.
227. Beh & Diamond, supra note 2, at 37–38.
228. 18 U.S.C. §116(2000).
229. Id.
230. Bruce A. Robinson, Female Genital Mutilation in North America & Europe, at http://www.religioustolerance.org/fem cira.htm (last updated Jan. 22, 2004). "FGM has ... been criminalized at the state level in California, Minnesota, North Dakota, Rhode Island, and Tennessee." Id.
231. 18U.S.C. §116.
232. Id.
233. Id.
234. Id. §116(c).
235. Id. §116.
236. Id. §116(b)(l).
237. See Beh & Diamond, supra note 2, at 46; FAUSTO-STERLING, supra note 1, at 58.
238. FAUSTO-STERLING, supra note 1, at 48, 51.
239. Id. at 109.
240. Id. at 52, 55, 58. Intersexed children with Congenital Adrenal Hyperplasia may develop problems with salt metabolism, which could be life threatening if not treated with cortisone. Id. at 52. Some intersexed babies may have an increased rate of urinary tract infections possibly leading to kidney damage. Id at 58.
241. Beh & Diamond, supra note 2, at 46; FAUSTO-STERLING, supra note 1, at 58.
242. Ramos Summary, supra note 54, at 4; Kaldera, supra note 1, at 4.
243. COLAPINTO, supra note 12, at 218.
244. Ramos, supra note 6.
245. 18U.S.C. §116.
246. Pub. L. No. 104-208, div. C, § 645(a), 110 Stat. 3009-709 (1996) (codified as amended at 18 U.S.C. § 116 (2000)). "The Congress finds that—(l) The practice of female genital mutilation is carried out by members of certain cultural and religious groups within the United States; (2) the practice of female genital mutilation often

results in the occurrence of physical and psychological health effects that harm the women involved; (3) such mutilation infringes upon the guarantees of rights secured by Federal and State law, both statutory and constitutional; (4) the unique circumstances surrounding the practice of female genital mutilation place it beyond the ability of any single State or local jurisdiction to control; (5) the practice of female genital mutilation can be prohibited without abridging the exercise of any rights guaranteed under the first amendment to the Constitution or under any other law; and (6) Congress has the affirmative power under section 8 of Article 1, the necessary and proper clause, section 5 of the fourteenth Amendment, as well as under the treaty clause, to the Constitution to enact such legislation." Id.

247. FAUSTO-STERLING, supra note 1, at 85–86.

248. See 18 U.S.C. §116.

249. Id.

250. *Craig v. Boren,* 429 U.S. 190, 197-98 (1976). Equal protection claims brought on the basis of gender must meet intermediate scrutiny; thus, the government must show that there is a legitimate state interest in treating the sexes differently, and that this statute is substantially related to a legitimate government interest. Id.

251. Convention on the Rights of the Child, G.A. Res. 44/25, UN GAOR, 44th Sess., Supp. No. 49, at 167, UN Doc. A/44/49 (1989), available at http://www.un.org/documents/ga/res/44/a44r025.htm

252. Id. The other country that did not sign the convention was Somalia. See Office of the United Nations High Commissioner for Human Rights, Status of the Ratification of the Convention on the Rights of the Child (Nov. 4, 2003), available at http://www.unhchr.ch/htrnl/menu2/6/crc/treaties/status-crc.htm

253. Convention on the Rights of the Child, supra note 250.

254. 200

255. Id.

256. Trials of War Criminals Before the Nuremberg Military Tribunals Under Control Council Law No. 10 (1946–1949) [Nuremberg Code], available at http://www 1.unm.edu/humanrts/instree/nuremberg.html [hereinafter Nuremberg Code]; *Grimes v. Kennedy Krieger Institute, Inc.* 782 A.2d 807 (2001). This case discusses experimental research on children in the United States without informed consent. Id. at 811. The court in that case stated, "The Nuremberg Code is the most complete and authoritative statement of the law of informed consent to human experimentation. It is also part of international common law and may be applied, in both civil and criminal cases, by state, federal and municipal courts in the United States." Id. at 835 [internal quotations omitted]. The court refers to the text of the Nuremberg Code to support its conclusion that the consent to the research was invalid, "The voluntary consent of the human subject is absolutely essential. This means that the person involved should have legal capacity to give consent; should be so situated as to be able to exercise free power of choice, without the intervention of any element

of force, fraud, deceit, duress, over-reaching, or other ulterior form of constraint or coercion; and should have sufficient knowledge and comprehension of the elements of the subject matter involved as to enable him to make an understanding and enlightened decision." Id.

257. Nuremberg Code, supra note 254.

258. In Ramos, the court explores the experimental nature of the surgery and its possible violation of the Nuremberg Code. Ramos Summary, supra note 54, at 6.

259. COLAPINTO, supra note 12, at 75.

260. Cruz Translation, supra note 100, at 25.

261. Id.; see Greenberg& Chase, supra note 18.

262. Cf Ryken Grattet & Valerie Jermess, Examining the Boundaries of Hate Crime Law: Disabilities and the 'Dilemma of Difference,' 91 J. CRIM. L. & CRIMINOLOGY 653 (2001) (exploring the susceptibility of minority groups to hate crimes).

263. Americans with Disabilties Act of 1990 [ADA], 42 U.S.C. § 12101, (2000). The ADA was enacted in the face of discrimination against individuals with disabilities in all areas of life. Id. The purpose of the ADA is to ensure inclusion of individuals with disabilities in employment, education, public accommodations, and government services. Id.

264. FAUSTO-STERLING, supra note 1.

265. Citation:

266. Kate Haas. *Who will make room for the intersexed?* 30 Am J Law Med 41 (2004). (File revised 29 July 2004)

INTRODUCTION TO: LABORING ON

Birth Transition in the United States

JAN CAMPBELL

Simonds and Rothman offer an interesting look at the transitions that have occurred in the United States in obstetric care. Moving from an era where midwifery was mainly absent to fifty years later when nurse-midwives began practicing in U.S. hospitals, childbirth has seen many changes. We've seen operating rooms replaced by birthing rooms, and cesarean section rates skyrocket from 5 percent in 1970 to 31.1 percent in 2006.

These authors cite the fact that childbirth is a natural process and a healthy natural event but also enlighten us that the risk factors of birthing make it anything but natural. Their discussion of the types of monitoring and interventions during labor and delivery illuminates the fact that these interventions are often unnecessary. Maternity care has become very medicalized. Simonds and Rothman take us through the perspective of the philosopher Descartes, who saw the application of a technological model of the human body as mind-body dualism. He saw the body as a machine, which breaks down and needs repair. The authors further guide us through patriarchal theory that historically posits that men are fathers who rule, and this idea colors our views of birth and family. Adding to these concepts the idea that medicine is disease oriented makes birthing something that is not always viewed as a natural process. The language of illness is often applied, as it might be in other parts of a hospital, with terms like "conditions" or "diagnosis of pregnancy" to "recovery from childbirth." The midwifery model grew as a response to the medical model, and the authors show the evolution of a back-to-nature perspective of the 1960s to the holistic approach today.

The reader is given a time line of events that looks at the medicalization of pregnancy and controlling pain to the era of home births and how nurse midwives and obstetricians feel about tailoring the needs of the birth to fit the patient.

LABORING ON

Birth Transition in the United States

WENDY SIMONDS AND BARBARA KATZ ROTHMAN

We have seen the return of the midwife. And the rise of the cesarean section. For fifty years there were almost no midwives to be found in most of the U.S. Then during the same period in which nurse-midwives began practicing in U.S. hospitals, while hospitals introduced "birthing rooms" to replace operating-room-like delivery rooms and the "natural childbirth" movement flourished, we also saw the cesarean section rate rise from 5% in 1970 to an astonishing and unprecedented 31.1% in 2006; it increased by a full 50% between 1996 and 2006 (Curtin and Kozak 1998, DeClercq et al. 2006, Hamilton et al. 2007, Martin et al. 2005).

Since the development of modern obstetrics, there has never been more talk of birth as a "healthy natural event," yet each individual birthing woman is now acquainted with her personal "risk factors," factors that doctors tell her make her birth less than healthy and far less than "natural." Eighty-five percent of women who birth in hospitals are strapped to fetal monitors (Martin et al. 2003), despite evidence that such monitoring produces unnecessary interventions (see Goer 1999, 2AA-A7, for a summary of the medical literature on this issue).

How did we come to this strange paradoxical position regarding childbirth in this country? Understanding these contradictions of contemporary U.S. maternity care is the goal of this reading.

Pregnancy and birth have different meanings to different people. What after all is a pregnancy?

Pregnancy is, sometimes, a contraceptive failure, a side effect of a not very reliable method of birth control. Pregnancy is the effect of a successful treatment for infertility. Pregnancy is a condition of a woman's body, to be distinguished from ovulation, menstruation and menopause. Pregnancy is the presence of a man's baby in a woman, as when a man wants a woman to bear him a son to carry on his name. W.I. Thomas famously said, "Situations defined as real are real in their consequences." How do we define, how do we give meaning to pregnancy, to birth? Who has the power to define?

The meaning of pregnancy is, like everything else, in the eye of the beholder, and in the U.S., the foremost "beholder" of pregnancy is the obstetrician. The obstetrical perspective on pregnancy and birth is held to be not just one way of looking at it, but to be the truth, the facts, science: other societies may have had beliefs about pregnancy, but we believe our medicine has the facts. But obstetrical knowledge, like all knowledge, comes from somewhere, it has a social, historical and political context. Medicine does not exist as "pure," free of culture or free of ideology. The context in which knowledge develops and is used shapes that knowledge. Doctors see pregnancy, childbirth, and women's entire procreative lives, from their perspective. Home-birth advocates and midwives offer a radically different—in some ways diametrically opposed—view. It is in the conflict between these two perspectives that the contradictions surrounding birth in this country arise.

The primary characteristic of the modern medical model of health and illness in general is that it is based on the ideology of technology, that ideology appropriate to technological society, with its values of efficiency and rationality, practical organization, systematizing, and controlling. The application of a technological model to the human body can be traced back to Rene Descartes' concept of mind-body dualism. For Descartes, the body was a machine, the structure and operation of which fell within the province of human knowledge, as distinguished from the mind, which God alone could know. Even though the Hippocratic principles state that the mind and body should be considered together, most physicians, whatever their philosophical views on the nature of the mind, behave in practice as if they were still Cartesian dualists (Dubos 1968, 76). The Cartesian model of the body as a machine operates to make the physician a technician, or mechanic. The body breaks down and needs repair; it can be repaired in the hospital as a car is in the shop; once "fixed," a person can be returned to the community. The earliest models in medicine were largely mechanical; later models worked more with chemistry and newer medical writing describes computer-like programming, but the basic point remains the same. Problems in the body are technical problems requiring technical solutions, whether it is a mechanical repair, a chemical rebalancing, or a "debugging" the system.

A second major ideological basis of the medical model comes from its history as a men's profession, growing out of a patriarchal history. Its values are those of men as the dominant social power; medicine sees pregnancy and birth through men's eyes—even now, as more and more women are trained in obstetrics, that history continues to cast its shadow. Medicine treats all patients, male and female, as "machines," in conformance with the ideology of technological society. The treatment of women patients is further affected by the ideology of patriarchal society. We mean something more subtle here than just "men rule." In a patriarchy, it is men as fathers who rule, and families take their name and their identity through fathers. Our society is not of course a simple patriarchy. But the history of patriarchy continues to color our understandings of birth and family.

One important consequence of its patriarchal history is that medicine has fared no better than other disciplines in arriving at a working model of women that does not take men as the comparative norm. Medicine has treated and in many instances overtly defined, normal female reproductive processes as diseases. Certainly U.S. medicine is disease oriented, and has been since its early formal organization. Yes, doctors are illness oriented, and yes they did and sometimes still do treat pregnancy, birth, menstruation and menopause as diseases. But knowing that is not enough. We must go beyond that and ask why. Medicine does not, after all, treat all of our biological functions as diseases: the digestive system, for example, is usually considered well unless shown otherwise. Neither a full nor an empty colon has been seen as a disease-like state, and normal bowel movements are not medically monitored. Why then were female reproductive processes singled out to make women "unwell," in a "delicate condition," constantly moving from one disease-like state to another?

The source of the pathology orientation of medicine toward women's health and re-production is a body-as-a-machine model (the ideology of technology) in which the male body is taken as the norm (the ideology of patriarchy). From that viewpoint, reproductive processes are stresses on the system, and thus disease-like.

Until the middle of the 1900s, doctors used the language of illness when discussing women's reproductive systems, with pregnancy seen as a disease, menopause as a deficiency disorder, childbirth as a surgical procedure. Contemporary physicians do not usually speak this way any more, regularly asserting that female reproductive functions are normal and healthy. However, they make these statements within the context of teaching the medical "management," "care," "supervision" and "treatment" of these "conditions." From the "diagnosis" of pregnancy, through the "management" of its "symptoms," on to "recovery" from childbirth, the disease imagery remains and continues to influence obstetric thinking and practice.

The contemporary midwifery model of birth grew in response to this medical approach. Coming together out of the "back to nature," movements of the 1960's, "hippy" communal life, the feminist movement, the patient's rights movement, religious fundamentalism, radical individualism—from a variety of strangely interrelated and sometimes apparently unrelated sources, a new midwifery began to appear in the U.S. Where the obstetric approach was "technological," the midwives were "holistic," where the obstetricians were patriarchal, the midwives were "women centered." In home births, birth centers, in midwifery practices in and out of hospitals all over the United States, midwives worked to redefine birth, to offer a different place to stand, a new—and maybe a very old—perspective on pregnancy, birth, mothers and babies.

We've done interviews with over 100 midwives and midwifery students—both direct-entry midwives who mostly practice home birth, and nurse-midwives, who mostly practice in hospitals—around the U.S., as well as with a smaller groups of women obstetricians (ten who were recommended to us by midwives) in Atlanta. In the rest of this article, we will offer brief a summary of the history of birth work in the U.S., and compare how members of these groups talked about one particular birth practice.

BIRTH IN THE U.S. IN HISTORICAL PERSPECTIVE

Midwives came over with the Pilgrims, and indeed the native peoples had their midwives before that. What is different about the United States, compared to other countries, is that it was virtually unique in the world in largely abolishing midwifery before reinventing it in a new form, as a branch of nursing. Other developed countries, like France, Germany, Japan, and the Netherlands, each maintained a form of midwifery. In some the midwives had more power, and in some less, but all have a continuous history of practicing midwives. There are continuing midwifery traditions all over the world, but their independence and their relationship to medical practice directly reflects the history of imperialism and colonization. The history of midwifery reflects world history: America won World War II and Japanese midwives lost status and power as Americans restructured Japanese hospitals; East and West Germany went separate ways in birth practices; countries colonized by the Dutch show a different midwifery than those colonized by the British. But it is in the United States that we see an attempt to simply abolish midwifery completely.

The beginning of the end of American midwifery goes back before the establishment of the United States, and has its roots in British and European history. The earliest sign of encroachment on midwifery came from the development of the barber-surgeons guilds. In England, for example, under the guild system that developed in the thirteenth century, the right to use surgical instruments belonged officially only to the surgeon. Thus, when giving birth was absolutely impossible, the midwife called in the barber-surgeon to perform an embryotomy (crushing the fetal skull, dismembering it in utero, and removing it piecemeal) or to remove the baby by cesarean section after the death of the mother. It was not within the technology of the barber-surgeon to deliver a live baby from a live mother. Not until the development of forceps in the 17th century were men involved in live births, and so became a genuine challenge to midwives. Interest in abnormal cases increased throughout the 17th and especially the 18th centuries; this may have been due to rapid urbanization and the resultant increase in pelvic deformities caused by rickets. (For a history of American midwifery, see Donegan 1978; Donnison 1977; For a history of European midwifery, see Bullough 1966).

In the early 17th century, the barber-surgeon Peter Chamberlen developed the obstetrical forceps, an instrument that enabled its user to deliver a child mechanically without necessarily destroying it first. The Chamberlen family kept the forceps secret for three generations, for their own financial gain, and only let it be known that they possessed some way of preventing the piecemeal extraction of an impacted fetus. The right to use instruments resided exclusively with men, and when the Chamberlens finally sold their design (or the design leaked out) it was for the use of the barber-surgeons, and not generally available to midwives.

It has frequently been assumed that the forceps were an enormous breakthrough in improving maternity care, but on careful reflection that seems unlikely. The physicians and surgeons did not have the opportunity to observe and learn the rudiments of normal birth, and were therefore at a decided disadvantage in handling difficult births. And unlike in the pre-forceps days, when a barber-surgeon was called in only if all hope of a live birth was gone, midwives were increasingly encouraged and instructed to call in the barber-surgeon prophylactically, whenever birth became difficult.

The midwives of the time expressed their concerns. Sarah Stone, an 18th century midwife and author of *The Complete Practice of Midwifery*, alleged that more mothers and children had died at the hands of raw recruits just out of their apprenticeship to the barber-surgeons than through the worst ignorance and stupidity of the midwife (Donnison 1977, 31). The noted midwife Elizabeth Nihell, author of *A Treatise on the Art of the Midwife*, in 1760 questioned the value of instrumentation as a result of her training in France at the Hotel-Dieu, where midwives practiced without male supervision or intervention (Donnison 1977, 33). Instruments were, in her opinion, rarely if ever necessary. The forceps of that time were of a primitive design, not originally curved to fit the birth canal, and so went high up into the birth canal; and were not sterilized. Injuries and infections were common. A journalist of the time, Philip Thicknesse, agreed with Elizabeth Nihell that the growing popularity of the man-midwife, the barber-surgeon, and his instruments was not because of his superior skills but because of the power of men to convince women of the dangers of childbirth and the incompetence of the midwives. The men were aided by the growing prestige of male birth attendants as a symbol of higher social status, possibly because of their higher fees. Not only did the men use their instruments unnecessarily, resulting in maternal and infant mortality and morbidity, puerperal fever and extraordinary birth injuries, but, Nihell complained, were so adept at concealing errors with "a cloud of hard words and scientific jargon" that the injured patient herself was convinced that she could not thank him enough for the mischief he had done (Donnison 1977, 34). "Meddlesome midwifery," as it was called at the time, was the forerunner of what later became known as "interventionist obstetrics."

Spurred on by the development of basic anatomical knowledge and increased understanding of the processes of reproduction, surgeons of the 1700s began to develop formal training programs in midwifery. Women midwives were systematically excluded from such programs. Women were not trained because men believed women to be inherently incompetent. The situation was far from simple however, and some men surgeons did try to provide training for the midwives, sharing with them the advances made in medical knowledge. Such attempts failed in the face of opposition from within medicine, supported by the prevailing beliefs about women's abilities to perform in a professional capacity. The result was a widening disparity between midwives and surgeons. As men developed newer and more sophisticated technologies were developed, they kept them from the women.

We cannot assume that midwives would have been incompetent to use these technologies. Rather, their basic experience with normal birth probably made them eminently more capable than the inexperienced men. For example, some historians believe that the first cesarean section recorded in the British Isles in which both mother and child survived was performed by an illiterate Irish midwife, Mary Dunally (Donnison 1977, 49). The training, experience and competence of the midwives of the 17th and 18th centuries varied enormously, and went largely unregulated. And the same was true of the training, experience and competence of the physicians and barber-surgeons.

As physicians gained near-complete ascendancy, the midwife was redefined from being a competitor of the physician-surgeon to being, in her new role, his assistant. Midwives lost autonomy over their work throughout most of Europe and in England, to a greater or lesser degree losing control over their own licensing, training requirements and the restrictions under which they functioned. Once physicians came to be socially defined as having expertise in the management of difficult or abnormal birth, midwifery effectively lost control over even normal birth. The deleterious results of the new obstetrics outweighed its benefits, particularly for normal and healthy pregnancies. The rise of obstetrics in the U.K., in Europe, and in cities throughout the U.S., was not associated with improved outcome for mothers and babies.

But once the surgeon or physician is held to be necessary "in case something goes wrong," then the midwife becomes dependent on the physician and his goodwill for her "backup" services. When physicians want to compete with midwives for clients, all they have to do is withhold backup services, that is, refuse to come to the aid of a midwife who calls for medical assistance. This is a pattern that began in the earliest days of the barber surgeon and continues right through to today.

Even when physicians are not in competition with midwives, but really need midwives to handle the cases that they, the physicians, wish to avoid—such as the rural poor or the tediously normal births—physicians still control midwives by setting the standards for training and regulating which instruments and procedures they may use, and for which they must call on their backup doctors. While these decisions are ostensibly made to bring about best possible health care for mother and child, by preventing "unqualified" persons from providing particular services, that is certainly not the way it always worked out. And again, this is a problem that repeats itself over and over in different eras.

The balance of power that has been achieved between medicine and midwifery varies across the world. It is only in the United States however, that midwifery actually failed to survive.

In the 19th and early 20th centuries, midwives and physicians in the U.S. were in direct competition for patients, and not only for their fees. Newer, more clinically oriented medical training demanded "teaching material," so that even immigrant and poor women were desired as patients (Ehrenreich and English 1973). Doctors used everything in their power to stop the midwives from practicing. They advertised, using racist pictures of "drunken, dirty" Irish midwives, and of hooked-nose, witch-like Jewish midwives. They played on immigrant women's desire to "become American," linking midwives with "old country" ways of doing things. The displacement of midwives can be better understood in terms of this competition than as an ideological struggle or as "scientific advancement." Physicians, unlike the unorganized, disenfranchised midwives, had access to the power of the state through their professional associations. They were thus able to draw women in with their advertising, but also to control licensing legislation, in state after state restricting the midwives' sphere of activity and imposing legal sanctions against them (Brack 1976, 20).

What did the medical takeover of birth mean for women and babies? Medicine would have us believe that it meant above all a safer birth. The profession of medicine claims the decline in maternal and infant mortality that we experienced in the 20th century was a result not so much of women's hard-won control over their own fertility, or even of better nutrition and sanitation, but rather of medical management per se. Medical expansion into the area of childbirth began, however, before the development of any of what are now considered to be the contributions of modern obstetrics: before asepsis, surgical technique, antibiotics, anesthesia. At the time when physicians were taking over control of childbirth in the U.S., the noninterventionist, supportive techniques of the midwife were safer for both the birthing woman and her baby.

In Washington, D.C., as the percentage of births reported by midwives shrank from 50% in 1903 to 15% in 1912, infant mortality in the first day, first week, and first month of life all increased. New York's dwindling corps of midwives did significantly better than did New York doctors in preventing both stillborns and puerperal sepsis (postpartum infection). And in Newark a midwifery program in 1914–1916 achieved maternal mortality rates as low as 1.7 per thousand, while in Boston, in many ways a comparable city but where midwives were banned, the rates were 6.5 per thousand. Infant mortality rates in Newark were 8.5 per thousand, contrasted with 36.4 in Boston (Kobrin 1966, 353). The situation was similar in England, where an analysis of the records of the Queen's Institute for Midwives for the years 1905–1925 found that the death rate rose in step with the proportion of cases to which midwives called the doctors (Donnison 1977, 120).

In sum, during the course of the late 1800's through the early 20th century, medicine gained virtually complete control of childbirth in U.S., beginning with the middle class and moving on to the poor and immigrant population. And it did this without any indication that it was capable of doing it well. Midwifery almost ceased to exist in this country, and for the first time in history, an entire society of women was attended in childbirth by men.

MEDICALIZED BIRTH

What did this medically attended birth look like, feel like, to the women who experienced it?

The standards for obstetrical intervention that gained acceptance in the 1920s and 30s remained in place through the 1970s, and shadows of those practices remain with us today. These practices can be traced back to a 1920 article in the *American Journal of Obstetrics and Gynecology*, "The Prophylactic Forceps Operation," by Joseph B. DeLee. DeLee's procedure for a routine, normal birth required sedating the woman through labor, and giving ether for the descent of the fetus. The baby was to be removed from the unconscious mother by forceps. An incision through the skin and muscle of the perineum, called an episiotomy, was to be done before the forceps were applied. Removal of the placenta was also to be obstetrically managed rather than spontaneous. Ergot or a derivative was to be injected to cause the uterus to clamp down and prevent postpartum hemorrhage.

Why were DeLee's procedures, rather than allowing the mother to push the baby out spontaneously, so widely accepted by the 1930s? On one level, we can answer this in terms of the needs of the still developing profession of obstetrics: the need for teaching material; the need to justify both the costs and the prestige of obstetrics by providing a special service that midwives and general practitioners had not provided; the need to routinize patients in a centralized facility. Consider, however, the medical rationale, the reasons doctors themselves gave. They thought that what they were doing was a reasonable response to the demands of labor. Just how did they understand labor, and what is this medical model of birth?

The use of forceps was to spare the baby's head, DeLee having famously compared labor to a baby's head being crushed in a door. The episiotomy was done to prevent tearing of the perineum, something that is almost inevitable with the use of forceps. Even without forceps use, however, U.S. physicians were finding tearing to be a problem, most likely owing to the use of the American-style delivery table, which required the supine position, with legs in stirrups (Haire, 1972). The clean cut of the episiotomy was held to be easier to repair than the jagged tear. DeLee further claimed that the stretching and tearing of the perineum resulted in such gynecological conditions as prolapsed uteri, tears in the vaginal wall, and sagging perineums. It wasn't until 1976 that an empirical study was done to determine the long-term effectiveness of episiotomies, and the results indicated that episiotomies caused rather than prevented these conditions (Brendsel, Peterson, and Mehl 1979). Episiotomies are still one of the most widely performed surgical procedure on women and every few years another study comes forth showing that they do not work (most recently, Hartmann et al, 2005). Most intriguingly perhaps, DeLee claimed that the episiotomy would restore "virginal conditions," making the mother "better than new." All through the 1970s obstetricians were heard to assure husbands, who were just then starting to routinely attend births, that they were sewing the woman up "good and tight."

For the baby, according to DeLee and his many followers, the labor was a dangerous, crushing threat, responsible for such conditions as epilepsy, cerebral palsy, "imbecility" and "idiocy," as well as being a direct cause of death. For the mother, birth was compared to falling on a pitchfork, driving the handle through her perineum. Using these analogies, DeLee was able to conclude that labor itself was pathological (DeLee 1920, 40).

The implication of the DeLee approach to birth for the mother is that she experienced the birth as an entirely medical event, not unlike any other surgical procedure. At the beginning of labor she was brought to the hospital and turned over to the hospital staff. The sedation most commonly used from the 1930s through the 1970s was "twilight sleep," a combination of morphine for pain relief in early labor, and then scopolamine, believed to be an amnesiac. A woman under twilight sleep can feel and respond to pain; the claim is only that she will not remember what happened. Women in twilight sleep therefore had to be restrained, or their uncontrolled thrashing could cause severe injuries, as the drugs left them in pain and disoriented. Obstetrical nursing texts offered warning pictures of women with battered faces who were improperly restrained and threw themselves out of bed.

The birth itself was not part of the mother's conscious experience, because she was made totally unconscious for the delivery. Such women required careful watching as they recovered from anesthesia. They were in no way competent to hold or even see their babies; it might be quite some time before they were told the birth was over (Guttmacher 1962). The babies themselves were born drugged and required careful medical attention. That drugged, comatose newborn was the source of the popular imagery of the doctor slapping the bottom of the dangling newborn, attempting to bring it around enough to breathe. It was several hours, or even days, before the mother and baby were "introduced."

While women were sometimes co-conspirators with doctors in the development of twilight sleep, so-called "painless" labors, and medicalization, other women fought this turn of events. When the DeLee approach developed in the 20s and 30s became dominant throughout the United States by the 1950s, a counter voice was raised, calling for a return to a more "natural" childbirth.

MAKING PAIN THE ISSUE

"Natural childbirth" is a slippery concept: one would be hard put to claim that anything people do is "natural." In the world of birth, "natural" is used for anything from a vaginal (as contrasted to a cesarean) birth, whether or not the woman was conscious, to a completely "nonmedicated" birth. "Prepared childbirth" is a more useful concept for viewing U.S.

hospital births; it has come to mean the use of breathing and/or relaxation techniques, and particularly, taking some "childbirth preparation course," perhaps six evenings, perhaps one or two days over a weekend, to learn about birth. Or perhaps, to be more accurate, to learn about the medical management of birth: Most of the preparation courses, many offered by the hospitals themselves, are designed to prepare women for the hospital experience they are expected to have.

And what is that experience? Largely it is understood in terms of pain: pain experienced and pain avoided. There are a number of reasons why pain became a central issue in hospitalized births. For one thing, birth in hospitals is almost certainly experienced as more painful than birth outside of hospitals. Before the pressures of the prepared-childbirth movement brought husbands or other companions into the labor room, laboring women were routinely left alone. Their only companionship might have been another laboring woman on the other side of a curtain. A nurse would stop in now and again, but for hour upon hour the woman lay alone, with no one to comfort her, hold her hand, rub her back, or just talk to her, and nothing to do to take her mind off her pain. Consider what a toothache feels like in the middle of the night, when you're all alone and just lying there, feeling it ache and watching the clock tick away hours.

Second, the physical management of birth made it more painful. Confinement to bed prolongs labor, and the comparatively inefficient contractions in the horizontal position may make it more painful. When a woman is upright, each contraction presses the baby down against her cervix, opening up the birth passage. When she is lying down, the weight of the baby presses on her spine, accomplishing nothing except to increase her discomfort.

Third, the mother's experience needed to be conceptualized as pain in order to justify medical control. Conceptualizing the mother's experience as work would have moved control to the mother. This was clearest in the medical management of the second stage of labor, pushing the baby out, in which the woman was so positioned as to make the experience as painful as possible and at the same time to minimize the value of her bearing-down efforts. In the lithotomy position, the baby must be moved (pushed or pulled) upward because of the curve of the birth canal. Doctors felt that this position gave them the most control, with total access to the woman's exposed genitals. But doctors' control came at the expense of mother's control. The lithotomy position rendered her totally unable to help herself, feeling like "a turtle on its back," or a "beached whale."

This is not to say that labor, even under optimal conditions, is not painful. It is. But there is a difference between experiencing pain and defining the entire situation only in terms of pain. Pain may be one of the sensations people experience in sexual activity, for example, but most do not take it as the key element in sex. Any particular stimulation or pressure produces many complex sensations, and pain may be part of what one feels. And birth does have much in common with orgasm: the hormone oxytocin is released; there are uterine contractions, nipple erection, and, under the best circumstances for birth, an orgasmic feeling (Gaskin 2003). But the lithotomy position, like the "missionary" position, put women flat on their backs and made attaining an orgasm—or any pleasurable feelings—a lot less likely.

WHAT HAPPENS AT HOME?

Midwifery focuses on pregnancy and birth as processes. Labor is *labor*, difficult *work*, but it is beautiful, normal, "natural" as midwives see it. They work to help women have birth experiences that are spiritual, beautiful, and worthwhile. Pain may be part of labor, risk may be part of giving birth, but they are not the central elements around which midwifery practice is built. When discussing what they're all about, the dominant theme for midwives is facilitating one of life's most meaningful events. Doctors, in contrast, with their risk-orientation, focus much more on the outcome: healthy baby, healthy mom.

To illustrate the differences in their philosophies, we will focus here on participants' views about the topic of home birth. (For an extended discussion of many more aspects of maternity care and birth attendants' discussions of their motivations and practice ideals, see Simonds, Rothman, and Norman 2007.) Home birth is, according to most studies, safer than hospital birth, but doctors in this country have continuously raised opposition to—and political leverage against—home birth.

The smear campaigns against home birth midwifery that U.S. doctors have orchestrated at various times in U.S. history have not, and do not, rely on data that show hospital birth to be safer than home birth, because such data are lacking. One study out of dozens recently showed a higher infant death rate in home births than in other settings (Pang et al. 2002), but critics of that study refute the claim because the authors did not clearly distinguish between intentional (planned) and unintentional home births (see, e.g., MANA press release 2003 and Vedam 2003). All other studies show superior outcomes in terms of maternal and infant morbidity for home births, and equivalent outcomes in terms of mortality (see, e.g., Goer 1999; Johnson and Daviss 2005; and Olsen 1997).

DIRECT-ENTRY MIDWIVES ON HOME BIRTH

Regardless of whether they first attend births at home or in hospitals, direct-entry midwives and midwifery students find that their experiences of home birth make them reconceptualize hospital birth negatively. Many do rotations in hospitals as part of their training, or have experience as labor and delivery nurses or as doulas. In one of the student focus group interviews, they sought to articulate the differences:

> ALLIE CORNELL: I've found that the difference between the home and hospital birth is much more profound in the States than in other places. And I've seen hospital births, like I was at [a public hospital in Atlanta] actually. It was my first

birth. And it was pretty—I mean, the midwives were wonderful, and I cried. It was a wonderful experience. … And then in Holland, I saw my first home birth, and was, of course, completely blown away with the difference that it was just a completely different world in terms of it being the woman's environment. The woman's in charge. The woman's the most comfortable she can possibly be. The midwife is the guest. But if you have a woman give birth in the hospital there [Holland], it's almost the same. It's not like you become a prisoner of the hospital who's completely given over all power. You're just—you're now in a slightly different setting. Your midwife is still your primary attendant. And you're still calling the shots. And you go home an hour or two after the birth. I mean, it wasn't this wholly different thing. … I still felt a difference, but I wondered how much of it was our way of doing hospital birth, rather than *just* the location.

PAULA DANIELS: Hmm. I've only seen two different births in two different hospitals. And I guess major things I noticed that disturbed me … [were] just watching how the focus was on the [EFM] machine … the nurses come in, look at the strip, and since I was a student nurse for one of them, she's like, "get the blood pressure"! So I'd get her vital signs and then I'd write 'em down, and the nurse left the room. I was like, this is really disturbing. First of all, she never even really looked at the woman. She looked at the machine. … I feel like, at least in this country, the hospital tends to take your power away. And your—any sense of self-confidence and any sense of—I mean, you're just completely vulnerable. … If it's a teaching hospital—there's people in and out you've never seen before, never will see again. Medical students catching your baby. It's just total craziness. And at home, in a home birth setting … it's your house and you've invited these people in to help you with your process, and it's *your* process.

RUTH RUSSELL: I want to say one other thing, which is about the actual birth of the baby and after that. That there is a *tremendous* difference in my experience. That at home, the baby's born, there's a respect for this sacred moment and time afterwards. And the family is seen as the—*the* unit—that's the whole focus, is the baby and those parents having their time. And that the midwife is monitoring quietly, but you know, doing what she needs to do to make sure that everything's okay, but that isn't the focus. Whereas in the hospital that I worked in, the baby was taken *right away* to the warmer, and the mother could only look from across the room at her baby. And that's the difference of night and day! That moment is taken away from her that she has worked so hard for.

These students contrasted hospital staffs professional indifference with the reverence and unobtrusiveness of midwifery. They depict hospital routines as routinizing, dehumanizing, and mundane—and as ultimately depriving women of real, true, wonderful birth experiences. The group agreed that hospital births don't have to be this way (as in Cornell's example of the hospital births she observed in the Netherlands), but that hospitals in the U.S. were unlikely ever to offer women the control over their births they could have at home.

Most obstetric and nurse-midwifery group practices (and most practices today are group practices) at best offer women the opportunity to meet all the providers who work together in the group. Meeting someone once or twice is not the same as knowing them. Knowing someone, midwives repeatedly say, means one is more likely to trust them and to feel safe with them. Home birth best exemplifies this ethic of "continuity of care." Home birth midwives describe presence through unobtrusiveness: there is something so forceful about not taking charge, and simply representing the values that can make someone else who believes in them too feel safe and protected. This is so different from medical paternalism. It is, truly about feeling connected with others while you feel most vulnerable, during what could be a potentially very isolating event.

Many home birth midwives (and advocates of home birth) feel that moving birth into an alien environment staffed primarily (or exclusively) by strangers exacerbates the very slow-downs and pathologies in labor that medicine seeks to "correct." We heard repeatedly how, especially for home birth midwives, taking part in hospital births means adapting to an institutionalized setting organized in ways they find philosophically alien. As Serena Davis said:

> Whether these protocols are always necessary or not—you have to fit into them. And sometimes when we see that some of the protocols are just absolutely ridiculous—I'm not going to—you know, I'm not going to say you have to *fight*. But, you know, because a lot of the people that are in the hospital are very territorial and they—sometimes they build up an attitude or a shield around themselves. … You don't have to do [that] at home, you know! One of the nice things about … having your baby at home is that you can labor how you want to, you can give birth how you want to. And what I mean by "how you want to" is basically what's the most effective for the mother. … Sometimes, when you're in the hospital, they don't want you to walk around, they don't want you to walk outside the bedroom. It's just a lot more rules, more regimens there. … In the hospital, they don't want you to deliver in any position: they want to be able to see, so they can manage. And that's what happens in hospitals: births are managed by machines, by people, by drugs; whereas at home, it's not being managed by anybody, you know, just the … the natural flow of the body.

Davis starts out by talking about how it's difficult for her in the hospital, but when she moves into discussing home birth, she shifts from talking about how she feels different at a home birth to talking about how the birthing woman ("you") experiences the birth.

Home birth midwives are especially identified with the women they work with, both in a personal idiosyncratic way (via the friendships that are formed) and in a kind of womanly solidarity based upon a shared view of birth. In hospitals, women may feel a connection with staff and staff may seek to connect with them, but everyone is subject to obeying institutional protocols. Even though most births follow the same general course of events, from contractions to pushing a baby out, home births are deroutinized. They are deroutinized mainly because they take place one at a time, but also because the over-riding philosophy, the general sensibility of everyone involved, is that births should not be routinized.

Home birth midwives emphasize that home birth is not "for everyone." They are care-ful not to speak in universals. They want every woman to at least have access to midwifery, but realize that deinstitutionalizing birth would be impossible given the entrenchment of obstetrics and the prevalence of medicalization.

Several home birth midwives we interviewed raised the humorous analogy of ordering a man to get an erection in a public setting to point out the absurdities of the ways in which birthing women are often bossed around and typically exposed in hospitals. Similarly, Ina May Gaskin (2003) describes an example used by midwife Lisa Goldstein in childbirth education classes to illustrate how difficult it can be to get one's body to perform under impersonal surveillance: "First she shows them a fifty-dollar bill. Then she places a medium-sized stainless-steel bowl on the floor. ... She then offers that bill to the first man who comes forward and pees in the bowl in front of everyone. In all the years she has repeated this routine, she has never handed over that fifty dollars to anyone" (174). Most midwives agree that hospitals can produce inhibitions in a way that one's own environment will not.

NURSE-MIDWIVES ON HOME BIRTH

Unlike the direct entry midwives, nurse-midwives begin their careers as nurses, and then have further education, based in hospitals, in midwifery and obstetrical care. Most nurse-midwives rarely receive training outside of hospitals, so home birth is something they first (and often only) imagine against a backdrop of hospital birth. Except for one group of nurse-midwives doing home birth we interviewed in New York, most of the nurse-midwives and nurse-midwifery students we interviewed intended, expected, or did practice in hospital settings. Most of them felt they couldn't imagine doing home births themselves (as midwives), because the level of responsibility they would have for the well-being of women and babies would be too daunting. They couldn't imagine birth as a situation for which they would not be responsible as *managers* for producing good outcomes. And they showed their fear of birth, which home birth midwives accept and view as integral but not central to, their work. Betsy Ettinger, for instance, recognized her uneasiness about home birth as a product of her training:

I think I have too much medicine and medical background in me to be comfortable in a home birth. Now, I was comfortable in a birthing center, but I had the safety net of a medical center across the street. And, I had some wonderful experiences in birthing centers—so beautiful—but I've had beautiful experiences in the hospital. And I guess—and maybe this is my rationale—but I think the birth experience can be a good experience anyplace.

Many nurse-midwives portray birth centers as an ideal compromise between the unknown perils that could happen and the level of constraint of the medical model. Birth centers are more convenient for midwives, too, because they tend to employ larger groups of midwives who can be on call less than they would be in a home birth practice. (However, because of malpractice insurance costs in the U.S., birth centers are risky business ventures.)

We also interviewed several nurse-midwives who were practicing, or had practiced, home birth midwifery. In their discussions of home birth they sounded no different from the direct-entry midwives. Nurse-midwives interviewed (by Rothman) in the 1970's talked about how doing home birth required a reconceptualization of birth; outside the medical context, the meaning of "progress" and the timetables used to assess it, would gradually relax until a paradigm shift had occurred, and risk was no longer the central structuring element of attending a woman in labor (see Rothman 1991).

OBSTETRICIANS ON HOME BIRTH

Most of the ten obstetricians we interviewed expressed an antipathy to home birth because they viewed birth as a potentially pathological series of obstacles, at best a "natural" process that could go wrong at any time and require correction via medical interventions that were not available outside of hospitals. Consider these responses to the question

"Have you ever seen a home birth?" and "What do you think about home birth?"

Harriet Murphy: I would have a heart attack if I had to observe a home birth. I would absolutely probably just wet my pants. I *never* would do a home birth. I would think that [only] an idiot would have a home delivery. ... I just can't understand why any reasonable person who loved their child would take a chance with having their child be born dead, which is what they're doing—even if it's a small chance. I have seen too many people go down the tubes in five minutes, and if you weren't in a hospital either the mother could be dead or the baby could be dead.

Lois Silverman: I think that nobody today should be laboring far from a room where they can have a c-section. The American College of OB-GYN recommendation is that you need—in an emergency, you need to have a c-section *done* in thirty minutes. And I think that anyone in labor ... *deserves* that level of care. ... I mean, you can be having a perfectly nat—normal labor at home, and you think you're just in hard labor, and your placenta abrupts from the strength of your contractions; it separates and you start hemorrhaging. Where are you? You're, like, not in the hospital! You don't have an IV. ... Your baby is most likely going to die, and you may not do so well afterwards yourself. I mean, I just don't think it's worth the risk.

Julie Elkmont: I don't believe in home births. ... It's risky. I know midwives do that. I don't particularly like that. I mean, what do you do when you are in trouble, and you're home, and things happen? There are patients that get in trouble at the very end, and now you're stuck at home and you're not in a hospital situation. I mean there's a lot of—there's a reason why moms aren't dying anymore. There's a reason why babies aren't dying anymore. ... We just don't have that anymore, because we have made a lot of changes. ... Why do you have to suffer when you are in labor? I guess if you get some kick out of it, or if you feel that you are a stronger woman. I think there are some patients, they feel that they are a better woman for it. It's like, okay, fine, if that's what makes you happy. ...

What do you do when somebody's bleeding, and you have no drugs to give that patient to help her stop bleeding and she is having a postpartum hemorrhage? What do you do? You're at home. You call an ambulance. You're wasting time. ... I have seen too many things happen. That's why I don't think it is necessarily good. But these stars, Hollywood stars, have their births at home, and have all these midwives, nothing bad—it's good that nothing bad has happened to them. Then everyone reads about it in the paper, and is like "oh, I want to be like so and so"!

Corrinne Wood-Daniels: Well, I do not support home deliveries. I think if a woman should choose not to have the benefit of medical intervention even when it clearly could save her life and the life of her baby, and if she makes that decision, then that is her choice. But she has to understand many of the life-threatening complications of obstetrics come with no warning.

These doctors equate home birth with the direst of consequences—life-threatening situations for babies and mothers, and they equate hospital birth with safety for babies and mothers. They see midwives and women who attempt home birth as misguided (even "idiots," as Murphy said or Elkmont implied when she talked about women imitating movie stars), irrationally choosing pain (Elkmont) or irresponsibly risking trouble that could spiral into irreparable emergency (all of them). Even when doctors say that women have the "right" to make this decision, closer attention reveals their frustration with what they see as poor decision-making (Elkmont and Wood-Daniels). Doctors may even frame the ideology of home birth as masochistic (Elkmont), or as a touchy-feely ruse, cheating women of care they deserve (Silverman).

Among the midwives and midwifery students we interviewed who worked outside of hospitals, few spoke about deaths or near-deaths they'd encountered as part of their work. None told of a death that would have been avoided had the mother been in a hospital. This could mean that midwives are reluctant to speak of such matters, but such situations are exceedingly rare, or presumably word would get out. Midwives are well aware of the attitude of the medical profession toward home birth and know that if something does go wrong; doctors and family members may well hold midwives and/or the women who choose them responsible.

Doctors' notion of risk inflates as a result of their interventive training and interventive experience as practitioners. They come to see their interventions as producing (good) results; they never imagine what situations might be like without viewing their (medical, interventive) actions as central. Midwives doing—and women having—home births know that risks exist; the difference is that they view these risks as acceptable, and ultimately preferable to the risks incurred by birthing in hospitals, which doctors do not acknowledge in the first place. Most of the doctors we interviewed did not seem aware that there was any other point of view on home birth but theirs—the story medicine tells about itself that it made birth safer for women and babies, and that home birth is a throwback to a dangerous past practice. This story simply is not true.

Doctors talked about how nice hospitals have become nowadays. Home, they think, can be approximated through cosmetic changes: nice furniture, fancy wood floors. Perhaps if environments are homelike enough, people feel more at home. But redecorating will not alter conventional power dynamics, as long as the precepts of obstetrical monitoring remain in place and the operating room is right down the hall from the LDR "suites." We don't mean to suggest that aesthetic improvements cannot improve people's experiences—they can—but they do not necessarily affect power differentials. They may, in fact, mask them.

Only three doctors we interviewed did not condemn home birth. Here are excerpts from two of their interviews:

> *Laurie Leland:* I do feel strongly that we need to … have access to things like an operating room if something went wrong. … You probably wouldn't find

me completely on the side of some lay midwives, or whatever. I don't want to jeopardize at all the health of the baby, and I realize that the health of the baby is more important than any—so the issue of trying to make it as natural a process as we can, but still having the benefits of—you know my experience in dealing—when the shit hits the fan on labor and delivery, it really hits the fan and you can't always predict who ... it's going to happen to. ... *Simonds:* Do you feel like home births are not safe? *Leland:* I don't know—that's—I feel sort of conflicted about that.

Fried: I'm a little uncomfortable with home birthing. You know, if someone's very low risk and has easy access to a hospital, I think it can be okay. ... I think it must be really *nice* to *not* be in a hospitalized medicalized setting. I think that that could be a real plus. *But,* having practiced high-risk obstetrics for so many years and seen such horrible disasters. ... It creates fear in me to think about it.

The differences between what Leland and Fried said about home birth and what the other doctors said was that these two recognized that home birth could be very appealing and different from hospital birth; they acknowledged ambivalence rather than taking a firm position on the issue; and they recognized that their ambivalence was empirically grounded and institutionally produced. Phyllis Fraser was the only doctor we interviewed who had observed a home birth. She said, "It was quite beautiful. ... It's not for everyone. But for those who want it, I think they should have the right to do it."

CONCLUSION

Inside the ideology of the medical model, undamaged babies are the end product of the birth process; to ensure a good product, ideally, one must be able to take total control over it should anything go awry. Medicalized thinkers (like Harper and many of the doctors) see access to and use of interventive techniques as providing them with the greatest amount of control they could possibly have, and they can only imagine the lack of such access and usage as inappropriate and dangerous. To reject the hospital, to question the medicalized formulation of the control issue, to them means inviting what they see as *unwarranted* risk. They simply cannot see outside the hospital box.

When we listened to many of the doctors talk about practicing obstetrics, we were reminded of other institutions that enjoy taken-for-granted supremacy and that can systematically produce negative, even violent effects that occur in such a way that they appear uninitiated by actors, because the institutions have ideological lives of its own. Routines and protocols become taken for granted and appear to need no justification or analysis. Militarism, for instance, comes to seem unauthored and inevitable (see, e.g., Enloe 1990, 2000), as do various forms of inequality (class-based, race-based, gender-based, sexual-identity-based, etc.) under capitalism. Milgram's (1974) experiments in which men and women thought they were administering electric shocks to others, Zimbardo's (1992) simulated prison, and actual "total institutions" like real prisons and mental hospitals (see Goffman 1961) show how easily, seemingly automatically, covert sadomasochistic dynamics are produced when hierarchical power structures become commonplace and taken for granted (see also Chancer 1992, and of course, Foucault 1973, 1977). Within such structures, people rarely question what's happening, and those who do tend to have the least power to effect change. Obstetrics is very much an example of this sort of sadomasochistic institution, even when the actual doctors are nice people with positive intentions. It has taken on a life of its own, as all institutions do. Its ideology and practices evidently do damage to people, but it cloaks itself in a scientific white coat and holds fast to its conceptions and methods. But obstetrics has changed in ways that mask its deleterious effects. Just as subtle or covert racism (or any "ism") may be more difficult to see and to combat, so it is with the sadomasochistic hegemony underlying medicalization.

A few doctors we interviewed could see outside the parameters in which they functioned, but they could only occasionally or murkily imagine a better way. And, for the most part, they felt that the changes that had occurred—wallpaper, hardwood floors, conscious women, the presence of significant others—showed that humanitarianism held sway and progress occurred progressively. So they inadvertently (rather than intentionally) tended to promote the reign of medical authority over women's bodies and pregnancy and birth experiences.

Midwives struggled continuously in their work to make compromises, to resist, or to avoid medicalizing women's pregnancies and birth experiences. Working in and outside of the system, they strove to honor the notion that birth is about facilitating women's growth, change, and self-realization, rather than managing risk, avoiding pain, and objectifying bodies.

DISCUSSION QUESTIONS

1. What are the ideologies that shape the medical model?
2. What are some of the very different meanings a pregnancy might have?
3. How is a nurse midwife's training different than that of a direct entry midwife?
4. What are the changes in hospital practice that women obstetricians recommend?
5. List some of the ways that obstetrical practice has increased risk and danger to mothers and babies in birth.

REFERENCES

Brack, Datha Clapper (1976). "Displaced: The Midwife by the Male Physician." *Women and Health* 1: 18–24.

Brendsel, Carol, Gail Peterson, and Lewis Mehl (1979). "Episiotomy: Facts, Fiction, Figures and Alternatives." In *Compulsory Hospitalization Or Freedom in Childbirth?* Leww Steward and David Stewart, eds. Marble Hill, MO: NAPSAC.

Bullough, Vern (1966). *The Development of Medicine as a Profession: The Contribution of the Medieval University to Modern Medicine.* New York: Karger.

Chancer, Lynn (1992). *Sadomasochism in Everyday Life: The Dynamics of Power and Powerlessness.* New Brunswick, NJ: Rutgers University Press.

Curtin, Sally C, and Lola Jean Kozak (1998). "Decline in U.S. Cesarean Delivery Rate Appears to Stall." *Birth* 25 (December): 259–262.

DeClercq, Eugene R., Ray Menacker, and Marian MacDorman et al. (2006). "Maternal Risk Profiles and the Primary Cesarean Rate on the United States, 1991—2002." *American Journal of Public Health* 96 (May): 867–72.

DeLee, Joseph B. (1920). "The Prophylactic Forceps Operation." *Journal of Obstetrics and Gynecology* 1: 34–44.

Donegan, Jane B. (1978). *Women and Men Midwives: Medicine, Morality and Misogyny in Early America.* Westport Conn: Greenwood Press.

Donnison, Jean (1977). *Midwives and Medical Men: A History of Inter-Professional Rivalries and Women's Rights.* New York: Schocken.

Dubos, Rene (1968). *Man, Medicine and Environment.* New York: New American Library.

Ehrenreich, Barbara, and Deirdre English (1973). *Witches, Midwives and Nurses: A History of Women Healers.* Old Westbury NY: Feminist Press.

Enloe, Cynthia (2000). *Maneuvers: The International Politics of Militarizing Women's Lives.* Berkeley, CA: University of California Press.

(1990). *Bananas, Beaches and Bases: Making Feminist Sense of International Politics.* Berkeley, CA: University of California Press.

Foucault, Michel (1977). *Discipline and Punish: The Birth of the Prison.* Alan Sheridan, tr. New York: Pantheon.

(1973). *The Birth of the Clinic: An Archaeology of Medical Perception.* A.M. Sheridan Smith, tr. New York: Vintage.

Gaskin, Ina May (2003). *Ina May's Guide to Childbirth.* New York: Bantam.

Goer, Henci (1999). *The Thinking Woman's Guide to a Better Birth.* New York: Berkley Publishing Group.

Goffman, Erving (1961). *Asylums: Essays on the Social Situation of Mental Patients and Other Inmates.* Garden City NY: Doubleday.

Guttmacher, Alan (1962). *Pregnancy and Birth: A Book for Expectant Parents.* New York: New American Library.

Haire, Doris (1972). *The Cultural Warping of Childbirth*. Seattle: International Childbirth Education Association.

Hamilton, Brady E., Joyce A. Martin, and Stephanie J. Ventura (2007). "Births: Preliminary Data for 2006." *National Vital Statistics Report* 56 (December 5). Hyattsville, MD: National Center for Health Statistics.

Hartmann K., M. Viswanathan, R. Palmieri, G. Gertlehner, J. Thorp, and K.N. Lohr (2005). "Outcomes of Routine Episiotomy: A Systematic *Review.*" *Journal of the American Medical Association* 293: 2141–8.

Johnson, K.C., and B.A. Daviss (2005). "Outcomes of Planned Home Births with Certified Professional Midwives: Large Prospective Study in North America," *British Medical Journal* 330(June 18): 1416–23.

Kobrin, Frances (1966). "The American Midwife Controversy: A Crisis in Professionalization." *Bulletin on the History of Medicine* 40: 350–363.

MANA press release (2003). "Obstetricians Use Dubious Method in Attempt to Discredit Home Birth." http://www.mana.org/WAHomeBirthStudy.html. (Feb. 11).

Martin, Joyce A., Brady E. Hamilton, Fay Menacker, Paul D. Sutton, and T.J. Mathews (2005). "Preliminary Births for 2004: Infant and Maternal Health." Hyattsville, MD: National Center for Health Statistics.

Martin, Joyce A., Brady E. Hamilton, Paul D. Sutton, Stephanie J. Ventura, Fay Menacker, and Martha L. Munson (2003). *National Vital Statistics Report, Births: Final Data 2002*. Hyattsville, MD: National Center for Health Statistics.

Milgram, Stanley (1974). *Obedience to Authority: An Experimental View*. New York: Harper & Row.

Olsen, O. (1997). "Meta-analysis of the Safety of Home Birth," *Birth* 24: 4–13.

Pang, J.W., J.D. Heffelfinger, G.J. Huang, T.J. Benedetti, and N.S. Weiss (2002). "Outcomes of Planned Home Birth in Washington State." *Obstetrics & Gynecology* 200 (August): 253–259.

Rothman, Barbara Katz 1(991 [1982]). *In Labor: Women and Power in the Birthplace*, revised edition. New York: WW Norton.

Simonds, Wendy, Barbara Katz Rothman, and Bari Meltzer Norman (2007). *Laboring On: Birth in Transition in the United States*. New York: Routledge.

Vedam, S. (2003). "Homebirth v. Hospital Birth: Questioning the Quality of Evidence for Safety." *Birth* 30 (1) (March): 57–63.

Zimbardo, Philip (1992). *Quiet Rage: The Stanford Prison Experiment*. Stanford, CA: Stanford University.

INTRODUCTION TO: INTIMATE FATHERHOOD

Exploring Attitudes

JAN CAMPBELL

In her article, Esther Dermott describes the meaning of the construction of fatherhood. She discusses the move from an emphasis on "fathers as financial providers to emotional nurturers" … and involves a consideration of many other factors in which fathering practices are accommodated, promoted or challenged. Dermott uses paradoxes to describe the current thinking about fatherhood by various institutions, social commentators, and culture.

Dermott offers five distinct ways in which fathers describe spending time with children. Additionally, she explores the idea that time and activities are important, but they are also significant for fulfilling the "ideas of good fatherhood." It was noted that fathers felt a good father-child relationship was possible as long as some time was given to it. She reported that fathers cited "caring about" as most significant and "caring for" as less significant, implying that they concentrated on activities that were "least work-like."

The article includes information on emotional closeness and its importance in communication and disclosure and tenets of verbal and physical expressions of feeling. Additionally, Dermott shows us the linkage between motherhood and fatherhood as described by the respondents. It depicts how gender was represented by the respondents as significant and how biology, specifically described as the biological imperative, also plays an important role. Added to this discussion was the idea of self-reflexivity—looking not just at how our relationships should be but also at a more creative way to construct them, producing a "narrative of the self."

INTIMATE FATHERHOOD

Exploring Attitudes

ESTHER DERMOTT

The setting is a seminar given by two senior male academics. The first speaker begins his talk by taking out of his pocket a bright blue child's watch, saying that he will rely on his son's dolphin watch to make sure that he doesn't go over time. The second speaker starts his talk more conventionally, mentioning his forthcoming book. After a comment from his co-presenter about his high rate of publication, he responds that any royalties will keep his children clothed and fed, adding that his productivity has gone down "since the kids arrived." The incident serves as an example of the extent to which fatherhood is now pervasive as a comfortable public identity.

It is the different, sometimes polarized, opinions about modern fatherhood, within and outside the academy that make it an intriguing topic of study. There is general agreement that the meaning of fatherhood has altered, but there is much less consensus over the extent of change and how modern fatherhood should be understood. Questions such as what involved fathering entails, whether the absence of fathers from families is problematic, whether breadwinning is an essential component of good fatherhood and if mothering and fathering are equal, all remain key areas of debate.

Thinking about fatherhood involves thinking about fatherhood, fathering and fathers. This means recognizing the construction of fatherhood at the level of meanings, especially the move from an emphasis on fathers as financial providers to emotional nurturers. It also involves a consideration of fathers' involvement, including the importance of pre-existing social categories as an influence on what fathers do and the extent to which various fathering practices are accommodated, promoted or challenged. Finally, it requires an acknowledgement of the diverse routes by which individual men become fathers.

A useful way of conceptualizing current thinking about fatherhood is as characterized by paradoxes. The first paradox (attention and absence) is that, at a time when levels of father absence from the family are unprecedented there is increasing attention paid to fathers and fatherhood by academics, policy makers and social commentators. The second paradox (creation and construction) is that while the tie between biological father and child is given primary status, there is also recognition that social fatherhood (without a biological link) is increasingly prevalent and that "good fathers" are made, not born. Thirdly, (culture and conduct) is the issue first raised by Ralph La Rossa in the 1980s, namely that while cultural representations of fatherhood suggest a new model of ever increasing involvement and a move towards equal parenthood, the conduct of fathers suggests much less change in men's activities and an obvious continuing division of labor between mothers and fathers. A better understanding of contemporary fatherhood requires moving beyond the binary positions suggested by these dominant paradoxes and towards a more nuanced approach.

FATHERING ACTIVITIES AND THE MEANING OF TIME

Fathers talked about spending time with children in five distinct ways. Firstly, there was direct "caring for" children. This fits reasonably well with understandings of unpaid work but is explicitly child related: this form of childcare consists of jobs, such as taking a child to school or finding their sports kit, which would not exist without children to require them. These tasks are referred to as "routine caring" because they occur at specific times in a day or during the week, and were seen as distinct activities in the mind of the interviewees. These are the kinds of tasks which are often absent in general lists of housework as they only apply to households where children are present.

Second, were mentions of day-to-day chores that merge into the general category of housework, such as cooking, tidying and cleaning. These are tasks which are not necessarily related to children, and are not prominent in most existing accounts of fatherhood. However, in households where children are present, their frequency, relative importance and status as an aspect of childcare mean that they have a qualitatively different, child-specific dimension. Cleaning may suddenly become an acknowledged task once a child is born compared to the relatively slovenly existence that can be enjoyed as an adult couple, or tidiness may disappear in the face of more explicit demands on time from children.

Third, is time spent together as a family: this "family time" covers a range of activities from going for a walk to visiting relatives to eating a meal together, but is marked out by the presence of both parents and, normally, all children. It also refers to a significant chunk of time, such as a Saturday, rather than what is actually happening, so that one period of "family time" can contain a number of different, unrelated activities.

Fourthly, there is being present at activities that involve a child—the often referred to "being there." This term can be taken to mean secondary activity without active engagement, for example, being in the home, absorbed in something else, but available for childcare if required either by a child or a partner. Here the term is also taken to mean devoting a period of time exclusively to participation in activity that is child related, such as a father attending a school parents' evening or going to sports day. Yet it can still be thought of as passive as it does not involve direct engagement between father and child: it is this criterion which marks out a fundamental difference between "being there" and the one-to-one, intensive time defined below.

Finally, there is intensive time. This would come under the heading "primary" engagement in the literature, in that during these periods children are the main focus for men. This can be a considerable portion of time, if a father and child spent time together in a specific activity, but more often occurs in shorter, more intense bursts. It is the importance of short periods that have some form of interaction but are not the object of a specific activity which are given especial attention here.

> I see my main activity in the evening, when I may or may not help with the bath or I may or may not help in various other ways, but most evenings—which is very important to me—at their different bedtimes, having read them a story (or maybe Felicity [wife] will read them a story), give them a cuddle and talk to them for five or ten minutes. (William)

To understand contemporary fatherhood requires not only an acknowledgement of the amount of time fathers spend in parenting activities and the kinds of activities to which time is dedicated, but also the significance they are given for fulfilling ideas of good fatherhood.

There is no formal contract laid down which specifies the number of hours that someone should spend engaged in the care of their own children. However, cultural expectations suggest that the heightened desire of fathers to develop an involved relationship with their children should correlate with a greater time commitment since time is considered the "ultimate parental resource."

Yet the total length of time spent in fathering work was not used by these men to calculate the quality of their fathering. They did not accept that time was a useful measurement of responsibility and commitment in relation to the nurturing of children, and comparing the length of time spent in individual childcare tasks did not help in assessing how important each was considered in contributing to the overall role of "good father." Further to this, fathers who spent relatively less time with their children did not express feelings of guilt about being worse fathers.

That involvement was not measured by these fathers simply in terms of time does not imply that it has no time component. The dominant impression is that a good father-child relationship is possible as long as some period of time is given over to it: time is not irrelevant to men's parenting. While some child centered tasks were merely listed, others were imbued with a deep significance for the fathering role. The aspects of parenting the fathers viewed as most significant indicated that "caring about" was more important than "caring for"; fathers concentrated on the aspects of parenting that were least "work-like" and downplayed the requirement to perform regular child maintenance activities. It was key that some amount of time was available and that times of special significance could be accommodated.

It was not the routine, transferable work of childcare that mattered nor the total amount of time spent with children that counted in these fathers' version of good fatherhood. The elements of parenthood most valued by these fathers were viewed as desirable because they develop and facilitate a strong parent-child relationship.

PERFORMING EMOTION

> If you listen to my father it was the classic, "oh when I was young I had to walk to get to school and had gruel to eat" and all the rest of it, it was a different set up. … I think he was as good a father as I was going to get, bearing in mind his background, but comparatively he is nothing like the father that I am to my children. (Vik)

> He [father] wasn't a fraction as involved with us as I have been with my children. He worked, he came home late from work, he went to sleep on the couch. (Jack)

A number of my interviewees made comments along these lines—that their fathering practices were both different and better to those they had experienced as children. More interesting, is what is included as justification for this upward trajectory, with comparisons acting as a foil to draw out the facets regarded as most significant to the men's concept of "good fathering." The men's fathers were typically characterized as failing to epitomize a more "modern" form of fatherhood and it was having an emotional bond between father and child that provided the contrast. It is the demonstration of emotion, through "openness," that is seen as the key in both fostering and demonstrating a good relationship between father and child. A "close" relationship constituting a positive model for their fathering was defined largely in terms of the recognition and expression of emotion. When mentions of specific activities were made they were used as a way of illustrating the existence, or non-existence, of this highly prized relationship.

Interviewees repeatedly contrasted the emotional remoteness of their own fathers to the closeness for which they were aiming.

I didn't want to be like my own dad. No, he's a nice guy and everything but he's a little bit distant with small children. He's a kind of intellectual, kind of academic guy and if people can't talk to him in long sentences with lots of subordinate clauses he doesn't tend to be that interested in them. So that excludes, obviously, children. I didn't want to be like that, I wanted to try and relate to kids on their own level. (Phil)

My father was very remote to me when I was very little ... [and] when I was starting to get stroppy [as a teenager]. I suppose, I was just, not wanting to be like that. (Simon)

I would say that he was close to me, but not in the way of showing emotions or talking about things, or like necessarily being very open about things. And so, I suppose, I always aspired to try to be more open with my children. I mean I'm not saying he was uninvolved or didn't care but I would have, well, I wanted to be really involved in what they do. (Gareth)

Gareth's statement does not present any specific problems in the relationship he experienced with his father, nor does he profess any negative feelings towards him. In fact, in this extract he uses a number of extremely positive terms to describe his father—he was very dedicated to his family, close to him, involved and caring—yet overall his father is still categorized as "quite distant." It seems contradictory to use the antonyms "distant" and "close" to describe his father in consecutive sentences but this ambiguity occurs because he is categorical in stating his father did feel emotion towards him but did not make him aware of this: a central plank in fulfilling the idea of being "really involved" with his own children means being open with them on an emotional level.

Emotional closeness is positive because emotional distance in today's society is viewed as negative. In this context, emotional involvement has been seen as crucial to fulfilling the idea of being a "good father" and emotional distance one expression of bad fatherhood. "Emotional" is though a shorthand term that requires more examination and positing simply an "emotional connection" as the basis of a new kind of fatherhood is a vague conclusion. There is a distinct difference between saying that a father has an emotional relationship with his child (which is not specific to contemporary fatherhood) and saying that closeness and openness are the basis of good fatherhood (which does seem to be a central component to nurturing fatherhood). On the whole, the existence of some kind of an emotional connection between father and child, which is regarded as absolutely necessary, is assumed to be present. It is the demonstration of emotion, through "openness," that is seen as key in both fostering and demonstrating a good relationship between father and child. The fatherhood which the interviewees reject is the image of the father who is reticent about expressing his feelings and is one step removed from the experiences and emotions of his child. Despite various positive qualities, the men's fathers are frequently characterized as failing in this way to epitomize a more "modern" fatherhood. These men are aiming for a fatherhood which is based upon both the verbal and physical expression of feeling. This "good" relationship with children places great emphasis on the importance of disclosure and was based on the ability of parents and children to communicate: talking, listening and understanding.

LINKING MOTHERHOOD AND FATHERHOOD

The prospect of a new fatherhood, which revises men's parental importance as fathers who make a greater contribution to childcare, could provide a challenge to the status of mothers and might be welcomed as a route to greater equality between men and women. Men becoming more like women with regard to parenthood could provide the other half of the transformation in gender roles, to balance women's growing similarity to men in terms of participation in paid work.

Alternatively, it has been suggested that mothers may resent the intrusion of men into their arena of expertise and therefore seek to limit fathers' parental contribution. It is argued that fathers can only respond to the options presented to them by mothers whereas women's preferences over the organization of parenting can be asserted.

Mothers were conspicuously present in fathers' accounts of their everyday lives and the men often presented a strong sense of partnership in their depictions of parenting. The argument that in order to understand either mothering or fathering they must be looked at in relation to each other makes particular sense in the light of interviews in which differences of opinion, relative levels of expertise, role distinctions and negotiations were openly on display.

When asked directly about differences between mothering and fathering, men's responses varied, including both absolute denials of any distinction and strong opinions that very real differences did exist. One group of fathers were adamant that it was all "just parenting,"

> This is quite naive but I suppose I don't really feel that there should be differences between mothering and fathering, I think there is parenting. (Jim)

Others were certain that gender was significant.

> Yes, in the sense that what Ruth [wife] does, she does almost naturally without thinking, she's very good at [it]. ... The kids need a mother more than they need a father. ... More people are like that than otherwise. ... I think [with] most of my friends that are parents the mother is more important than the father. (George)

[The] shift in some of the gendered assumptions surrounding parenthood accompanied by a recognition of ongoing differences perhaps explains why the majority of fathers were either circumspect or uncertain:

> Broadly speaking, yeah, I see it as parenting. Although, there are definitely, there are different things that we give to the children. Well, I don't know how much of it is personality and how much of it is, you know, gender, I don't know. Ermm. I don't think I can answer actually. (Tony)

> I think she [wife] sees there are differences between men and women, which probably I think there are as well. But if you're just talking about how people relate to one another then I don't really see different roles for the parents. I mean she has some things that she does, that are more to her personality rather than because she is a mother or, it's difficult to unscramble those things. (Gareth)

These interviewees wanted to maintain that, while there may be an underlying difference between men and women as parents, this does not undermine the fundamental equality of fathers and mothers. While mothers may be seen as having closer emotional ties with children and doing more in terms of practical childcare, men still need to be considered as parental peers.

A better understanding of these, somewhat confusing, accounts is possible once the rationale behind what the fathers said is explored; that is, how their views on the similarities and differences between fathers and mothers were justified. When fathers acknowledged some kind of distinction between mothers and fathers, they referred to biology, personal preference, and the influence of social forces in order to explain differences in levels of everyday engagement in childcare and orientations to children between mothers and fathers.

BIOLOGY AS TRUMPS

The most frequently voiced reason to explain the contrast between mothering and fathering was the existence of a biological imperative towards a particular division of labor. Among the fathers I interviewed, Hugh epitomized this viewpoint.

> I think that the way which people bring up their children is entirely up to them and I have no views, I really genuinely have no views as to whether it is better or worse. I am a traditionalist in the sense of what I, we, have done for ourselves. I also believe there is a strong evolutionary impulse to do what we have done.

While Hugh uses the idea of evolution—a primordial drive—other respondents were more specific in defining the distinction between fathers and mothers as resulting from the early period of child development, due to women's role in childbirth and breastfeeding and a concomitant psychological attachment.

> The mother is really the point of contact with the child, particularly in the first nine months, a year say. The father really has pretty limited input … particularly if she [the mother] is breastfeeding. I mean you can change the odd nappy and things like that, give your wife a bit of respite, particularly if the child is difficult … but there is a pretty limited amount that you can do. (Bill)

> Obviously fathering and mothering are not the same and clearly at different stages of the child's development they are not the same. I don't think I, I can't be as close to a small child as a mother is, it's very obvious for her, in times of deep distress it will be the mother that they ask for. (Michael)

Opinions of this kind resonate with the majority view that it is women who should stay at home when children are young. A particular, unique maternal bond is invoked and used to illustrate the "naturalness" of a division of labor between provider and nurturer. This is unsurprising given that comparisons with the natural world are commonly invoked at the popular level to justify dominant practices. However, although the move from biological fact through psychology to social prescription is strong, it can be problematized. Two examples from the interviewees illustrate this point. The way in which biology is manipulated into the realm of the social is perhaps best indicated by the comments of George. As quoted above, George believed that in the lives of his children, his wife was a more important figure than he was and he went on to locate the source of this difference as originating in "the fact of giving birth." Employing a similar turn of phrase to a number of other interviewees, the importance of mothers was grounded in the act of childbirth which engendered, in his view, a special connection. Yet, this was a rather surprising pronouncement from George, given that his wife had not given birth to their two adopted children. When presented with this apparent contradiction George insisted that, nevertheless, there was a singular bond between his wife and their adopted children, grounded in the biological fact of motherhood. Although George claimed that it is giving birth which leads to a distinctive mother-child connection, he in fact articulates the way in which women as potential mothers are considered to have an intrinsic maternalism which is triggered by the mere presence of children. This illustrates the way in which biology can refer to specific biological processes such as gestation and childbirth as well as chosen practices that are specific to one sex such as breastfeeding; but there is space too for biological associations to be made which draw on more general allusions to womanhood and, through their absence, to manhood. It is also noteworthy that some fathers who mentioned biological differences were dismissive of the impact of biology and early parenting practices on the forms of parenting provided by mothers and fathers in the long term.

With the exception of the first year in the child's life I don't think I do see much distinction really. There are distinctions in the first twelve months.

Derek acknowledged that in the early period of a child's life the roles of mother and father were not the same, but felt that this was a clearly demarcated stage, one that did not have later repercussions. In contrast Bill used the initial phase of intense mother-child activity as the rationale for his view that "the mothering role, is, the traditional mother." The biological appears definitive and so can be presented as responsible for the origins of difference, but as Derek's comment indicates it is still open to interpretation.

SELF-REFLEXIVITY

Proponents of reflexive modernity, such as Giddens and Beck, point to reflexivity as central to the "project of the self," suggesting that in contemporary society individualized responses to circumstances are foregrounded. It is this emphasis on self-reflexivity which provides a backdrop for the emergence of a transformed intimacy around the "pure relationship" based around the ideals of autonomy and democracy. Older traditions no longer hold weight and individuals instead get to produce their own guidelines for living. An increased range of social possibilities means that life-style options have to be negotiated and re-negotiated, producing a "narrative of the self." In terms of personal life, a diminishing of certainties around how relationships *should* operate is associated with the requirement to be more creative in how we think about ourselves and how we construct our relation-ships. The dynamics of contemporary life mean that individuals increasingly encounter challenges to the idea that personal life is experienced as distinctly mapped life stages and this disrupts previous understandings of "the family." This results in a breakdown in the uniformity of social categories (such as "father").

I would argue that existing data shows that much of the "thinking about" fatherhood results in the adoption of familiar patterns of action rather than radical change. While some contexts for fathering do prompt critical reflection that can be properly termed self-reflexivity, often the thinking that goes on does not present a challenge to existing modes of behavior.

The move from non-father to father does not itself entail self-reflexivity, although it is easy to see how this association occurs, since becoming a father means acquiring a new social status and often does involve "thinking about" a whole range of behaviors and identities. Fathers speak about evaluating the meaning of relationships with family members and friends; they weigh up competing demands for their time in a new light; and they document changes in themselves that are attributed to their new identity. These are evidenced by judgments, for example, about with whom to spend leisure time and the pros and cons of moving house or taking on a new job opportunity. The presence of a child means that different decisions are taken about a whole range of issues and becoming a father is also the catalyst for awareness about, previously unthought of, new possibilities. Deciphering the extent to which individuals are reflexive about their beliefs and behaviors is difficult when relying on interview data since, by their nature, interviews encourage participants to reflect on their personal circumstances and therefore tend to emphasize reflexivity, but it is clear from the fathers' accounts that the transition to parenthood is often associated with rethinking relationships, priorities and men's sense of self. However, significantly, these reflections do not necessarily challenge the status quo. The shock of the new is more likely to result in individuals seeking out commonly available patterns of fathering behavior rather than creating fresh models. The movement from non-parent to parent, although it prompts a renegotiation of the way in which day-to-day life is organized, is not necessarily about reflexivity in its true sense, because this alteration in status is a recognized rite of passage which is associated with well defined modes of behavior. It may be of interest to explore when "thinking about" something occurs, but this can be categorized as reflexivity only in a weak, non-transformative form. Men may reflect on their fatherhood as a significant point of transition, but this does not mean that there is critical reflection on the concept of fatherhood.

Possibilities for critical reflection occur when men are parenting in allegedly "fragile" situations, as these more tenuous positions can permit the reformulation of the aims and practices of fatherhood. Genuine reflexivity is a feature of some non-resident fathers' parenting since, if they are to have a meaningful relationship with their children it often means adjusting their view of fathering. Likewise the negotiation that is required in becoming a gay father and doing fatherhood, means that these men are more likely to think critically about the meaning and practice of contemporary fatherhood.

DISCUSSION QUESTIONS

1. Why does Dermott say that contemporary fatherhood is characterized by paradoxes?
2. Fathers are classified as spending time with their children in five different ways. Think of specific activities that could fit into each of the five categories.
3. Why is emotion considered so important for being a good father?
4. Do you agree with Jim that mothers and fathers are all "just parents"?
5. What does Dermott mean by "critical reflexivity"? Why does she suggest that it is more likely to occur when fatherhood is "fragile"?

INTRODUCTION TO: THE TRANSFORMATION OF THE LESBIAN/GAY MOVEMENT

JAN CAMPBELL

Elizabeth Armstrong begins her chronology of events in the lesbian/gay movement by relating the significance of the Lesbian/Gay/Bisexual/Transgender Freedom Day Parade and Celebration held since 1970 in San Francisco, the birthplace of the national movement. The gay identity movement had its origin in the early 1970s, and Armstrong shows us the evolution of this identity and the vast changes that occurred in this social movement.

This writing demonstrates how important the ideas of inclusion and diversity were to the understanding of what took place in the early years in the metamorphosis of the movement. She maintains that the movement was framed in the idea that gay/lesbian/bisexual/transgender issues revolved around the fact that differences ("we are different from straight people") were also defined paradoxically as points of similarity ("we must all be the same") to the point that there is diversity within the community ("as individuals, we are also different from one another"). This focuses on the unified but diverse movement that was and is exemplified by the symbolism of the parade.

From this early beginning, change occurred with various types of interest groups and organizations, albeit some very diverse but also complementary, which developed identities to influence this social movement, thus effecting social and political change.

THE TRANSFORMATION OF THE LESBIAN/GAY MOVEMENT

ELIZABETH A. ARMSTRONG

very year in San Francisco, the last Sunday in June is devoted to the Lesbian/Gay/
Bisexual/Transgender Freedom Day Parade and Celebration. The parade brings
several hundred thousand people into the streets to participate in a collective
contemplation of contemporary lesbian and gay life. It is impossible to absorb the entire
spectacle. Parade contingents represent the diversity of lesbian and gay organizations and
display myriad variations on lesbian and gay identity. Onlookers read the banners with
organization names and the signs that designate individual identities. As the contingents
pass, people's comments range from amusement to erotic appreciation, from deep respect
to downright disgust. The community relishes the spectacle—an enacted, moving list—a
literal field of organizations and identities. The parade's public display of identity is powerful although, of course, ephemeral. But the organizations that participate in the parade are
not so fleeting. Most are permanent. This is an annual celebration of the organizational
infrastructure that grounds the life of San Francisco's lesbian/gay/bisexual/transgender
communities.

Neither the parade nor the organizations in it existed before 1970. Thus, the parade
reflects the proliferation and diversification of lesbian/gay organizations in the last thirty
years. Since 1950, such organizations in San Francisco have evolved from a tiny underground bar subculture of uncertain legality into a sprawling, interlocking set of visible
organizations that influence virtually every aspect of life in the city. From 1964 to 1994

the number of nonprofit homosexual organizations in San Francisco increased from 6 to 276.[1]

This book examines this evolution in gay life, gay organizations, and gay identity. The story of this evolution is not a tale of smooth, gradual development. Instead, it occurred in two historic ruptures. Throughout the 1950s and 1960s, public homosexual organizations were limited to a tiny number of organizations that thought of themselves as "homophile." Homophile organizations modeled themselves on interest group politics and hoped to improve life for homosexuals by educating the mainstream public. They had names that conveyed little explicit information about sexual identity, such as the Society for Individual Rights, the Daughters of Bilitis, and the Mattachine Society.

The first rupture occurred in 1969, when gay liberation made its dramatic appearance. Gay liberation defined itself in opposition to the existing homophile project. Like other parts of the New Left, gay liberation was complex and contradictory. The most radical strand of gay liberation, which I refer to as "gay power," sought a total transformation of society.[2] Sexual liberation was defined as merely one aspect of a broader social transformation. Building gay identity was seen as a step toward eliminating social categories altogether.

The second rupture, which occurred in the early 1970s, was less dramatic but even more significant. At that point, affirming gay identity and celebrating diversity replaced societal transformation as goals, marking the origins of a gay identity movement. This shift in logic sparked the rapid proliferation of a vast diversity of new gay organizations. These new organizations had more specific titles, reflecting a continuously unfolding variety of new identities and subidentities, such as Affirmation Gay/Lesbian Mormons Gay Asian Pacific Alliance, Straights for Gay Rights, and Gay American Indians.[3] Organization names now included elaborate identity information and represented specialized subidentities. This turn toward identity building was accompanied by rapid political consolidation and the explosive growth of a commercial sub-culture oriented around sex. For the first time, gay organizations agreed upon a national gay rights agenda and moved aggressively to pursue common goals in the political arena.

These vast changes in the gay community present a fascinating puzzle for those wishing to understand the social forces that hold social movements together. In the lesbian/gay movement, which scholars have referred to as the "quintessential identity movement," we find a paradox.[4] Contrary to the assumptions and expectations of many experts on social movements, the focus on identity building and identity elaboration has not proved to be paralyzing or divisive for the gay movement. Paradoxically, the unity and diversity of the gay community seem inextricably interconnected. Therefore, by looking closely at this "quintessential" identity movement we can better understand a phenomenon that is common to many contemporary social movements.

In this book, I argue that the key to understanding the paradox of gay identity lies in its historical origins. The ability of the gay movement to balance commitment to a group identity with the protection of individual differences was built into the movement as it crystallized in the early 1970s. The movement would not have coalesced when and as it did without the development of homophile politics before 1969, the cultural innovations made available by the New Left, the sudden decline of the New Left in the early 1970s and the efforts of activists in the early 1970s to ensure that the gay movement survive. Each of these processes contributed in a crucial way to the movement that formed in the early 1970s. In isolation, these processes would have been insufficient. Only because they all happened in sequence did they lead to the forming of a gay identity movement.

Homophile organizing in the 1950s and 1960s began the process of transforming homosexual identity from a private group consciousness into a public collective identity. It established the legitimacy of creating public organizations of homosexuals and the notion that homosexuals were a group deserving rights that could be won by engaging in interest group politics. But homophile politics could not have generated the visible public identity needed for truly effective use of interest group politics, nor could it have justified a proliferation and diversification of organizations. The encounter between established homophile organizing and the New Left produced gay liberation and provided homosexual activists with the cultural tools that made "coming out" possible. The decline of the New Left reduced the plausibility of revolutionary socialist ideas and cleared the way for an identity-focused "gay pride" movement.

By defining the primary goal of gay politics as the expansion of the range of ways to express gay identity, the gay movement was able to balance interest group and identity politics. This way of understanding the goal of gay politics highlighted the most individualistic aspects of identity politics. Other movements understood identity politics as endorsing the creation of communities of similarity. In contrast, the gay movement focused on freedom of individual expression, making it hypocritical to exclude any form of gay political expression. Gay interest group politics—pursuing gay rights—was defined as one possible way to express gay identity. Activists were thus able to reframe a potential liability as an advantage, redefining the community's diversity as strength. "Difference" was defined, paradoxically, as a point of similarity. Gays and lesbians were all individuals in search of freedom of expression. Instead of extrapolating from "what we share is that we are all different from straight people" to the notion that "we must all be the same," the gay identity movement acknowledged, "yes, together we are different from straight people, but as individuals we are also different from one other." Individualism, which one would expect to hamper collective action, in this case structured and motivated it.

The vision of a unified but diverse movement was further reinforced by the discovery that a common, well-understood kind of cultural event, a parade, provided experiential evidence for the claim that unity and diversity were not in contradiction. Lesbian/gay freedom day parades provided an articulated structure linking, gay organizations while allowing an unfettered display of diversity. Unlike a march, which requires agreement on a set of political demands, a parade needs only the willingness of participants to be associated with each other.

This book tells the story of how, in the early 1970s, a tiny group of gay activists created a new understanding of same-gender sexual experience that would have far-reaching implications. This model of identity influenced the ways people all around the country and the globe make sense of same-gender sexual desires, practices, and relationships. It enabled the spectacular cultural, political, organizational, and commercial successes of the gay movement in the 1970s and 1980s. The movement was culturally generative; its very logic challenged members to produce more variants of gay identity. The new framework shaped what was possible and what was not possible for the gay movement to accomplish. Movement claims to universality and diversity made it difficult for those excluded to identify the ways the movement reflected the particular experiences of a cohort of white, middle-class American men. The gay identity movement enabled an impressive gay response to the AIDS epidemic, which led to the emergence of a competing set of AIDS organizations. Internal contradictions embedded in the movement at the moment of founding continue to shape debates in gay politics today and provide the fissures that may lead to the possible demise or transformation of the movement.

I focus on San Francisco because it, along with a few other major urban centers in the United States, served as the birthplace of what has become a national (and even international) lesbian/gay movement. The frameworks forged in these core cities diffused to smaller cities and towns around the country. Evidence of this diffusion can be seen in the proliferation of freedom day parades, the ubiquity of the language of coming out, and the spread of gay rights politics. Those who have studied lesbian and gay life in smaller towns might argue that the assumptions of the urban-centered gay movement do not describe gay life outside of big cities. This lack of fit does not negate the reality that, in the early 1970s, a hegemonic understanding of same gender sexual experience crystallized in a few urban centers in the United States and that others, even those whose experience it describes less well, have now to contend with it.[5] The chapter proceeds by outlining a cultural institutional approach to social movements, followed by a description of how lesbian/gay San Francisco changed over time, and concludes with an overview of the arguments presented in the book.

DESCRIBING THE LESBIAN/GAY FIELD

Lesbian/gay organizations in San Francisco proliferated over time. Activists founded the first nonprofit homosexual organizations in the 1950s. Organizations accumulated slowly in the 1950s and 1960s, accelerated in the 1970s, exploded in the 1980s, and declined slightly in the late 1980s and early 1990s (see figure 1.1).[6] However, this simple quantitative story does not capture the complexity of changes over time. Close analysis revealed dramatic change in the types of organizations created at different moments in the development of the field.

Public homosexual organizations founded before 1969 were shaped by an interest group political logic (see table 1.1).[7] Activists at the time referred to their organizations as "homophile organizations." Between 1969 and 1971 new organizations saw themselves as participating in the gay liberation movement. Gay liberation organizations were torn between a redistributive political logic and an identity political logic. Beginning around 1970, new organizations began to clearly reflect an identity political logic.

Figure 1.2 shows the changing representation of these organizations over time. In the 1950s and 1960s, homophile organizations were the only public homosexual organizations. The tiny numbers and beleaguered state of organizing suggest that the field at this

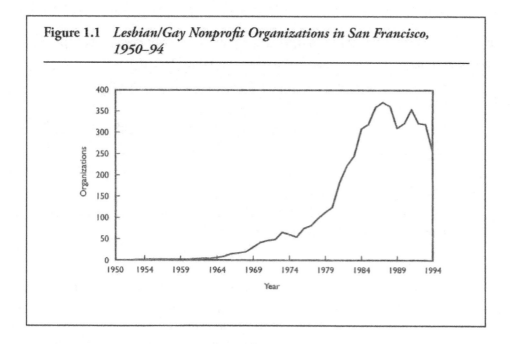

Figure 1.1 *Lesbian/Gay Nonprofit Organizations in San Francisco, 1950–94*

time was emerging, rather than fully formed. In the years 1970 and 1971, homophile, gay liberation, and gay identity organizations were all founded, with no one kind achieving numerical dominance, suggesting instability and competition among political logics. In 1971 and 1972 gay identity organizations began to outnumber homophile and gay liberation organizations. Gay identity organizations dominated after 1972, while other kinds of organizations fell by the wayside. The proliferation of gay identity organizations beginning in the early 1970s reflected a crystallization of the field around an identity political logic.

To understand the meaning of this transformation, it is necessary to understand the political logics shaping the gay movement and how these three logics were reflected in the various kinds of gay organizations. Table 1.2 summarizes these distinct political logics. and organizations that did not fall into any of the categories (5).

Interest group politics assumes that American society is composed of intersecting constituencies, each of which has a fair opportunity to influence policy according to its interests.[8] Problems arise but are corrected through reform when a group builds a unified voice and a voting bloc and is thus able to effect policy change. Discrimination against groups is targeted through advocating for rights. Change should and can be effectively achieved by using the channels made available in a democratic society, including lobbying and influencing electoral outcomes. With a focus on influencing elite groups, interest group organizations frequently locate in the nation's capital and direct attention toward building a national movement. Interest group organizations tend to be formally structured and bureaucratic. Their legitimacy increases with the size and unity of their constituency, so interest group politics tends to produce large single-issue organizations, each of which at-

Table 1.1 *Homophile, Gay Liberation, Gay Identity, and Other Lesbian/ Gay Organizations Founded in San Francisco, by Time Period*

Year	Homophile	Gay Liberation	Gay Identity	Other*	Total
1953–68	15 (71)	0 (0)	0 (0)	6 (29)	21
1969–71	2 (6)	12 (33)	12(33)	i o pa)	36
1972–94	0 (0)	11 (1)	859 (95)	31 (4)	901
Total	17 (2)	23 (2)	871 (91)	47 (5)	958

Note Percentages are in parentheses.

* "Other" organizations include motorcycle clubs (29), queer organizations (13), and organizations that did not fall into any of the categories (5).

tempts to monopolize a particular cause (e.g., the American Association of Retired Persons [AARP] and the National Rifle Association [NRA]). Multiple organizations representing the same constituency tend to see each other as competitors.

Typically, when we think about social movements, we think about politics organized around a logic of redistribution. Based on a Marxist analysis of society, a redistributive model sees structural inequality, particularly economic inequality, as the underlying problem that social movements must address. From an interest group perspective, society is seen as basically just, although in need of reform. Within a redistributive model, society is seen as exploitative. The goal of political change is to transform the structure of society in ways that lessen material injustice. Elite groups are seen as controlling economic and political rules, with the implication that meaningful change must usually be initiated through noninstitutionalized channels. This, movements based on a redistributive politics typically engage in marches, rallies, demonstrations, boycotts, and strikes. Social movement organizations tend to be less formally structured, less bureaucratic, and more ephemeral than interest group organizations. While unity within the interest group model is conveyed by the size and strength of large single-issue organizations, solidarity within mass movements

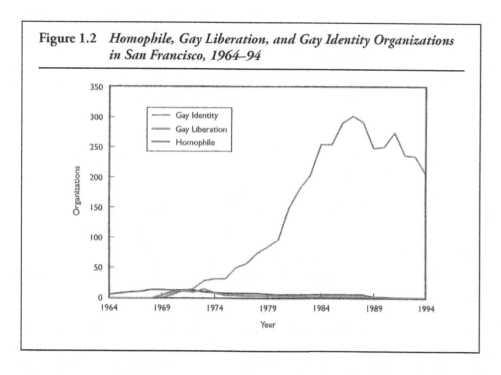

Figure 1.2 *Homophile, Gay Liberation, and Gay Identity Organizations in San Francisco, 1964–94*

tends to be measured by the size, frequency, and complexity of the events movements can sustain. Participation is organized around ideology or structural position, not around identity. The difference between mobilizing participants based on structural position rather than identity is subtle but important. Those mobilized around structural position are organized through criticizing the system for relegating them to a particular category, while organizing in behalf of identity is about affirming and solidifying the category.

Identity politics rejects both the notion that society is basically just but in need of reform and the idea that society is exploitative and in need of structural overhaul. In the identity model, the fundamental problem with society is alienation.[9] People are estranged from society and from themselves. They lack sources of meaning and are blocked from expressing themselves in an authentic manner. The goal of political change is thus to reduce alienation by making society more connected, meaningful, and authentic. This quest for authenticity may involve the creation and affirmation of collective identities. In his investigation of the New Left, Doug Rossinow argues that "individuals define their politics along lines of race, gender, ethnicity, and sexual identity, in part to make themselves feel rooted, real, solid."[10] The affirmation of previously marginalized or stigmatized identities is seen as creating spaces for people to express themselves. Within this framework, according to Kauffman, "identity itself—its elaboration, expression, or affirmation—is and should be a fundamental focus of political work."[11] While interest group politics suggests lobbying for legislative change and redistributive politics implies mass demonstration, identity politics suggests that creating and expressing alternative selves and alternative communities is the way to achieve change. Change happens from the bottom up, through the creation of

Table 1.2 Interest Group, Redistributive, and Identity Political Logics

	Interest Group	Redistributive	Identity
Problem	discrimination	structural inequality	alienation
Goal	reform; rights	societal transformation	authenticity, broadened range of expression
Strategy	lobbying, influencing elections	mass movement (demonstrations, boycotts, strikes)	prefigurative politics
Organizations	few, large, professional, bureaucratic	ephemeral social movement organizations	many, small, informal, diverse, egalitarian
Identity seen as	means to end	means to end	end in itself

the desired society in miniature. Wini Breines referred to this feature of the New Left as "prefigurative politics"; movement communities are supposed to "prefigure" the ideal society.[12] The transformation of individuals is central, as it is believed that, as Pamela Allen puts it, "a human politics will not grow from people who fear honest human relationships but through ones who are willing to share of their total selves."[13]

Differences in the logics guiding the movement were reflected in differences among the organizations constituting the movement at each point in time (see table 1.3). The logic organizing the field shaped the goals, strategies, size, formality, display of identity, and degree of psychological focus of the organizations produced. In addition, political logic also shaped relationships among organizations, the total numbers of organizations produced, and the likelihood of organizations being similar to or different from each other.

THE CRYSTALLIZATION OF A GAY IDENTITY MOVEMENT, 1971–1973

Between the hard conservatives and the intolerant radicals, young Gays are finding the middle ground productive. From coast to coast, they are building new organizations modeled after New York's highly successful and active Gay Activists Alliance. The formula: just enough structure and planning to have a sound foundation but not so much that action is impossible. Also, most new groups are limiting their activity to gay-oriented issues, rather than tackling all the world's ills at once. It seems to be a formula that can win the wide spread support that the GLF's were never able to get.

The Advocate *(Los Angeles gay newspaper), editorial, September 29, 1971*

Chapter 4 explained how gay organizing survived the decline of the New Left. This chapter provides the next piece of the puzzle by explaining how gay organizing then began to thrive. In chapter 4 I showed that the existence of contradictory political logics within gay liberation allowed the movement to survive a dramatic moment of ideological pruning. However, the survival of gay organizing did not guarantee its growth. Differences between gay rights, premised on an interest group logic, and gay pride, which drew on an identity logic, could have proved to be debilitating. Binding gay individuals and the various strands of gay politics into a coherent political project presented activists with a challenge.

A coherent political project did emerge, and rapidly. Activists settled on a way to organize that reconciled the seemingly contradictory parts of the project in the early 1970s. The movement coalesced around the simultaneous pursuit of gay rights, gay pride, and sexual expression. That something new was coming together was evident to close observers at the time, such as the Advocate editorialist quoted in this chapter's epigraph. Sociologist Laud Humphreys noted in 1970 that "the old-line, civil-libertarian thesis and the gay liberationist antithesis began to produce a synthesis."[14]

How were the potentially contradictory aspects of gay politics reconciled? In this chapter, I show that the identity logic provided the cultural resources needed to defuse the threat posed by conflicting visions of the goals and strategies of gay organizing. By seeing meaningful social change as a product of individual self-expression, an identity logic suggested that positive change could occur even if differences were not resolved. Change would occur simply through broadening the range of authentic expression possible in society. Differences thus seemed less threatening and could be celebrated instead of resolved. Not all movements drawing on an identity logic highlight its individualistic side. Identity logic more typically gave rise to a concern with the internal homogeneity of identity categories. That the gay movement managed to play with both meanings of the term "identity" (sameness and individuality) provided a powerful and generative ambiguity. The vision of a unified but diverse movement became real as activists developed practices and rituals that substantiated the rhetoric—most notably, the annual lesbian/gay freedom day parade. The parade, through hits very structure, conveys the message of unity through diversity.

Cultural and political approaches were thus defined as complementary—some groups could focus primarily on gay rights, while others expressed gay pride, without forcing a decision about which should be the goal. Affirming gay cultural identity provided gay rights with the identity needed to claim a place on the American political scene. In turn, gay rights created space for the elaboration of gay identity. But even those who could not agree with a gay rights agenda could be included (although in a marginal place in the movement). Interest group politics was not the glue holding the project together. The glue was provided by shared gay identity and the celebration of its expression. The movement became an "identity movement."

This analysis of the timing and nature of the transformation of the gay movement in the early 1970s differs in several key ways from how this transition is generally described in the social movements and sexuality literatures. That a transition occurred in the 1970s is widely accepted.[15] While some, like Laud Humphreys, agree with the dating of the transition in the very early 1970s, others, like Steven Seidman, date the transition to later in the decade.[16] With the exception of Humphreys, most others see the transformation as happening gradually. For example, Seidman claims that "gay liberation came to an end by the mid-1970s."[17] These other scholars, in contrast to the approach taken here, do not see the transformation in terms of a sudden crystallization of a new field.

In addition, sexuality and social movement scholars have seen gay rights and gay pride as seamlessly compatible. In virtually all of the scholarship on the gay movement, the politics of pride, display, coming out, and community building are seen to fit naturally with an interest group/gay rights politics. Seidman talks of the turn to "community building and winning civil rights."[18] John D'Emilio links gay rights and identity politics: "Gay rights activists retained a central emphasis on coming out; they engaged in militant, angry protests; they adopted the language of pride and self-affirmation."[19] Mary Bernstein explains that the "lesbian and gay movement [had] been altered from a movement for cultural transformation through sexual liberation to one that seeks achievement of political rights through a narrow, ethnic-like interest-group politics."[20] Because scholars have seen the fit between rights and pride politics as natural and obvious, they have missed the political work involved in producing this fit.

Without analyzing precisely how the movement that took shape in the 1970s merged interest group and identity politics, it is difficult to understand how it produced and supported such a diverse array of organizations. Interest group politics is suited for pursuing group rights, but not for building and displaying identity. An identity logic made the building and displaying of identity through building organizations and hosting events like the annual freedom day parade meaningful and possible.

While gay movement experts take for granted the synergistic relationship between community development and the pursuit of rights, they have not articulated the theoretical implications of this fit. They have not pointed out that this relationship defies the categories of political process theories of movements. By straddling the boundaries of the cultural and the political not to mention the commercial, the gay identity movement refuses to be contained within a narrow definition of a "social movement." As we will see in chapter 6, the multifaceted nature of this project fueled its growth. The power of this project lay not only in the strength of a narrow political rights movement but also in the generative nature of its identity politics. Understanding the nature of this project, and of the synergy among its various components, is crucial to understanding the success of the gay identity movement in the 1970s and beyond. The first section below provides evidence of field crystallization in the early 1970s. The second section discusses the challenge of arriving at this consensus and the nature of the field formed.

The comments discussed above provide one indication of the crystallization of the gay identity movement in the early 1970s. These observations were substantiated by a variety of other indicators of field formation. It was when I noticed the synchronicity of these indicators that I began to organize this story around this crucial moment in the history of the gay field.

The creation of the freedom day parade provided one indication of field formation. If the event had occurred only once, or only sporadically, or had stayed geographically localized, or varied over time in structure and organization, I would not attribute so much salience to its birth. But freedom day parades happen in all major cities and some small towns in the United States each year, employing the language and structure settled on in the early 1970s. San Francisco's gay community has organized a freedom day parade every year since 1972. Each year the language of "pride," "celebration," "unity," and "diversity" appears in parade themes and mission statements. Freedom day parades involved political, social, and commercial organizations from the early years. The participation of all these kinds of organizations shows that the collective project was not conceived in a narrowly political way.

Taken alone, the founding of the parade would not necessarily signify the crystallization of a new field. But 1972 also marked the first time, after years of effort, that a national conference of homosexual organizations reached a consensus on a political platform.[21] In February, at "A National Coalition of Gay Organizations," jointly sponsored by New York's Gay Activists Alliance and Chicago's Gay Alliance, eighty-five organizations from eighteen states agreed on a gay rights platform in preparation for the 1972 elections.[22] Never before had a national conference of gay organizations been able to agree on a gay stance. Throughout the late 1960s multiple attempts had failed to produce such a consensus.[23]

In addition, as I discussed in chapters 1 and 4, the creation of the parade and the new political consensus coincided with the sudden appearance of entirely new kinds of gay organizations. These organizations included gay religious organizations (e.g., the Metropolitan Community Church, founded 1970), gay self-help organizations (e.g., Gay Alcoholics Anonymous, founded 1971), gay hobby organizations (e.g., San Francisco Front Runners, founded 1974), and gay parenting groups (e.g., Lesbian Mother Union, founded 1971). The use of bold sexual identity terminology in organization names illustrated their new devotion to pride and identity building. The sudden explosion of support groups, which were unheard of before 1970, created contexts in which individuals could discover and express their authentic selves. The proliferation of varieties of gay organizations, both in terms of function and identity, suggested the salience of the vision of a unified but diverse movement. Most gay organizations created after 1972 proclaimed gay identity and the particular function or identity of the organization (e.g., Gay History Film Project, Slightly Older Lesbians). These new organizations were made imaginable, appealing, and obvious by the crystallization of a gay identity movement. While activists and community members may not have noted these new organizations until the mid to late 1970s, their distinctiveness was evident in the names and goals of organizations beginning in 1970. It is the proliferation and diversification of this particular kind of organization that accounts for the shape and size of the organizational infrastructure of the community to this day.

The changing density of various kinds of homosexual organizations provided yet another confirmation of the timing of the consolidation of the gay identity movement. Figure 5.1 shows the decline of homophile and gay liberation organizations and the emergence of the new kind of gay organizations, which I refer to as "gay identity organizations." Note that by 1972, gay identity organizations began to dominate. The existence of multiple kinds of organizations from 1969 to 1972 indicates the unsettled nature of the field and the contestation between multiple political logics that characterized those years. As the gay identity movement coalesced, gay identity organizations began to dominate. Homophile and gay liberation organizations declined.

The creation of resource guides in the early 1970s provided still another indicator of field crystallization. To build my organizational data set, I scoured archives, bookstores, libraries, and secondary sources for lists of lesbian/gay organizations. I found that while bar guides were published consistently throughout the 1960s, the first guides to list both nonprofit and commercial organizations were published in 1972. Gayellow Pages, the first national annual guide to both nonprofit and commercial organizations, was first published in 1973. Organizational researchers see the existence of resource guides as a good indicator of the existence of a field.[24] Guides provide evidence that participants are aware of being involved in a common enterprise. Guides also reveal the ways that participants conceived of their enterprise. That these guides listed nonprofit organizations, including

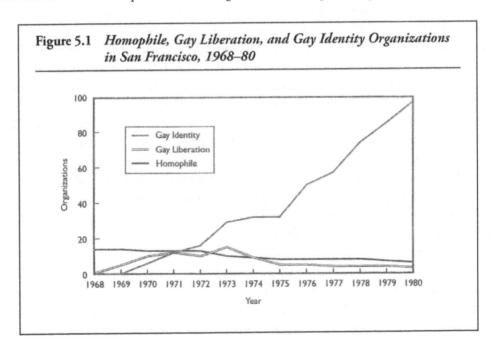

Figure 5.1 *Homophile, Gay Liberation, and Gay Identity Organizations in San Francisco, 1968–80*

both cultural and rights organizations, as well as commercial organizations, such as bars and bathhouses, showed that gay activists saw their project in terms of the expansion of all kinds of gay social space.

"UNITY THROUGH DIVERSITY"

How did this field finally lock in? What was the nature of this consensus? Answering these questions requires a deeper understanding of the challenges faced by activists as the New Left receded. I show that activists faced conflicting visions of the goals and strategies of gay organizing, but that the identity logic provided gay activists with a cultural framework that allowed for the finessing of the contradictions between these visions.

We have grown to accept the conflation of gay pride and gay rights as inevitable; it is difficult to imagine that they were not always natural bedfellows. However, they are based on fundamentally different notions about the nature of the oppression of homosexuals and how this oppression should be addressed. Gay pride, based on an identity logic, asserts that the goal of gay politics should be building a public, positive gay identity through coming out and identity display. Gay rights politics defines the goal of gay politics as battling discrimination through interest group politics. In 1970 and 1971, activists battled over the differences between these approaches. In his history of homosexual politics, Toby Marotta devoted a chapter of more than thirty dense pages to the conflict between "pride" and "rights" orientations in the Gay Activists Alliance in New York.[25] Gay pride advocates saw gay rights as missing the point, as they believed that fundamental change involved broadening the repertoire of acceptable cultural expression. Activist-analyst Peter Fisher, in a 1971 paper for a political science seminar, articulated this position:

> What use … was the passage of legislation that would enable homosexuals to be openly gay without fear of losing their jobs, if there was no way to be gay outside of the tawdry bar scene? What must be developed in order for political gains to be meaningful was a new life style, an integral gay counterculture which could draw uptight gays out of their closets of secrecy and shame into a new expressive and creative way of life. What was needed, in effect, was the initiation of a grand social experiment, the creation of a new society within the old.[26]

Fisher's vision of "the creation of a new society within the old" beautifully illustrates that gay pride politics was premised on the prefigurative politics of the identity logic. The resonance with the vision of Students for a Democratic Society (SDS) is striking. Greg Calvert, an officer of SDS, wrote in 1966: "While struggling to liberate the world, we would create the liberated world in our midst. While fighting to destroy the power that had created the loveless anti-community, we would ourselves create the community of love—The Beloved Community."[27] In contrast, those focused on gay rights, such as GAA's

Marty Robinson, felt that those focused on cultural expression mistakenly believed they could "dance their way to revolution." Marotta explains that gay rights advocates felt that too much focus on the expressive "diverted energy and attention from important political enterprises."[28]

Complicating matters further was the fact that gay pride and gay rights were not the only models available for thinking about how homosexuals ought to act in pursuit of their interests. Many gay men were primarily interested in participating in gay social life. This understanding of gay interest was at odds with rights politics, which saw gay interests as dependent upon passing antidiscrimination legislation. This orientation toward partying was also at odds with the gay pride agenda; it was unconcerned with achieving social change through a politics of visibility. The pursuit to sex all outside of every existing definition of political action. But it is collective action because the vitality of this sexual culture depended upon the health of commercial organizations. The pursuit of sex and sociality thus present compelling alternative way of structuring the collective project. In Chapter 2 we saw that the history of this subcultural logic of organization extended back at least to the 1930s and presented homophile activists with a challenging alternative to their vision of a public interest group movement throughout the 1950s and 1960s.

This diversity of ways of envisioning a gay collective project was matched by individual-level diversity among gay men and lesbians. The success of gay liberation had intensified the internal diversity that had plagued homosexual organizing since its inception. Homosexuals came from all different kinds of backgrounds and were diverse in terms of ideology. Before gay liberation, this lack of shared socialization was overcome by the tight control homosexual subcultures maintained over the boundaries of their world and the processes of socialization into it.[29] With the sudden visibility of the gay movement in the early 1970s, the numbers of those identifying as gay grew fast. Many of these new converts lacked experience either in the New Left or in the gay sexual subculture. There were simply more people, from more different walks of life, willing and able to identify as gay. In addition, the movements of the 1960s left the whole society, including homosexuals, ideologically polarized.

Thus, at this crucial moment, three distinct visions about the nature and goals of gay collective action existed: gay rights, gay pride, and sexual pleasure seeking.[30] We saw above that these agendas became linked into one coherent project. The linking of these three agendas was not inevitable. As has been seen in other movements, cleavages can develop, weakening the movement as a whole. In the women's movement, the politics of cultural affirmation and the pursuit of rights developed into distinct, competing fields, referred to as "cultural feminism" and "liberal feminism." Each saw its analysis of women's oppression as correct and the analysis of the other as irrelevant or even harmful to the cause. The seductions of pure pleasure seeking might have eliminated all interest in gay rights or gay pride. Or interest group politics might have come to dominate, restricting the diversification of the community and slowing organizational proliferation.

The political logic of identity made it possible to reconcile pride, rights, and sexual expression. I show this through a close analysis of an important movement statement made by New York's Gay Activists Alliance leader Jim Owles, published in the April 1971 issue of the Gay Activist. In his 1972 analysis of homosexual liberation, Laud Humphreys identified this statement as one of "great significance."[31] Humphreys saw it as revealing "certain characteristics of the synthesis that has formed around one-issue organizations."[32]

Jim Owles recognized the tremendous growth of the gay movement and the resulting problem of the diversification of gay organizations. Other movement leaders were aware of the contradictions as well. Owles described the variety of approaches:

> There are gay organizations of all types. Some are politically oriented, some are socially oriented, some devote their energies to much needed public education about homosexuals, and some are focusing on the problem of reconciling homosexuality and religion. Some groups have adopted specific ideological platforms, while others attempt to encompass gay people from all areas of the political spectrum.[33]

Owles only describes ideological diversity here—not race, class, or gender diversity. Race, class, and gender differences were not seen by white male leaders as serious obstacles to forming a coherent gay movement. Movement leaders were primarily concerned with trying to move beyond the ideological polarization of the 1960s and with garnering the support of middle-class white gay men who might have been alienated by the extremes of gay power.

After describing the diversity of gay organizations, Owles acknowledged that this diversity could potentially lead to destructive conflict. He moved quickly to emphasizing the possibilities for cooperation:

> Although there is a potential for disagreement among the many gay organizations with regard to ideology and priorities, this is greatly outweighed by the numerous areas of potential cooperation and mutual effort.[34]

Owles felt that responding to this diversity by attempting to create an ideologically homogeneous movement would be a mistake. He asserted that:

> Few of us are anxious to see a uniform and monolithic movement develop out of the foundations we have laid. We have seen other mass movements develop in this direction in the past, only to be torn apart by internal struggles over ideology and leadership, eventually to fail in achieving their goals.[35]

Owles saw efforts to develop ideological consensus to be dangerous, potentially leading to movement factionalization. His leeriness about homogenization was shaped by the value placed on individual expression within gay liberation and by the movement's late position in the cycle of protest.

After rejecting a "uniform and monolithic movement," Owles further discredited "uniformity" by pointing out that "one of society's favorite myths about gay people is that we are all alike." With this statement, Owles hinted at a view of homosexual oppression resting primarily on homosexual cultural invisibility, suggesting his reliance on an identity political logic. Owles claimed that "we" are aware of the diversity of homosexuals: "We ourselves know that there are all types of gay people, with all types of interests, and from all types of backgrounds."[36] Expression of this diversity is thus positive as it has the consequence of dismantling stereotypes of gays.

Owles then boldly asserted that the diversity he described:

> is our strength, not a weakness. There is room in the gay liberation movement for every gay person to make his or her own type of contribution toward creating a society and a world in which we will all be free to be ourselves.[37]

Movement diversity was defined as strength, not weakness. Owles argued for the movement to embrace diversity instead of trying to resolve or deny it.

That Owles relied on an identity political logic is evident in his assertion that the goal of gay politics is "creating a society ... in which we will all be free to be ourselves." It was this vision of change that made it possible to see diversity as strength. From a political worldview in which the ultimate end is individual self-expression, the presence of diversity is evidence of movement toward that goal. In a worldview in which the end goal is eliminating discriminatory law, the presence of ideological diversity could be seen as hindering the likelihood of achieving policy change. Thus, framing diversity as strength is made possible within an identity political logic.

Defining diversity as strength makes sense within a political logic that sees change as emerging out of the aggregation of individual actions. In closing, Owles restated his commitment to a movement composed of multiple and varied forms of political expression:

> The way we will build an effective national movement is by every gay person making his or her own particular contribution, and by gay individuals and organizations working together when possible.[38]

With diversity defined as strength, gay pride, gay rights, and sexual expression all became perfectly acceptable forms of gay politics. All furthered the gay movement.

In order for gay identity to be meaningful, activists also needed to define a minimal set of shared characteristics. After all, the term "identity" implies likeness as well as individual uniqueness. The first premise was that gay men and lesbians had a core of shared experience simply because of shared same gender sexual attraction. The experience of growing up "closeted," combined with the subsequent experience of developing a gay identity, joining a gay community, and coming out to family, friends, and coworkers was presumed to produce feelings of commonality. The second premise was that supporting gay rights logically followed the adoption of a positive, public gay identity. While it was understood that ideological consensus was impossible, gay rights were seen as a lowest common denominator set of political goals. Such activists as Owles went to great lengths to emphasize that the gay rights agenda fit with political philosophies across the spectrum. Gays from the political right or left could endorse gay rights. A third point of agreement placed participation in a liberated, active sexual subculture at the center of gay male identity. But because a diverse movement would be built out of the aggregated contributions of all gay individuals, however they defined their contribution to the collective project, even those who disagreed with gay rights or with the role of sex in gay life could find a place in the movement.

DISPLAYING UNITY THROUGH DIVERSITY: THE GAY FREEDOM DAY PARADE

The creation of the gay freedom day parade illustrated that an identity movement that defined itself in terms of its diversity could produce large collective action events. That the founders of the event commemorating the Stonewall riots eventually arrived at "parade" for the form of the event, after initially calling for a "demonstration," illustrated the emerging dominance of an identity logic. In turn, the immediate success of the parade contributed to the consolidation of the gay identity movement.

The annual freedom day parade was born at the Eastern Regional Conference of Homophile Organizations in the fall of 1969. Activist Craig Rodwell proposed that the Stonewall riots be commemorated with an "annual reminder."[39] The resolution establishing "Christopher Street Liberation Day" read as follows:

> We propose that a demonstration be held annually on the last Saturday in June in New York City to commemorate the 1969 spontaneous demonstrations on Christopher Street and this demonstration be called CHRISTOPHER STREET LIBERATION DAY. No dress or age regulations shall be made for this demonstration. We also propose that we contact Homophile organizations throughout the country and suggest that they hold parallel demonstrations on that day.[40]

The "annual reminder" was originally intended to be a "demonstration," not a "parade" or "celebration."

In preparation for the first event, which was to take place on June 28, 1970, in New York, activists struggled to find a form for the event that could motivate the participation of a diverse constituency. Disagreement over the shape of the event was fierce. The Gay Activists Alliance, Marotta explains, wanted "to make homosexuals aware of the need to exercise political power and to confront politicians and public officials with evidence of the gay voting bloc. Instead of a picnic in the park, they wanted a program of speeches by political leaders and politicians."[41] In contrast, Craig Rod well and others wanted to emphasize the importance of "affirming liberated gay life styles and celebrating gay community."[42] The victory of the identity affirmation perspective was evident in the Christopher Street Liberation Day Umbrella Committee's welcome message:

> Welcome to the first anniversary celebration of the Gay Liberation movement. We are united today to affirm our pride, our life-style, and our commitment to each other. Despite political and social differences we may have, we are united on this common ground: For the first time in history we are together as The Homosexual Community.[43]

All references to "demonstration" were dropped and replaced by the language of "celebration" and "pride." The language of "political and social differences" and "unity," which would become ubiquitous, emerged. While this first event did not include floats and more closely resembled a march than a parade, it was certainly not a political demonstration as it was originally conceived. Until the day of the event, it was unclear whether gay organizations would support the event. By the time of the march, every major gay political group in New York had signed on as a sponsor.[44] The use of essentially the same welcome message the next year suggests that key activists felt that the framing worked to motivate the participation of the whole community.[45]

The first San Francisco gay freedom day parade, called "Christopher Street West," was held in 1972 with about fifty thousand participants.[46] Organizers were aware of the implications of the different possible formats for the event:

> More speakers had not been allowed in an attempt to avoid political or protest activities and to keep the parade from becoming a demonstration. It had been the Christopher Street West S.F. committee's contention that a demonstration as such in San Francisco would prove a flop and would alienate most gay community members here. Their contention was supported by gay community leaders who had been involved in the parade, who commented to the Advocate that only a non-political Gay Pride celebration would be able to unite all spectrums of the community.[47]

Leaders were committed to unifying the community and were convinced that a parade was precisely the right format to accomplish this goal. They felt that the "nonpolitical" character of a parade would make it appealing to all parts of the community.

San Francisco's first freedom day parade was quite successful. The format of a parade and the goal of a gay pride celebration enticed a diverse group to participate in the event. According to the Advocate:

Almost every spectrum of the gay community was pulled together in the parade, including every San Francisco gay organization except the Daughters of Bilitis, the Council on Religion and the Homosexual, and the Gay Sunshine Collective, some of whose members participated as individuals.[48]

Drag queens, gay businesses, entertainers, religious groups, prison groups, gay organizations, reigning "royalty," leather men, radicals, street people, conservatives, lesbians, and "hunky guys" were all represented in parade contingents.[49]

There were some who were critical of the turn away from radical politics toward a politics of identity display. The *Advocate* mentioned that "isolated and small groups of radicals … began shouting that they had been denied the right to address the crowd."[50] These radicals were already in the minority by 1972.

Since it took the form of a "pride parade" there has been little debate within the community about the assumptions underlying the event. That is not to say the staging of the parade has been without conflict. There have been many battles about the parade.[51] However, the conflicts have not generally been about whether the parade should exist or whether the event should be a political demonstration. The value of the parade is usually accepted as given. That the event was originally intended to be a political demonstration has been forgotten. Conflicts about the parade have typically reinforced the sense of its inevitability. Most of the conflicts have been about issues of inclusion (of bisexuals and transgendered people) or status within the event (the ordering of contingents and locations of booths). And of course, there have been conflicts about the public representation of sexual diversity: Should we highlight those who are most different from mainstream society (drag queens, people into S/M)? Or should we emphasize those who are ever so conventional (lesbian/gay parents, employees, bicyclists)? Every so often some group complains that the parade has become too much of a "party." But even those who think the parade should be more political rarely suggest that the parade be transformed into a demonstration.

Activists discovered a form of collective action that conveyed both unity and diversity. The fit between the parade as a form and the message displayed was perfect. A parade by definition involves display, and the form of the parade worked beautifully to display newly visible collective and individual identities. Even if one participated with a different intention, the audience tried to "read" one's identity. By convention, parades consist of identifiable groups or contingents. When the contingents were different from each other, the event was more successful as an exhibition or show. By participating in the same parade, the contingents appeared unified.

To participate in the parade, individuals needed to form a contingent or to pick a contingent with which to march. The parade demanded the display of both shared gay identities and secondary, modifying identities. That everyone needed a contingent, a secondary identity, constructed diversity as a point of commonality. Everyone brought one or more additional identities into the community with them. The demand for display of both individual and organizational identities also produced a continual diversification of the community, as people searched for different variations of gay identity to contribute to the spectacle.

In this new arena, the existence of multiple organizations is unambiguously positive. Gone were the homophile concerns about organizational competition. The more organizations, the more contingents there were to participate in the parade. The more different the contingents were from each other, the better the show. The existence of many organizations was now seen as evidence of community richness and strength rather than as evidence of fragmentation and division.

The structure of the parade and the relationships between organizations can be described as articulated. Something that is articulated is expressed in parts, but is also systematically interrelated. Each contingent or organization expresses its position without restraint but does not claim to represent the gay movement as a whole. Organizations were linked by shared gay identity. Beyond this basic point of commonality, participation in the parade and in the movement meant simply accepting the diversity of goals and identities expressed by others. Real political differences were finessed. Groups that disagreed with each other—say a radical group and a Republican group—have usually been separated from one another in the parade. That such politically disparate groups participated conveyed the message that political differences were not threatening. Shared gay identity was asserted to be a more fundamental commonality. By stumbling upon a way to integrate the various aspects of the project, activists solved the final obstacle to the creation of a new kind of movement—a gay identity movement. They forged a field. The next chapter shows that this consensus allowed the movement to grow rapidly in the 1970s.

APPENDIX

Constructing a Database of San Francisco's Lesbian/Gay Organizations

A database of San Francisco's lesbian/gay organizations formed the evidentiary base for this book. I constructed this database by coding resource guides and directories. These provided a great source of data because they conveyed a rich picture of how actors within the field defined participation in the collective project. Institutional theorists have pointed out that guides are an indicator of field institutionalization because the very existence of guides suggests "the development of a mutual awareness among participants in a set of organizations that they are involved in a common enterprise."[52]

The quality of the database and the analysis based on it rests on the quality of the decisions made while identifying, locating, and coding the research guides. These decisions were necessary to translate the guides into a form amenable to systematic description and analysis.[53]

Guides found were of four general types—national guides, local guides, women's guides, and bar guides. National guides listed both nonprofit and commercial organizations for every major city in the United States. Local guides listed only San Francisco organizations. In addition to providing information on many of the same organizations listed in the national guides, local guides listed smaller, more obscure organizations. Women's guides included lesbian organizations that were sometimes missed by national and local guides. Bar guides listed only commercial establishments, thus offering relatively little information on nonprofit organizations. In addition to using the guides as sources for organizational information, I also coded every mention of a homosexual organization in the central publication of San Francisco's homophile community, the *Vector*, from December 1964 through June 1971, to compensate for the lack of guides before 1972.

Inclusion and Exclusion of Organizations

After choosing which guides to code, I decided which organizations listed in the guides to include in the data set. Institutional theory suggested including all listed organizations in order to best reveal how actors understood the boundaries of the collective project. If I had followed this approach, my data set would have been quite unwieldy. I began in this fashion, but the database rapidly grew to twenty-five hundred organizations, with indications that it would grow substantially larger. Guides listed organizations and services that were clearly not gay (e.g., the city bus service), organizations located outside of San Francisco, and both commercial and nonprofit organizations.

Screening organizations before including them in the data set, while unfortunately imposing my own categories on the data, was necessary. I constructed inclusion rules with the intent of doing as little violence as possible to the construction of the world emerging through the guides.

To be included in the data set, the organization had to meet the following criteria:

- define in its name or mission statement that the organization was for or composed of sexual or gender minority individuals (including, but not limited to, those who defined themselves as homosexual, homophile, lesbian, gay, bisexual, queer, transvestite, transsexual, transgender, leather, BDSM, or sex workers)
- be nonprofit
- be in existence at some point from January 1, 1964, through December 31, 1994
- be located in the city of San Francisco
- have a name, be more formal than a friendship network, be publicly accessible, and have the intention of being permanent
- be clearly distinct from other organizations in the data set
- have a minimum amount of information available including, but not limited to, a name and some information on the purposes of the organization.

The decision to exclude commercial organizations was highly problematic as it was quite clear that actors saw both commercial and nonprofit organizations as full participants in their project. That actors made no distinction between commercial and nonprofit organizations became clear as I attempted to identify commercial organizations with the intention of excluding them. Many for-profit organizations, such as newspapers, magazines, and bookstores, engaged in gay identity building activities in ways indistinguishable with nonprofit organizations. Dennis Altman points out that many gay merchants see their businesses in terms of community building. He observes:

> What is striking is the profusion of services and institutions, many of which straddle both movement and commercial activities. ... Starting a business is often a way of integrating one's working and one's social life, and to start a gay hotel or a women's restaurant can be a way of expressing commitment to the gay community.[54]

In spite of these compelling reasons to include commercial organizations in the core data set, I felt that I had to separate the for-profit and not-for-profit organizations. With commercial organizations moved to a related dataset, it was possible to make sense out of what looked like pure organizational chaos. The identity political logic was more purely in evidence in the nonprofit organizations, which were not simultaneously shaped by the logic of profit seeking. I incorporated the second data set into the analysis at crucial moments in the book.

The decision to exclude nongay organizations was also problematic. Given my contention throughout the book that the gay/nongay divide was central to the way actors defined their world, excluding these organizations potentially eliminated evidence contrary to my claim. But after analyzing the kinds of nongay organizations listed in the guides and how they were listed, I decided that excluding these organizations could be done with integrity. Usually the guides listed nongay organizations under separate headings such as "Emergency Numbers" or "Financial Assistance" as opposed to "Gay/ Lesbian Publications and Media," clearly indicating that the makers of the guides did not think of these organizations as gay. The cognitive divide between gay and nongay that made construction of these guides relevant and possible was reproduced within the guides. Nongay organizations included in the guides tended to be of a certain type: crisis services, such as suicide lines, available to all; city or state services available to all; organizations providing general information or services; inclusive community centers; organizations geared to other constituencies (such as youth, runaways, older people, Jewish people) that might include gay people; or inclusive mainstream churches. The inclusion of these organizations asserted that gays in San Francisco were entitled to the full range of public services available to heterosexuals. This revealed a view of gay San Francisco as embedded within and connected to the mainstream institutions of the city.

In addition to general service organizations, guides also listed two other groups of non-gay organizations: AIDS and feminist organizations. That these organizations were seen to be of particular interest to lesbians and gay men was not surprising, given the numbers of gay men with AIDS and the connections between lesbianism and feminism. However, it was clear that many of these organizations did not define themselves as lesbian or gay organizations. I included organizations that identified as gay or lesbian while excluding those that indicated that they did not. For example, AIDS organizations that served all constituencies were excluded, while gay AIDS organizations were included.

Table A.2 *Organizational Information Collected*	
Organization name	
Address	
Phone	
Year of first mention	year organization first mentioned in a resource guide
Founding date	date (month and year) organization founded, if available
Year of last mention	year organization last mentioned in a resource guide
Disbanding date	date (month and year) organization disbanded, if available
Source	all issues of all resource guides that listed organization
Description	how organization described itself in resource guides or organization flyer
Function	organizational goal or function, from information in resource guide or
	organization flyer
Gender	gender of participants (men, women, men and women, or transgender)

INFORMATION COLLECTED ABOUT EACH ORGANIZATION

Information collected from resource guides on each organization is described in table A.2.

Note that I collected both the actual founding and disbanding dates and the dates of listing in the resource guides. Ultimately, I was able to find actual founding and disbanding dates for only 150 of the 958 organizations in the core data set. For the sake of consistency, all analysis is done based on dates of listing rather than on actual founding and disbanding dates. In order to make sure the dates of listing in the guides map onto actual founding dates in a meaningful fashion, I compared dates of first mention in resource guides with actual founding dates. The 150 organizations for which I had an actual founding date were listed in the guides, on average, 2.8 years after they were founded. Some 71 percent (107/150) were listed in guides within two years of founding.

It would have been useful to collect systematic data on changes in organizational names and missions, organizational size and membership, organizational structure, and the fit between organizational presentation and reality (whether the actual composition of the membership matched the claims that the organization made about its membership). At the time these data were collected, this information could have been collected only through intensive archival investigation. Preliminary efforts suggested that it might have taken several hours to research each of the 958 organizations in the data set. Given the revolution in internet usage that has taken place in the intervening years, the barriers to obtaining much of this information have been substantially reduced. However, even now, some of this information, particularly the highly interesting information on membership rates, may simply not be available.

DISCUSSION QUESTIONS

1. Parades are not generally the kinds of events that social movements promote. How does San Francisco's L/G/B/T Freedom Day Parade contribute in some way to social change? How does it represent the ideal of "unity through diversity"?

2. What are the two "ruptures" that Armstrong identifies, and how are they related to shifts in the gay/lesbian movement, and the organizations that comprise it?

3. Explain the different "political logics" associated with the various organizations that Armstrong included in her research. How, specifically, did she decide to include or exclude organizations?

NOTES

1. Numbers derived from an exhaustive database of San Francisco's lesbian/gay organizations. See the appendix for details on the construction of this database.

2. Marotta developed an even more complex categorization of the strains of gay liberation ideology in *The Politics of Homosexuality* (Boston: Houghton Milflin, 1981).

3. "Marching in the Pride Parade? Here's How to Find Your Contingent ...," *San Francisco Bay Times,* June 15, 1995, 8.

4. Mary Bernstein, "Celebration and Suppression: The Strategic Uses of Identity by the Lesbian and Gay Movement," *American Journal of Sociology* 103 (1997); Alberto Melucci, *Nomads of the Present: Social Movements and Individual Needs in Contemporary Society* (Philadelphia: Temple University Press, 1989).

5. Some might argue that instead of a case study of San Francisco, I should have focused on the dynamics of the movement at the national level. To this critique I would respond that during the 1950s through the late 1970s a national-level gay movement existed only in an extremely attenuated form. The political activism that would ultimately produce a national movement occurred in a few core cities. San Francisco was not the only site of these processes, but it was a very important one. It is through understanding what happened in San Francisco, and other major urban areas, that the birth of a national gay movement can be understood. The crystallization of the movement on the national level in the late 1970s, which was marked by the first gay march on Washington in 1979, built on the city-level organizing of the 1950s, 1960s, and 1970s.

6. Others could also argue that the focus on San Francisco is misplaced given that New York was the site of the famous Stonewall uprising. Movement legend implies that all gay political and cultural accomplishments since 1969 can be traced back to this event. However, even a cursory examination of the history challenges this view. Gay liberation developed in San Francisco before the Stonewall uprising in New York, suggesting that the view of Stonewall as the one and only "ground zero" is incorrect. A focus on San Francisco provides a corrective to the assumption that the gay movement diffused from one point. The movement appeared simultaneously in several different cities. While there were multiple origin points, they were not independent. Particularly in late 1969 and 1970, ideological battles spanned the continent, with gay liberation groups in New York critiquing the agendas and plans of gay liberation groups in San Francisco. The spread of goals and strategies of organizing seemed to be virtually instantaneous. For example, the idea for a gay takeover of Alpine County in California in 1969 was debated not only by West Coast gay liberationists, but also by New York groups (see chapter 4). Given the intensity of this interaction and feedback, I do not treat San Francisco as a completely independent case. Particularly in my analysis of the years 1969 and 1970, I reference movement events on both coasts.

7. Readers familiar with population ecology theory will observe that the density of lesbian/gay organizations follows the expected pattern of "initially low rates of growth, which accelerate over time, reach a maximum rate, and then slowly decline." David J. Tucker et al., "Ecological and Institutional Sources of Change in Organizational Populations," in *Ecological Models of Organization,* ed. Glenn R. Carroll (Cambridge: Ballinger, 1988), 127. Initially, founding increases the legitimacy of a particular organizational form. Eventually, as the population approaches the environment's carrying capacity, competitive processes kick in, halting the expansion of the size of the population. See Glenn R. Carroll, ed., *Ecological Models of Organization* (Cambridge: Ballinger, 1988); Glenn R. Carroll and Michael T. Hannan, "Density Dependence in the Evolution of Populations of Newspaper Organizations," *American Sociological Review* 54 (1989); Michael T. Hannan and John Freeman, "Density Dependence in the Growth of Organizational Populations," in *Ecological Models of Organizations,* ed. Glenn R. Carroll (Cambridge: Ballinger, 1988); Michael T. Hannan and John Freeman, "The Ecology

of Organizational Mortality: American Labor Unions, 1836–1985," *American Journal of Sociology* 94 (1988); Hannan and Freeman, *Organizational Ecology;* Hannan and Freeman, "The Population Ecology of Organizations." This perspective was of limited usefulness for several reasons. It does not provide a theory of the source of organizational innovations. Its measurement of institutionalization is circular and it assumes a static carrying capacity. Fundamentally, this perspective is not a theory that can do justice to the complex processes of the construction of meaning systems. See Lynne G. Zucker, "Combining Institutional Theory and Population Ecology: No Legitimacy, No History," *American Sociological Review* 54 (1989), for a critique of this approach.

8. The desire for public recognition distinguished these homosexual organizations from those classified as "other." Homosexual organizations founded before 1969 with the desire for public recognition can be classified as homophile organizations. In addition to bars, restaurants, bathhouses, and cafes, there were also private homosexual social groups, organizations are discussed in more detail in Chapter 2.

9. Clemens, *The People's Lobby;* McAdam, *Political Process.*

10. Wini Breines, *Community and Organization in the New Left, 1962–1968: The Great Refusal (New* Brunswick: Rutgers University Press, 1989); Doug Rossinow, *The Politics of Authenticity* (New York: Columbia University Press, 1998).

11. Rossinow, *The Politics of Authenticity,* 343.

12. Kauffman, "The Anti-politics of Identity," *67.*

13. Breines, *Community and Organization.*

14. Pamela Allen, *Free Space: A Perspective on the Small Group in Women's Liberation* (Washington, N.J.: Times Change, 1970), 14.

15. Laud Humphreys, *Out of the Closets: The Sociology of Homosexual Liberation* (Englewood Cliffs, N.J.: Prentice-Hall, 1972), 123.

16. Dennis Altman, *The Homosexualization of America* (Boston: Beacon, 1982); Mary Bernstein, "Celebration and Suppression: The Strategic Uses of Identity by the Lesbian and Gay Movement," *American Journal of Sociology* 103 (1997): 532; John D'Emilio, "After Stonewall," in *Making Trouble: Essays on Gay History, Politics, and the University,* ed. John D'Emilio (New York: Routledge 1992); John D'Emilio, "Gay Politics, Gay Community: San Francisco's Experience," in *Making Trouble: Essays on Gay History, Politics, and the University,* ed. John D'Emilio (New York: Routledge, 1992); Steven Epstein, "Gay Politics, Ethnic Identity: The Limits of Social Constructionism," *Socialist Review* 17, no. 2 (1987); Jeffrey EscofBer, "Sexual Revolution and the Politics of Gay Identity," *Socialist Review,* no. 82/83 (July-October 1985); Joshua Gamson, "Must Identity Movements Self-Destruct? A Queer Dilemma," in *Social Perspectives in Lesbian and Gay Studies: A Reader,* ed. Peter M. Nardi and Beth E. Schneider (London: Routledge, [1995] 1998); William Paul, "Minority Status for Gay People: Majority Reaction and Social Context," in *Homosexuality: Social, Psychological, and Biological Issues,* ed. William Paul, et al. (Beverly Hills: Sage, 1982); Steven Seidman, "Identity and Politics in a 'Postmodern' Gay Culture: Some Historical and Conceptual Notes," in *Fear of a Queer*

Planet: Queer Politics and Social Theory, ed. Michael Warner (Minneapolis: University of Minnesota Press, 1993); Urvashi Vaid, *Virtual Equality: The Mainstreaming of Gay and Lesbian Liberation* (New York: Anchor, 1995). "

17. Seidman, "Identity and Politics," 117.
18. Ibid.
19. Ibid.
20. D'Emilio, "After Stonewall," 246.
21. Bernstein, "Celebration and Suppression," 532.
22. Dudley Clendinen and Adam Nagoumey acknowledge the unprecedented feat of arriving at a gay rights agenda. However, they emphasize that the conference was quite contentious and that the participants disagreed about more issues than they could agree upon. They also suggest that this event planted seeds for future conflict within the gay movement. Clendinen and Nagoumey, *Out for Good: The Struggle to Build a Gay Rights Movement in America* (New York: Simon and Schuster, 1999), 136–38. See also Humphreys, *Out of the Closets,* 168.
23. Humphreys, *Out of the Closets,* 165.
24. John D'Emilio, *Sexual Politics, Sexual Communities: The Making of a Homosexual Minority in the United States, 1940–1970* (Chicago: University of Chicago Press, 1983).
25. Paul J. DiMaggio and Walter W. Powell, "The Iron Cage Revisited: Institutional Isomorphism and Collective Rationality," in *The New Institutionalism in Organizational Analysis,* ed. Walter W. Powell and Paul J. DiMaggio (Chicago: University of Chicago Press, [1983] 1991); John Mohr, "Community, Bureaucracy, and Social Relief: An Institutional Analysis of Organizational Forms in New York City, 1888–1917" (Ph.D. diss., Department of Sociology, Yale University, 1992), 42.
26. See Toby Marotta, *The Politics of Homosexuality* (Boston: Houghton Mifflin, 1981), chap. 7, "Conflicts between Political and Cultural Leaders," esp. 191.
27. Quoted in ibid.
28. *New Left Notes,* November 26, 1966, quoted in Wind Breines, *Community and Organization in the New Left, 1962–1968: The Great Refusal* (New Brunswick: Rutgers University Press, 1989), 48.
29. Marotta, *The Politics of Homosexuality,* 173.
30. The way a lesbian bar community in the 1950s socialized newcomers is beautifully described in Elizabeth Lapovsky Kennedy and Madeline D. Davis, *Boots of Leather, Slippers of Gold: The History of a Lesbian Community* (New York: Routledge, 1993), 80.
31. A marginalized minority continued to espouse the gay power vision, representing a fourth logic of organizing.
32. Humphreys, *Out of the Closets,* 126.
33. Ibid.
34. Ibid., 127.
35. Ibid.
36. Ibid.

37. Ibid.

38. Ibid.

39. Ibid.

40. Clendinen and Nagourney, *Out for Good,* 62; Marotta, *The Politics of Homosexuality,* 164.

41. Marotta, *The Politics of Homosexuality,* 164.

42. Ibid., 167.

43. Ibid.

44. Ibid.

45. Ibid., 169.

46. Humphreys, *Out of the Closets,* 5.

47. "Christopher Street West S.F. Gay Parade," *Advocate,* July 19, 1972, 3; Susan Stryker and Jim Van Buskirk, *Gay by the Bay: A History of Queer Culture in the San Francisco Bay Area* (San Francisco: Chronicle, 1996); Greg L. Pennington, "A Parade Almanac," *San Francisco Lesbian/Gay Freedom Parade and Celebration Magazine,* June 25, 1989, 15. The 1972 event was the first sizeable commemoration of Stonewall to take place in San Francisco. In 1970, "20 to 30 people marched down Polk Street from Aquatic Park to City Hall." Stryker and Van Buskirk, *Gay by the Bay, 67. See also* Pennington, "A Parade Almanac," 8. In 1971 there was no event at all. Stryker and Van Buskirk, *Gay by the Bay, 67;* Pennington, "A Parade Almanac," 8. "Christopher Street: West S.F. Gay Parade," 3.

48. Ibid.

49. Ibid.

50. Ibid., 10.

51. For a discussion of Chicago's lesbian/gay freedom day parade, see Richard K. Herrell, "The Symbolic Strategies of Chicago's Gay and Lesbian Pride Day Parade," in *Gay Culture in America: Essays from the Field,* ed. Gilbert Herdt (Boston: Beacon, 1992).

52. Paul J. DiMaggio and Walter W. Powell, "The Iron Cage Revisited: Institutional Isomorphism and Collective Rationality," in *The New Institutionalism in Organizational Analysis,* ed. Walter W. Powell and Paul J. DiMaggio (Chicago: University of Chicago Press, [1983] 1991), 65.

53. Scholarship participates in affirming the reality of the objects it turns its gaze upon, even when the gaze is purportedly neutral. According to Steven Seidman, "Social constructionism, at least the historical scholarship of the late 1970s through the 1980s, often served as a kind of celebration of the coming of age of a gay ethnic minority." Seidman, "Identity and Politics in a 'Postmodern' Gay Culture: Some Historical and Conceptual Notes," in *Fear of a Queer Planet: Queer Politics and Social Theory,* ed. Michael Warner (Minneapolis: University of Minnesota Press, 1993), 127. By studying the formation of the lesbian/gay field I inevitably participate in solidifying the field. The enthusiasm for this project expressed by community members encountered in doing this research suggests both that they recognized that this research advanced their agenda of identity

solidification and that they felt (or assumed) that my understanding of the boundaries and nature of the project matched their own views.

54. Dennis Altman, *The Homosexualization of America* (Boston: Beacon, 1982), 19.

INTRODUCTION TO:
PARAPHILIAS ACROSS CULTURES

Contexts and Controversies

JAN CAMPBELL

In this article, the authors provide a comprehensive look at paraphilias (sexual deviances or atypical behaviors) to explain the variations, definitions, and differentiations of normal versus abnormal sexual behaviors in various cultures. The authors explain how places in the world may view "deviant" behaviors in various ways over time and space. Some behaviors may be qualified or quantified and defined akin to a particular culture, such as collectivistic or egocentric types, so that understanding cultural differences is key to understanding sexual behaviors and the ways in which the individual thinks.

This work also describes not only the cultural differences in behaviors but also the biological differences, psychiatric diagnoses, and religious tenets and ways to explain behavior. This article is an enlightening look at a fascinating topic and helps us understand a topic steeped in contrasts.

PARAPHILIAS ACROSS CULTURES

Contexts and Controversies

DINESH BHUGRA, DMITRI POPELYUK, AND ISABEL MCMULLEN

Cultures define and describe what is normal and what is deviant. These defini-tions of normality vary across cultures and are influenced by a number of factors, such as religion. Cultures have been described in various ways, including sex-positive where the sexual act itself is seen as important for pleasure, or sex-negative where the sexual act is seen only as for procreative purposes. The role and development of paraphilias across cultures is also variable, with cultures defining what is legal or illegal. Such differences make collection of epidemiological data and comparison across paraphilias problematic. This discussion suggests that characteristics of cultures may influence the rate of reporting paraphilias, as well as the rate of paraphilias themselves. Furthermore, with increased industrialization and urbanization, fami-lies will become more nuclear, with attitudes toward sex and paraphilias changing as well. This review also explores whether paraphilias can be seen as culture-bound syndromes, and recommends consideration of a number of conceptual issues regard-ing the diagnosis and prevalence of paraphilias as future cross-cultural studies on this topic are developed.

Humans are sexual animals, but vary across cultures in their propensity to use sex as a non-procreative and pleasurable activity. Sexual behaviors in the non-procreative tradition differ across partners; depend on the availability of partners, fantasies, and opportunities; and are influenced by cultural norms, mores or morals, religion, religious taboos, types of societies, and expectations of its members.

Normal and abnormal behaviors are defined and differentiated by the society and culture, with the culture defining deviance—what is "abnormal" versus what merely contravenes the norms of society. However, this distinction is not always an easy or clear one. Within the abnormal, particularly with regard to what is considered sexual, a substantial range exists—for example, from a man dressing in women's clothes for a dress party, to occasionally dressing up for sexual pleasure, to wanting to be dressed all the time. In all of these situations, the basic premise of cross-dressing remains the same, but the degree, intention, and purpose vary. In a similar way, Bhugra and de Silva (1996) noted that uniforms represent symbols that may extend from fashion, to fetish, to fantasy.

Furthermore, some types of "deviant" sexual behavior may be readily quantified; for example, sexual "addiction" might be assessed by the person's number of sexual partners, compared against various established norms. However, other types of behavior are difficult to quantify for any number of reasons. Individuals may withhold information relevant to the particular sexual behavior, especially if illegal. In addition, societies that encourage the medicalization of deviant behaviors may view them primarily as psychopathologies—an approach that may clash with social and statistical norms. As an example of some of these issues, homosexuality, originally seen as a mental illness in the West, was removed from the *Diagnostic and Statistical Manual of Mental Disorders* in 1973 (American Psychiatric Association [APA], 1973). Yet, in several cultures, even now it is considered a mental illness. Further complications arise because of the influence of religious and religious institution-induced norms and expectations. Such expectations may result in egodystonic homosexuality (where an individual is uncomfortable with his or her orientation), which may be deemed a mental illness. In this regard, the distinction between sexual behavior, sexual fantasy, and sexual orientation becomes relevant. Where heterosexual outlets may not be available (e.g., in boarding schools or prisons), a person with a heterosexual orientation may engage in homosexual behavior while carrying on with heterosexual fantasies. Researchers and clinicians must, therefore, not only consider the "end" sexual behavior, but the person's fantasies and preferences as well. Thus, both culture and circumstance may influence "end" behaviors, but not necessarily the person's desires or orientations. Such problems of definition and quantification apply to many types of sexual behaviors, including fetishes and other paraphilias.

Paraphilias have, in the past, been described as fetishes, deviancies, or sexual minority behaviors. Although such classes of behaviors are prevalent across all nations, cultures, and societies, they may, in some cultures, be considered normal (e.g., masturbation), subcultural (within homosexual or transgender groups), or individual. Although some authors (e.g., Gagnon & Simon, 1967) argue that the consensual nature of deviance should also be taken into account in defining such behaviors, statistical norms, prevalences, and legal statuses may also play important roles within any society.

In this article, we discuss ways in which culture influences fetishes and other paraphilias, including their understanding and identification. Further, we contend that because cultures differ along a number of dimensions, including the attitude toward sex as a non-procreative and pleasurable activity, the reported rates of paraphilias are likely to be higher in some societies than in others. Specifically, in societies that stress egocentric or individualistic values, social mores are more likely to be constrained by legal factors than norms, thereby making paraphilias appear more common because they are more likely to be reported to and seen by clinicians. We do not argue that legal constraints cause certain behaviors to be labelled as paraphilic, but rather the reverse. We also explore the relationship between culture and the biology of paraphilias and briefly discuss culture-bound syndromes that may contribute to paraphilias and other sexual problems. We focus on specific fetishes and other problem behaviors to demonstrate these basic conceptual principles. Finally, as we discuss these issues, we avoid the use of the term "sexual deviance" to the extent possible, as this label carries moralistic overtones.

CULTURAL CONSIDERATIONS

Understanding Culture and the Individual

Culture is constituted of explicit and implicit patterns of acquired behaviors that are transmitted through symbols (Kroeber & Kluckhohn, 1952). The essential core of culture is seen as consisting of traditional ideas and values. Culture can exist at the level of observable phenomena (within the community) and at the level of ideas, either individual or collective, with the latter represented by an organized system of knowledge and beliefs (Keesing, 1976).

With respect to ideas, the individual and the collective influence one other. As part of the process of acculturation (e.g., when cultures having different values impinge upon a single individual), the individual's core values may not necessarily change, but peripheral values—behavior, dress, and diet—may do so. Castillo (1995) suggested that "enculturation" allows an individual to learn language, follow a religion, and develop road maps of behaviors, attitudes, and patterns of experiencing. Tseng (1997) further emphasized that the habitual act of thinking in a particular language or following a particular set of religious values physically structures (or restructures) the neural networks in the brain, thereby affecting cognitions and forming cognitive schema (Sperry, 1987). This societal-cultural interaction with the individual is not static, but fluid; there may be stages when the individual changes very rapidly, followed by a plateau, before further change occurs. Thus, the growth and change of the individual in a culture will be influenced by a number of factors, including the differences among the values of the cultures, the amount of time spent in the different cultures, and family and individual factors that contribute to the rate of enculturation.

Types of Cultures

Hofstede (1980, 1984) broadly divided cultures into sociocentric (collectivist) or ego-centric (individualistic). Sociocentric cultures believe in "we-ness," and people from birth onward are integrated into strong cohesive ingroups, which throughout their lifetime continue to protect them in exchange for unquestioning loyalty. Collectivism emphasizes "we-consciousness," with the focus on collective identity, emotional interdependence, group solidarity, and sharing duties and obligations. The focus is also on the need for stable and predetermined friendships, and decisions are made by the group and the kin.

Egocentric cultures emphasize loose ties between individuals, where members of society are expected to look after themselves and their immediate family. Individualism believes in "I-ness, I-conscious" with a focus on autonomy, emotional independence, individual initiative, right to privacy, pleasure-seeking, financial security, and need for specific friendship.

Key differences exist between collectivist and individualistic societies in a number of areas. Apart from attitudes, differences in behaviors and relationships mean that the individual's response to social expectations will vary. For example, in a collectivist society, prior to conducting business, a relationship of trust is established between the two parties. As Hofstede (2001) stated, to the collectivist mind, only "real" persons are worthy of trust and, via these persons, their friends and colleagues; legal entities or companies do not stand worthy of trust (p. 239). Thus, personal relationships (in collectivist societies) prevail over the task and the company. In sociocentric or collectivist societies, where the individual's identity (and ego) is subsumed in the kinship-based identity, tensions will develop around non-procreative, pleasure-based sexual behaviors. Furthermore, kinship-based societies are more likely to impact an individual's moral values, thereby complicating attitudes toward sex, sexuality, and sexual behavior.

A separate dimension on which national cultures differ systematically is related to masculinity-femininity. Some cultures support flexible and equal gender roles, and others do not. These national differences can be measured, and they affect not only interpersonal relationships, but also factors in an individual's work choices and goals. Hofstede (2001, p. 293) cautioned that the masculinity-femininity dimension should not be confused with the individualism-collectivism dimension, as they measure different things. Both dimensions produce norms for societies, but each places a different emphasis on aspects of relationships and social role expectations. However, cultures with high masculine indexes tend to score high on individualism, emphasize financial rewards and masculine work and features, and extend limited sympathy for the weak. Feminine societies, on the other hand, are relationship oriented and focus on minimum social and emotional differentiation.

In addition to individualism-collectivism and masculinity-femininity, Hofstede (2001, p. 25) identified three other cultural dimensions for analysis: power distance, uncertainty avoidance, and long-term versus short-term orientation. Power distance is a measure of the interpersonal power or influence between a superior and a subordinate and reflects the degree of inequality between individuals. The concept of uncertainty avoidance relies on the fact that extreme uncertainty causes intolerable anxiety, with different societies adapting in different ways to uncertainty. The strategies to manage uncertainty are both rational and non-rational and may include laws, religion, and technology. Societies with lower work stress, low levels of anxiety in the population, and shared happiness and more subjective elements of well-being score low on the uncertainty index. Finally, cultures may differ on long- versus short-term orientation, with those that are long term giving greater value to preparation for the long-term futures and goals. Although evidence supports these cultural dimensions (Hofstede, 2001), it is not clear whether any particular hierarchical arrangement exists for them.

Given Hofstede's (2001) five dimensions, it may be that cultures with specific combinations of these dimensions are at greater risk for fetishes and other problem-related sexual behaviors. For example, cultures that are masculine, individualistic, have low power distance, have low short-term orientation, and have low uncertainty avoidance may present a combination of conditions ripe for the expression of paraphilic behavior. Although cross-cultural comparisons using such factors to predict the presence of fetishes and other paraphilic behaviors have not been undertaken, this kind of cultural analysis may prove fruitful in understanding cultural factors that account for variability in sexual fetishes and other problematic sexual behaviors.

Disease Versus Illness

From a cultural standpoint, one of the major challenges toward understanding fetishes and other problematic sexual behaviors lies in how they are viewed: as "unusual," "abnormal," "deviant," "sick," and so on. Cultures can differentiate normality from abnormality through expert opinion, deviation from the mean, and assessing the function or social judgment of the individual—this last strategy relegating the behavior or problem to the classification of psychopathology (Offer & Sabshin, 1966).

One common tool, based on the psychopathological model, used for identifying fetishes and other paraphilic behavior has been the *DSM* (APA, 2000). In this diagnostic system, exhibitionism, fetishism, frotteurism, pedophilia, sexual masochism, sexual sadism, transvestic fetishism, voyeurism, and paraphilia not otherwise specified are included under the broad rubric of paraphilias. In the *DSM-IV-TR,* the essential features of paraphilias are their recurrent, intense sexually arousing fantasies, sexual urges or behaviors involving non-human objects, suffering, or humiliation of oneself or one's partner or children or other non-consenting persons occurring over at least six months. Paraphilic fantasies may be occasional or regular, and the individual may or may not act on them. Generally, fetishes and paraphilias serve a common purpose—all are intended to induce sexual arousal. As a result of the arousal, some individuals may feel guilt or shame, whereas others feel none—this latter scenario suggesting the presence of an underlying personality disorder.

Given the psychopathological approach, the question arises as to whether paraphilias represent a "disease" state, so it is initially useful to compare the concepts of "disease" versus "illness" in the context of paraphilias (Eisenberg, 1977). Disease has been noted as "dis-ease," related to pathology, and diagnosed and managed by trained physicians. Nevertheless, even "disease" may have a relativistic nature about it. For example, in psychiatric diagnoses that are "cross-cultural," the clinician must be aware of the impact of cultural factors and norms on help-seeking and diagnosis. Similarly, successful management of a psychiatric disease will be influenced by factors such as expectations, past experiences, and cultural-specific explanatory models (Bhugra & Gupta, in press). When the disease begins to affect others around the patient and leads to certain behaviors as a result, it becomes an "illness" (Eisenberg, 1977). Thus, disease as an entity reflects the underlying psychopathology or pathophysiology, whereas illness constitutes the set of behaviors surrounding the disease that affects those around the patient—behaviors that are likely to be dictated by social and cultural factors (Eisenberg, 1977; Kleinman, 1980). Bhugra and Bhui (2001) noted that the universalistic approach, which argues that all psychiatric disorders are identical across cultures, does not sit easily when cultural influences related to "illness" are taken into account.

The diagnosis of paraphilias is typically based on behaviors, sexual urges, or fantasies that cause clinically significant distress or impairment in social, occupational, or other areas of functioning. Relationships and functioning may suffer if the individual's actions create problems in forming or sustaining relationships or with the legal system. Especially for voyeurism, frotteurism, exhibitionism, and pedophilia, the individual is more likely to experience legal difficulties. Thus, virtually all these categories of paraphilias can be seen as "illnesses," as they affect others around the individual. Yet, since the underlying pathology for these paraphilias is not always clear, the identification of these patterns of behavior as "disease" needs to be re-examined with more data.

However, not all paraphilias necessarily fall into the illness category either. Some types of paraphilias, such as sadomasochism, will affect other people, especially if the behavior is non-consensual or illegal. But, at this point, Gagnon and Simon's (1967) consideration of the relationship between the two individuals and their mutual consent becomes useful. For example, what if the sadomasochism is mutually consensual? Or, consider the man interested in cross-dressing in females' clothes: This behavior may not represent an "illness" until it results in criminal behavior (e.g., stealing women's clothing that then leads to an arrest). The psychiatric approach would, therefore, focus on the "illness" aspects of the paraphilia—that is, how the behavior affects others.

Because paraphilias are more likely to be illnesses rather than diseases, treatment strategies may need to reflect this. Paraphilic conditions—as illnesses—are likely to be chronic, increase in frequency under psycho-social stressors, and decrease with advancing age. Furthermore, the clinicians' efforts may be negatively perceived by the patient and viewed as legitimizing the suppression of non-normative behaviors that threaten social norms—a reaction that may differ depending on the patient's cultural context. Thus, assessment and management strategies of paraphilias across cultures need to take into account the distinction between disease and illness, along with the conditions that typically accompany illness across various cultures.

Sexual Attitudes and Behaviors Across Cultures

In a classic volume, Bullough (1976) highlighted differences in sexual attitudes and behaviors across societies and cultures. In his work, he noted that sexual activities have been either encouraged or proscribed through the assumptions of the philosophy and religion of the culture. Tolerance of certain sexual behaviors is linked with these sexual assumptions girded by cultural values and creation myths. Bullough stated that, even though heterosexual coitus is prevalent for the majority of adults in human societies, societies themselves differ about the variety of sexual behaviors that will be tolerated (p. 16). Although inevitably society will view heterosexual intercourse as essential, insight into deviant sexuality can be garnered through its legal codes, religious proscriptions, and literary and philosophical descriptions. Thus, what constitutes deviation may differ not only over time or within different segments of culture, but also from one individual to another within a single culture. Furthermore, the state's stated norms for the society may actually vary from the actual or even accepted norms. Ford and Beach (1965), from information derived from the Human Relations Area Files, concluded that both wide agreement and wide variation in sexual attitudes and behaviors occur both across and within cultures. For example, although some societies condoned and encouraged sexual impulses of children, others forbade and punished such behavior. In yet another twist, although masturbation was condemned by some societies, this did not prevent most adults from engaging in the behavior.

Bullough (1976, p. 94) further noted that one influential factor in setting sexual outlooks is the attitude toward the opposite sex, especially toward women—that is, attitudes toward sexual conduct will be influenced by gender roles, gender role expectations, and the specific expectations within the sexual dyad. Such attitudinal factors might contribute to an understanding of the greater prevalence of paraphilias in men. For example, as the role of women has often focused on producing children, women's sexual needs have frequently been discounted or ignored, whereas the sexual needs of the male have almost always been paramount. In such male sexual-centric systems, fetishistic behavior, especially when it does not affect others, may serve the purpose of increasing the man's arousal, thereby increasing the chances of successful conception.

Sex-Positive and Sex-Negative Cultures

Bullough (1976) viewed societies and cultures as either sex-positive or sex-negative. Sex-negative cultures see semen loss, even in coitus, as a weakness; and sexual asceticism is encouraged. Sex-positive cultures, on the other hand, emphasize, among other things, the pleasurable, rewarding, and non-procreative aspects of sex.

A brief historic overview of Western culture can serve to illustrate how attitudes can undergo significant change and how religious values may affect these attitudes.

From Greek and Roman times, when sexual activity and alternative sexual behaviors were acknowledged and accepted, to early days of Christianity, a massive shift in attitudes toward sexuality occurred. Ascetic ideals were increasingly promoted by the Christian religious teachings of the time (Bullough, 1976, p. 167). Furthermore, in order for societies (or subgroups within those societies) to survive and flourish, it was imperative that men not lose semen and couples procreate as necessary. Accordingly, in order to channel the thoughts of their followers, early theologians focused on selected aspects of sex, emphasizing the good of sex within marriage while condemning it outside marriage (p. 168). Early Christianity generally disapproved of non-procreative sex (p. 181) and Bullough, while acknowledging the possibility of some (mis)interpretations, postulated that the dominant reason for this attitude was related to competition between parallel, but competing, religious systems. However, even marriage was not a license for sexual activity (p. 185), the ideal being to reject all sexual desire. In such a context, sexual activity was interpreted as a duty rather than a source for pleasure.

In contrast, Bullough (1976, p. 205) identified Islam as leaning more toward a sex-positive position, especially as sexual traditions of pre-Islamic Arabs were more accepting of sex. Women were to be sought out for wedlock but not debauchery, and mention is made of transvestism and transsexualism in historic documents (p. 234). However, in this tradition, the role of women both sexually and otherwise was typically seen as inferior to that of men—a view that typically counters sex-positive attitudes.

Hinduism, both a religion and a philosophy, was seen as sex-positive, as evidenced by the Kama Sutra and temple carvings depicting sex acts. The Kama Sutra covers most aspects of human courtship and mating, as do many other erotic classics of the Hindu religion (Bullough, 1976, p. 246). There were, of course, sexual prohibitions among Hindus: for example, incest was taboo, adultery looked down upon, and intercaste relations discouraged, yet transvestism, transsexualism, and other forms of "deviance" were tolerated. Special appendages were available to change the shape of the penis, and bestiality was also tolerated under some conditions (p. 265). Bullough (p. 273) noted that it was important in the Indian subcontinent for the male to express his femininity and the female her masculinity since, otherwise, neither would be able to understand the specific nature of the opposite sex. However, male seed was seen as precious, as it was presumably the result of a complicated process of turning food into semen, which made it "biologically" expensive (see Bhugra & Buchanan, 1989). Even today, semen loss anxiety is widely prevalent in the Indian subcontinent.

As changes in societies have occurred, attitudes toward sexuality, sexual activity, and the purpose of such activity have also changed. In early centuries, religion was more likely to define, reinforce, and modify sexual attitudes and concepts. These concepts and attitudes began to change with the development of challenges to religion and new ideas, both philosophical and scientific. In 19th-century England, these changing attitudes were both spurred by and reflected in the growth of erotic and pornographic novels and materials, ideas of sex drawn from Darwinism, the influence of colonialism, the growth of special brothels related to flagellation, and homosexual prostitutes. Sexual activity underwent a redefinition from an obligation to a necessity (Bullough, 1976, p. 495).

In the first part of the 21st century, attitudes toward sex, the sexual act, and paraphilias remain variable across the globe. For example, in some countries, consensual homosexual acts among adults remain illegal and even a capital offense, whereas, in others, homosexual acts over the age of 14 are considered acceptable. Although by and large greater acceptance of women's sexuality has occurred over the past decades, this too remains vastly different across cultures. Scientific advances, increased tolerance, the changing role of religion, and organized propaganda and media for new sexualities have all contributed to changing values and attitudes. Nevertheless, for some societies even today, a long-term sequel of colonial laws and systems that have remained in place for hundreds of years have prevented change from occurring.

Sociocultural Theory of Human Sexuality

Supporting an important role for social and cultural expectations, Reiss (1986) noted that sexual practices are linked with kinship patterns and power structures within the society, an idea consistent with Hofstede's (2001) suggestions. Reiss argued that sexual practices follow shared cultural scripts, which may promote one kind of sexual behavior while discouraging others. These sexual scripts may be both innate and learned—for example, heterosexual attraction may be innate, but specific "end" behaviors may be learned through culture. The contents of sexual scripts are also influenced by social class, age, religious practice, and educational and economic status. Other culture-specific factors, such as caste as in Hindu society, may also play a role. Sexual attraction, and the mores governing it, is both individual and social—that is, in the way it is accepted, tolerated, or rejected by the society at large. Reiss emphasized that sexual scripts determine what people find erotically arousing, with arousal learned in response to social and cultural stimuli. Thus, kinship-based and gender-based ties allow individuals to form long-lasting relationships based on support systems, the needs of the kinship, and the rearing of children. Gender roles and gender role expectations are also important determinants of sexual scripts. Members of the more powerful sex (generally male), argued Reiss, will secure control of major social institutions and shape gender roles (which impact sexual attitudes and behaviors), an idea that fits with Hofstede's (2001) cultural dimension of masculinity and femininity.

Table 1. *Types of Deviance and Cultural-Biological Influences*

Deviance	Type	Cultural Influences	Biological Influences
Normal	Masturbation	+ + +	+
	Oral sex	+ + +	?
	Premarital sex	+ + +	?
Subcultural	Fetishism	+	?
	Sadomasochism	+	?
	Transsexualism	+	+ +
	Transvestism	+ +	?
Individual	Exhibitionist	+	?
	Rape	7	?
	Incest	?	?

+ = positive correlation present; ? = unknown.

However, as Segall, Dasen, Berry, and Poortinga (1990) pointed out, sexual attraction and arousal is also biological, making the interaction between the social scripts and biology of great interest to both social science researchers and biomedical communities. Ultimately, then, in addition to the role played by the type of culture—for example, whether sociocentric or egocentric—underlying biological factors (sex of the person, biological mechanisms of arousal, etc.) may play a role in the genesis of certain types of paraphilias (see Table 1)—conditions characterized by unusual sexually attracting stimuli for the purpose of sexual arousal.

Indeed, the importance of biological factors to the aetiology of some paraphilias may actually be greater than social factors. This view, one that combines biological, individual, and *cultural* differences may enable researchers to develop models of aetiology, diagnosis, and management of attraction, arousal, and paraphilia that are more focused and effective. Too often, the role of cultural factors, while given lip-service, has not been afforded serious attention in the understanding of human sexual behavior. In the following section, we focus on the role that culture may play in the development of fetishes.

SEXUAL ATTRACTION, AROUSAL, AND BEHAVIORS ACROSS CULTURES

There are few, if any, standards of what constitutes "sexually attractive and arousing." From size to color of the eyes and hair, individual notions of attraction remain just that—individual. However, these characteristics may also be strongly influenced by sexual preference and societal norms. In most societies, the physical beauty of the female form receives more attention than that of the male, although this pattern may be undergoing change. This preoccupation with the female form may reflect patriarchal social systems, be related to the importance of arousal to the male for sexual performance, and help explain why men are more likely to become aroused by objects and, thus, develop fetishes. Ford and Beach (1965) pointed out that selected family traits may include plump body shape, small ankles, elongated labia majora, large clitoris, or pendulous breasts; and these may become objects of attraction for the males.

Permitted sexual activities also vary significantly across cultures. As an example, some societies tolerate bestiality, particularly among teenage males (although seen as unnatural, silly, disgusting, and inferior to normal sexual activity), but do so primarily in the absence of more appropriate sexual outlets. Ford and Beach (1965) noted that at least four societies allowed such contact without condemnation. Similarly, although adult masturbation is tolerated in some cultures and encouraged in others, attitudes toward female masturbation have generally remained negative.

In societies that are restrictive in their attitudes to sex, teenagers publicly suppress their sexual desires, and sexual activity is usually absent. In less restrictive societies, teenagers find ways to circumvent barriers, even though restrictions are enforced and punishment may occur. In semi-restrictive societies, formal restrictions on certain kinds of sexual activity may still exist but are not applied or enforced very seriously. Sexual experimentation occurs, but usually in secrecy or semi-secrecy, and punishment is unlikely. Permissive societies will tolerate sexual activity in teenagers, but absolute proscriptions on certain activities, such as incest, persist. In restrictive societies, girls are expected to be virgins until they marry whereas in other societies, if such expectations exist, these are less obvious. As a result of differences in permissiveness, the onset of partnered sexual activity will develop somewhat more rapidly in certain societies in comparison with others.

Social expectations related to the location of sexual activity also come into play. Ford and Beach (1965) noted that, in most societies, sexual intercourse occurs in seclusion and, if allowed in public, is proscribed around children. Where people live in un-partitioned multiple dwellings, outdoor sex may be allowed. In some settings, sexual intercourse can occur only at night (even if the individuals do not prefer it), as the sexual act is shameful and daytime coitus is too risky. In fact, some societies believe that children resulting from daytime sex may be born blind. These social restrictions on where sex can occur also contribute to the onset and development of sexual behaviors over various cultures.

Finally, in most cultures, sexual intercourse is preceded by some degree of foreplay—that is, sensory and sexual stimulation intended to induce arousal. This stimulation may be visual, tactile, or otherwise. When visual, it may be the sight of the partner or parts of his or her body or clothing, but these may vary across cultures (Bhugra, 2000). Kissing as part of sexual foreplay is common in the West but virtually unknown in other parts of the world (Ford & Beach, 1965). There are some cultures where penetration was the key element to intercourse, and neither foreplay nor afterplay was recorded. Ford and Beach pointed out that physical pain and biting are sometimes permitted as part of sexual foreplay and, therefore, such behaviors are likely to be readily incorporated into the sexual repertoire. Thus, individuals learn about methods of sexual arousal and sexual activity from their cultural habits and, in order to avoid being labelled and treated as deviant, they conform to prevalent and expected mores.

Given that attraction, arousal, and sexual behavioral development vary in response to cultural restrictions, the next section briefly presents selected paraphilias and then attempts to view their development from a cultural lens. In doing so, we quite intentionally overlook other aetiological views of paraphilic development, including biological, learning, or cognitive-developmental models. In addition, data relevant to these paraphilias are almost exclusively derived from Western samples and based on Western assumptions.

PREVALENCE OF PARAPHILIAS AND OTHER PROBLEM SEXUAL BEHAVIORS: CULTURAL CONSIDERATIONS

Examples of Prevalence and Culturally Derived Risk Factors

Even in societies friendly to sex research (as may occur in parts of the West), reliable studies examining the prevalence of paraphilias are scarce for obvious reason: The activities may themselves be illegal and, even if legal, people may be too embarrassed to acknowledge that they indulge in these behaviors. Clinic populations are likely to consist of individuals referred for legal reasons, rather than seeking help on their own. In non-Western societies, prevalence data are nonexistent, thereby making cross-cultural comparisons very difficult. In the following section, we offer a broad overview of the prevalence of selected paraphilias primarily as background for the broader discussion of cultural context; we do not intend to provide an exhaustive review of this topic.

One strategy devised to investigate the relative prevalence of various paraphilias has been to use indirect measures. For example, Dietz and Evans (1982) used cover images and content of pornographic magazines as an index of the relative prevalence of specific paraphilias. They concluded that, although some pornography is consumed for curiosity value, the imagery of pornography is likely to correspond to the pre-existing fantasies of the consumer (Stoller, 1975, 1979). Dietz and Evans identified the most common imagery as bondage and domination. Furthermore, magazines of any type usually depicted women wearing high heels and lingerie. Although this procedure represents an interesting strategy, it suffers from several problems, including that these images may be used for fantasy and not actual behavior, and that many cultures neither have nor permit such materials.

More recently, in Sweden in 1996, 2,450 randomly selected 18- to 60-year-old individuals participated in a broad survey of sexuality and health. Included were questions dealing with paraphilias and other problem sexual behaviors (Langstrom & Hanson, 2006; Langstrom & Seto, 2006; Langstrom & Zucker, 2005). Langstrom and Seto (2006) found that 3.1% of respondents reported at least one incident of being sexually aroused by exposing their genitals to a stranger, and 7.7% acknowledged at least one incident of being sexually aroused by spying on others having sex. These behaviors were related to gender (male), having more psychological problems, lower satisfaction with life, and greater drug and alcohol use. These individuals were also twice more likely to become sexually aroused easily and to have had same-sex partners. Not surprisingly, they were also more likely to have had sexual fantasies related to paraphiliac behaviors. Men were twice as likely than women to expose themselves and nearly three times more likely to indulge in voyeuristic behavior, and these behaviors were associated with masturbation frequency and pornographic use, but not sexual abuse. These researchers also indicated that immigrant status was not a significant correlate of either paraphilic-like behavior—a finding that suggests possible cultural differences in prevalence of paraphilias. However, without detailed knowledge of the immigrant groups, it is impossible to verify such ideas. Another interesting survey finding was that some paraphilias were related to early family environment—for example, separation from parents. Since family and, therefore, developmental environments differ greatly across cultures, cultural differences on such variables might well be critical to understanding the aetiology of paraphilias.

From the same data set, Langstrom and Zucker (2005) reported that almost 2.8% of men and 0.4% of women acknowledged at least one episode of transvestic fetishism. Again, separation from parents, same-sex sexual experiences, getting easily sexually aroused, pornography use, and higher frequency of masturbation were associated with this fetish and these individuals were also more likely to have been separated from parents in childhood, to have been sexually abused, and to report other paraphilic behaviors such as exhibitionism and voyeurism. As with other paraphilias, migrant groups to Sweden were less likely to report tranvestic fetishism, with the lower prevalence reflecting several possibilities: a genuinely lower rate; a lack of understanding of its "illness" status in the West; or hesitancy toward admitting to a behavior that might signal weakness, embarrass their cultural group, or expose them to legal challenges. Although the numbers were small, this study raises further questions about the role of separation from parents, childhood sexual abuse, general sexual arousability, and same-sex relationships in the aetiology of paraphilias—that is, it might be hypothesized that in cultures where these characteristics are less probable, the prevalence of such paraphilic behaviors would also be less probable.

Once again relying on the same sample, Langstrom and Hanson (2006) noted an association between hyper-sexuality and paraphilic disorders. While recognizing the challenges of denning hypersexuality, they reported that men falling into this group were more likely to be young, to experience separation from parents, and to live in major cities. They had an earlier onset of sexual activity, were more likely to pay for sex, and reported higher frequencies of same-sex behavior, exhibitionism, voyeurism, and sadomasochism. Interestingly, they were less satisfied with their sex lives and indulged in more risk-taking behaviors such as drinking, smoking, drug abuse, and gambling. Clearly then, paraphilic tendencies are associated with many other behaviors and social variables and, although it is not known whether or how such factors contribute to paraphilias, cultures that differ significantly on these factors may be more or less prone to paraphilic behaviors. Furthermore, cultures that have strong proscriptions toward extramarital sexual activity may provide fewer occasions for the development of such problematic sexual behaviors. Specifically, it is theoretically possible that men with hypersexuality need stronger arousal stimuli as a result of conditioning behavior and cultural mores that allow such behaviors to play out, and may be more likely to exhibit paraphiliac tendencies.

Gender Differences

Gender differences in the prevalence of paraphilias are well-known. Baldwin and Baldwin (1997) proposed a hypothesis to explain this difference by arguing that biological and social factors operate together. Males are often more interested in physical sexuality than females (Blumstein & Schwartz, 1983; Greer & Buss, 1994; Laumann, Gagnon, Michael, & Michaels, 1994; Sprecher, 1989; Sprecher & McKinney, 1993). Men think of sex more frequently (Laumann et al., 1994) and emphasize the physical pleasure of sex (Frazier & Esterly, 1990), whereas women are less likely to engage in sexual intercourse without an emotional attachment (Carroll, Volk, & Hyde, 1985). Furthermore, from a developmental perspective, the male child develops differently from the female child. Boys learn genital pleasure more readily and perhaps earlier (Galenson & Roiphe, 1974), and parents often apply double standards in encouraging boys toward sexuality while proscribing it for girls. Non-coital learning through peers and other sources influence male attitudes toward sex, sexuality, masturbation, and erections. Pubertal girls, on the other hand, often learn about genitalia and sex in an embarrassing way. These roles related to sex, gender, sexual activity, and masturbation are strongly influenced by cultural values, as are the perceived purpose and inherent pleasure related to sexual intercourse.

A Specific Paraphilia Defined Within Cultural Context: Pedophilia

Seto (2004) provided a recent review of pedophilia and sexual offenses against children. Pedophilia is a recurrent sexual interest in prepubescent children, reflected in persistent thoughts, fantasies, urges, sexual arousal, and behavior (APA, 2000). In its strongest form, Seto argued, pedophilia reflects an exclusive preference for prepubescent children to the total exclusion of sexual interest in adults. Most research in this area has been conducted on either offender samples or on people who have identified themselves as pedophiles. In one survey, 71% of male pedophiles reported an attraction to boys aged 12 to 14 years, and only 12% preferred girls aged 8 to 10 years. Nearly one half had fantasies about sex (Wilson & Cox, 1983). Interestingly, Seto, Cantor, and Blanchard (2006) argued that child pornography can be used as a valid indicator of diagnosis of pedophilia, but its use may be related to fantasy and arousal rather than actual behavior with children. However, in cultures where pornography is illegal, even this indicator is not available.

Although ancient Greece and Rome allowed adult-child sex, studies on other cultures are rare. Current notions of child molestation were well-known in some cultures in the past (Green, 2002). In today's view, the definition of pedophilia is tied directly to the cultural definition of "age of consent": Different cultures and societies allow different ages of consent for homosexual and heterosexual activity and, within some countries, variation is seen as well. In Western societies, pedophilia is viewed as an aberration, and significant effort has been expended to identify characteristics of pedophiles. For example, they have been shown to be deficient in social skills (Emmers-Sommer et al., 2004), shy, unassertive, and passive (Langevin, 1983), and socially withdrawn (Bard et al., 1987; Langevin et al., 1985). Family variables are correlated as well; pedophiles have troubled childhoods (see McAnulty, 2006), may have been abused sexually as children, are associated with poor parenting, discontinuities in parenting (as seen in the Swedish sample discussed above, Langstrom & Seto, 2006), and serious family dysfunction (Marshall, 1989; Marshall, Hudson, & Hodkinson, 1993). Given these factors, we wonder, for example, whether certain family environments, which differ considerably across cultures, may be more or less likely to result in pedophilia. Extended families, with the focus on kinships, with more parenting figures, and with lower propensity toward family dysfunction, may result in a society having a lower predilection for pedophilia.

Cultures and the Meaning of Fetishes

Kaplan (2006), whose view is primarily psychoanalytic, suggested that, in general, the need to transform something unfamiliar and intangible into something familiar and tangible is one of the major principles of the fetishism strategy (p. 1). In its classical (nonsexual) sense, fetishism is related to the practice of worshipping, and the origins of the word relate to artificial objects, feathers, or wooden carvings; etymologic origins also refer to false values, worship of useless objects, fictitious, false, artificial, or simulated (p. 2). Kaplan noted that a "fetishist" is one who is irrationally devoted to these (bizarre) worship practices. Within a more sexual context, rubber, leather, and latex and other materials have all been identified as objects of sexual "worship" and desire.

The fetishism strategy is worth consideration in understanding the cultural influence on the development of paraphilias. Kaplan (2006, p. 5) described fetishism as a mental strategy or defence that enables a person to transform something or someone with its own enigmatic energy and immaterial essence into something or someone that is material and tangibly real—a form of being that makes the something or someone controllable.

Using exhibitionism as an illustration of a paraphilia, it might be argued that reality shows enable a form of narcissistic behavior linked with a desire to put oneself on show—hence a form of exhibitionism. Kaplan (2006, p. 5) argued that such shows also dehumanize its participants, thus making them into commodities. Under these circumstances, why is it that people fall for this trap and allow themselves to be "fetishized" in such a way? This externalized fetish at one level must serve a purpose—perhaps not necessarily or always sexual, but certainly as an object that may be commodified and used for excitement. As Kaplan indicated, the commodity is a non-living entity with no life of its own, but by virtue of the mechanical stereotyped representation of actual human beings, the commodity eventually becomes a fetish. Kaplan (p. 6) noted that fetishism transforms ambiguity and uncertainty into something knowable and certain. Her argument was that a fetish is reassuring, external, and used to control the uncontrollable energies of the unknown. The unknowingness and uncontrollability of energies is not necessarily greater in the traditional societies where (nonsexual) fetishistic objects emerge. However, one might view the sexualization of fetishistic objects as an individual's attempt to deal with internalized (uncontrollable and sexual) urges. Thus, sexualization of the objects into fetishes allows individuals to deal with internal anxiety and ambiguity—an idea that is consistent with Hofstede's (1980) cultural dimension of anxiety management through avoiding uncertainty (which may, by the way, occur at either the individual or societal level). Although this general sexual strategy should be possible in any given culture, as we have suggested, individual cultures provide different stimuli for arousal and also set up barriers that inhibit the development of other types of sexual attraction and arousal.

Kaplan (2006) suggested that "fetishism allows certain details into the foreground of experience … to mask and disguise other features that are thus cast into the shadows and margins and background" (p. 6). The obvious presence, attraction, and purpose of the fetish, therefore, become masked, with the mask itself often becoming more dramatic and obvious. Using necrophilia as an example, Kaplan continued that, in using and seeing dead bodies as fetishes, there is a transformation of the living into the dead. Furthermore, "the more dangerous and unpredictable the threat of desire, the more deadened or distanced from human experience the fetish object must be" (p. 7). The full identity of the sexual object is alive with unpredictable realities. The dead object, therefore, becomes knowable and predictable, thereby reducing both external and internal anxiety.

Analogous Fetishes Manifested in Culturally Specific Ways?

Given the aforementioned strategy and purpose of fetishism strategy, one might expect sexual fetishes to appear across cultures, although the content and the object of the fetishes may well be influenced by cultures and thus may well vary. Kaplan (2006, pp. 35–50) used the example of foot binding of Chinese females as a cultural fetish. This practice began in the 21st century BC, and in its earliest days was confined to the upper classes, specifically to concubines, dancing girls, and the ruler's mistresses; it did not initially appear among commoners and was localized to specific geographical regions. However, the practice spread widely across China—a phenomenon attributed to a generalized anxiety about the erosion of the clearly defined places for women and, with it, the male fear of competition from women and deterioration of patriarchal order (Ping, 2000). The control of women in this manner may be associated with a fetishistic desire on the part of the male, who can exert control over the object. However, why the feet and not other parts of the body? Is it because feet symbolize servility, yet are highly visible? In a more recent development, one might suggest that the female obsession (urged and encouraged by the male) with high heel shoes—which trap and injure the feet—is a modern foot binding exercise practiced in the West. Furthermore, shoe designers are generally male, and their perception of what female beauty is or ought to be both fetishizes and commodifies the woman and her body parts. Thus, the male gaze focuses not only on the shoes, but on the woman's whole body shape, particularly the legs and hips, all of which are impacted by the wearing of the shoes, and all of which reinforce the fetishistic desire in the male.

The previous comparison indicates that, although some paraphilias may be recognizable across cultures, their aetiologies and specific manifestations may be quite different. Wearing stilettos is by and large a Western phenomenon. Thus, in cultures where high heels or stockings are not used and seen, it is unlikely that these fetishes will emerge, as people have generally not been exposed to these as sexual stimuli. Yet, the question remains, however, why, despite these apparent fetish adaptations across cultures, some cultures do not appear to have any objects or practices analogous to them.

Normalizing Behavior That Might Be Considered Fetishistic

Cultures may sometimes "normalize" behavior that might otherwise be considered fetishistic. For example, Herdt (1981, 1984) reported that among the Sambians of Papua New Guinea, young boys, upon reaching puberty, fellate older men of the tribe and swallow the semen in order to gain strength. Nowhere else would this be viewed as normal. These young males spend 10 or more years of their life in exclusively homosexual relations, during which they are taught to fear the polluting effects of women (Herdt, 1981; Stoller & Herdt, 1985). However, once in heterosexual marriages, these homoerotic experiences appear to become irrelevant.

Baldwin and Baldwin (1989) observed that, among the Sambians, sexual expression is restricted to highly ritualized patterns. These authors argued that after 7 to 10 years of "heterosexual" childhood, young males enter homoerotic interactions, with homosexual behavior seen as a means to an end. Cognitive refraining that semen is important for growth and strength means that these behaviors become highly desired. Thus, the initiation of sexual behavior in this culture is socially guided. Baldwin and Baldwin (1989) also noted the aversive side of this ritual behavior: The homosexual behavior is not necessarily to be enjoyed—that is, the implication is that unless these boys perform fellatio, they will not become strong and masculine. The young males are generally introduced to the females of the tribe while still engaging in the homosexual behavior, with the adolescent period bringing males and females together even more. Baldwin and Baldwin (1989) noted that further initiation rituals specifically present females as objects of sexual desire and interest, providing the basis for a cognitive restructuring that promotes heterosexual conditioning. This gradual introduction to heterosexual behavior allows new behaviors to be learned in successive approximations. Baldwin and Baldwin (1989) suggested that Sambian males have numerous additional socialization experiences through which they gain more heterosocial and heterosexual orientation prior to marriage.

This illustration of reorientation from homosexual to heterosexual confirms that cultures provide different foci in the range of sexual behaviors. Overall, "normalization" of certain behaviors allows behaviors that might otherwise be considered "deviant" to be redefined according to social norms and mores. In a tribe like the Sambians, a general sociocentric orientation coupled with the importance of kinship, rather than inherent biological factors, determines how people should behave sexually—initially from fear of pollution by the female to the heterosocial and heterosexual attraction characterized by both a behavioral and a cognitive shift.

Furthermore, the Sambians are not expected to be sensitive and all-enveloping in their marital state, thus allowing them to function in a heterosocial way. Thus, cultures that place an emphasis on marriage as companionship rather than on an all-encompassing marital relationship may also allow individuals to develop sexual behaviors in a different way. Sambian males may continue to have same-sex fantasies, but their behavior is likely to be heterosexual.

As part of her study of fetishism, Kaplan (2006, p. 52) argued that the female form is often used to demonstrate fetishistic emblem. These images reflect the vulnerability of the female form and also the reflection of the male gaze on her. Tattooing, flesh-piercing, and self-cutting may be seen as body fetishistic behavior, with overtones of sexuality and sexual worship; such patterns are found in many cultures and subcultures but often take different forms. Kaplan suggested that "long before fetishism was named as a perversion of the sexual life, religious pundits, anthropologists, philosophers, poets and economists employed the concept of fetishism to illuminate a vast assortment of cultural activities" (p. 93). The assertion here is that objects of fetishism are reflections of the culture in which they are found. Whether the specific culture then dictates fetishistic behavior or whether the behavior appears de novo and then influences the culture represents an interactive process that is not fully understood. Interestingly, cultures that have bred and nourished the fetishism strategy as espoused by Kaplan have been long-standing (p. 177) and likely to be Euro-American. The relationship between the fetishism strategy (which, in part, reduces anxiety) and the moral restraints placed by society on such behavioral strategies pulls the individual and the culture in opposing directions.

THE ROLE OF SEXUAL FETISHES

Sexual fetish may make the male more potent by improving his sexual arousal. The question then is, "Why are fetishes considered a problem if they allow the man to perform better and increase the chances for reproduction?" The answers may be various, and typically include the idea that they objectify the female form or cause social and functional impairment. Yet, the question then follows as to why they should be considered aberrations, particularly in cultures that espouse sexual functioning primarily for procreation and reproduction.

It is possible that in sociocentric cultures where sexual intercourse is primarily for procreation, the presence or development of sexual fetishes may be either genuinely lower or reported less often—reliable data are lacking. In cultures that are egocentric and where the primary purpose of sex is pleasure, the sexual fetish leads to the commodification of the female object, thereby increasing arousal for the purpose of pleasure.

In psychoanalytic terms, the main objective of sexual fetishism in these cultures may be that of conquering and subsuming the fetishistic object—a process that can be both exciting and arousing.

The sexual fetishist uses his fetish both to tame and to subdue the otherwise unpredictable erotic vitalities of his sexual partner (Kaplan, 2006, p. 111). The fact that these erotic vitalities are seen as unpredictable may push the male and his gaze toward a lifeless or nearly lifeless body (in necrophilia or rape) or toward fetishistic objects in order to produce arousal. Kaplan (p. 111) posited that this energy may be ambiguous and the fetishistic object, therefore, presents a liberating factor, especially if seen as erotic. The question then is whether this erotic freedom or liberation is present across all cultures; and the secondary question is, if so, is the extent of liberation then the same? The answer to the first question is "probably," but the answer to the second one has to be "no." The question of probability can be linked with the cultural values on sexual activity and the purpose of the sexual activity, whether it is procreative or pleasurable. With increased globalization and urbanization, sex-negative cultures may be changing and the perceived or real freedom experienced by the members of these cultures may encourage them to be more experimental in their sexual activity; however, evidence supporting such an hypothesis has yet to be collected.

CULTURE AND BIOLOGY

The relationship between culture and biology is complex, and only recently have attempts been made to understand this interaction. During the intrauterine period, the human brain develops in a male direction through the action of testosterone, and in a female direction through the absence of this hormone (Swaab, 2007). Swaab further argued that the social environment has little effect on sex differences in cognition and aggression. As Swaab emphasized, if gender identity, sexual orientation, cognitions, and aggressive and other behaviors are programmed into the brain in a sexually differentiated way, then what is the role of the culture? Such a position might also argue that the prevalence of certain sexual fetishes might also then be similar across cultures, as they are primarily biologically driven. However, the interaction between biology and culture requires further exploration, and if we introduce the factors of pleasure and enjoyment in the context of sexual experience and activity, interesting notions emerge.

Berridge and Kringlebach (2008) reported that brain mechanisms of affect, motivation, and emotion are particularly relevant factors influenced by developmental experiences. These authors argued that the rewarding stimulus is a composite process, with the active processes of the brain reacting to the stimulus causing the reward. They divided the major components of the rewards into liking (core of conscious types—the latter cognitively elaborates core reaction through brain mechanisms)—wanting (motivation for reward, which includes incentive salience and conscious wanting), and learning (both explicitly and implicitly; p. 458). These different psychological components are mediated by partly dissociable brain substrates. The reactions of pleasure and displeasure are common in human lives, but pleasure is more than a sensation. Berridge and Kringlebach (2008) observed that pleasure always requires the activity of hedonic brain systems to give a "hedonic gloss" onto a sensation to make it liked. They saw this as consistent, as pleasure's role has a "reward" sensation attached to it. There is no doubt that some stimuli have a greater ability to generate pleasure or displeasure than others. Pleasure, of course, is also related to survival and procreation (Kringlebach, 2008; Panksepp, 1998; Rolls, 2005). Therefore, the pleasure from eating and sex and the displeasure related to certain tastes or smells—or sexual practices—play a significant role in human emotions. Higher order pleasures such as artistic, musical, and altruistic pleasures may depend on learning and are more specifically culture influenced.

Cognitive capacity elaborates mental representations of pleasure and displeasure as do the neural networks underlying it. Interestingly, cognitive schemas among humans are strongly influenced by culture, so the understanding of this interaction becomes critical. The occurrence of pleasure is coded by neural activity in many brain sites (Kringlebach, 2005) and, although the coding of pleasure and its causation often go hand in hand, it may not be identical (Berridge & Kringlebach, 2008). Pleasure inevitably is both behavioral and cognitive, and it may also be personal or social. The socially derived pleasure may be related to the same stimuli as the personal pleasure or to different stimuli, such as kinship-based or other reward systems. In sexual fetishism or in paraphilias, both the behavioral and cognitive aspects will work toward increasing pleasure and the rewards may be personal, social (e.g., subcultures), or both; or the personal and the social may be at odds with one another.

Various brain structures mediate this reward, with the orbitofrontal cortex the presumed apex of pleasure representation (Kringlebach, 2005) and other systems (e.g., dopamine) and structures (e.g., subcortical) involved as well (see Berridge & Kringlebach, 2008).

Disruption of these and other neural systems has been related to paraphilia. For example, in a case study involving two paraphilics, Casanova, Mannheim, and Kruesi (2002) found pathological changes in the hippocampus similar to those reported after persistent stress or long-term chronic glucocorticoid administration in a case study. Using a different approach, the study of abnormal sex offenders (with a diagnosis of paraphilia) has revealed unusual EEG recordings and anatomical differences in a number of specific frontal and temporal lobe areas (Flor-Henry, Lang, & Frenzel, 1988; Flor-Henry, Lang, Koles, & Frenzel, 1991; Hucker et al., 1986; Kirenskaya-Berus & Tkachenko, 2003). In some instances, specific abnormalities were associated with particular paraphilias (Hucker et al., 1988; Wright, Nobrega, Langevin, & Wortzman, 1990). Other studies, however, failed to find any abnormalities at all (Garnett, Nahmias, Wortzman, Langevin, & Dickey, 1988; Hendricks et al., 1988; Langevin, Lang, Wortzman, Frenzel, & Wright, 1989; Langevin, Wortzman, Dickey, Wright, & Handy, 1988; Langevin, Wortzman, Wright, & Handy, 1989), and overall results are mixed (Krueger & Kaplan, 2001).

In addition to the previously mentioned neurological studies, other research has identified neuro-developmental factors associated with various paraphilias, including low IQ, increased rates of non-right-handedness, delayed memory recall, and childhood head injury (Blanchard et al., 2007; Blanchard et al., 2002; Blanchard et al., 2003; Cantor et al., 2004; Cantor, Blanchard, Robichaud, & Christensen, 2005; Cantor et al., 2008; Rahman & Symeonides, 2008; Schiffer et al., 2008). In a recent review, Blanchard et al. (2006) suggested that, in some instances, deviant sexual behaviors result from pathogenic factors, which may impede normal psychosexual development, although others recommend caution given the incompleteness of the data (Rahman, 2005).

From the previously discussed lines of research, we might conclude that affect, reward, and pleasure become programmed to certain kinds of stimuli through experience; that this programming occurs within specific brain structures presumably as a neuro-developmental process; and that paraphilias are sometimes associated with certain brain abnormalities that may disrupt normal neural and psychosexual development. However, what is decidedly absent from this perspective is any effort to study these developmental factors and paraphilias within a cross-cultural framework. The findings reported earlier have been obtained mainly from Western samples—would similar relationships between paraphilias, brain abnormalities, and various neuro-developmental indexes be evident in non-Western groups? Are the neural anomalies thus far identified related to specific paraphilias; to their cross-cultural analogues (e.g., foot binding and stilettos); to behaviors that in one culture are considered paraphilic, although not in another; or to a general disinhibition of abnormal behavior. Cross-cultural investigations could provide key insights into the role of biological-neural factors in the aetiology of paraphilias, providing models that integrate the two approaches.

Culture-Bound Syndromes

In this final section, we discuss several psychiatric conditions, especially ones related to sexual behaviors that are heavily influenced by cultures. Culture-bound syndromes came to prominence in the early part of the 20th century. There remains an inherent danger that medical communities are too easily fascinated by exotic syndromes, turning culturally sanctioned activity into colorful, high-profile conditions (Davis, 1996). The result is that selected features of the sexuality of other cultural and ethnic groups may be viewed from the perspective of Western medicine—a tradition that attempts to "fix" conditions that are viewed as abnormal and that is sometimes less tolerant of different or unusual sexual acts and forms of sexual desire (especially those that deviate from procreative potential).

Culture-bound syndromes have been seen as rare, exotic, unpredictable, and even chaotic (Bhugra & Jacob, 1997). Two such syndromes are *dhat* (or semen loss anxiety) and *koro*. Semen loss anxiety is generally reported from the median subcontinent of India (Wig, 1960) and is based on the Ayurvedic concept of food turning into blood, which turns into marrow, which turns into flesh, which turns into semen, thereby making semen an incredibly precious *dhatu* (metal; Bhugra & Buchanan, 1989; see also Bhugra, Sumithipala, & Siribadanna, 2007, for a review). Patients having depression or "underlying weakness" as a result of semen loss due to masturbation or nocturnal emissions are typically the ones who will seek out help. Bhugra et al. argued that, although this represents a cultural explanation of depression and anxiety, it is not necessarily culture-bound, as it was reported widely and treated in the United Kingdom and the United States until the mid-19th century. Industrialization, scientific progress, and the shift away from traditional models of explanation have resulted in the disappearance of this syndrome in the West. Similar culturally explained symptoms have been reported from China, Singapore, and France. A second syndrome is *koro* (shrinking penis syndrome), often reported from China and countries of Southeast Asia. The term probably originates from the Japanese word meaning tortoise. Accompanied by feelings of panic, worry, and guilt, it generally occurs in epidemic form.

Both *dhat* and *koro* are generally reported from low- and middle-income countries and, although not paraphilias as such, they illustrate the difficulty in trying to understand the role of culture in the presentation of symptoms and help-seeking. Thus, certain paraphilias may increase or decrease with changes in globalization, urbanization, and industrialization.

CONCLUSIONS ABOUT CULTURE, FETISH, AND PARAPHILIA

In Western societies, a wide range of sexual behaviors are described in a number of surveys and studies. However, not only are such data often not available from other societies, the accuracy of the data that do exist is often questionable. For something as intimate and secretive as sexual behavior and fantasies, especially when they border on the illegal or problematic, accurate prevalence rates may be difficult to ascertain. Nevertheless, the understanding of strongly depends on reliable epidemiological data.

Even so, not all cultures appear to manifest fetishes or certain paraphilic practices, or view them as an issue. That in itself may be a reflection of first, whether the culture sees itself as sex-positive or sex-negative, and second, whether the function of the sexual intercourse is pleasure or procreation. Furthermore, other characteristics of the society may play important roles; for example, paraphilias may be more common in egocentric and sex-positive cultures where sexual intercourse is predominantly practiced for pleasure and arousal becomes a predominant theme. In contrast, sociocentric, kinship-based, pre-industrialized societies that emphasize sex for reproduction may well have rates of paraphilia different from those reported from the West.

The lack of data regarding sexual fetishes and paraphilias from low- and middle-income countries presents a formidable challenge to future research on this topic. This lack may reflect several factors including lack of awareness of such behaviors, the behaviors not being a legal issue, or people's use of alternative health care providers (especially traditional healers who advertise themselves as sexologists in some countries); or perhaps the behaviors that constitute paraphilias in sociocentric and rural settings are so different from those reported in the Western literature that they are not recognized or reported as such. Transvestism, more common across cultures than previously assumed, may be one such example, as various types of clothing (women's, uniforms, etc.) may represent anything from fashion, to fantasy, to fetish (Bhugra & de Silva, 1996).

When fetishes and paraphilias are attributed to organic or pathophysiological factors, such as brain irregularities or trauma, their occurrence should be studied cross-culturally so as to establish "culture-free" relationships between presumed cause and effect. Nevertheless, once physical or organic causes are ruled out, sociocultural factors are likely to play a key role in the genesis and maintenance of at least some paraphilias. The heterogeneity of sexual practices both within and across cultures suggests that their development both within societies and within individuals needs to be studied from a cross-cultural perspective (see Table 2). More exploration of these ideas across different cultural symptoms is much needed in understanding human sexuality.

Table 2. *Interaction Between Individuals and Cultures*

Variable	Sex-Positive and Non-Procreative	Sex-Negative and Procreative
Sociocentric individual Pleasure	+ + +	+ + ?
Egocentric individual Pleasure		? + + +

+ = positive correlation present; - = negative correlation present; ? = unknown.

REFERENCES

American Psychiatric Association. (1973). Homosexuality and sexual orientation disturbance: Proposed change in *DSM-II* (6th printing, p. 44). Position statement (retired). Retrieved February 28, 2010, from www.psychiatryonline.com/DSMPDF/DSM-II_ Homosexuality_Revision. pdf

American Psychiatric Association. (2000). *Diagnostic and statistical manual of mental disorders* (4th ed., text rev.). Washington, DC: Author.

Baldwin, J. D., & Baldwin, J. I. (1989). The socialization of homosexuality and heterosexuality in a non-Western society. *Archives of Sexual Behavior, 18,* 13–29.

Baldwin, J. D., & Baldwin, J. I. (1997). Gender differences in sexual interest. *Archives of Sexual Behavior, 26,* 181–210.

Bard, L. A., Carter, D. L., Cerce, D. D., Knight, R., Rosenberg, R., & Schneider, B. (1987). A descriptive study of rapists and child molesters: Developmental, clinical and criminal characteristics. *Behavioral Science and the Law, 5,* 203–220.

Berridge, K. C, & Kringlebach, M. L. (2008). Affective neuroscience of pleasure: Reward in humans and animals. *Psychopharmacology, 199,* 457–480.

Bhugra, D. (2000). Disturbances in objects of desire: Cross-cultural issues. *Sexual & Relationship Therapy, 15,* 67–78.

Bhugra, D., & Buchanan, A. (1989). Impotence in ancient Indian texts: Implications for modern diagnosis. *Sexual and Marital Therapy, 4,* 87–91.

Bhugra, D., & Bhui, K. S. (2001). *Cross cultural psychiatry: A practical guide.* London: Arnold.

Bhugra, D., & de Silva, P. (1996). Uniforms: Fact, fashion, fantasy or fetish. *Sexual and Marital Therapy, 11, 393–106.*

Bhugra, D., & Gupta, S. (in press). Culture and its influence on diagnosis and management. In C. Morgan and D. Bhugra (Eds.), *Principles of social psychiatry.* London: Wiley-Blackwell.

Bhugra, D., & Jacob, K. S. (1997). Culture-bound syndromes. In D. Bhugra & A. Munro (Eds.), *Troublesome disguises: Under-diagnosed psychiatric syndromes* (pp. 296–334). Oxford, England: Blackwell.

Bhugra, D., Sumithipala, A., & Siribadanna, S. (2007). Culture-bound syndromes: A re-evaluation. In D. Bhugra & K. S. Bhui (Eds.), *Textbook of cultural psychiatry (pp. 141–156).* Cambridge, England: Cambridge University Press.

Blanchard, R., Christensen, B. K., Strong, S. M., Cantor, J. M., Kuban, M. E., Klassen, P. E., … Blak, T. (2002). Retrospective self-reports of childhood accidents causing unconsciousness in phallometrically diagnosed pedophiles. *Archives of Sexual Behavior, 31,* 511–526.

Blanchard, R., Kolla, N. J., Cantor, J., Klassen, P. E., Dickey, R., Kuban, M. E., & Blak, M. (2007). IQ, handedness, and pedophilia in adult male patients stratified by referral source. *Sexual Abuse: Journal of Research and Treatment, 19,* 285–309.

Blanchard, R., Kuban, M. E., Blak, T., Cantor, J. M., Klassen, P., & Dickey, R. (2006). Phallometric comparison of pedophilic interest in nonadmitting sexual offenders against stepdaughters, biological daughters, other biologically related girls, and unrelated girls. *Sexual Abuse: Journal of Research and Treatment, 18,* 1–14.

Blanchard, R., Kuban, M. E., Klassen, P., Dickey, R., Christensen, B. K., Cantor, J. M., et al. (2003). Self-reported head injuries before and after age 13 in pedophilic and nonpedophilic men referred for clinical assessment. *Archives of Sexual Behavior, 32,* 573–581.

Blumstein, P., & Schwartz, R. (1983). *American couples: Money, work, sex.* New York: Pocket Books.

Bullough, V. L. (1976). *Sexual variance in society and history.* Chicago: University of Chicago Press.

Cantor, J. M., Blanchard, R., Christensen, B. K., Dickey, R., Klassen, P. E., Beckstead, A. L., et al. (2004). Intelligence, memory, and handedness in pedophilia. *Neuropsychology, 18,* 3–14.

Cantor, J. M., Blanchard, R., Robichaud, L. K., & Christensen, B. K. (2005). Quantitative reanalysis of aggregate data on IQ in sexual offenders. *Psychological Bulletin, 131,* 555–568.

Cantor, J. M., Kabani, N., Christensen, B. K., Zipursky, R. B., Barbaree, H. E., Dickey, R. ... Blanchard, R. (2008). Cerebral white matter deficiencies in pedophilic men. *Journal of Psychiatric Research, 42,* 167–183.

Carroll, J. L., Volk, K., & Hyde, J. (1985). Differences between males and females in motives for engaging in sexual intercourse. *Archives of Sexual Behavior, 14,* 131–139.

Casanova, M. H., Mannheim, G., & Kruesi, M. (2002). Hippocampal pathology in two mentally ill paraphiliacs. *Psychiatry Research: Neuroimaging, 115,* 79–89.

Castillo, R. (1995). Culture, trance and the mind-brain. *Anthropology of Consciousness, 6,* 17–34.

Davis, D. (1996). Cultural sensitivity and the sexual disorders of *DSM-IV.* In J. E. Mezzich, A. Kleinman, H. Fabrega, & D. Parron (Eds.), *Culture and psychiatric diagnosis* (pp. 191–208). Washington, DC: American Psychiatric Association.

Dietz, P. E., & Evans, B. (1982). Pornographic imagery and prevalence of paraphilia. *American Journal of Psychology, 139,* 1493–1495.

Eisenberg, L. (1977). Disease and illness: Distinction between professional and popular ideas of sickness. *Culture, Medicine, and Psychiatry, 1,* 9–21.

Emmers-Sommer, T. M., Allen, M., Bourhis, J., Sahlstein, E., Laskowski, K., Falato, W., et al. (2004). A meta-analysis of the relationship between social skills and sexual offenders. *Communication Reports, 17,* 1–10.

Flor-Henry, P., Lang, R. A., & Frenzel, R. R. (1988). Quantitative EEG investigation of genital exhibitionism. *Sexual Abuse: A Journal of Research and Treatment, 1,* 49.

Flor-Henry, P., Lang, R. A., Koles, Z. J., & Frenzel, R. R. (1991). Quantitative EEG studies of paedophilia. *International Journal of Psychophysiology, 10,* 253–258.

Ford, C. A., & Beach, F. A. (1965). *Patterns of sexual behavior.* New York: Harper & Row.

Frazier, P., & Esterly, E. (1990). Correlates of relationship beliefs:Gender, relationship experience and relationship satisfaction. *Journal of Social and Personal Relationships, 7,* 331–352.

Gagnon, J. H., & Simon, W. (Eds.) (1967). *Sexual deviance.* New York: Harper & Row.

Galenson, E., & Roiphe, H. (1974). The emergence of genital awareness during the second year of life. In R. C. Friedman, R. M. Richart, & R. L. V. Wiele (Eds.), *Sex differences in behavior: A conference* (pp. 223–231). New York: Wiley.

Garnett, E. S., Nahmias, C, Wortzman, G., Langevin, R., & Dickey, R. (1988). Positron emission tomography and sexual arousal in a sadist and two controls. *Sexual Abuse: A Journal of Research and Treatment, 1,* 387–399.

Green, R. (2002). Is paedophilia a mental disorder? *Archives of Sexual Behavior, 31,* 467–471.

Greer, A., & Buss, D. (1994). Tactics for promoting sexual encounters. *Journal of Sex Research, 31,* 185–201.

Hendricks, S., Fitzpatrick, D., Hartmann, K., Quaife, M. A.,Stratbucker, R. A., & Graber, B. (1988). Brain structure and function in sexual molesters of children and adolescents. *Journal of Clinical Psychiatry, 49,* 108–112.

Herdt, G. H. (1981). *Guardians of the flute: Idioms of masculinity.* New York: McGraw-Hill.

Herdt, G. H. (Ed.). (1984). *Ritualized homosexuality in Melanesia.* Berkeley: University of California Press.

Hofstede, G. (1980). *Culture's consequences: International differences in work-related values.* Beverly Hills: Sage.

Hofstede, G. (1984). *Culture's consequences: International differences in work-related values* (Abridged ed.). Beverly Hills: Sage.

Hofstede, G. (2001). *Culture's consequences: Comparing values, behaviors, institutions and organizations across nations* (2nd ed.). Thousand Oaks, CA: Sage.

Hucker, S., Langevin, R., Dickey, R., Handy, L., Chambers, J.,Wright, S., … Wortzman, G. (1988). Cerebral damage and dysfunction in sexually aggressive men. *Annals of Sex Research, I,* 33–17.

Hucker, S., Langevin, R., Wortzman, G., Bain, J., Handy, L.,Chambers, J., & Wright, S. (1986). Neuropsychological impairment in paedophiles. *Canadian Journal of Behavior Science, 18,* 440–148.

Kaplan, L. J. (2006). *Cultures of fetishism.* New York: PalgraveMacmillan.

Keesing, R. M. (1976). *Cultural anthropology: A contemporary perspective.* New York: Holt, Rinehart & Winston.

Kirenskaya-Berus, A. V., & Tkachenko, A. A. (2003). Characteristic features of EEG spectral characteristics in persons with deviant sexual behaviour. *Human Physiology, 29,* 273–287.

Kleinman, A. (1980). *Patients and healers in the context of culture.* Berkeley: University of California Press.

Kringlebach, M. L. (2005). The human orbitofrontal cortex: Linking reward to hedonic experience. *Nature Reviews Neuroscience, 6,* 691–702.

Kringlebach, M. L. (2008). The hedonic brain: A functional neuroa-natomy of human pleasure. In M. L. Kringlebach & K. C. Berridge (Eds.), *Pleasures of the brain* (pp. 202–221). Oxford, England: Oxford University Press.

Kroeber, A., & Kluckhohn, C. (1952). *Culture: A critical review of concepts and definition* [Papers of the Peabody Museum of American Archaeology and Ethnology]. Cambridge, MA: Peabody Museum of American Archaeology and Ethnography.

Krueger, R. B., & Kaplan, M. S. (2001). The paraphilic and hypersexual disorders: An overview. *Journal of Psychiatric Practice, 7,* 391–403.

Langevin, R. (1983). *Sexual strands: Understanding and treating sexual anomalies in men.* Hillsdale, NJ: Lawrence Erlbaum Associates, Inc.

Langevin, R., Hucker, S., Handy, L., Purins, J., Russon, A., &Hook, H. (1985). Erotic preference and aggression in pedophilia. In R. Langevin (Ed.), *Erotic preference, gender identity and aggression inmen* (pp. 137–160). Hillsdale, NJ: Lawrence Erlbaum Associates Publishers.

Langevin, R., Lang, R., Wortzman, G., Frenzel, R. R., & Wright, P. (1989). An examination of brain damage and dysfunction in genital exhibitionists. *Annals of Sex Research, 2,* 77—87.

Langevin, R., Wortzman, G., Dickey, R., Wright, P., & Handy, L. (1988). Neuropsychological impairment in incest offenders. *Sexual Abuse: A Journal of Research and Treatment, 1,* 401–415.

Langevin, R., Wortzman, G., Wright, P., & Handy, L. (1989). Studies of brain damage and dysfunction in sex offenders. *Sexual Abuse: Journal of Research and Treatment, 2,* 163–179.

Langstrom, N., & Hanson, R. (2006). High rates of sexual behavior in the general population: Correlates and predictors. *Archives of Sexual Behavior, 35,* 37–52.

Langstrom, N., & Seto, M. C. (2006). Exhibitionistic and voyeuristic behavior in a Swedish national population survey. *Archives of Sexual Behavior, 35,* 427–135.

Langstrom, N., & Zucker, K. J. (2005). Transvestic fetishism in the general population: Prevalence and correlates. *Journal of Sex and Marital Therapy, 31,* 87–95.

Laumann, E. O., Gagnon, J. H., Michael, R. T., & Michaels, S. (1994). *The social organization of sexuality: Sexual practices in the United* Marshall, W. L. (1989). Intimacy, loneliness and sexual offenders. *Behavior Research and Therapy, 27,* 491–503.

Marshall, W. L., Hudson, S., & Hodkinson, S. (1993). The importance of attachment bonds in the development of juvenile sex offending. In H. E. Barbaree, W. L. Marshall, & S. Hudson (Eds.), *The juvenile sex offender* (pp. 164—181). New York: Guilford.

McAnulty, R. D. (2006). Paedophilia. In R. D. McAnulty & M. M. Burnette (Eds.), *Sex and sexuality* (Vol. 3, pp. 81–96). Westport, CT: Praeger.

Offer, D., & Sabshin, M. (1966). *Normality—Theoretical and clinical concepts of mental health.* New York: Basic Books.

Panksepp, J. (1998). *Affective neuroscience: The foundations of human and animal emotions.* Oxford, England: Oxford University Press.

Ping, W. (2000). *Aching for beauty: Footbinding in China.* Minneapolis: University of Minnesota Press.

Rahman, Q. (2005). The neurodevelopment of human sexual orientation. *Neuroscience and Biobehavioral Reviews, 29,* 1057–1066.

Rahman, Q., & Symeonides, D. J. (2008). Neurodevelopmental correlates of paraphilic sexual interests in men. *Archives of Sexual Behavior, 37,* 166–172.

Reiss, I. L. (1986). *Journey into sexuality: An exploratory voyage.* Englewood Cliffs, NJ: Prentice Hall.

Rolls, E. T. (2005). *Emotion explained.* Oxford, England: Oxford University Press.

Schiffer, B., Krueger, T., Paul, T., de Greiff, A., Forsting, M., Leygraf, N., …Gizewski, E. (2008). Brain response to visual sexual stimuli in homosexual pedophiles. *Journal of Psychiatry & Neuroscience, 33,* 23–33.

Segall, M. H., Dasen, P. R., Berry, J. W., & Poortinga, Y. H. (1990). *Human behavior in global perspective.* Elmsford, NY: Pergamon.

Seto, M. C. (2004). Pedophilia and sexual offences against children. *Annual Review of Sex Research, 15,* 321–361.

Seto, M. C, Cantor, J. M., & Blanchard, R. (2006). Child pornography offenses are a valid diagnostic indicator of pedophilia. *Journal of Abnormal Psychology, 115,* 610–615.

Sperry, R. W. (1987). Structure and significance of the consciousness revolution. *Journal of Mind and Behavior, 8,* 37–65.

Sprecher, S. (1989). Premarital sexual standards for different categories of individuals. *Journal of Sex Research, 26,* 232–248.

Sprecher, S., & McKinney, K. (1993). *Sexuality.* Newbury Park, CA: Sage.

Stoller, R. J. (1975). *Perversion: The erotic form of hatred.* New York: Pantheon.

Stoller, R. J. (1979). *Sexual excitement: Dynamics of erotic life.* New York: Pantheon.

Stoller, R. J., & Herdt, G. (1985). Theories of origin of male homosexuality: A cross-cultural look. *Archives of General Psychiatry, 42,* 399–404.

Swaab, D. F. (2007). Sexual differentiation of the brain and behavior. *Best Practice & Research: Clinical Endocrinology & Metabolism, 27,*431–444.

Tseng, W.-S. (1997). Introduction: Understanding culture. In W.-S. Tseng & J. Streltzer (Eds.), *Culture and psychopathology: A guide to clinical assessment* (pp. 1–22). New York: Brunner/ Mazel.

Wig, N. N. (1960). Problems of mental health in India. *Journal of Clinical and Social Psychology, 17,* 48–53.

Wilson, G., & Cox, D. (1983). *The child-lovers: A study of paedophiles in society.* London: Peter Owen.

Wright, P., Nobrega, J., Langevin, R., & Wortzman, G. (1990). Brain density and symmetry in pedophilic and sexually aggressive offenders. *Sexual Abuse: A Journal of Research and Treatment, 3,* 319–328

INTRODUCTION TO: SEXUAL ABUSE AND THE WHOLESOME FAMILY

JAN CAMPBELL

K erwin Kaye examines the idea of sexual familial abuse from the perspectives of pre-feminist narratives, second-wave feminism, post-feminist psychology, and contemporary state discourse as represented in U.S. Supreme Court rulings. The Child Abuse Prevention and Treatment Act of 1974 was the first federal acknowledgement that sexual abuse occurred within the family. Kaye explicitly exposes the issue of abuse as problematic when framed in notions that "family wholesomeness" and "intact families" were used to describe how the abused should ultimately be returned to their abusers and the family. This writing takes us through eras from the pre-feminist ideas of child abuse, which are described as "Lolita" fables, to post-feminist critiques of the seductive child and to individual deviance (in the abuser), rather than looking at power imbalances in the family.

The work focuses on the portrayal of sexual abuse victims and concentrates more on the female survivors than male survivors. Kaye investigates the relationships between trends in the representation of sexual abuse victims and then discerns differing political projects in the formulations of feminists, psychologists, and policy makers.

The ideas portrayed in Kaye's work bring awareness to renaming certain acts in order to better clarify and understand how phrasing can color one's view of an event. She uses Brownmiller's phrase "father rape" to show how this phrase precluded victim blaming. The questions for discussion and critical thinking at the end of the work are thought provoking.

SEXUAL ABUSE AND THE WHOLESOME FAMILY

KERWIN KAYE

T he first U.S. federal acknowledgement that sexual abuse occurred within the family came in 1974 with the passage of the Child Abuse Prevention and Treatment Act (CAPTA 1974). Official recognition for victims marked a major break with earlier psychological discourses that emphasized the culpability of sexually abused children. Notably, this legislative change occurred only after feminist activism had drawn significant public attention to the topic. Indeed, the initial version of CAPTA focused entirely upon the physical abuse of children and did not include sexual abuse within its purview; lawmakers added sexual abuse to the bill as something of an after-thought (Nelson 1984). A dramatic rise in reports of sexual abuse soon followed the passage of CAPTA, surprising both lawmakers and the child protection agencies who were required by the legislation to investigate each claim.[2] The adoption of CAPTA and the resulting rise in reported cases of sexual abuse gave feminists a degree of state legitimation as they struggled to reveal the pervasive and painful nature of sexual victimization within the family. In some cases, feminist ties with the state were direct, as many of the early feminist writers and activists held positions within the rapidly expanding child protection agencies. These positions placed them in contact with many sexual abuse cases and also conferred something of an expert status upon them. Although feminist activists certainly did not receive federal funding in support of their work, the feminist victory in securing state recognition established a context of relatively strong ambient support for their ideas.

Nevertheless, feminist perspectives on sexual abuse remained marginal within both state discourse concerning abuse and within the overall field of psychology. Although feminist activism gained state recognition of sexual abuse and was also successful in pushing psychology toward acknowledging and addressing the issue, neither the state nor clinical psychology became decidedly feminist as a result. Within the dominant streams of psychology, for example, analysis of male power within the family is generally infrequent and poorly elaborated, and critical analysis of societal reactions to survivors (including their treatment within the legal system) is virtually nonexistent. Although a number of important exceptions exist within the field, clinical psychology typically pays little attention to the connections between what survivors of sexual abuse experience and the social structures that both facilitate the abuse and shape survivors' postabuse experiences.[3] Instead, the individualizing approaches favored within the dominant trends of clinical psychology work to divide survivors' experience of sexual victimization from broader questions of power and sexuality. Psychological authorities advise survivors that they are not alone in their suffering, yet the therapeutic community that survivors are invited to participate in generally focuses upon interpersonal support, not political challenge (Armstrong 1994).

Furthermore, clinical psychology's apparent lack of engagement with the sociopolitical realm conceals a politically conservative project that reinforces the privileged status of nuclear families. By focusing upon the presumed deviance of survivors, psychological accounts move to contain public narrations of abuse within a framework that does not threaten the prevailing idea of family "wholesomeness." Survivors of abuse are thus encouraged to return to the same familial configurations that produced their initial maltreatment, neatly curtailing the radical potential for actual political and structural change generated by a shared recognition of collective suffering.

This chapter provides a critical genealogical assessment of the portrayal of incestuous abuse through the lenses of four competing discourses: prefeminist narratives, early second-wave feminism, postfeminist psychology, and finally contemporary state discourse as represented in U.S. Supreme Court rulings. I begin with a brief discussion of the prefeminist narrative of child sexual abuse as a "Lolita" fable. Feminists in the 1970s attempted, with some success, to undermine this narrative and to reconstitute child sexual abuse as a political problem of male dominance and of the subjugation of women within patriarchal families. Postfeminist psychology largely accepted feminist critiques of the seductive child, but within an apolitical framework that focused upon individual deviance rather than systemic power imbalances, and which furthermore presented sexual abuse as something to cure in the individual. Last, I examine the concerns of the state as represented in the language from various twentieth-century Supreme Court rulings that have shaped the regulation of sexual abuse within the family. I argue that the relationships among dominant discourses within psychology and the policy-making level of the state serve to reform but defend the "wholesomeness" of the male-dominated nuclear family, ensuring its long-term survival in the face of a crisis caused by the rebellion of those oppressed within its structures.

Mirroring the contemporary literature on sexual abuse, this chapter focuses upon the portrayal of sexual abuse victims, and like the literature, it therefore concentrates more upon female than male survivors.[4] Arguably, it is this very fixation upon survivors that is most problematic: The psychological state of victims is pathologized and regulated while the emotional and relational patterns of offenders are normalized and subject to significantly less scrutiny (McKinnon 1995, 32). Yet by investigating the relationship between trends in the representation of sexual abuse victims, it becomes possible to discern differing political projects implicit within the distinct formulations of feminists, psychologists, and policy makers. This task is particularly necessary in relation to psychological and state discourses, where apparent and overt support for victims masks gender and familial ideologies that disempower victims and others who might be at risk of abuse. Yet feminist activism should not limit itself to discursive objectives. This chapter therefore concludes with some brief suggestions for the creation of familial structures that would mitigate against abuse by empowering the people within them.

HISTORICAL DEFINITIONS: THE "SEDUCTIVE" CHILD

A number of conceptions regarding the specific harms of incest emerged in the early twentieth century. These proposals typically revolved around a set of concerns that had little to do with potential injury to the child. Hegemonic discourses regularly treated children as active instigators rather than as victims whose suffering lay at the center of concern. For example, during English parliamentary debates in 1908, proponents of the Punishment of Incest Act focused on the possibility that a deformed or illegitimate offspring would result from such a union, or the danger that a sexualized parent-child bond would foster rivalries within the family.[5] This formulation essentially treated incest as a form of adultery, and situated sexual abuse survivors in terms of the danger they posed for the reproductive success and emotional stability of the "normal" family unit. Abuse victims were identified as willing partners, sexual deviants who needed to be controlled.

Although a feminist campaign against carnal abuse within the family occurred from the 1870s to 1930s, it had little success in changing this aspect of the public debate (Gordon 1989; Hooper 1992). Some lawmakers did align themselves with the feminist campaign against sexual abuse, speaking in favor of guarding children (especially girls) from emotional suffering, but even this objective was frequently framed in relation to "the strengthening of the fabric of the family" (Bell 1993, 136), rather than in terms of promoting the wellbeing of children. In sharp contrast to present-day representations, comments regarding children's suffering were notably brief, and little elaboration was offered as to the nature of the pain these children might experience. The voice of victims was, in fact, nowhere present in these early debates.

The view within medical psychiatry and clinical psychology reinforced these themes. Freud's famous revision concerning sexual abuse—in which he first proposed that women developed psychological disorders as a result of "sexual shock" from a caretaker's "seduction" (1896, quoted in Ward 1985, 104–6; see also Rush 1980, 87–8), and then later argued that women's Oedipal desires caused them to imagine that they were seduced (1900, quoted in Ward 1985, 110–14; see also Rush 1980, 93–6; Masson 1984)—undermined abuse victims' credibility. In this context, Bender and Blau's 1937 comment, which would be favorably cited in the professional literature for the next 35 years, is not surprising:

> [F]requently we considered the possibility that the child might have been the actual seducer rather than the one innocently seduced. … The experience offers an opportunity for the child to test out in reality, an infantile fantasy; it [sic] probably finds the consequences less severe, and in fact actually gratifying to a pleasure sense. The emotional balance is thus in favor of contentment. (quoted in Ward 1985, 90)

From Freud until the feminist challenge of the 1970s, psychological wisdom generally focused upon the presumed "closeness of the external event to the unconscious fantasy" (Lewis and Sarrel 1969, 618, quoted in Ward 1985, 146). Like state narratives, psychology of the mid-twentieth century portrayed the survivor of sexual abuse as an oversexed and delinquent "Lolita" who actively (though perhaps unconsciously) seduced her abuser. At the same time, psychologists followed Freud in claiming that actual (as opposed to imagined) seduction was not a very common occurrence, perhaps "one in a million" (Weinberg 1955, quoted in Gordon 1988, 60), an opinion cited as recently as 1975 (by Freedman et al. 1975, quoted in Russell 1986, 388).[6]

By the time second-wave feminists began to seriously engage with the issue, the movement for sexual liberation had inspired a few psychologists to take this line of thinking toward its logical conclusion. This minority forged a "pro-incest" position, one which argued that incest could be "educative" for children and encouraged "mild forms of sex play" between parents and children (Constantine and Constantine 1973).[7] The second-wave feminist identification of incest as sexual abuse arose within and against this social environment.

SECOND-WAVE FEMINISM: ESTABLISHING INCEST AS ABUSE

Second-wave feminists were forced to counter prior portrayals of children as seducers in their attempt to establish that incest was a form of abuse. Significantly, feminist discussion concerning childhood sexual abuse began within the movement opposing sexual assault. Feminist women began speaking out publicly against rape, and the attitudes and silences that serve to perpetuate it, in the mid- to late-1960s. By the mid-1970s, the sexual abuse of girls was increasingly mentioned within these speakouts as an all-too-common aspect of women's overall sexual victimization (Rush 1974; Dinsmore 1991, 13; Jenkins, 1998,

125–8). The historical emergence of incest as a topic within the broader context of sexual assault definitively shaped the feminist challenge to psychological and state orthodoxies.

Feminist analysis of sexual assault challenged a legitimizing ideology similar to that found within the incest literature. The dominant ideology concerning rape presumed that if a woman was not entirely chaste, she must be a "whore" who wanted sex at all times and therefore could not be violated.[8] For example, in one instance, a prominent lawyer began a rape trial by spinning a bottle and showing the jury how difficult it was to insert a pencil into this "resisting" orifice, thereby suggesting that the woman had consented to the assault (Margolin 1972, quoted in Donat and D'Emilio 1998). Thus, in cases of stranger rape, as in cases of incestuous abuse, the fact of the sexual assault might itself be used as evidence against the woman's character, with the mere accomplishment of the sexual act placing the woman into the whore category (Herman 1981, 187; Ward 1985, 159). To counter this virgin/whore dichotomy, feminists emphasized the intensely unwanted and traumatic nature of rape, establishing that the event was not pleasurably sexual for the victim, and instead linking it to other types of aggressive attack through such terms as "sexual violence" and "sexual assault."

The parallels between stranger rape and incestuous abuse—the fact that men are overwhelmingly the perpetrators and the justification that the victims "wanted the sex"—lead early second-wave feminists to emphasize the similarities between the events, or even to subsume one within the other. Incest became a form of rape, as in Susan Brownmiller's early discussion of "father rape" (1975, 271–82). The resultant terminology effectively precluded victim-blaming, as in Butler's comment that "[A]ggressors … sexually assault their own children" (1978, 10). Such a claim would have been difficult to make within the seduction-oriented terminology that was provided by the prior experts on incest.

While clarifying questions of force and coercion, the process of renaming linked the experience of child incest victims with adults who were assaulted by strangers in less interpersonally and psychodynamically complex situations. Brownmiller's phrase "father rape," for example, is revealing on this point in that the word "father" is an adjective, suggesting that the unmodified term "rape" retained its primary meaning in relation to rape from a stranger. The phrase thereby placed the abuse of children within a category that emphasized a vastly different set of circumstances. Elizabeth Ward likewise titled her book *Father-Daughter Rape* and argued, "I believe that the sexual use of a child's body/being is the same as the phenomenon of adult rape. Terms like 'sexual abuse,' 'molestation' and 'interference' are diminuations of 'rape': They imply that something *less* than rape occurred" (emphasis in original 1985, 79). The definitional inclusion of sexual abuse as a form of rape redefined the notion of what constituted sexual assault in relation to a broader set of circumstances, yet it also utilized the earlier meanings associated with stranger rape to politically situate the child as an unwilling victim rather than addressing the possibility of any form of collusion (with all of the additional forms of suffering, confusion, and guilt that such collusion typically brings). Although feminists at times acknowledged differences between "stranger rape" and "father rape" (e.g., Ward 1985, 99–100), the need to proclaim the child's status as victim generally took precedence over these considerations in labeling and framing the experience of sexual abuse.[9]

Framing the issue of incestuous abuse in relation to stranger rape could make it difficult to fully incorporate the experiences of abused children. Feminists often discounted questions of children's agency within abusive situations, specifically undertheorizing the surface-level participation of some victims in order to counter prior victim-blaming interpretations. As more recent feminist examinations have shown, victims display a variety of means of resistance or accommodation in abusive situations. For example, in some instances, a victim may actively initiate specific sexual episodes, particularly once a pattern has been established (Wilson 1993, 93–4, 103–8; see also Scott 1988, 96). Other victims may begin to use sex "as a bargaining point in order to obtain the rewards of 'affection,' 'the right to stay up late,' or 'a bit more freedom'" (Kitzinger 1997, 172). In these cases, the abusive dynamic offers victims some small modicum of power within the family (Herman and Hirschman 1977, 748). Still other victims may allow themselves to get caught up in whatever sexual pleasure is available as a means to avoid unpleasant emotional feelings (Dinsmore 1991, 25). Although most contemporary perspectives would nevertheless emphasize the facts of parental/adult power and responsibility (see Finkelhor 1979; Russell 1984, 266–8), during the early 1970s, ruminations upon such possibilities ran the risk of being taken as admissions of culpability.

Rather than focusing on the significance of a child's potential pleasure or desire (whether affectional, sensual, or sexual), early second-wave feminists tended to emphasize the unequivocally oppositional or "unknowing" state of the victims in order to avoid enabling others in more hegemonic positions to claim that children offered "consent." Elizabeth Ward, for example, speaks only of the "powerlessness (which is read as passivity) of the girl victims" (1985, 99). She similarly identifies any potential pleasure as a "likely genital reaction" deriving from a "mind-split" (152), a formulation that carefully avoids the suggestion that the child's subjectivity might in some way be engaged. Ward's conclusion—that "Passivity (being coerced) can thus co-exist with the experience of pleasure" (153)—crucially depends upon the elimination of all subjective elements of pleasure within the context of abuse.

Sandra Butler's solo work similarly discounts the possibility of conscious involvement on the part of victims, though her framework grants that there might be some abusive situations in which a child more actively participates. Butler's reasoning focuses upon the sexual knowledge of the child:

> [A] child … is unable to alter or understand the adult's behavior because of his or her powerlessness in the family and early stage of psychological development. This type of incest is non consensual because the child has not yet developed an understanding of sexuality that allows him or her to make a free and fully conscious response to the adult's behavior. (1978, 4–5)

Butler's focus upon a presumed lack of sexual knowledge does not require that victims find abusive sexual interchange entirely repulsive. It is supplemented, however, by an understanding in which a victim's potentially positive (or conflicted) feelings can exist only in relation to a "child's inability to make or understand sexual decisions" (1978, 30). However true this might be in any given case, the act of requiring a victim's ignorance in order to define the event as "abuse" effectively repudiates the possibility that a girl might "knowingly" participate in her abuse in any manner, and thus limits possible subjectivities that a victim might claim while still maintaining a guiltless status.

There were, however, ruptures within this theoretical narrative, particularly within the first-person accounts that actually constituted the greater part of many texts (Armstrong 1978; Butler 1978; Brady 1979; and to a lesser extent, Ward 1985). Attention to the victims' perspectives was needed to counter the claim that incest was "relatively harmless" (as per Bender and Blau, above), and to act "as a political tool for giving voice to women's real experiences" of incest over and against the prior silencing myths (Armstrong 1994, 24). Questions of childhood agency were frequently raised in much more direct ways within these first-person accounts than within the feminist theory that surrounded and contextualized them. Although many of the survivors told of situations that indeed fit the framework of forced and thoroughly unwanted sex, others described situations involving various forms of abuser deception, manipulation, or emotional bribery that in one way or another coerced cooperation from the victims.

Stories from those who experienced some degree of pleasure or desire within the abuse were, in fact, not deeply hidden within the feminist texts. In the first few pages of her book, for example, Elizabeth Ward quotes extensively from a woman who felt affection toward her abusing father, and who additionally reports sometimes enjoying the sex. Nor are these facts insignificant details within this victim's account, as it was the presence of physical pleasure that gave cause for a deeply discrediting perception of self: "I did start to come, I did have orgasms. I remember now, I did start to come because that's where the guilt came from: I started to look forward to it" (Ward 1985, 10). Significantly, it was precisely this woman's subjective pleasure and sense of agency, the very elements that the early theoretical frameworks attempted to elide, that generated the most internal conflict:

> The conflict was knowing it was wrong, knowing he was my father ... and at the same time, enjoying sex. And knowing that he'd love me if I did this. I felt guilt for a long time. I can now accept that it *was* rape ... but I still can't help feeling that I'm responsible ... why didn't I get out, otherwise? And because I enjoyed it sometimes. (ellipses and emphasis in original, Ward 1985, 13)

The ambivalence this girl felt complicated her relationship with her father, making her sense of unease that much more difficult to resolve. Having a sense of agency in the situation felt deeply implicating, despite a recognition that she ultimately did not have power in the situation ("it was rape").

Although the denial of children's agency may have been a political necessity, it made it difficult to theorize the relationship between a child's ability to act (however narrowly exercised) and the nature and impact of the abuse. Ward's analysis, for example, leads her to misidentify the sources of shame that some victims experience. She argues that "The Daughters, in expressing shame, are speaking of *what has been done to them.* They are speaking of humiliation, of powerlessness. They are speaking of the effect of having a Father use and abuse their very bodies against their will" (emphasis in original, 1985, 151). This formulation holds well when considering some of the stories that Ward presents, cases in which the sex was thoroughly unwanted, but it ignores situations in which the shame results from a sense of (limited) power and chosen (although coerced) involvement in the situation. Because feminist theoretical frameworks created space for guiltlessness only in relation to a victim's undiscerning agreement or simple acquiescence to power, it left crucial aspects of the victim-blaming paradigm untouched. The possibility of a child's conscious complicity was simply repudiated at a theoretical level, rather than acknowledged and addressed. The stance implicitly forced survivors who had lived through such situations to either deny their experience of agency or to internalize an unaddressed (and, most probably, intense) sense of self-blame.

Not all early second-wave feminists relied upon analyses that displayed this shortcoming. Feminist psychiatrist Judith Herman developed a framework that more completely emphasized the overwhelming power parents have over their children, a formulation that enables her to more fully examine the occasional participation of survivors. Herman argues:

> Because a child is powerless in relation to an adult, she is not free to refuse a sexual advance. Therefore, any sexual relationship between the two must necessarily take on some of the coercive characteristics of a rape, even if, as is usually the case, the adult uses positive enticements rather than force to establish the relationship. This is particularly true of incest between a parent and child: it is a rape in the sense that it is a coerced sexual relationship. The question of whether force is involved is largely irrelevant, since force is rarely necessary to obtain compliance. The parent's authority over the child is usually sufficient to compel obedience. Similarly, the question of a child's "consent" is irrelevant. Because the child does not have the power to withhold consent, she does not have the power to grant it. (Herman 1981, 27; see also Finkelhor 1979)

By emphasizing the overwhelming coercive power of the family environment, Herman is able to address abusive situations that extend beyond directly coerced sex, to include the possibility of a victim's more active awareness and sexual participation.[10]

But although Herman's emphasis on structural inequality offers possibilities for the recognition of divergent survivor subjectivities, it still does not permit those survivors who participated in their abuse to fully acknowledge their own experience. Herman's text informs victims that they are not to blame, yet they are not given a means with which to deal with their own potential ambivalences, to take credit (or responsibility) for any real choices they have made. The need to resituate blame onto the offender again appears through the assertion that children should not be seen as participating in acts that are fundamentally coercive, yet little attempt is made to grapple with the subjective engagements that can arise within such situations. Through this reactive process, the previous portrayal of incest survivors as seductresses (and of rape victims as sluts) continued to shape the portrayal of survivors, leading early feminists away from examining a full range of survivor subjectivities.

A contrast with a more contemporary feminist analysis of sexual abuse is instructive. Feminist psychologist Sharon Lamb, for example, comments provocatively upon the relationship between perceived agency and self-blame that many victims experience:

> [S]elf-blame sometimes is healing, and in some part appropriate. … Victims' sense of overresponsibility, though sometimes harmful and other times pathological, should not be dismissed. At its core are real moments of responsibility, times when they made poor choices, foolish decisions. Almost every victim, except those of the most horrendous crimes, will speak of these moments. It is crucial in working with victims to tease out the accurate level of responsibility. (1996, 179–80)

Lamb notes the importance of careful reflection upon the numerous social constraints that frequently present victims with "choiceless choices" within their families (1996, 37). Nevertheless, Lamb emphasizes that victims do indeed make decisions, a perspective that allows survivors to more deeply assess the meaning of their own actions and possible involvement. Although this type of self-examination is indeed challenging, it continues to undercut the unrestricted sense of responsibility generated within the victim-blaming framework. Indeed, Lamb's formulation rests upon the assumption that a victim is basically not to blame for any abuse: Abusers are fully responsible for their own actions, whatever decisions a victim might make.

Lamb's intervention is important, however, because it challenges other difficulties that are latent within Herman's analysis that focuses upon the coercive capacity of adults (Herman 1981). Although it is an important corrective, it nevertheless simplified analyses of family dynamics by claiming that children have no power whatsoever. Herman's framework is thus compatible with other formulations that conceive of childhood as being entirely free from the stain of sex, formulations that naturalize children's "innocent" lack of power and circumvent any recognition of the socially mediated inequities that exist within male-female and adult-child relations. Although we must continue to emphasize establishing adult (male) blame for abuse, we must not ignore a victim's control, however partial, over her or his own behavior. As will be seen, many clinical psychologists have adopted this seemingly more flexible definition of sexual abuse in a manner that pushes the analysis toward a simplistic (and falsely apolitical) focus upon "age appropriateness" and "sexual innocence," and away from questions of power and coercion.

Early second-wave feminist texts clearly work against any sort of apolitical focus upon children. Typical is Rush, who speaks of abuse survivors as "victims of the family structure, they are also victims of the utter dependency of children—economically, physically, socially, legally, and of the violent nexus between power and sex, the instrument of rape, by which women and girl-children are controlled in a male supremacist society" (1984, 95). Far from idealizing the male-dominated nuclear family, feminists tended toward the view that "incest is integral to 'normal family life'" and that the family "is in fact one of the most dangerous places female children (and women) can be" (Anonymous 1985). Yet despite a universal emphasis on political critique within the texts, the pictorial representations on

Figure 9-1.

 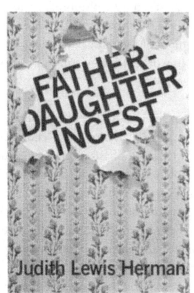

Book covers from two early feminist texts on the sexual abuse of children (Rush 1980; Herman 1981). Rush's cover features a haphazardly abandoned teddy bear (perhaps suggesting that the victim had been playing with the stuffed animal immediately prior to the abuse, which occurs off-camera). On Herman's book, the words "Father-Daughter Incest" violently tear apart picturesque wallpaper that seems to invoke conventional idealized notions of domesticity. These photos achieve impact through their disruption to notions of familial bliss (Kitzinger similarly examined book covers for these themes, 1997).

the covers of the early books frequently reflected a contrary preoccupation with themes of childlike innocence and familial bliss (see Figure 9–1). Publishers, who presumably chose the images, apparently thought it easier to market an image of "ruptured domestic bliss" than to develop a cover that reflected the actual analysis within the books: that abuse resulted from the very form of normative (i.e., male-dominant) domesticity idealized on the book cover.

Although the texts identified the isolated, male-dominated family as a primary source of danger for children, especially girls, the cover art promoted a view that idealized childhood as being properly nested within a protective (and implicitly patriarchal) family.

Ethical claims emphasizing the improper violation of a virginal sphere, and hence deemphasizing imbalanced power relations between victims and abusers, are, not surprisingly, rare within the early feminist writings. An atypical comment by Butler to the effect that "The most devastating result of the imposition of adult sexuality upon a child unable to determine the appropriateness of his or her response is *the irretrievable loss of the child's inviolability* and trust in the adults in his or her life" (emphasis added, 1978, 5) is, in fact, an anomaly within the literature. What the early second-wave feminist framings share with later psychological accounts, however, is an analysis that denies the relevance of a survivor's agency. Although this emphasis is useful in establishing adult (male) blame for the abuse, it tends to ignore a victim's control, however limited and partial, over her or his own behavior. Denying the relevance of children's ability to act within abusive situations, even in limited ways, enabled latter commentators to claim a feminist stance while covertly inserting more familialist discourses into their accounts. These new discourses similarly denied the possibility of childhood agency, but did so in a way that reified patriarchal power, as will be seen below.

CLINICAL PSYCHOLOGY: "INNOCENCE LOST" AS SEXUAL STAIN

With the advent of state funding, child protection agencies were given a primary role in defining the issue of sexual abuse and the needs of victims. Earlier psychoanalytic interpretations were rapidly pushed aside in favor of feminist-influenced frameworks that acknowledged the frequent occurrence and generally traumatic effects of sexual abuse. Although the notion of child victimization was incorporated into the literature, however, other feminist insights regarding the determining influence of male power were pushed aside. Most clinicians instead began to search for the causes of incestuous abuse in "dysfunctional family dynamics." By spreading the focus upon the entire family dynamic, this family-systems approach tended to redirect therapeutic attention away from the male perpetrator and toward the "collusive" mother, whose sexual and emotional distance was often said to "cause" the husband to seek out sexual comfort in his daughter (or son). The child victim also received a good deal of blame within these approaches as earlier

Freudian-inspired theories of Oedipal seductiveness continued to hold sway (Armstrong 1990, 1994; McKinnon 1995). At present, ongoing feminist criticism has lead the majority of psychologists to distance themselves from the most egregious types of victim and mother blaming, and they have increasingly acknowledged and emphasized the male perpetrator's responsibility for his own behavior (see Sturkie 1986). Nevertheless, the majority of clinical approaches remain committed to a search for "dysfunctional behavior." By arguing that sexual abuse results from faulty interpersonal dynamics, psychological discourse individualizes the problem, effectively ignoring the propensity for abuse that lies within conventional (i.e., male-dominant) family forms.

The impact this political allegiance has on the representation of victims is significant. Even when psychologists adopt a feminist perspective regarding the blamelessness of children (and mothers), they frequently do not frame the violation in terms of sexual coercion. Whereas earlier feminists had portrayed sexual abuse survivors as victims of a male power structure, clinical psychologists more frequently portray survivors in relation to the "betrayal of trust" experienced when an adult caretaker abuses a victim. Without denying that a child may indeed experience a tremendous sense of betrayal when a parent mistreats her or him, it is important to note the manner in which this framework highlights a violation of parental norms—norms that remain nonproblematic—rather than repudiating abuse as a not-too-surprising outcome of excessive parental (and especially paternal) power. The power of men within families is thus subjected to critique only in its "abusive" manifestations, while its day-to-day workings are rendered invisible.

For example, Summit speaks of the "betrayal ... by someone who is ordinarily idealized as a protective, altruistic, loving, parental figure," without specifying that the social source for this idealized image lies in hetero- and family-normative culture (1983, 184). Similarly, he suggests that a child idealizes her parents because to do otherwise "is tantamount to abandonment and annihilation" (1983, 184), a formulation that fails to examine the social sources of juvenile dependency: the relative isolation of children within nuclear families, the lack of economic and social options for runaway children, and the existence of cultural and legal systems that identify children as parental property. The possibility for less stratified power relations within the family is never raised, effectively naturalizing parental (and paternal) power. A primary focus upon the "betrayal" of children stands in implicit contrast to modernist images of domestic bliss, a vision that is heavily gendered in favor of male power. Disapproval of abusive fathers here focuses upon their failure to uphold their role within the arrangement, rather than upon the failings of the arrangement itself.

The other source of trauma frequently identified within the clinical literature is the presumed loss of "childhood innocence" that occurs with the abuse. With titles such as *Betrayal of Innocence* (Forward and Buck 1981), "Shattered Innocence" (Kohn 1987), *The Right to Innocence* (Engel 1991), *Innocence Destroyed* (Renovoize 1993), *Shattered Innocence* (Weiner and Kurpius 1995), and *Stolen Innocence* (Toldson 1997), many clinical psychologists took what existed as an aberrant concept within the feminist literature and developed it into a primary axis of concentration. Though the issue of coercion is

sometimes mentioned in these clinical texts, the primary source of trauma is often identified as "an abnormal event interrupting the normal development process" (Berliner and
Stevens 1982), "an intrusion into presexual personhood" (Hancock and Mains 1987,
32), or being "prematurely introduced to sexuality" (Sgroi 1982, 114). Within much of
the clinical literature, the emphasis shifts decidedly toward themes of lost childhood innocence, invoking images of formerly "pure" victims whose loss is permanent and total.
Emphasizing the inappropriateness of sex beneath a certain age again removes the focus
on coercion, this time placing it on the idea of "underage sex." Sexual abuse is here framed
as a genderless imposition by an individually deviant adult (who just happens to more
frequently be male) upon a child (who just happens to more frequently be female).

Although the image of asexual innocence seems to support the blameless status of
children, in practice it continues to stigmatize those children who do not appear to be
"pure." This is a key point, as many children who are sexually abused gain early sexual
knowledge and act in sexual ways that are not deemed appropriate by the virginal standards
of innocence. As noted by feminist sociologist Jenny Kitzinger, the imagery of childhood
innocence can thereby cause great harm to the survivors of sexual abuse. Kitzinger writes:

> [I]nnocence is a double-edged sword in the fight against sexual abuse because
> it stigmatizes the "knowing" child. The romanticization of childhood innocence
> excludes those who do not conform to the ideal. ... This penalizes the child who
> sexually responds to the abuse or who appears flirtatious and sexually aware.
> (1997, 168; see also Kitzinger 1988; Alcoff 1996, 130–1; Kincaid 1998)

The notion of childhood innocence thus functions in a way that closely parallels cultural ideals of female virginity. Within this frame, the no-longer-virginal child becomes
"damaged goods" and no longer merits the limited protections offered by claims of innocence. As Kitzinger notes, "If the violation of innocence is the criterion against which
the act of sexual abuse is judged, then violating a 'knowing' child becomes a lesser offense
than violating an 'innocent' child. ... Indeed, a child who is known to be a victim of sexual
abuse is often a target of further exploitation" (1997, 168–9).[11] The notion of sexual abuse
as "lost innocence" finds further expression in the idea that victims necessarily share common characteristics, exhibiting what has been called a "sexual abuse syndrome" (Summit
1983). The idea that all abuse is in some sense "the same" decontextualizes the events from
their distinctive social environment and encourages an approach that does not examine
the particularities of an individual's experience. Within this unitary definitional structure,
sexual abuse is seen as a form of sexual staining, one that leaves its victims unable to
achieve a normative heterosexuality. The phrase "sexual abuse victim" here ceases to be a
descriptive categorical grouping and instead takes on qualities of a diagnostic term, one
that purports to explain all manner of (sexual) deviance. Sexual abuse thus gains salience
within a wide variety of sexual contexts, standing equally well as an explanation for
prostitution, lesbianism, heterosexual "promiscuity," or abstinence. Holding these diverse

outcomes together is a framework that identifies a sexual abuse survivor as someone who has been violated and thereby forever placed outside of the virginal, sexually innocent "norm." In contrast, although early feminist writers focused upon the overall structures of male dominance that generated abuse, they did not assume any uniformity of response from the victims. Far from generating a singular list of effects or "symptoms," early feminist works are characterized by the wide variety of situations and reactions that were presented (if not fully theorized).

The focus upon sexual abuse as a sexual offense, rather than as an abuse of power, is most noticeably seen in the way in which psychologists often devote a great deal of attention to the purported sexual deviance of abuse survivors. "In fact," suggest Herman and Hirschman in their early review, "failure to marry or promiscuity seems to be the only criterion generally accepted in the literature as conclusive evidence that the victim has been harmed" (1977, 739). While the contemporary research is more extensive and describes some emotional states that may well present difficulties for many survivors—confusion about sexual identity, negative reactions to sexual arousal and activity—implicit judgments are made in these discussions regarding the value of particular forms of sexual being and expression: "Confused" identities are not "healthy," nor are negative associations with sex. And as Herman and Hirschman noted, psychological writings frequently continue to problematize sexual "excess" at either end of the spectrum. Social patterns such as promiscuity or asexuality are thus rendered as symptoms in need of treatment, primarily because of their incompatibility with the conventional sexual and familial structures that the dominant forms of psychology assume to be necessary for personal fulfillment. Finkelhor and Browne, for example, list "promiscuity" and "prostitution," as well as "difficulty in arousal" and "avoidance of or phobic reactions to sexual intimacy" in their table of "Traumagenic Dynamics in the Impact of Child Sexual Abuse" (1986, 186). Presumably, an individual who slept with three different people in a week would be labeled "promiscuous," while an individual who slept with the same partner seven times during the same week would not. Similarly, a person who masturbates regularly may be reproached for "avoiding sexual intimacy," while a person who has infrequent sex with a partner is less likely to be so labeled. Thus, by pathologizing both abstinence and licentiousness, many psychologists covertly reinforce ideologies that sanction only normative, monogamous sexual relations. As Saunders argues in a slightly different context (this volume), aspects of a survivor's personality that are simply nonnormative—and that may in fact be highly adaptive—are understood through this process to be "tragic" results of abuse.

The implicit understanding that defines sexual abuse as a form of sexual staining and loss of innocence also reveals itself in the assumption that all sexual abuse victims are inescapably and permanently damaged. Totalizing comments to the effect that victims are filled with "magical expectations" (Sgroi 1982, 126), are "inwardly seething with anger and hostility" (Porter, et al. 1982), "have unusual and dysfunctional needs to control or dominate" (Finkelhor and Browne 1986, 193), or are inevitably "the dominant females" (James and Nasjleti 1983, 6) are common and establish survivors as deviants against whom normalcy can be measured. Similarly, universal declarations such as "[R]egardless of its form and the child's response, incest is a devastating experience and leaves a devastating mark on its victim" (Dinsmore 1991, 21), or blanket assertions to the effect that "Incest is a traumatic event that leaves its victims scarred into adulthood" (Lindberg and Distad 1985, 334) reinforce a sense that sexual abuse causes a stigma that irrevocably attaches itself to the victim. Lengthy lists detailing the "effects" of sexual abuse (for example, Hall and Lloyd 1993, 67; Finkelhor and Browne 1986, 186–7) likewise frame sexual abuse victims as necessarily having problems that need to be resolved. This focus upon deviance establishes sexual abuse survivors as separate Others; they are in some sense "damaged goods" whose worth has been decreased by the fact of having been assaulted (Haaken 1998, 77; McKinnon 1995; Kitzinger 1997, 168–9). The therapeutic treatment of sexual abuse can thus become another means of policing the sexual behavior of survivors (a process that can extend into institutionalization, as seen in some of the instances presented by Ericcson; this volume).

Admittedly, victims of abuse may at times be attracted toward labels of psychological disease precisely because they postulate survivor deviance. Pathological designations offer a targeted, unitary explanation for all social suffering as well as an implicit promise to ease the distress once the problem is diagnosed. "Healing from the abuse" becomes the goal within this work, but it is important to examine the kind of social world that is being theorized in such formulations. As noted previously, clinical psychology frequently operates under an assumption that the effects of the "dysfunctional" past must be exorcised for the survivor to properly adjust to an implicitly "functional" present. Adult survivors must therefore perform a tremendous amount of emotional labor in order to successfully enact the very sexual and relational scripts that caused their initial suffering. Survivors are deemed "well-adjusted" precisely to the extent that their behavior conforms to models that take no account of their experiences.

Christine Dinsmore's integration of feminist principles within her therapeutic work leads to an alternate approach. Within her perspective, suffering is not automatically positioned as something to be overcome or "worked through." Her model instead suggests that some of the lessons learned through coping with abuse may be useful, although others may not:

> In my work with incest survivors, we examine survival behaviors and at-
> tempt to determine which of these skills, if any, may in fact still be useful. ...
> In other words, we do not assume that all survival skills acquired as a result of
> an abusive childhood are debilitating and need to be eradicated. Just as children
> need to learn skills to survive their childhoods, women need to learn to survive
> the patriarchy. (1991, 24; see also Hall and Lloyd 1993, 92–3)

Rather than narrowly scrutinizing the disposition and behavior of survivors for evidence of "dysfunctional" behavior, suffering becomes an investigatory tool that might be

used to shed light on normative social practices. The perceptions and practices of survivors become potentially visionary tools forged in opposition to abusive patterns that have deep social roots.

As these comments suggest, challenging the presumed deviance of sexual abuse victims requires reexamining the presumed normalcy of society. Such an investigation must necessarily situate abuse within a larger social and political context, and examine the ways in which sexual abuse is structured into the most commonplace and mundane patterns of male dominance. This approach therefore questions the very salience of the survivor/nonsurvivor distinction, invoking the categories in a much more qualified and contingent sense, rather than automatically assuming complete dissimilarity between victims and "nonvictims." The category "sexual abuse survivor" instead becomes useful to invoke at some times (when emphasizing patterns unique to families in which coercive sexualities are enacted) and useful to deconstruct at others (when highlighting the diversity of abusive situations, or when emphasizing the commonalties between abusive situations and other sexist patterns that are generally taken for granted).

To be clear, nothing within my analysis is intended as a commentary upon the efficacy of counseling for particular individuals. While clinical psychology tends to presume that the power differentials between women and men arise out of localized interpersonal dynamics—thereby ignoring the impact of systemic, society-wide oppressions upon families—it is of course true that many sexual abuse victims benefit from counseling, including the most individualized and depoliticized variants. For some survivors, therapy may provide them their only opportunity to speak about their experiences, an opportunity to reformulate their history in an environment where it is strongly emphasized that they are not to blame for their victimization. For others, the widespread encouragement psychology offers for setting boundaries and for identifying and pursuing one's desires may prove extremely beneficial, even life-altering, offering a much-needed challenge to the effects of gender, sexual, and antichild oppression manifested in both the abuse and in the broader society. By supporting a model of behavior in which individuals are encouraged to identify and pursue their own interests, clinical psychology can help to undermine certain elements of status-based hierarchical arrangements (male over female, adult over child) that have proven dangerous for victims, even as it works to support other aspects of these hierarchies (the nuclear family).

SEXUAL ABUSE AND THE STATE

With the passage of CAPTA in 1974, the federal government threatened to significantly cut funding for human services to any state that did not possess a mandatory reporting law, essentially forcing states to adopt such legislation. CAPTA similarly required the states to investigate these reports and to protect children who were deemed to be living in abusive situations. As documented in Barbara Nelson's historical study, Making an Issue of Child

Abuse (1984), the inclusion of sexual abuse within CAPTA resulted most immediately from last-minute lobbying pressure from child welfare agencies that pushed for a more inclusive definition of child abuse.[12] As noted previously, none of the legislative actors who initiated and passed CAPTA expected the tremendously large number of reports that would rapidly follow. Far from being a legislative priority, lawmakers essentially stumbled into a situation in which much more governmental activity concerning sexual abuse (and child abuse more generally) was generated than was ever expected. Notably, these augmented levels of state intervention have not been welcome among all quarters. CAPTA itself was nearly allowed to expire at the beginning of the Reagan presidency in 1982. Instead, funds to child welfare agencies, along with nearly all other health and human service agencies, were cut by 30 percent (Krugman 1997).

The tentative status of sexual abuse as a state concern can be seen in other ways as well. U.S. Supreme Court rulings with precedents extending to the 1920s have consistently ruled in favor of the relatively unrestricted rights of parents to control their children. As the court itself noted in a 1979 decision, "Our jurisprudence historically has reflected Western civilization concepts of the family as a unit with broad parental authority over minor children" *(Parham v. J.R.* 1979). These rulings were reaffirmed as recently as 2000 in *Troxel v. Granville,* in which the Court ruled "the interests of parents in the care, custody, and control of their children … is perhaps the oldest of the fundamental liberties recognized by this court." This history of legal precedent strongly supports "the sanctity of a man's home and the privacies of life" *(Boyd v. United States* 1886) and establishes a "private realm of family life which the state cannot enter" *(Prince v. Massachusetts* 1944).

This right to familial privacy is not absolute. U.S. law recognizes the state's power to interfere with parents' control over their children, "particularly where the children need to be protected from their own parents" (Croft 1997). However, the history of legal support for the "privacy" of family life raises the legal standards for state intervention in cases of abuse, significantly attenuating the state's willingness to intercede on behalf of children. The primacy of the family reveals itself through the disparity with which the state treats incestuous sexual abuse and nonfamilial sexual abuse: Incestuous offenders are generally dealt with by social service agencies or in civic court, although nonfamilial offenders are handled through the criminal justice system (Fisher 1998; see also Armstrong 1994). Indeed, child victims are frequently left in the custody of their abusers, placing them in further danger (Berliner 1993). Legislators have also proven willing to back down to minimally organized pressure from those seeking to protect the familialist order, both in relation to those who claim that false memories of sexual abuse are regularly "implanted" by therapeutic suggestion and in relation to those who argue that sexual abuse accusations are frequently falsified during custody disputes (Armstrong 1994; Myers 1994).

At best, then, the state has shown contradictory tendencies in relation to sexual abuse. On the one hand, it has supported intervention into the family through mandatory reporting laws and funding for social service agencies, creating through this process a base of professionals who are generally committed to strong legislative action on these issues. On the other hand, the state has proven reluctant to extend its mandate too far into the realm of family life. As might be expected, the result of these tensions has been far heavier state intervention against poor families than among those who are better able to mobilize legal protections (Armstrong 1994). While the effects of this situation clearly offer victims many advantages over the previous judicial regime that failed to identify sexual abuse, it clearly does not represent a complete break with the patriarchal norms of the past. Within the context of a society that advantages men, the right to familial privacy most directly limits any "undue interference" men might otherwise encounter in controlling their families.

State discourse concerning sexual abuse survivors further reveals the interests at play in governance over families. Before considering state discourses more fully, however, it must first be acknowledged that in many ways the language of the state is the language of clinical psychology. Given that the state directly funds the work of many social workers, psychologists, and psychiatrists, and given the way in which these professionals frequently exercise legal authority in their role as child welfare advocates of various sorts, the dominant views within psychology must indeed be seen as a significant part of the state apparatus. Indeed, the hegemony of psychological perspectives in discussions of sexual abuse is in no small part due to this state support and the role of psychology within the state. All the same, it is interesting to note that in those relatively limited instances when policy makers are directly called upon to describe sexual abuse survivors, the portrayals typically invoke even more stigmatizing representations of victims than are present within most clinical psychological imagery. For example, in a 1982 case referring to the making of child pornography, the U.S. Supreme Court cited several psychiatric studies of victims of child pornography, and of familial sexual abuse more generally, concluding flatly that "sexually exploited children are unable to develop healthy, affectionate relationships in later life, have sexual dysfunction, and have a tendency to become sexual abusers as adults" (*New York v. Ferber* 1982). This definitive and overarching conclusion was reiterated in a declaration by the U.S. Congress in 1999 (HR 107 1999).

Examining the views of psychologists and those of most upper-level policy makers suggests further contrasts between the two groups. Not only do policy makers tend to hold opinions that stigmatize survivors to a greater degree, but they also situate the issue of sexual abuse within a set of concerns that are different from those that prevail within psychology. While clinicians tend to assume that normative familial arrangements are necessary for personal fulfillment, the U.S. Supreme Court has ruled that "the best interests of the child" do not constitute a sufficient reason for the state to intervene into the private life of the family (*Troxel v. Granville* 2000). Instead, the Court held that the sanctity of family life requires a higher standard be satisfied in authorizing state action—that of social reproduction. As the Court comments, "A democratic society rests, for its continuance, upon the healthy, well-rounded growth of young people into full maturity as citizens, with all that implies. It may secure this against impeding restraints and dangers, within a broad range of selection" (*Prince v. Massachusetts* 1944). As noted previously, the 1982 case of *New York v. Ferber* argued that sexual abuse threatens the ability of children to later develop "healthy, affectionate" relationships, to carry on a "functional" sex life rather than a "dysfunctional" one, and to not become abusive (and, presumably, thereby injure others' ability to carry out either of the former activities). It is thus the threat to the family, to "healthy, functional" relationships, that triggers state intervention, and not simply a threat to a victim's personal safety or well-being.

The social and physical perpetuation of society through the family unit has been at issue even since the 1908 Punishment of Incest Act in Great Britain, which showed a similar concern. There are, however, two important differences between the Victorian legislation and contemporary dialogues: (1) the discourse of concern has shifted from physical to social reproduction, and (2) the child is no longer viewed as a sexual competitor for the father's affection, and is instead seen as an innocent victim, someone whose sexual innocence defines the abhorrent nature of the crime. Although contemporary state discourse places more emphasis on the suffering of children, it does so only within the framework of promoting the well-being of "democratic society," for which familial and sexual "normalcy" are apparent prerequisites.[13]

By emphasizing the absolute deviance of survivors, the state justifies its regulation of family life through county agencies such as Child Protective Services as well as the simultaneous freedom it gives to "functional" families (particularly when they are white and nonpoor). But although the state is clearly concerned with maintaining the relative independence of familial units (which typically amounts to freedom for the men within such units), its basic willingness to intervene in at least some cases of abuse shows it has an interest in limiting the enactment of power within the familial hierarchy. Actions that are judged to cause problems in relation to the future social and physical reproduction of society are deemed unacceptable and labeled as abusive, not just by psychologists, but by the full power of the state. As with the literature within clinical psychology, the Supreme Court's decisions move beyond an expression of concern for victims toward a prescription of healthy relationships and functional sex lives, that is to say, toward the reproduction of the modern family. Although interventions by the therapeutic state indeed undermine male familial authority in certain limited ways, they offer discourses that obfuscate male-dominant gender relations, and that discipline victims in ways that support the recreation of the very same familial and sexual structures that enabled the initial abuse. Action against abuse is thus best seen as a reformist attempt to restrict the harm caused by the patriarchal family in order to better reassure its ongoing continuance.

CONCLUSION

Remedying this situation clearly requires challenging state-therapeutic discourses. Yet such activism should not limit itself to discursive objectives. As Linda Gordon argues,

Probably the most important single contribution to the prevention of incest would be the strengthening of mothers. By increasing their ability to support themselves and their social and psychological self-esteem, allowing them to choose independence if that is necessary to protect themselves and their daughters, men's sexual exploitation could be checked. (1988, 62)

Numerous feminist commentators have noted a connection between women's ability to challenge wife abuse and their financial situation (see Brandwein 1999, for example), and it seems only reasonable to presume that similar dynamics exist in relation to sexual abuse. Strengthening the welfare system, instituting a more progressive tax structure, or introducing the idea of comparable worth are all difficult but eminently practical actions that would enable many poor mothers to prevent the abuse of their children. Increasing children's material opportunities outside the familial home, by providing better quality alternative and foster care, supporting shelter and food programs for runaways, and allowing teenagers to economically support themselves would similarly disrupt both male and parental power. Recognizing ways in which psychological and state discourses reinscribe the normative, male-dominant, heterosexual family should lead to action against not only the discursive manifestations of this dangerous inequity, but its material foundations as well.

DISCUSSION QUESTIONS

1. What social circumstances helped prompt passage of the CAPTA, and official acknowledgement of child sexual abuse claims, in general?
2. Why, historically, has the state played a passive role in acknowledging and curbing familial incest and abuse?
3. Why, according to the author, are terms like "molestation" and "abuse" used instead of "rape" when dealing with child violation? Why is terminology, in general, important in the sociological response to such abuse?

NOTES

1. I would like to thank Clare Corcoran, Astrea Davidson, Ali Luterman, Penelope Saunders, Ali Miller, and most especially Laurie Schaffner and Elizabeth Bernstein for their tireless work in helping me to produce this essay, from thinking through the initial ideas to editing the final text.
2. The rise in reports of sexual abuse was much more sudden than the rise in reports of child abuse as a whole. For example, from 1976 to 1983, reports of sexual abuse in the U.S. increased nearly tenfold (from 7,559 to 71,961), while reports including all

forms of abuse during approximately the same time period increased by 150 percent (Berrickand Gilbert 1991). Similarly, from 1980 to 1986, reports of sexual abuse more than tripled (resulting in approximately 155,000 reports of sexual abuse), while reports of physical abuse and neglect rose by 58 percent (National Center on Child Abuse and Neglect 1988).

3. For key exceptions, see, for example, MacLeod and Saraga 1988; Dinsmore 1991; Wilson 1993; Lamb 1996, 1999; Haaken 1998, 1999.

4. A slightly different analysis arises when male survivors are considered; Haaken 1999, 23–6.

5. See Hooper 1992, 60; Bell 1993, 126–49; see also Bailey and Blackburn 1979; Jackson 2000, 46–50, 120–2.

6. For feminist reviews of this literature, see Rush 1980, 97–103; Ward 1985, 139–61; Breines and Gordon 1983; Masson 1988; Summit 1988; Costin 1992; Olafson *etal.* 1993; McKinnon 1995.

7. See also DeMott 1980; "Attacking the Last Taboo" 1980; Leo 1981. For critiques, see Finkelhor 1979; Rush 1980; Janus 1981; Russell 1984, 1986; Armstrong 1994.

8. See, for example, Connell and Wilson 1974, 128–30; Brownmiller 1975, 220, 370–1, 385; Butler 1978, 165–8; Griffin 1979, 10–17.

9. Herman and Hirschman were extremely critical of Brownmiller on this point, and their comments merit quoting at length: Stressing the coercive aspect of the situation, she [Brownmiller] calls it "father rape." To label it thus is to understate the complexity of the relationship. The father's sexual approach is clearly an abuse of power and authority, and the daughter almost always understands it as such. But, unlike rape, it occurs in the context of a caring relationship. The victim feels overwhelmed by her father's superior power and unable to resist him; she may feel disgust, loathing, and shame. But at the same time she often feels that this is the only kind of love she can get, and prefers it to no love at all. The daughter is not raped, but seduced. In fact, to describe what occurs as a rape is to minimize the harm to the child, for what is involved here is not simply an assault, it is a betrayal. A woman who has been raped can cope with the experience in the same way that she would react to any other intentionally cruel and harmful attack. She is not socially or psychologically dependent upon the rapist. She is free to hate him. But the daughter who has been molested is dependent on her father for protection and care. ... She must endure it and find what compensations she can (1977, 748). Herman and Hirschman's observations are quite astute, and foreshadow some of the analysis that follows in this essay. Unfortunately, while these comments appear in their jointly authored essay in Signs, Herman chooses not to include these remarks in her booklength monograph where she instead argues that "it is a rape in the sense that it is a coerced sexual relationship" (1981, 27). More generally as well, the above views formed a decidedly minoritarian opinion among most feminists writing on the topic.

10. Herman's earlier work with Hirschman (1977) is even more explicit in noting the agency of victims in responding to abuse, albeit from within a very narrowed range of options.

Arguing that a victim "must endure it [the abuse], and find in it what compensations she can" (748), Herman and Hirschman utilize language which portrays victims as extremely active in negotiating the terms of their abuse with whatever resources they may have at their disposal. They note, for example, that many of the daughters effectively replaced their mothers and became their fathers' surrogate wives. They were also deputy mothers to the younger children and were generally given some authority over them. While they resented being exploited and robbed of the freedom ordinarily granted to dependent children, they did gain some feeling of value and importance from the role they were given. (748) While making clear that results such as these do not represent attractive bargains for victims, such an analysis incorporates a sense of a victim's agency into the overall approach.

11. As Schaffner points out (this volume), the protections of "childhood" are also applied disparately with regard to both race and gender. To the extent that the image of childhood innocence offers any sense of protection at all, it is severely mitigated in relation to girls who are not white and (at least) middle class. While innocence is applied somewhat ambivalently to even these girls, as seen previously, whiteness and class respectability nevertheless seem to be prerequisites for any of innocence's shield. See also Wilson (1993).

12. This information is somewhat buried in Nelson's discussion but can be gathered by examining the differing definitions of abuse within the initial legislation passed by the Senate in 1973 and the final legislation as signed into law in 1974 (106–7, 114–7). For an additional historical treatment of the passage of CAPTA, see Weisberg 1984.

13. It is notable, in this regard, that the Supreme Court originally ruled that homosexuality did not merit constitutional protection precisely because "No connection between family, marriage, or procreation on the one hand and homosexual activity on the other [was] demonstrated" *(Bowers v. Hardwick* 1986). In over turning this decision (*Lawrence v. Texas* 2003), the Court held that the right to privacy extended beyond the realm of the family, further noting favorably that the case "does not involve whether the government must give formal recognition to any relationship that homosexual persons seek to enter." Thus, while engaging in homosexuality is now recognized as a legal right, the court does not yet find that same-sex partnerships could constitute a family as such. Given that same-sex couples are not defined as part of that which helps to uphold democratic society, but are merely allowed to exist within the private sphere, it follows that the state is allowed to promote and reward heterosexual marriages while denying benefits to homosexual partnerships. Similarly, while Lawrence permits sexual practices to exist within the private sphere, it leaves untouched the notion that families are to have greater access to privacy than are nonfamilies. While the content of such a distinction is unclear, the state could theoretically decide to establish a lower threshold of intervention into the lives of children living with same-sex couples than for those living with heterosexual parents. It could, for example, decide that living with a same-sex couple constitutes a threat to a child's ability to later form a proper family—therefore

removing the child from its home—even while holding that homosexuality itself would not be prosecuted. However unlikely this scenario, the distinction between familial and nonfamilial rights to privacy must be noted.

REFERENCES

Anonymous. 1985. "Best Kept Secret?" In *Women Against Violence Against Women,* Dusty Rhodes and Sandra McNeil, eds., London, UK: Onlywomen Press, pp. 159–164

Armstrong, Louise. 1994. *Rocking the Cradle of Sexual Politics: What Happened When Women Said Incest.* New York: Addison-Wesley.

Bailey, Victor, and Sheila Blackburn. 1979. "The Punishment of Incest Act 1908: A Case Study of Law Creation." *Criminal Law Review* 20: 708–718.

Bell, Vikki. 1993. *Interrogating Incest: Feminism, Foucault and the Law.* New York: Routledge.

Bender, Lauretta, and Abraham Blau. 1937. "The Reactions of Children to Sexual Relations with Adults." *American Journal of Orthopsychiatry* 7: 500–518.

Berliner, Lucy, and Doris Stevens. 1982. "Clinical Issues in Child Sexual Abuse." In *Social Work and Child Sexual Abuse: Journal of Social Work and Human Sexuality,* Vol. I n. 1/2, Conte and Shore, eds. New York: Haworth Press, pp. 556–562.

Berrick, Jill, and Neil Gilbert. 1991. *With the Best of Intentions: The Child Sexual Abuse Prevention Movement.* New York: The Guilford Press.

Bowers v. Hardwick. 478 U.S. 186 (1986).

Boyd v. United States. 116 U.S. 616 (1886).

Brady, Kathleen. 1979. *Father's Days.* New York: Seaview.

Brandwein, Ruth, ed. 1999. *Battered Women, Children, and Welfare Reform.* Thousand Oaks, CA: Sage Publications.

Breines, Wini, and Linda Gordon. 1983. "The New Scholarship on Family Violence." *Signs* 8(3): 490–531.

Brownmiller, Susan. 1975. *Against Our Will: Men, Women and Rape.* New York: Bantam.

Butler, Sandra. 1978. *Conspiracy of Silence: The Trauma of Incest.* San Francisco: New Glide Publications.

Child Abuse Treatment and Prevention Act (CAPTA). *Public Law* 93–247 (1978).

Connell, Noreen, and Cassandra Wilson, eds. 1974. *Rape: The First Sourcebook for Women* by New York Radical Feminists. New York: New American Library.

Constantine, Larry, and Joan M. Constantine. 1973. *Group Marriage.* New York: Macmillan.

Costin, Lela B. 1992. "Cruelty to Children: A Dormant Issue and Its Rediscovery, 1920–1960." *Social Service Review* 66(2): 177–198.

DeMott, Benjamin. 1980. "The Pro-Incest Lobby." *Psychology Today,* March. 11–16.

Dinsmore, Christine. 1991. *From Surviving to Thriving: Incest, Feminism, and Recovery.* Albany, NY: State University of New York Press.

Donat, Patricia, and John D'Emilio. 1998. "A Feminist Redefinition of Rape and Sexual Assault: Historical Foundations for Change." *In Confronting Rape and Sexual Assault,* Mary Odem and Jody Clay-Warner, eds. Wilmington, DE: *Scholarly Resources,* pp. 35–49.

Engel, Beverly. 1991. *The Right to Innocence: Healing the Trauma of Childhood Sexual Abuse.* New Haven, CT: Ivy Books.

Finkelhor, David. 1979. "What's Wrong with Sex Between Adults and Children? Ethics and the Problem of Sexual Abuse." *American Journal of Orthopsychiatry* 49(4): 692–697.

Finkelhor, David, and Angela Brown. 1986. "Initial and Long-Term Effects: A Conceptual Overview." In *A Sourcebook on Child Sexual Abuse,* David Finkelhor *et al.* eds. Beverly Hills, CA: Sage Publications, pp. 180–98.

Fisher, Nancy. 1998. "Defending the Symbolic Boundaries of the Family: Legal Discourse on Child Sexual Abuse." Paper presented at the 93rd Annual Meeting of the American Sociological Association. San Francisco: CA.

Forward, Susan, and Craig Buck. 1981. *Betrayal of Innocence: Incest and Its Devastation.* New York: Penguin.

Freedman, Alfred M., H. I. Kaplan, and B. J. Sadock, eds. 1975. *Comprehensive Textbook of Psychiatry.* Baltimore: Williams & Wilkins.

Gordon, Linda. 1989. *Heroes of Their Own Lives: The Politics and History of Family Violence.* London, UK: Virago.

Gordon, Linda. 1988. "The Politics and History of Child Sexual Abuse: Notes from American History." *Feminist Review* 28: 56–64.

Griffin, Susan. 1979. *Rape: The Politics of Consciousness.* San Francisco: Harper and Row.

Haaken, Janice. 1999. "Heretical Texts: The Courage to Heal and the Incest Survivor Movement." In *New Versions of Victims: Feminists Struggle with the Concept,* Sharon Lamb, ed. New York: New York University Press, pp. 13–41.

Haaken, Janice. 1998. *Pillar of Salt: Gender, Memory, and the Perils of Looking Back.* New Brunswick, NJ: Rutgers University Press.

Hall, Liz, and Siobhan Lloyd. 1993. *Surviving Child Sexual Abuse: A Handbook for Helping Women Challenge Their Past.* Washington, DC: Falmer Press.

Hancock, Maxine, and Karen Mains. 1987. *Child Sexual Abuse: Hope for Healing.* Wheaton, IL: Harold Shaw Publishing.

Herman, Judith. 1981. *Father-Daughter Incest.* Cambridge, MA: Harvard University Press.

Herman, Judith, and Lisa Hirschman. 1977. "Father-Daughter Incest." *Signs* 2(4): 735–756.

Hooper, Carol-Ann. 1992. "Child Sexual Abuse and the Regulation of Women: Variations on a Theme." In *Regulating Womanhood: Historical Essays on Marriage, Motherhood and Sexuality,* Carol Smart, ed. New York: Routledge. pp. 53–77.

Jackson, Louise. 2000. *Child Sexual Abuse in Victorian England.* New York: Routledge.

James, Beverly, and Maria Nasjleti. 1983. *Treating Sexually Abused Children and Their Families.* Palo Alto, CA: Consulting Psychologists Press.

Janus, Sam. 1981. *The Death of Innocence: How Our Children Are Endangered by the New Sexual Freedom.* New York: William Morrow.

Jenkins, Henry, ed. 1998. *The Children's Culture Reader*. New York: New York University Press.

Kitzinger, Jenny. 1997. "Who Are You Kidding? Children, Power, and the Struggle Against Sexual Abuse." In *Constructing and Reconstructing Childhood*, Allison James and Alan Prout, eds. Washington, DC: Falmer Press, pp. 165–189.

Kohn, Alfie. 1987. "Shattered Innocence." *Psychology Today* 21 (February): 54–58.

Krugman, Richard. 1997. "Child Protection Policy." In *The Battered Child*, Mary Heifer, Ruth Kempe, and Richard Krugman, eds. Chicago, IL: University of Chicago Press, pp. 627–641.

Lamb, Sharon, ed. 1999. *New Versions of Victims: Feminists Struggle with the Concept*. New York: New York University Press.

Lamb, Sharon. 1996. *The Trouble with Blame: Victims, Perpetrators, and Responsibility*. Cambridge, MA: Harvard University Press.

Lawrence v. Texas. No. 02–102 (2003).

Leo, John. 1981. "Cradle-to-Grave Intimacy: Some Researchers Openly Argue that Anything Goes' for Children." *Time*, September 7: 69.

Lewis, Melvin, and Phillip Sarrel. 1969. "Some Psychological Aspects of Seduction, Incest and Rape in Childhood." *Journal of American Academy of Child Psychiatry* 8: 606–619.

Lindberg, Frederick, and Lois Distad. 1985. "Post-traumatic Stress Disorders in Women Who Experienced Childhood Incest." *Child Abuse and Neglect* 9: 329–334.

Macleod, Mary, and Esther Saraga. 1998. "Challenging the Orthodoxy: Towards a Feminist Theory and Practice." *Feminist Review* 28 (January): 16–55.

Margolin, D. 1972. "Rape: The Facts." Women: A Journal of Liberation 3: 19–22.

Masson, Jeffrey. 1984. *The Assault on Truth: Freud's Suppression of the Seduction Theory*. Harmondsworth, UK: Penguin.

McKinnon, Susan. 1995. "American Kinship/American Incest: Asymmetries in a Scientific Discourse." In *Naturalizing Power: Essays in Feminist Cultural Analysis*, Sylvia Yanagisako and Carol Delancy, eds. New York: Routledge. pp. 25–46.

Myers, John, ed. 1994. *The Backlash: Child Protection Under Fire*. Newbury Park, CA: Sage.

National Center on Child Abuse and Neglect. 1988. *Study of National Incidence and Prevalence of Child Abuse and Neglect*. Washington, DC: U.S. Department of Health and Human Services.

Nelson, Barbara. 1984. *Making an Issue of Child Abuse: Political Agenda Setting for Social Problems*. Chicago, IL: University of Chicago Press.

New York v. Ferber. 458 U.S. *747*, 759 (1982).

Olafson, Erna, D.L. Corwin, and R.C. Summit. 1993. "Modern History of Child Sexual Abuse Awareness: Cycles of Discovery and Suppression." *Child Abuse and Neglect* 17: 7–24.

Parham v. J.R. 444 U.S. 584 (1979).

Porter, Francis, Linda Blick, and Suzanne Sgroi. 1982. "Treatment of the Sexually Abused Child. "In *Handbook of Clinical Intervention in Child Sexual Abuse*, Suzanne Sgroi, ed. Lexington, MA: Lexington Books, pp. 109–145.

Prince v. Massachusetts. 321 U.S. 158 (1944).

Renovoize, Jean. 1993. *Innocence Destroyed: A Study of Child Sexual Abuse*. New York: Routledge.

Rush, Florence. 1980. *The Best Kept Secret: Sexual Abuse of Children*. New York: McGraw-Hill.

Russell, Diana. 1986. *The Secret Trauma: Incest in the Lives of Girls and Women*. New York: Basic.

Russell, Diana. 1984. *Sexual Exploitation: Rape, Child Sexual Abuse, and Workplace Harassment*. Beverly Hills, CA: Sage Publications.

Scott, Ann. 1988."Feminism and the Seductiveness of the 'Real Event.'" *Feminist Review IS:* 88–102.

Sgroi, Suzanne. 1982. "Family Treatment of Child Sexual Abuse." In *Social Work and Child Sexual Abuse: Journal of Social Work and Human Sexuality, Vol.* I, Issue 1 and 2, Jon Conte and David Shore, eds. New York: Haworth Press.

Sturkie, Kinly. 1986. "Treating Incest Victims and Their Families." In *Incest as Child Abuse: Research and Applications*. Brenda Vander Mey and Ronald Neff, eds. New York: Praeger. pp. 126–167.

Summit, Ronald. 1983. "The Child Sexual Abuse Accommodation Syndrome." *Child Abuse and Neglect 7: 177–193.*

Toldson, Ivory, ed. 1997. *Stolen Innocence: Preventing, Healing and Recovering from Child Molestation*. New York: CPHC Press and Products. *Troxelv. Granville.* 530 U.S. 57 (2000).

Ward, Elizabeth. 1985. *Father-Daughter Rape*. New York: Grove Press.

Weiner, Niel, and Sharon Kurpius. 1995. *Shattered Innocence: A Practical Guide for Counseling Women Survivors of Childhood Sexual Abuse*. New York: Taylor Francis.

Weinberg, Kirson S. 1955. *Incest Behavior*. New York: Citadel Press.

Weisberg, D. Kelly. 1984. "The' Discovery' of Sexual Abuse." *UC Davis Law Review* 18: 1–57.

Wilson, Melba. 1993. *Crossing the Boundary: Black Women Survive Incest*. Seattle, WA: Seal Press.

INTRODUCTION TO: MOMENTS OF INTIMACY

Norms, Values, and Everyday Commitments

JAN CAMPBELL

I n his article, Jeffrey Weeks shows how our homogeneity in friendship has become the tie that binds and affirms identity and belonging. These friendships produce fluid network families comprised of friends, lovers, ex-lovers, biological kin, and children. In looking at this new emphasis on friendship, it becomes apparent that these "bridging ties" allow for, according to Weeks, "balancing autonomy and relatedness, flexibility and responsibility, negotiation and commitment." He gives us a view of how this works in the non-heterosexual world.

Weeks cites examples from various authors in his work, which reinforces the theme of family as a noun, an adjective, and even a verb. Family may not always be fixed but rather a sort of composite of relational interactions with persons interpreted to be family.

MOMENTS OF INTIMACY

Norms, Values, and Everyday Commitments

JEFFREY WEEKS

I nformal, local, contextualized relationships are important for underpinning the emergent norms of a diverse society. These are sustained by what Spencer and Pahl (2006) have called the 'hidden solidarities' that are a major source of social capital in the contemporary world. I want to look in a little more detail at a crucial aspect of this, the significance of friendship, and its links with changing family forms. This link has been most evident in the developing culture of the non-heterosexual world (Weston 1991; Weeks et al. 2001), but as various writers have indicated (e.g., Pahl 2000; Roseneil 2004; Roseneil and Budgeon 2004; Vernon 2005) it has profound implications for wider personal relationships, challenging narrow interpretations of what constitutes family and intimate life.

I do not want to exaggerate the cultural significance of television series such as *Friends, Sex in the City* or *This Life,* which have concentrated on young attached (and usually highly attractive) people living or interacting with one another in intense, often family-like and sexually relaxed contexts, but they are popular because they echo new realities about the importance of friendships. Research commissioned by the food manufacturer Dolmio and published in 2006 has found that increasingly the boundaries of friendships and families are dissolving for young people, who often spend more time with friends than with family.

Apparently, *67* percent of Britons now feel their best friend is part of their family, and whereas twenty-five years earlier half the population sought to keep friends and family apart, in 2006 only 15 percent sought to do so. This has given rise to the rather ghastly neologism of 'framilies', which people feel happy to identify with. Here is 32-year-old Kirsten:

> My relatives live in Australia, which makes my friends all the more important. My framily and I eat together once a week, and I speak to most of them everyday. These people understand me and I understand them. We all feel comfortable around each other and I don't have to make too much of an effort. I don't see my framily as a replacement for my blood family. They're an addition to my family. (Mowbray 2006: 19)

What is interesting about this quotation is that it echoes much of the language used about lesbian and gay friendships. The non-heterosexual world, I have argued elsewhere, is sustained by the intricately woven but durable strands of a 'friendship ethic' (Weeks et al. 2001: ch. 3). Of all our relationships, claims Sullivan (1998: 176), 'Friendship is the most common and most natural. In its universality it even trumps family.' Peter Nardi (1999), reflecting on the significance of gay male friendships, describes them as the basis for 'invincible communities'. They provide the strength for gays to develop fully creative lives, and the protection against a potentially hostile world. Even more strongly, Michel Foucault saw in gay friendships the really subversive outcome of the gay revolution since the 1970s. 'Society and the institutions that frame it have limited the possibility of relationships [to marriage] because a rich relational world would be very complex to manage' (quoted in Vernon 2005: 134). Gay friendships open up new possibilities of loving, befriending and relating which challenge the narrow solidarities of traditional families, and contribute to the development of Blasius' (1994) distinctive 'gay ethos'. Lesbians and gay men who may feel excluded from the traditional nuclear family can ground their emotional security and daily needs in strong friendships, where the boundaries between friendships and sexual relationships are often blurred. Lovers can become friends, friends lovers, and significant others are not necessarily sexual partners in a 'queering' of conventional boundaries (Roseneil 2000, 2004; Roseneil and Budgeon 2004).

Friendships provide a web of support and security which is particularly important in times of rapid change. They flourish when broad identities are undermined or shattered in periods of rapid social change, or at turning points in people's lives, or when lives are lived at odds with social norms (Weeks 1995: 145–6; Weeks et al. 2001). Friendships are, like Paris, a 'movable feast', they can be sustained over time and place and distance, yet they can allow individuals who live at the margins to feel constantly affirmed and confirmed in who and what they are through evolving life experiences. They offer the possibility of developing new patterns of intimacy and commitment, based on choice (because friendship is by definition elective, not given) and some degree of equality (because friendships are peer relationships, tend to homogeneity, and can be escaped from if differences become divisions). All these features give a special meaning and intensity to friendship in the lives of those who live on the edge. Friends can provide emotional and material support, but also affirm identity and belonging.

But this is not simply an LGBT (lesbian, gay, bisexual, transgendered) experience. Friendships, for example, have been widely portrayed as central to women's experiences, underpinned as they are by an ethic of reciprocity (see Harrison 2004). So in periods of social upheaval it is not surprising that heterosexuals and non-heterosexuals alike are giving a new emphasis to friendship. The 'bonding ties' of traditional families can be too restrictive, enclosed, protective and limiting for the post-traditional individual. The 'bridging ties' and flexibility provided by friendship, families of choice or 'personal communities' where friendships and families overlap provide flexible and effective ways of negotiating risk and uncertainty, and of providing care and support (Allan 1996; Pahl 2000; Roseneil 2004; Budgeon 2006; Spencer and Pahl 2006). Friendships provide the space for exploration of who or what you are, and what you want to become. This is true at all stages of the life cycle, from the first tentative stages of exploring sexuality and identity, through the pleasures and crises of relationships, to the problems of aging and potential loneliness of old age—those fateful or critical moments (Giddens 1992; Thomson et al. 2002) in a life which force individuals to reassess who and what they are, and to find ways of adapting to new situations.

Friendships are more than crutches for those who society barely acknowledges or accepts. They offer the opportunity for alternatives. In our study of non-heterosexual families of choice, fluid network families composed of friends, lovers, ex-lovers, biological kin, and increasingly children (Weeks et al. 2001), we found a range of life experiments in which individuals sought to balance autonomy and relatedness, flexibility and responsibility, negotiation and commitment. The language of 'family' used by many lesbian and gay people may be seen as both a challenge to conventional definitions and an attempt to broaden these; as a hankering for legitimacy and an attempt to build something new; as an identification with existing patterns and a more or less conscious effort to subvert them. The new narratives that many non-heterosexual women and men tell about families of choice and intimate life are creating a new public space where old and new forms jostle for meaning, and where new patterns of relationships are being invented (for US comparisons cf. Weston 1991; Carrington 1999).

Everyone, an American gay writer has argued, has the right to shape family forms that fit his or her needs (Goss 1997: 19), and this is like a leitmotiv for the emergence of 'new families'. Many LGBT people, traditionally seen as excluded from the scope of conventional family life, are simultaneously rethinking the meaning of same-sex relationships, and developing new meanings of family. Even the most passionate theoretical advocates of the rights of non-heterosexual people to form their own 'families' are careful to emphasize the dimensions of difference. Goss writes: 'In fact, we are Queering the notion of family and creating families reflective of our life choices. Our expanded pluralist uses of family are politically destructive of the ethic of traditional family values' (Goss 1997: 12). Others are not so certain that it is not a surrender to heteronormativity (Roseneil and Budgeon

2004). But more crucially, the emergence of non-heterosexual families of choice has to be seen as part of the wider pluralization of forms of family life that has been a central theme of this world we have made. If there are indeed so many types of family, why should same-sex families be ignored (Stacey 1996: 15)? Non-heterosexual relationships and families of choice are part of a wider struggle over meaning, both participating in and reflecting a wider transformation of family relationships. If the future of marriage is a critical ground of contestation in the wider world, it is hardly surprising that lesbians and gays should focus their demands on it. If parenting is perceived as in major need of rethinking, then why should non-heterosexuals be excluded from the debate? If families get ever more complex as a result of divorce, remarriage, recombination, step-parenting, surrogacy and so on, why should the chosen families of lesbians and gays, including with increasing frequency children, be denied a voice (Weeks et al. 2001)?

As Morgan (1996, 1999) has suggested, it is more useful today to see family in terms of a set of social practices rather than a fixed institution to which we belong. From this perspective 'family' may be seen as less of a noun and more as an adjective or a verb. '"Family" represents a constructed quality of human interaction or an active process rather than a thing-like object of social investigation', writes Morgan (1999: 16). This approach displaces the idea that the family is a fixed and timeless entity of which one is either a member, or excluded from. We may see it instead as a series of practical everyday activities which we live: through activities such as mutual care, the division of labor in the home, looking after dependants and 'relations', all of which practices LGBT people regularly engage in. 'Family' is about particular sorts of relational interactions rather than simply private activities in a privileged sphere. Instead of being an objective phenomenon, 'family' may be interpreted as a subjective set of activities whose meanings are made by those who participate in them. Family practices focus on everyday interactions with close and loved ones, and move away from fixed boundaries of co-residence, marriage, ethnicity and obligation that defined the male breadwinning family. It registers the ways in which our networks of care and affection are not simply given by virtue of blood and marriage, but are negotiated and shaped by us (Williams 2004: 17). From this perspective, it is less important whether we are in a family than whether we do family-type things. Following Judith Butler (1990) we can describe family practices as 'performative', with families constructed through their constant iterative enactment. We live family rather than dwell within it.

This allows us to recognize and begin to understand the fluidity of everyday life practices, and the way doing family is related to the ways we do or perform gender, sexuality, work, caring and the other activities that make up the totality of life experiences. Family life is a historically specific, contextualized set of activities, intimately linked with other social practices. From this perspective there is no theoretical reason to exclude non-heterosexual everyday practices—or anyone else's—from the pantheon of family and kin.

Having said that it is important at the same time to acknowledge that diversity in family forms does not necessarily mean diversity in family lifestyles or moral guidelines.

The study of step-families by Ribbens McCarthy and her colleagues (2003) pin-points the continuing power of family discourse and ideals. Although family can be accepted as an accumulation of practices, people act as if it were a coherent unity, involving commitment, togetherness, putting the family first, mutual support and responsibility. The idea of the family as a loose, diffuse alliance or network across households was largely held by white, middle-class liberal interviewees, but others wanted a more closely defined boundaried unit. 'Being there for you' was a complex notion, but at the heart of it was a set of relationships that offered a sense of security, a unit in which children could be reared. Even step-families are communities of need rather than elective affinities, argue Ribbens McCarthy et al. (2003: 50–2). Gabb substantiates this to some extent in her study of lesbian parents in Yorkshire. She did not find any particular resonance of the friends as family model, and was critical of what she calls the 'community narrative' which normalizes it (2004: 168, 174). For her sample, 'blood was thicker than water.'

Again, we can see in this the complex coexistence of attitudes. On the one hand there is clearly an awareness of the fluidity and flexibility of intimate arrangements that are able to adapt not simply to non-heterosexuality but to key moments in heterosexual life—especially marriage breakup and remarriage, and the complexity of step-parenting arrangements that then emerge. On the other hand, there is a strong urge for what Giddens (1991) calls 'ontological security', based on a strong narrative of belonging and identity that can make sense of the past and present, and allow for planning for the future. A sense of family, embodying connectedness and belonging, provides that. But for some, as Ribbens McCarthy et al. and Gabb illustrate, this is necessarily embodied in the tight relationship of parent and child rather than the expansiveness of 'families we choose.'

We can draw a couple of useful observations from this. In the first place, while we can agree with those who argue that the shifting patterns of friendship represent a significant destabilization of the homosexual/heterosexual binary insofar as friendships and 'families of choice' cut across the gay/straight divide (e.g. Roseneil 2000; Roseneil and Budgeon 2004), they do not necessarily lead to the dissolution of what are seen as core values of family life. Rather they are reformulated for new times. Second, as Henning Bech (1992, 1997) suggested some years ago, referring to the first, Danish, experiments with legalizing same-sex partnerships, it is a step towards the end of the homosexual—but of the heterosexual too. It begins to make meaningless the categorical distinctions of which marriage was a key marker. That puts into some perspective the debate over the significance of same-sex marriage.

DISCUSSION QUESTIONS

1. Describe what research has found about how gay men and lesbians think of "family."
2. The author cites a researcher who has suggested that it is more useful today to see family in terms of a set of social practices rather than a fixed institution to which we

belong. Do you agree? What advantages and disadvantages of this approach come to mind?

REFERENCES

Allan, G. (1996) *Kinship and Friendship in Modern Britain,* Oxford: Oxford University Press.

Bech, H. (1992) 'Report from a Rotten State: "Marriage" and "Homosexuality" in "Denmark"', in Plummer (ed.) 1992, 134–50.

Bech, H. (1997) *When Men Meet: Homosexuality and Modernity,* Cambridge: Polity Press.

Blasius, M. (1994) *Gay and Lesbian Politics: Sexuality and the Emergence of a New Ethic,* Philadelphia, PA: Temple University Press.

Budgeon, S. (2006) 'Friendship and Formations of Sociality in Late Modernity: The Challenge of "Post Traditional Intimacy"', *Sociological Research Online* 11 (3), at: http://www.socresonline.org.Uk/ll/3/budgeon.html.

Butler, J. (1990) *Gender Trouble: Feminism and the Subversion of Identity,* London: Routledge.

Carrington, C. (1999) *No Place like Home: Relationships and Family Life among Lesbians and Gay Men,* Chicago, IL and London: The University of Chicago Press.

Giddens, A. (1991) *Modernity and Self identity,* Cambridge: Polity Press.

Giddens, A. (1992) *The Transformation of Intimacy: Sexuality, Love and Eroticism in Modern Societies,* Cambridge: Polity Press.

Goss, R.E. (1997) 'Queering Procreative Privilege: Coming Out as Families', in Goss and Strongheart (eds) 1997.

Harrison, K. (2004) 'The Role of Female Friends in the Management of Affairs', in Duncombe *et al.* (eds) 2004, 203–22.

Morgan, D. (1999) 'What Does a Transsexual Want? The Encounter between Psychoanalysis and Transsexualism', in More and Whittle (eds) 1999, 219–239. Morgan, D.H.J. (1996) *Family Connections,* Cambridge: Polity Press.

Morgan, D.H.J. (1999) 'Risk and Family Practices: Accounting for Change and Fluidity in Family Life', in Silva and Smart (eds) 1999, 13–30.

Mowbray, N. (2006) 'Now We can All Play Happy "Framilies"', *Observer,* 9 April.

Nardi, P. (1999) *Gay Men's Friendships: Invincible Communities,* Chicago, IL: Chicago University Press.

Pahl, R. (2000) *On Friendship,* Cambridge: Polity Press.

Ribbens McCarthy, J., Edwards, R. and Gillies, V. (2003) *Making Families: Moral Tales of Parenting and Step-parenting,* Durham: Sociology Press.

Roseneil, S. (2000) 'Queer Frameworks and Queer Tendencies: Towards an Understanding of Postmodern Transformations of Sexuality', *Sociological Research Online* 5 (3) at http://www.socresonline.org.Uk/5/3/roseneil.html.

Roseneil, S. (2004) 'Why We Should Care About Friends: An Argument for Queering the Care Imaginary in Social Policy', *Social Policy and Society* 3 (4), 409–19.

Roseneil, S. and Budgeon, S. (2004) 'Beyond the Conventional Family: Intimacy, Care and Community in the 21st Century', *Current Sociology* 52 (2), 135–59.

Spencer, L. and Pahl, R. (2006) *Rethinking Friendship: Hidden Solidarities Today,* Princeton, NJ, and Woodstock: Princeton University Press.

Stacey, J. (1996) *In the Name of the Family: Rethinking Family Values in the Postmodern Age,* Boston, MA: Beacon Press.

Sullivan, A. (1998) *Love Undetectable: Reflections on Friendship, Sex and Survival,* London: Chatto & Windus.

Thomson, R., Bell, R., Holland, J., Henderson, S., McGrellis, S. and Sharpe, S. (2002) 'Critical Moments: Choice, Chance and Opportunity in Young People's Narratives of Transit', *Sociology* 36 (2), 235–54.

Vernon, M. (2005) *The Philosophy of Friendship,* Basingstoke: Palgrave Macmillan.

Weeks, J. (1995) *Invented Moralities: Sexual Values in an Age of Uncertainty,* Cambridge: Polity Press.

Weeks, J., Heaphy B. and Donovan, C. (2001) *Same Sex Intimacies: Families of Choice and other Life Experiments,* London: Routledge.

Weston, K. (1991) *Families We Choose: Lesbians, Gays, Kinship,* New York: Columbia University Press.

Williams, F. (2004) *Rethinking Families,* ESRC CAVA Research Group, London: Calouste Gulbenkian Foundation.

INTRODUCTION TO: THE WEDDING-INDUSTRIAL COMPLEX

JAN CAMPBELL

This article describes the way in which heterosexuality and male-to-female sex roles are portrayed in the "recession-proof" industry we know as weddings. Ingraham exposes the reader to the globalization of all facets of constructing a wedding, from the products produced outside the U.S. to marketing and the distribution of goods and services, which ultimately produce what has been called the transnational wedding industrial complex. Even with goods and services produced in countries that help keep the cost of production low, it is estimated that revenues from the wedding market in the United States in 2005 ranged from $25 billion to $125 billion.

Ingraham continues the dialogue by indicating that the wedding alone is a huge conglomerate, but that the household goods represent up to 90 percent of the registry business. Even though newlyweds only make up about 2.6 percent of all households in the U.S., they account for 75 percent of all fine china, 29 percent of tableware, and 21 percent of the jewelry sold each year. An even bolder statement conveys the fact that the average American wedding costs the equivalent to one year of education at a private, four-year college or university.

One of the most astounding aspects of this article is the comparison of what $27,000 will buy in the parts of the world where the wedding goods and services are produced. This article is truly an eye-opener.

THE WEDDING-INDUSTRIAL COMPLEX

CHRYS INGRAHAM

T he heterosexual imaginary naturalizes male to female social relations, rituals, and organized practices and conceals the operation of heterosexuality in structuring gender across race, class, and sexuality. This way of seeing closes off any critical analysis of heterosexuality as an organizing institution and for the ends it serves.[1] By leaving heterosexuality unexamined as an institution we do not explore how it is learned, what it keeps in place, and the interests it serves in the way it is currently practiced. And, perhaps more importantly, by treating it as taken-for-granted and as natural we lose our ability to make conscious choices—a crucial ingredient for democratic life. Through the use of the heterosexual imaginary, we hold up the institution of heterosexuality as timeless, independent of relations of ruling, devoid of historical variation, and as "just the way it is" while creating social practices that reinforce the illusion that as long as one complies with this prevailing and naturalized structure—"it's just the way it is"—all will be right in the world. This illusion is commonly known as romance. Romancing heterosexuality is creating an illusory sexual identity category that defines perceived female to male socio-sexual relations. The white wedding as a pervasive social practice relies on the heterosexual imaginary and has become a significant site for the development of a range of social problems.

Referred to by Wall Street analysts as "recession-proof," the wedding industry has reached such proportions that it can be more accurately described as a wedding-industrial complex. This structure reflects the close association among weddings, the transnational wedding industry, labor, global economics, marriage, the state, finance, religion, media, the World Wide Web, and popular culture. The scope of this chapter is to provide an overview of the various components of this complex in order to make visible the historical and material foundation upon which the operation of the heterosexual imaginary depends.

THE TRANSNATIONAL WEDDING INDUSTRY

Several significant shifts have occurred in the wedding industry over the past fifteen years, inflating the average price of a white wedding by approximately 38 percent. Perhaps the most significant development has been the increased globalization of the wedding industry. Globalization is a complex and highly debated concept that refers to a relatively recent development in advanced capitalism. Capitalism, by definition, requires expanding markets and cheaper production costs in order to increase profits. To this end, producers must locate new consumers either by creating new desires and wants or by expanding into previously untapped regions or markets. Globalization describes the processes by which production, distribution, and markets have made use of global relationships and resources to this end. For example, products formerly made in the U.S. (local) at a higher cost are now being manufactured at a lower cost outside of the U.S. (global), e.g., U.S. wedding gown production in China. These lower costs frequently include paying workers substandard wages, child labor, sexual abuse and slavery, as well as exposure to toxins and excessive work hours. In addition to the role of the global economy in providing cheap labor and materials for the wedding industry, globalization has provided a variety of expanded markets for what can now be considered the transnational wedding industrial complex.

Globalization also involves cultural, social, economic, and political changes. Examples of these aspects include everything from the desire for white weddings by people in Japan to the westernization of non-western cultures. Governments and business work together to implement world trade policies that affect how business is conducted within and between countries. These policies significantly influence national and international migratory patterns resulting from poverty and production changes and increase struggles over immigration and immigration laws. For the wedding industry, the proliferation of satellite media, the growth of the World Wide Web, increased marketing of weddings around the world, the increasing trend toward destination weddings, and the vast use of outsourcing by the textile industry have combined to link global economics with the development of global culture(s).

As of 2005, industry estimates of the total annual revenues of 'the *primary* wedding market in the United States range from a conservative $50 billion

> **FACT**
>
> If American retailers paid only 25 cents more per garment, the total in Bangladesh would be $898 million—more than eight times current U.S. aid. *Source:* National Labor Committee, 2007 www.nlcnet.org

per year to a more generous assessment of $125 billion.[2] While this latter figure seems excessive, it is not unrealistic given that the wedding industry has, in recent years, benefited from the increased availability of cheap labor and has expanded to include destination weddings and a variety of global markets including Japan, India, Kenya, parts of South Asia, and South Africa. The availability of data regarding the size of the wedding industry is problematic in that most of their facts and figures are collected by the industry itself and not by more neutral data-gathering sources. However, by comparing each of the industry estimates against census data and marketing surveys, the most concise assessment establishes the current size of the U.S. based wedding industry at closer to $125 billion in revenues per year. If this assessment is accurate and the white wedding industry functioned as one company, it would place among the top 15 *Fortune* 500 U.S. corporations.

This multibillion-dollar wedding industry includes the sale of a diverse range of products, most of which are produced outside of the U.S.—wedding gowns and apparel, diamonds, honeymoon travel and apparel, destination weddings, and household equipment. Also included in this market are invitations and paper products, flowers, receptions, photos, video, gifts, home furnishings, wedding cakes, catering and food supplies, alcohol, calligraphy, jewelry, party supplies, hair styling, makeup, manicures, music, books, and wedding accessories, e.g., ring pillows, silver, chauffeurs, and limousines.[3] Although newly-weds make up only 2.6 percent of all American households, "they account for 75 percent of all the fine china, 29 percent of the tableware, and 21 percent of the jewelry and watches sold in this country every year."[4] Newlyweds and potential newlyweds are among the nation's largest consumers of major appliances, furniture, and consumer electronics, as well as tableware, linens, small appliances, and cookware, often obtaining these items as wedding presents selected through a registry. Household goods represent up to 90 percent of the registry business, and nearly 93 percent of engaged couples register their wedding gift choices. With nearly 10,000 weddings cancelled each year, even insurers have entered the primary wedding market by offering to cover the cost of any monies spent on the wedding preparation "if wedding bells don't ring." Fireman's Fund Insurance Company offers "Weddingsurance" for wedding catastrophes such as flood or fire but not for "change of heart."[5]

In fact, attach the words wedding or bridal to nearly any item and its price goes up. To increase market share in an ever-shrinking marriage market, the wedding industry has expanded the wedding season to include what they are now calling the "engagement season." With the vast majority of engagements occurring in November and December, customers are now the targets of wedding marketers from the engagement period through the leading wedding months of June, August, May and July.

According to industry estimates, the average wedding in the United States costs $27,852, with some regional variations. For instance, in the New York metro area the average times current US wedding increases to $38,852 with numerous examples of weddings costing more than $100,000. In the South, the cost drops to $18,624 and on the West Coast, to $24,918.[6] Considered in relation to what Americans earn, the cost of the average wedding represents 62.3 percent of the median earnings of a white family and 92 percent for black and Hispanic families. The fact that 40 percent of Americans earn less than $25,000 per year[7] means the average cost of a wedding approximates a year's earnings for many Americans.

To put these costs into perspective consider the following comparisons. The price tag for the average white wedding in the U.S. is equivalent to one year of education at a private four year college or nearly four years of school at a public college or university;[8] about the same to purchase a new fully-equipped Honda Accord, Ford Mustang GT Shelby, or Toyota Tundra truck;[9] or the down payment on a house. Given the extent to which the wedding industry has become globalized, and that nearly one half of the world lives on $2 per day, consider what else the average cost of a white wedding in the U.S. would buy in those locations where many wedding products are made.[10]

> "Unfortunately, sometimes the debt lasts longer than the marriage," he says.
>
> —Howard Dvorkin, Consolidated Credit Counseling, Ft. Lauderdale, FL

What $27,852 Will Buy Where Wedding Products Are Produced

- Food for 3,000 people in South Asia.
- Cost to build 12 wells for people in southeast Asia, Africa, and Latin America.
- Medicine for 10,000 children for one year in Africa.
- At wages of 12 cents per hour to sew wedding gowns, the cost to pay 111 workers for one year.
- At wages of $28 per week for mining diamonds in South Africa, the cost to pay 19 workers for one year.

"It Won't Be a Stylish Marriage ... I Can't Afford a Carriage ..."

Following the publication of the first edition of *White Weddings* and other recent wedding studies, a variety of media outlets became interested in exploring the issue of wedding debt. Most notable among these was an article published on the front page of the *Sunday New York Times*[11] and titled "For Richer or Poorer, to Our Visa Card Limit" by Jennifer Bayot.

Wedding bills are weighing down couples and their parents long after the "I do's," and many have been forced to seek financial counseling as a result, according to credit counseling agencies. Young couples with modest incomes are having the most trouble repaying. Whether they celebrate lavishly or modestly, they are more likely than ever to pay for their weddings without help from their parents. And even when parents pay, what more and more people expect of nice weddings is increasingly more elaborate for both the richer and the poorer. And so, with debt do they start.[12]

In this article, Bayot interviewed couples about their wedding choices and discovered that most were spending far beyond their ability to pay. Pundits, experts, and research studies since this article indicate that financial pressures for newlyweds are playing a prominent role in divorce among newly married couples.[13] While the level of debt incurred by newlyweds receives plenty of media attention, this coverage has had little effect on wedding consumption patterns. Not only has the size of the industry tripled in the past 15 years, the number of marriages has actually decreased indicating that couples are spending more to marry than ever before. Another trend contributing to the wedding debt experience is that 32 percent of

Author Interview, July 2003:

I was interviewed on WOR Talk Radio for their early morning commuter show. One caller responded to questions about the size of the wedding industry with this commentary:

"I don't care how excessive it is [the cost of weddings], I spent $40,000 on each of my three daughters' weddings and I'd do it all again. Today, they are all still married and I have beautiful grandchildren."

wedding expenses are paid for by the couple themselves. Only 30 percent of parents are paying the whole cost of weddings and 15 percent of the costs are shared.[14]

In an interview for an article in the *Boston Globe*, one couple referred to the newlywed experience with the wedding industry as "wedding hell."[15] The article described a fairly typical encounter with the wedding industry. Working against classic arguments such as "It's the happiest day of your life" and "It's a once-in-a-lifetime thing," the newlyweds in this article struggled to plan a wedding that would not exceed $5,000. What they found shocked them. After weeks of bartering with reception halls and caterers who were either unwilling to negotiate or were priced out of reach, the bride said, "I was exhausted. Planning a wedding is a full-time job, a second one for me[16]—and not even as rewarding. My fiancé and I were feeling like the victims of highway robbers with sanctioned routines."[17] The final blow was attending a crowded bridal show where they had to "register" for numerous mailing lists and the bride was given a "silly sticker," which proclaimed her "a very important bride," and told her to fill out fifty-eight coupons for special prizes. "These people must think *bride* is synonymous with *stupid,*" she thought. In the end, this couple decided not to get married yet and instead to put their $5,000 toward the purchase of a house, where, in the end, they could hold their own wedding and reception.

WHO ARE THE TARGETS OF THE WEDDING INDUSTRY?

Who marries and who are the consumers of this enormous industry? On average, newlyweds are getting older. According to the 2000 U.S. Census Bureau, the average age for brides had risen from 20 in 1960 to 25; for grooms from 23 to 26.8 years. By 2006, the average age increased further to 27 for brides and 29 for grooms. The age of first marriage has been rising steadily at a rate slightly greater than one year every decade for first marriages. One of the primary factors delaying the age of first marriages is the social acceptance of couples living together prior to marriage, from 500,000 in 1970 to 5.5 million in 2005 or 9 percent of all heterosexual couples.[18] While this has made marriage less necessary other couples are delaying wedding to finish college, graduate school, or to pursue career opportunities. For the privileged classes, the economic necessity of marriage has steadily decreased something that causes the wedding industry great concern.

As the total number of marriages and remarriages declined from 2,342,000 in 1996, to 2,253,750 by 2006[19] and the marriage rate has decreased from 8.8 to 7.8 per 1000 persons, the wedding industry has sought new opportunities for growth. Currently, the industry is encouraged by the projections for "echo boomers"—the children of "baby boomers"—that indicate that the annual number of marriages will once again increase. Considering how much growth has occurred in the wedding industry, it is clear that weddings are still a sizeable niche market! all again.

Today, they Contributing to the health of the wedding industry, the large and complex remarriage market "includes some married people who want to reaffirm their vows in second ceremonies,"[20] people who are divorced, as well as a growing population of widowed seniors who are remarrying. The current divorce rate of 4.3 per 1000 persons is a per capita rate and is based on the total population of persons of marriageable age. Since not all people are "marriageable," this figure is probably higher than 4.3 and increases the size of the wedding market. As of 2005, 4 out of every 5 people who have been divorced remarry and 50 percent of all marriages are remarriages for at least one of the participants.[21] The average age for divorced women who remarry is 35, and the average for divorced men is 39 with 75 percent of divorced women remarrying within ten years.[22] Even though remarriage weddings tend to be smaller, the wedding industry estimates that they total up to 40 percent of their revenues, evidence that at least one sector in American society actually benefits from divorce. In fact, without remarriages, the wedding industry would be substantially smaller.

Since 65 percent of remarriages include children from a prior relationship, the remarried market also incorporates revenues (and practices) affiliated with family. For example, this market now includes "familymoons"—post-wedding vacations that include family members and children. Additionally, people who are remarrying increasingly take advantage of another recent trend—destination weddings. Destination weddings—where the couple invite family and friends to travel to a distant location for a combined wedding/vacation—have emerged as the fastest growing segment of the wedding industry, growing from 3 percent to 16 percent of the total wedding market.

According to the wedding industry, today's newlyweds are also more likely to be dual-earner couples, with 83 percent of brides and 89 percent of grooms working; they earn a combined income currently one third greater than the median household income, at $65,076.[23] Factoring in the age and financial standing of many of those remarrying, the probability of higher incomes increases, as does the focus of the wedding market on the consumption patterns of these newlyweds. Additionally, many young couples own houses and many of the home furnishings they need before they marry. The effect of all these factors is a dramatic change in the wedding market and its strategies.

Fascinating, right? But there's something missing from this picture of the white wedding market. In researching data on the wedding industry, a striking pattern emerges. Almost without exception, most state and industry analysts have overlooked the effects of race and class on consumption. In other words, they have focused mainly on the *white* wedding market—those patterns attributable primarily to middle-to-upper-middle class whites. When recalculated to account for differences along racial, ethnic, and class lines, industry market data reveal significantly greater buying power and a very different relationship to marriage among middle to upper class whites than for any other group. The following paragraphs offer a race and class comparison of people who are of marriageable age in the U.S. as a way to illustrate the scope and target of the wedding industry.

The 78 percent marriage rate for Americans cited in wedding industry and census materials is primarily applicable to whites and Asians and is significantly lower for Hispanics (*67* percent) and even lower yet for blacks (42 percent). While blacks used to marry much younger, they now marry considerably later than the national average, if they marry at all. Twenty-five percent of black women and less than 12 percent of black men have married by their early twenties, and more than 43.3 percent of black men and 41.9 percent of black women have never married, compared to 27.4 percent for white men and 20.7 percent for white women[24]

The typical black couple spends an average of $12,152 on a wedding, much less than the national average of $27,852. Blacks and Hispanics spend less on weddings and marry less often than whites and Asians. Is this the result of wedding market targeting? Or does the meaning of marriage change depending on one's racial and ethnic affiliation? And, on what assumptions are these data based?

NEVER MARRIED	BLACK	WHITE
Women	43.4%	22.8%
Men	46.8%	30.2%

Source: U.S. Census Bureau 2006

Comparing marriage rates to socioeconomic status—income, educational attainment, housing, mobility, and social characteristics—provides a more complete picture of the wedding market. Consider the average combined income for marrieds from black and Hispanic groups. As of 2004, married couples from within these groups had significantly lower levels of income than whites, earning 79 percent of what whites earn. While this might explain the lower levels of expenditure on a wedding, it does not explain the lower marriage rate.

Another important difference between these groups is their degree of poverty. For example, for their numbers, blacks and Hispanics are disproportionately poor compared with whites and Asians. For instance, poverty rates for blacks and Hispanics greatly exceed the national average of 12.7 percent; 24.7 percent of blacks and 21.9 percent of Hispanics had earnings below the national poverty threshold[25] as compared with 8.6 percent of whites and 9.8 percent of Asians.[26]

A key influence on earning potential is education and here again we find significant differences between groups. While black and Hispanic high school graduation rates approach parity with whites, only 42 percent complete four or more years of college as compared with whites who graduate at a rate of 62 percent.[27] The result, of course, is that whites and Asians have greater earning potential than do blacks and Hispanics. Again, while this explains why wedding expenditure is lower for these groups, it does not explain why they marry in significantly lower numbers.

SOCIOECONOMICS FACTORS			
	Median Earnings	Poverty Rates	College Degree
Black	$30,134	24.7%	17.6%
Hispanic	$34,241	21.9%	12.1%
White	$48,977	8.6%	30.6%
Asian	$57,518	9.8%	49.4%

Source: U.S. Census Bureau 2006

As Americans we assume that most people not only desire marriage but that most people do, eventually, marry. Yet, except for some regional variations, the national rate of marriage in the U.S. has declined by about 30 percent in the past 20 years to 52 percent of the nation's estimated 106 million households.[28] Considered in relation to differences in marriage patterns across race and social class, a cursory examination of these data lead one to question if marriage is the universal practice we assume it is and to question what its frequency has to do with one's race and social class standing. Additionally, the data on marriage comes from a variety of legitimate sources that omit data on the complexities of racial and ethnic categories as well as the rising numbers of mixed marriages.

To understand the complexities influencing marriage patterns, researchers have uncovered a variety of factors. Of particular importance is what some researchers call the "marriage penalty."[29] This is not the same as the marriage penalty tax that Congress has been working to eliminate but is, instead, a concept created to explain the contradictory relationship the (working) poor have to marriage. Among those earning minimum wage or living near or below the poverty line, marriage disqualifies many for the complex array of benefits they need to survive. For single mothers—blacks, 48 percent; Hispanics, 25 percent; and whites, 14 percent—who are disproportionately poor and at risk, this is of critical importance in their relationship to marriage. For those living below the federally established poverty threshold, they are eligible for food stamps, Temporary Assistance to Needy Families (TANF), child tax credits, and Earned Income Tax Credit (EITC). While nearly 60 percent of single mothers live with a partner, marital status actually disqualifies some of them for assistance. Take, for example, what the Economic Policy Institute wrote about the Earned Income Tax Credit (EITC), a measure intended to provide income tax relief for the poor.

> The EITC also creates a substantial marriage penalty since combined incomes determine eligibility and benefits. If a householder with two dependent children and an income of $10,000, marries a partner with an income of $20,000, their combined disposable income would be reduced by more than $3,000. The penalty is even more severe if both partners had dependent children.[30]

In addition to this assessment, others have offered similar conclusions concerning the effect of marriage on poor families.[31] In their view, the average poor family of four living at or near the poverty threshold risks the loss of—by some estimates—as much as $6,000. In other words, a working husband's earnings (the majority of the poor work) may not be enough to qualify for tax relief and "too much" to qualify for a host of social programs including food stamps, school meals, and child care. Due in part to the inadequacies of tax laws, poverty assistance policies, and the lack of child care programs, not to mention poverty threshold calculations that have not been updated since 1964, marriage among the poor, whether young or elderly, places them at a significant disadvantage. As the latest census data indicate, an increasing number of couples are choosing to live together (cohabitation) without "benefit" of marriage in order to avoid losing valuable assistance, Social Security income, and important tax breaks.

Put simply, marriage frequency drops dramatically as its economic and material benefits decrease. While middle class women no longer "need" to marry for financial security, poor women do not participate in part because it puts them at greater risk economically.

Either way, just considering the economic value of marriage it comes as no surprise that the number of annual marriages is declining. Contrasted against the rising expenditures on weddings, it is possible to conclude that the primary target of the wedding industry is people who place higher up on the socioeconomic scale. The lower one's socioeconomic level, the less likely they are to marry and the less they will pay for a wedding. Considering weddings from an economic standpoint, it is possible to conclude that the white wedding industry targets privileged whites more prominently than any other group. Comparing whites and Asians for earnings and earning potential, the deciding factor in focusing on whites is population size. Asians are still a minority group within the American population.

Given the focus of the wedding industry, wedding advertisers, and the pervasive images of white weddings in popular culture, the comments of a 12-year-old African American boy recently interviewed for an article in *The Washington Post* are particularly insightful.

> "Marriage is for white people." That's what one of my students told me some years back when I taught a career exploration class for sixth-graders … in southeast Washington. I was pleasantly surprised when the boys in the class stated that being a good father was a very important goal to them, more meaningful than making money or having a fancy title.

"That's wonderful!" I told my class. "I think I'll invite some couples in to talk about being married and rearing children." "Oh, no," objected one student. "We're not interested in the part about marriage. Only about how to be good fathers." That's when the other boy chimed in, speaking as if the words left a nasty taste in his mouth: "Marriage is for white people."[32]

As if to echo the sentiments of the industry, this child's perception is consistent with what the marketers themselves believe. They are aware that the combined earnings of black or Hispanic newlyweds is usually significantly lower than those of whites and are likely to remain lower throughout the course of the marriage (which is also shorter). Wedding marketers know that white middle-class women are more likely to consume wedding products than any other group. They target their marketing campaigns to white women who have the means to consume their products. Even within the advertising industry there is considerable evidence of racial segregation and of institutional racism affecting who is hired and what images and strategies are used in wedding advertising.[33] Throughout the wedding industry, images of white women and couples are pervasive and set both a race and class standard for who marries and who has a white wedding. To attract a broader range of consumers, the wedding industry must appeal to non-material needs such as romance, kinship, beauty, morality, consumerism, affection, and sexual identity. These aspects play a central role in the massive revenues the industry earns.

The reality regarding marriage is that it primarily privileges the privileged, those who are able to secure and maintain goods, property, and credit. Marriages among those in the middle class or above generally increase the earning potential of the couple. Certainly, for middle- to upper-class white women, marriage signals financial security with married women earning 37 percent more than single women.[34] The rewards and benefits afforded these couples and their families—from health insurance to health club discounts to lavish weddings are substantial.

An examination of the wedding industry and its marketing efforts offers considerable evidence regarding the interests at stake in marriage in American society. Throughout the 80s and 90s politicians used lower marriage rates among the nation's lower classes to justify welfare policies and cuts in social services. They claimed that the lack of marriage in these communities was an indicator of poor family values. As we enter the 21st century, more political "solutions" have been devised to "encourage" heterosexual marriage as a way to reduce dependency on government assistance. The most recent of these was a $1.5 billion grant to poor communities in the hope that increasing the number of marriages among the poor would allow public officials to claim they had reduced public assistance claims.[35] The reality is that marriage itself does not lift the poor out of poverty; it just reduces the number of eligible recipients. It is clear from a brief examination of the material landscape for poor families that opportunities for employment that pay a living wage, safe neighborhoods, inexpensive housing, access to affordable child care and education are the path to prosperity. A close examination of the seemingly benign wedding market offers evidence regarding the economics of marriage and the interests at stake in preserving its power.

A major tension regarding the future of marriage has emerged in the struggle between social conservatives seeking to preserve the status quo regarding marriage and recent efforts on the part of legal and social advocates for same sex marriage. Studying the various facets of the wedding industry quickly reveals the massive market forces invested in the outcome of this battle. The transnational wedding industry, already expanding its global market share, stands to make substantial gains if same sex marriage becomes legal in the U.S. Massachusetts, where same sex marriage has been legal since May 2004, has allowed 10,400 same sex marriages and the wedding industry there has been in full bloom.[36] In California, where same-sex marriage was upheld by the courts in 2008 and where there is no restriction on out-of-state marriages, estimates are that the annual revenues from same-sex weddings will be $685 million per year (enough to pull California out of its debt crisis). With same sex civil unions legal in Vermont, and same sex marriage initiatives erupting throughout the U.S., the American wedding industry is already building markets and reaping the benefits. Same sex wedding expos have emerged all over the country as have honeymoon marketing, wedding consulting, and advertising to same sex couples. Major newspapers such as the *New York Times* have changed their wedding pages to "weddings and celebrations," regularly including same sex couples, and *Modern Bride* magazine has featured a spread on same sex weddings. Combined with the legalization of same sex marriage in Canada, the Netherlands, England, and Spain, the transnational wedding industry is experiencing rapid and unprecedented growth. All of this is occurring at the same time that federal and state governments in the U.S. are seeking permanent bans on same sex marriage. The conflict between the interests of the wedding industry, consumerism, transnational capitalism, with those who seek to consolidate heterosexual power and privilege vis a vis marriage is clearly visible. The important question is: which forces will carry the most weight in the outcome of this struggle—market or social?

PRIMARY WEDDING MARKET BACKGROUND: WHITE WEDDING GOWNS

Probably the most important wedding purchase is the bride's gown. Industry analysts have noted that most brides would do without many things to plan a wedding and stay within budget, but they would not scrimp when it comes to the purchase of the wedding gown. With the national average expenditure at $922 for the gown and $265 for the veil, the bride's apparel becomes the centerpiece of the white wedding. Most of us have heard the various phrases associated with the bride and her gown, the symbolic significance attached to how she looks and how beautiful her gown is.

Prior to Queen Victoria's wedding in 1840, white wedding gowns were not the norm. Brides occasionally wore white but more frequently were wed in black or gray dresses.[37] If the bride's family had the money and the means, she would wear a dress made from brocades of gold and silver, yellow and blue. Puritan women, for example, wore gray. When Queen Victoria was wed in a white gown, she captured the imaginations of many when this powerful president over the British Empire, who many thought of as "plain," married a handsome Prince.

She became a real-life Cinderella and she did so in an opulent ceremony where she wore a luxurious and beautiful (by nineteenth-century standards) *white* wedding gown. Following this grand event, many white Western middle-class brides, already captivated by a growing consumer culture and romance novels, imitated Victoria and adopted the white wedding gown. By the turn of the century, white had not only become the standard but had also become laden with symbolism—it stood for purity, virginity, innocence, and promise, as well as power and privilege.

Queen Elizabeth II's wedding to Prince Philip in 1947 once again seized the attention of people around the world. This post-World War II extravaganza was not only a wedding of royalty and affluence, but it came at a time following the devastation and gloom of the war when many Westerners were desperately seeking images of hope, prosperity, and order. The romances and lives of celebrities had become mainstream popular culture fare and royal weddings gave the public images upon which they could aspire. Even though advertisers had been using images of beautiful white brides to sell products since the early 1900s, these celebrity weddings renewed the linkage of romance with consumerism at a time when weddings and the U.S. economy were both booming. For years to come, these two royal spectacles secured the promise of, and romance with, the white wedding so prevalent today.

Continuing this powerful tradition in recent years were the weddings of two preeminent princess brides: Princess Grace and Princess Diana. These blond-haired, blue-eyed, real-life princess Barbies married during the mass media era. The former Grace Kelly was a beautiful, famous, internationally acclaimed film star who met a handsome prince, Prince Rainier of Monaco, married in a wedding extravaganza filmed by MGM in April 1956, and went off to live "happily ever after" as Princess Grace of Monaco.[38] For many Americans,

Grace Kelly, born in Philadelphia to Irish immigrant parents, represented the merging of the Hollywood fairy-tale happy ending and the American dream of possibility and wealth. The headlines proclaimed that even a little girl from Philadelphia could become a princess.

Lady Diana Spencer, previously unknown to the public, married one of the most affluent, famous, and eligible bachelors of the late twentieth century, Prince Charles. Also blond, blue-eyed, and beautiful, the nineteen-year-old Lady Diana became the wife of the future king of England. Their wedding was a globally televised public spectacle watched by 750 million people from all parts of the world.[39] In both weddings the brides wore extraordinarily elaborate and expensive white wedding gowns and were married in ceremonies befitting a queen—extravagant, luxurious, and opulent. These modern-day Cinderellas captured the imagination of people from all over the world, regardless of gender, race, social class, nation, and sexual identity.

Diana's wedding and gown have had a profound influence on the wedding industry. The wedding of Diana and Charles became the exemplar of the ultimate fantasy of what a wedding should be.

The marriage of conspicuous consumption with the promise of love and romance combines to create a highly lucrative but virtually invisible transnational wedding industry that is interdependent with the historical needs of capitalism. In this context, the wedding gown becomes fetishized, creating a "recession-proof" market where social relations become alienated in favor of the pursuit of the ultimate commodity—the couture or couture-like wedding gown that promises eternal love and romance for all regardless of race, class, nationality, or sexual identity.

WEDDING GOWN PRODUCTION

With world trade agreements such as the North American Free Trade Agreement (NAFTA), and the World Trade Organization (WTO), textile production has become largely an offshore industry. That is, the vast majority of wedding gowns are not made in the U.S. any longer. Instead, the vast majority of bridal gowns are produced by women workers in China who are 15 to 30 years old and earn an average of $12 per day. As designers and manufacturers pursue cheaper labor in their quest for profits, the "race to the bottom"—locating the lowest possible cost for production—frequently takes them to countries intent on competing for heir business even if it means lowering already low wage rates. The result is that most textile and shoe production occurs in China with significant competition coming from Guatemala, Mexico, Taiwan, the Commonwealth of Northern Mariana Islands (a U.S. protectorate), Saipan, and Bangladesh. Currently, Latin American production is high at $19 per day and Bangladesh has the lowest rate at $9 per day, making them the most attractive to a wide variety of companies.

While bridal gown manufacturers remove labels from their dresses, bridesmaid gowns frequently still have them. A look at the portion of tags bridesmaid gown-sellers leave in the dresses reveals that most are sewn in Mexico and China. Estimates by consumer advocates and industry specialists suggest that somewhere in the vicinity of 80–90 percent of all wedding gowns are produced outside the U.S. in subcontracted factories where labor standards are nowhere near what they are in the U.S. and no unions or regulators keep watch. Elson and Pearson quote from an investment brochure that uses racism and sexism to attract multinational corporations:

The manual dexterity of the oriental female is famous the world over. Her hands are small and she works fast with extreme care. Who, therefore, could be better qualified by *nature and inheritance* to contribute to the efficiency of a bench-assembly production line than the oriental girl?[40]

The recruitment of U.S. companies to contract offshore labor benefits manufacturers on many levels: cheap labor, low overhead, fewer regulations, and higher profits. And with the proliferation of free trade agreements labor and environmental abuses abound. Particularly in locations such as the free trade zone in Mexico where proximity to the U.S. and economic relations between the U.S. government and Mexico make this a largely unregulated location, occupational hazards, toxic exposure and dumping, sexual harassment, and labor abuses produce immeasurable negative costs to the people and lands in these areas.

In 1996, then Secretary of Labor Robert Reich (under President Clinton) gathered industry leaders together to head off a labor and offshore manufacturing crisis precipitated by the National Labor Committee's (NLC) exposure of sweatshop use by The Gap and by Wal-Mart's Kathie Lee Gifford clothing line. In a press release that coincided with the holiday season and the anniversary of the Triangle Shirtwaist Factory fire in New York City in 1909 in which 145 women died as a result of sweatshop working conditions, Reich released a "no sweat" initiative in the form of a Trendsetter's List. This directory of garment manufacturers and retailers provided consumers with a list of companies committed to taking "additional steps to ensure their goods are not made in sweatshop conditions."[41] While the list was extensive, the only wedding gown manufacturer in evidence was designer Jessica McClintock.

The Asian Immigrant Women's Association (AIWA) launched a full-scale campaign to force McClintock to pay her workers $10,000 in back wages. When they saw McClintock's name on the Trendsetters' List they contacted the Labor Department and threatened to expose the company for labor abuses. Rather than risk media exposure, McClintock settled with the workers over the back pay they were owed.[42]

Each of these events happened prior to the publication of the first edition of this book. At that time, with the exception of an investigation into

From *Bridal Gown Guide* E-Mail, 1998, p.6:

"After several weeks of gown shopping, I have learned that this experience is not for the faint of heart or the uninformed. I was not about to plunk down 60% deposit only to find out that the dress was made by a noname company in a sweatshop in China."

labor abuses on the part of one leading dress manufacturer by the Union of Needletrades, Industrial and Textile Employees (UNITE), little was being done by designers or governments to ensure legal and humane treatment of wedding apparel textile workers. Compared to major corporations such as Nike, Mattel, and Wal-Mart, most of these smaller textile operations were overlooked and unexamined.

Lifting the Veil A Special Report, a white paper distributed by UNITE, documented the sweatshop practices of the Alfred Angelo Company.[43] Alfred Angelo, a Philadelphia-based gown manufacturer founded by the Piccione family in 1940, has had a long-standing reputation in the design and production of wedding and prom gowns and bridesmaid and mother-of-the-bride dresses. Under labels such as Christian Dior, Michele Piccione Couture, Tina Michele, Dance-Allure, Flirtations, Bridallure, and Alfred Angelo Bridals, the company sells gowns and dresses through a variety of retail outlets.

In a survey conducted by UNITE of three factories in Guatemala, it was discovered that Alfred Angelo gowns were being made by thirteen-year-olds in factories with widespread violations of their country's child labor, wage, and hour laws and under life-threatening safety conditions. At two of the firms, fourteen- and fifteen-year-olds worked as long as ten hours a day earning $20.80 a week.

Even though sales volumes had risen steadily, according to UNITE, Alfred Angelo had planned to eliminate jobs in the United States and move all of its work to Guatemala. With annual sales at $59 million in 1996, the company still sought to use Chinese subcontractors to assemble dresses. UNITE reported that there was "no way of knowing the conditions under which the clothes are made" and that Alfred Angelo's primary motivation was "greed." Angelo laborers in the U.S. "allied themselves with the exploited workers in Guatemala and China" in an effort to convince the Piccione family to put corporate responsibility ahead of corporate greed.

In June 1997 the Alfred Angelo Company apologized for late deliveries and cited union trouble as the reason. They blamed the problems on "militant and negative responses from UNITE apparel union, which has directly contributed to the delay of shipments to our customers."[44] At the time, a sagging bridal retail market had contributed to sales declines, and companies like Alfred Angelo were pressured by discount bridal retailers who "undercut their prices on gowns," as well as by "rising couture stars like Amsale."[45] In the Spring 1998 bridal fashion review in New York, Alfred Angelo was conspicuously absent, leaving many with the impression that the company was having difficulty recovering from these setbacks.

Today, a world-wide social movement to stop a host of abuses by multinational corporations in the name of free trade has raised significant levels of awareness regarding these issues. Protests on everything from labor and human rights violations to environmental degradation have occurred at each meeting of the World Trade Organization and at the G8, an annual political summit meeting of the heads of government where trade issues are priorities. A number of organizations including the National Labor Committee, the New York State Labor/Religion Coalition, and Global Exchange[46] as well as several media outlets including *Dateline NBC, 20/20,* and *60 Minutes* have made it their mission to expose and confront the massive abuses companies have committed in the textile industry. For example, these organizations have made it well-known that Mexican and Asian workers are frequently young, female, live in cramped dormitory settings, experience significant levels of sexual abuse, and are paid extremely low wages under very poor working conditions.[47] Yet, despite dramatic efforts to raise public awareness regarding these practices, the current Bush administration has abandoned any effort to address sweatshop conditions, human rights and environmental abuses under a host of free trade agreements. Emblematic of their position (or lack thereof) was the high-profile Abramoff lobbying and political finance scandal that emerged during the Bush years. Federal investigations into Abramoff's dealings revealed that he had traded favors with Republican Congressman Tom DeLay, a leading representative of the Bush administration, to stop legislation banning sex shops and sweatshops that forced employees to have abortions in the U.S. Commonwealth of the Northern Mariana Islands.

While most free trade debates and protests have occurred in the West, the most powerful player to emerge in the globalization of the textile industry is China. The Chinese government has declared textiles and apparel to be a major industrial sector in their economy. As such they have spent tens of billions of dollars to create a highly competitive textile industry that has become the leading player in this drama. They have provided loan forgiveness to businesses, subsidized utility, land, and shipping costs, export tax rebates, and created some of the lowest wages for textile workers anywhere in the world. These practices have created highly competitive incentives and low costs for the textile and apparel industry, luring the vast majority of wedding gown designers to produce their products in China. Additionally, the Chinese government has established a significant block to any outside scrutiny or standards of accountability on the level of human rights and labor practices making doing business with the Chinese even more attractive to companies that desire low costs and less public accountability. The Chinese have under-priced their textile production and have outpaced countries such as Bangladesh and India which have lower wage rates. According to the United Nations, China exports apparel at prices 58 percent lower than other countries. Currently, China controls between 60 and 85 percent of the global apparel market and with it the vast majority of wedding apparel production.[48]

CONCLUSION

The contemporary white wedding under transnational capitalism is, in effect, a mass-marketed, homogeneous, assembly-line production with little resemblance to the Utopian vision many participants hold. The engine driving the wedding market has mostly to do with romancing heterosexuality in the interests of capitalism. The social relations at stake—love, community, commitment, and family—become alienated from the production of the wedding spectacle, while practices reinforcing a heterogendered and globalized racial division of labor, white supremacy, the private sphere as women's work, and women as property are reinforced.

The design of these rituals secures a heterogendered division of labor with the bride, socialized since childhood, as the domestic planner, showpiece of the groom's potential wealth and producer of future workers, while the groom represents the final decision maker—patriarchal authority—and passive recipient of the bride's service. He's in charge of the honeymoon travel (adventure) plans. The system also sets up the bride as primary consumer and the marriage promise as integral to the accumulation of private property, particularly for whites, who have significant economic advantage in American society.

The heterosexual imaginary circulating throughout the wedding-industrial complex masks the global, racial, class, and sexual hierarchies are secured. For instance, in nearly all of the examples offered here, the wedding industry depends upon the availability of cheap labor from developing nations with majority populations made up of people of color. The wealth garnered by white transnational corporations both relies on racial hierarchies, exploiting people and resources of communities of color (Africa, China, Haiti, Mexico, South Asia), and perpetuates them in the marketing of the wedding industry.

DISCUSSION QUESTIONS

1. What is the heterosexual imaginary and how does it use romance?
2. What is the wedding industrial complex and what is its relationship to the white wedding?
3. How does the heterosexual imaginary mask issues of labor, race, class, and sexuality?
4. Develop a case study of Disney, Mattel, DeBeer Diamonds, or any other or ganization in the wedding-industrial complex and explain how the historical and material conditions of these organizations depend upon the heterosexual imaginary and contribute to an array of social problems.

NOTES

1. Ingraham 1994, 1999.
2. Fairchild Bridal Group, 2006; Fields and Fields, 2005.
3. Fairchild Bridal Group, 2006; Fields and Fields, 2005, McMurray, Shane, 2005.
4. Dogar, 1997; *Bride's* Magazine Millennium Report, 1999, Fairchild Bridal Group, 2005.
5. Haggarty, 1993; http://www.pbs.org/wnet/moneyshow/cover/061501.html.
6. McMurray, Shane, 2005; Fairchild Bridal Group, 2006, Fields and Fields, 2005.
7. U.S. Bureau of Census, 2000.; *National Vital Statistics Reports, 2006.*
8. College Board, 2004.

9. www.auto.consumerguide.com/auto
10. PovertyMap.net, World Bank.org, worldonfire.org, http://news.bbc.co.uk/2/hi/africa/3189299.stm, http://www.professionaljeweler.com/archives/news/2004/042704story.html, http://www.globalwitness.org/campaigns/dia-monds/index.php, www.nlc.org
11. July 13, 2003
12. Bayot, 2003, p. 1.
13. Orman, 2006, Preventingdivorce.com, Poortman, 2005.
14. McMurray, Shane, 2005; Fairchild Bridal Group, 2005.
15. With, 1996.
16. Note: it is important to notice that the labor of planning the standard white wedding in the U.S. is the equivalent of a second job for the bride-to-be. This sets up an expectation that she be able to work outside the home full time while working a "second shift" at home. See Hochschild, *The Second Shift, 1990.*
17. With 1996, 85:1.
18. CDC, *National Vital Statistics Reports,* 2003.
19. Bride's 1996; U.S. Bureau of the Census 1996.
20. Dewitt, 1992.
21. CDC, *National Vital Statistics Reports,* 2003.
22. Bramlett and Mosher, 2001, p. 9.
23. U.S. Census Bureau, 2004 Current Population Survey.
24. U.S. Census Bureau, 2006.
25. The poverty threshold is the federal guideline that assesses the level of earnings below which one cannot afford to purchase the resources necessary for survival. People who have an income below the federally established poverty line have no discretionary disposable income.
26. National Poverty Center, University of Michigan, 2006, U.S. Bureau of Census, 2005.
27. The Journal of Blacks in Higher Education, June 19, 2006.
28. Francese, August 2, 2000.
29. Besharov and Sullivan 1996; Steurle 1995.
30. Cherry, 2000.
31. DeParle, 2005; Ehrenreich, 2002; Hays, 2004; Shipler, 2005
32. Jones, March 26, 2006, p. B1.
33. Sanders, 2006.
34. Poissant, 1993.
35. Bush's Healthy Marriage Initiative: Kirkpatrick, David; Pear, Robert, "Bush Plans $1.5 Billion Drive for Promotion of Marriage," *New York Times,* January 14, 2004; Brezosky, Lynn, "Attorney General Hosts Summits On Helping Low- Income Families," Associated Press, October 21, 2004.
36. Kibbe2006, Al.
37. Queen Victoria (1819–1901)

38. Grace Kelly 1929–1982.

39. BBC estimates, 1981.

40. Elson and Pearson 1981, 93.

41. U.S. Department of Labor 1996.

42. Cacas 1994.

43. Sailer 1997.

44. Fields 1997.

45. Fields 1997.

46. See Appendix for listing of organizations addressing sweatshop and labor abuses. June 1997.

47. National Council of Textile Organizations, "The China Threat," www.ncto.org/ threat/ index.asp, January 2006.

INTRODUCTION TO: RAPE WORK

Victims, Gender, and Emotions in Organization and Community Context

JAN CAMPBELL

Martin's work focuses on the view of the rape victim in the organizational context, defines what constitutes responsive and unresponsive treatment, and takes a close look at the legal and medical communities. She discusses how these institutions create conditions for rape work that does not necessarily serve the victim.

In citing examples of her premise, Patricia Martin looks first at the criminal justice system, which has often blamed the victim for the crime. Women's behaviors are often assaulted as the real issue, rather than the behaviors of the perpetrator. She believes these are not ill-willed people who place the blame, but social constructs that often supersede personal beliefs and cause victim blame. The rape workers often work with procedures that can take time, may be unresponsive to immediate needs of the victim, and are sometimes not gentle in their responses. She maintains that the process of rape work necessitates hearing the victim and empowering her in every way. The author cites researchers in the sexual assault arena, like Mary Koss, who maintain that many workers are required to give unresponsive treatment. They may be aloof, challenging, or unexpressive as a matter of policy. There are exceptions to these examples and Martin cites the SANE (Sexual Assault Nurse Examiner) programs, which help victims of rape by providing expediency and fewer interruptions in the exams.

By deconstructing the institutional ideas and barriers that are in place, Martin identifies work that needs to be done to perform tasks in a more compassionate and timely manner so that we may aid the healing process for these victims.

RAPE WORK

Victims, Gender, and Emotions in Organization and Community Context

PATRICIA YANCEY MARTIN

Rape work entails varied activities that are both made possible and constrained by jobs, organizations, communities, and institutions; its only common element is a focus on rape. While many positive changes have occurred in the recent past, many rape victims are still treated unresponsively. Rape workers' unresponsive treatment of victims is largely a product of the organizations within which they work and of the institutions that give the organizations legitimacy. In this article I discuss how views of rape and rape victims are constructed in an organizational context, define what constitutes responsive and unresponsive treatment, and look closely at how the legal and medical institutions create conditions for that does not, ultimately, serve rape victims. I conclude by examining the case of rape exams in hospitals; given the institutional and organizational influence on rape work, it is worthwhile to investigate whether hospitals should be performing rape exams at all.

ORGANIZATIONS AND VICTIM-BLAME

Despite beliefs to the contrary, the public tends to hold the victims of crime responsible for their bad fortune. For instance, jurors routinely disbelieve plaintiffs who lodge criminal charges against corporations, for example, when asserting the corporation's failure to enforce its own safety standards. Jurors side with corporations, rather than the plaintiffs, much of the time, Valerie Hans (2000) found, and defend their decisions with reasons such as, "They should have been more careful" or "They knew the work was dangerous when they took the job." Women who are stalked have difficulty getting police and prosecutors to believe they are in danger. These officials frame women as provoking the stalker or view the victims' concerns as evidence of a lover's spat, not a serious crime (Dunn 2002). In failing to understand stalking from the victim's experience, they misunderstand and downplay its seriousness.

Similar dynamics occur around rape. Public opinion routinely exonerates rapists and blames rape victims, with rationales such as, "She should not have gone there alone," "What was she doing there anyway?" or "She should have known this would happen if she went to his apartment." Beliefs like these depict raped women (and girls) as having invited their assault by how they dressed, behaved, talked, and so forth. They shift attention away from the *rapist's violence,* away from the fact that *he obtained sex by force or perpetrated violence in a sexual way.* Does "where she was" or "whether she was alone" exonerate a man *who forced* a woman to have sex against her will?

It is no surprise that organizations that do incorporate victim-blame into their rules and routines that in turn shape workers' actions. Some of these encourage subtle forms of victim blame, others blatant ones. A subtle example would be framing victims as unable to help with their cases; a blatant example, subjecting victims to polygraph tests. Mainstream discourse also works to hold victims responsible. Discourse such as this fosters "self-blame," encouraging victims to repress rather than deal with their hurt and anger. Judges who underestimate the seriousness of rape can communicate a message of victim blame. Because she's not pretty, what *made* you rape her? Comments such as this from court officials as well as law enforcement and medical professionals harm victims more than the rape itself, some of my informants say.

In my work I assert that the central cause of unresponsive is *not* biased, ill-willed workers but, rather, jobs, organizations, and their situational context.[1] Organizational conditions influence entire categories of people to treat victims unresponsively, regardless of their personal inclinations and beliefs. Even empathetic workers act unresponsively when employers tell them to.[2] Given our society's tendency to blame victims, can mainstream organizations treat rape victims responsively? I think they can if they "own rape," as I discuss shortly.

ORGANIZATIONS AND RESPONSIVENESS TO RAPE VICTIMS

Being responsive to rape victims means making their welfare a key concern, high in the organization's list of priorities. Basically, it means helping victims to recover from the assault and to obtain justice. Most mainstream organizations fail to make victims' interests a high priority. Rape workers are paid to do a job, only some aspects of which concern rape victims. Most of them work with many different victims and their encounters with them are not, as a rule, unduly traumatizing (although the emotional demands of are heavier in some occupations). They know what to do and the procedures to follow, unlike victims who often have no idea of what is happening. They have resources and the power to make decisions about "probable cause," whether a rape can be proved "beyond a reasonable doubt," and how to do rape exams. And yet, rape workers often are unaware that treating victims as if they are lying is harmful or that treating them gently, apologizing for their experience, and comforting them aids recovery. Being responsive to rape victims in mainstream organizations is challenging but it can be done.

According to psychologist and rape expert Mary Koss (1993b: 1066), rape victims need to be treated responsively, with the first premise stating: *avoid blaming them.* The first and most important principle for rape workers to follow, Koss says, is to *assure a victim that the rape was not her fault.* Sadly, many mainstream workers do the opposite, by focusing on the victims' behavior, judgment, dress, and so forth, instead of the rapist's actions. Koss admonishes ers to "provide a supportive non-stigmatizing view of rape as a criminal victimization," an environment in which victims can "overcome cognitive and behavioral avoidance," and to offer "information about trauma reactions and the expectation that symptoms will improve." They should comfort a victim, express regret that the crime was done to her ("I am so sorry this happened to you"), show empathic understanding and interaction, validate her feelings and confirm her experience, counteract self-blame and promote self-esteem, and share her grief. They should empower her in every feasible way (Koss 1993b: 1065; see also Herman 1992). Although these practices are neither complicated nor demanding, few mainstream organizations tell their staff to follow them and, indeed, some tell them *not* to. According to Tyler (1990), crime victims who are heard, taken seriously, and treated respectfully feel that justice is achieved even when the 'instrumental' outcome (e.g., conviction) is not in their favor (Tyler 1990). That is, being listened to and taken seriously makes them feel the process was just. Konradi and Burger (2000) find a similar dynamic among rape victims who are able to participate meaningfully in sentencing hearings for their attacker. Most mainstream contexts fail to embrace such practices although some do better than others.

Unresponsive treatment is the opposite of responsive treatment. It is behavior that Koss admonishes us to *avoid:* challenging rather than validating victims' experiences, remaining aloof rather than sharing their grief, remaining silent rather than expressing empathy, comfort, or support. Many jobs *require* workers to act in this manner, encouraging unresponsiveness as a matter of policy.

Owning rape is central. Against the odds, some mainstream organizations nevertheless treat victims responsively. Most that do so "own rape." Rather than trying to avoid and rid themselves of this nuisance crime and its victims, they make rape a focal concern. They affirm the importance of validating and comforting victims and of catching, filing charges on, and prosecuting rapists. They adopt a feminist understanding of rape, seeing it from the victim's rather than the apist's perspective. Rape work is valorized by the organization's frames and activities. Procedurally, organizations that own rape train their staff about rape, require them to be sensitive when relating to victims, and dedicate special staff, facilities, procedures, or units to rape work. They frame as a way to "do good," help victims recover, and achieve justice (Martin and Powell 1994). They do not express a preference for to go away.

Contrarily, organizations that do not own rape regularly fail to train their staff about rape or establish special units, appoint special staff, or make rape victims a high priority. They complain about the time, effort, and bother of rape victims and cases and depict victims as too unreliable and emotional. Many of them rotate rape cases through staff to prevent "burnout" and the "burden of these cases," although they know that this practice lowers effectiveness. Ironically, such actions often add to rather than alleviate the "burden" that rape cases pose.

Institutions determine the obligations and options of organizations and workers, including how to behave. Institutions grant legitimacy to organizations. The *legal institution* gives legitimacy to law enforcement, prosecutors, judges, defense attorneys and jurors to investigate rapes, arrest rapists, sentence rapists, question victims, file legal charges, prosecute rapists, and so forth. The *medical institution* gives legitimacy to physicians and nurses to treat injured and sick "patients" and to examine, touch, and remove evidence from the bodies of rape victims. The ways in which the workers in these institutions handle these responsibilities can give us insight into how the institutions can create the conditions for that is unresponsive rather than responsive.

THE LEGAL INSTITUTION

Alice Vachss (1993), a former prosecutor of sexual assault cases, says the pursuit of justice for victims is a minor consideration in the legal handling of rape cases. For many reasons, she says, prosecutors and judges "collaborate" with defense attorneys and rapists to let rapists off the hook. Rape prosecution is like a chess game that the contenders try to win. In this game, the legal institution pits the state against the person accused of a crime. The prosecutor tries to prove that the defendant is guilty of rape beyond a reasonable doubt, and the defense attorney does all that is feasible to challenge the prosecutor's case. The judge is supposed to assure that the contenders play by the standards of U.S. statutory and case law. In this game, rape victims become pawns in the hands of the contenders, especially prosecutor and defense attorney.

For many reasons, most legal work about rape is done by law enforcement (LE). As Rebecca Campbell and colleagues (1999) say, most rape victims never get a day in court. Fewer than half of cases reported to law enforcement proceed beyond the reporting stage. As a rule, law enforcement makes arrests in a third or fewer cases and a case cannot be referred to the prosecutor without a defendant.[3] Patricia Frazier and Beth Haney (1996) report that prosecutors filed charges on a majority of cases referred to them but the eventual number represented a small percentage of the rapes reported to the police (sixteen percent). Most rape cases are settled by plea bargains, often with the charge reduced to a lesser degree. Almost none result in jury trials—three percent, according to Frazier and Haney (1996:618). Given law enforcement's critical role in rape cases, police officers' decision-making processes about probable cause, investigation, and arrest are key to outcomes. After reviewing research on how police and prosecutors make decisions in rape cases, Frazier and Haney conclude that *neither group accurately knows what the bases of their decisions are.*

In practice, the standard of proof in rape cases is high. U.S. rape laws are written from the standpoint of the rapist, not the victim, according to feminist political theorist and lawyer Catherine MacKinnon (1987, 1989). As a result, victims' interests are not fully taken into account. Furthermore, the U.S. legal and justice system is guided by adversarial rules that hinder cooperation and prevent an unfettered search for the truth. Also, as noted previously, the legal institution has been historically biased in favor of men and masculinity/ies over women and femininity/ies—thus lowering women's odds of obtaining justice.[4] Conditions such as the foregoing mean that rape victims are routinely sold out before the case against their rapist gets off the ground. The prosecutor who "talks them [rape victims] out of it," as the police officer quoted earlier described, engages in such a practice. These conditions affirm the famous claim of British judge Lord Hale that "rape is easy to allege but difficult to prove." In the United States today, as in the past, few accused rapists are convicted of rape.

Rape prosecution is complicated by gender. Most rapists are men (or boys) and most victims are women (or girls); thus, rape litigation epitomizes the classic dilemma of whose word to accept: His or hers. Historically, women were not even allowed to testify in court and men had rights of sexual access to women's bodies whether or not the women consented. Assumptions in a society with a *pro-rape culture* that presumes men's *right* to have sex with women and women's *responsibility* to control men's sexual behavior affect dynamics in legal organizations.[6]

I argue that the obligations of their organizations and jobs encourage legal workers to *collaborate with* rapists and *settle cheap* rather than focus on helping rape victims and obtaining justice. Conditions that foster this result are reviewed later. One reason is that the burden of proof that falls on the state in rape cases is, by extension, a burden for rape victims as the state's key and usually only witness. The state must prove beyond a reasonable doubt that the accused *forced* sex on a woman while *knowing that she did not consent.* Only two legal issues are contested in rape cases: identification and consent.

Identification is an issue in stranger rapes where a victim is acknowledged to have been raped by someone she did not know. The defense does not contest whether a rape occurred but it does challenge the state's claim that the accused committed it. The victim's account, other witnesses' accounts, and physical evidence (e.g., semen, hairs, blood, saliva, DNA) become determinative elements in such cases. Recent progress with DNA results makes identification less problematic at the prosecution stage but if the victim does not know her rapist, finding and arresting her attacker are problematic. When a woman is physically injured from a rape, prosecutors find it easier to convince jurors that a "true rape" occurred (see later). When she is not physically injured or is injured only slightly, jurors are, as a rule, less apt to convict.

Consent. National data from both victim surveys and the FBI's Uniform Crime Report data show a minority of rapes committed by strangers, with sixty to eighty percent by nonstrangers—including intimates, friends, or others known to the victim.[5] In these cases, the primary legal issue is *consent.* Did the victim consent, or agree, to have sex with her attacker? One might assume that whether a woman truly consented is the concern. That assumption would be wrong. Rape is adjudicated from the *standpoint of the accused,* not the victim. Catherine MacKinnon (1989) explains that the legal question in rape is *not,* "Did the man use force to have sex with the woman (or girl), against her will?" but, rather, "Did the man have reason to *believe* [or convincingly say he believed] the woman (girl) consented to have sex?" Given this standard, defense attorneys routinely allege that victims *led rapists to believe they consented.* Whether a woman actually consented is less critical than the "acceptability" of a defendant's claim that he believed she did. Given this dynamic, legal officials' collaboration that lets rapists off the hook—and fosters a "second assault" of rape victims—is unsurprising.

Some prosecutors refuse to file charges or prosecute a rape case even when they believe a "real rape" occurred, when they are not skeptical, and when they empathize with the victim. Their organizations' goals, political vulnerability, untrained and overburdened staff, low odds of winning, and organizational frames prompt them to make victims' welfare and prosecuting rape cases a low level priority. As a result, prosecutors also collaborate with defense attorneys, judges, and rapists to sell out victims. LE officers who half-heartedly "build a case," pursue a rapist, or conduct inexpert victim interviews do so as well.

How and why do legal workers collaborate with rapists? The organization's frames provide one answer: in the legal system, the *victim of rape* and the *witness to rape* are one and the same. The conflation of these statuses represents a dilemma that legal workers resolve primarily by treating the *victim as witness* while ignoring the needs of *witness as victim.* The resolution might not matter if victims had no need for responsive treatment. But we know they do in order to make the transition from victim to survivor (Konradi and Burger 2000; Koss 1993a; Dunn 2001, 2002).

VICTIMS

Stereotypically, crime victims are viewed as deserving compassion and sympathy. If a friend tells about an experience of being a crime victim, we do not challenge her story. We accept her account and express sympathy rather than test her story's consistency, linearity, and credibility by making her go over it again and again. Yet legal processors do precisely the latter to rape victims. Victims need to be believed and respected, not condescended to, brushed off, or told what they're feeling.

Why do legal and justice officials regularly fail to act responsively? If legal system employers required workers to believe rape victims, accept whatever they say, and comfort them, they would do so. But they require other tasks, such as protect and collect evidence, build a case, prove a case, defend the accused—actions that prompt them to treat rape victims as witnesses *to* more than victims *of* rape. The predicament of having victim and witness in the same person helps to explain legal organizations' un-responsiveness. Barbara Stenross and Sherryl Kleinman (1989) found that male police detectives viewed crime victims, especially rape victims, as needing to be "coddled" and expecting "kid glove" treatment. Because their obligation is to build a case and produce a good witness, these perceptions make them uncomfortable. Some rape workers prefer "gamesmanship" with criminals over emotionally demanding work with victims because they perceive the latter as more difficult and less fun.

WITNESSES

Legal officials need witnesses to build and win cases. Without a victim's first-hand account, their legal case may be in jeopardy. A victim's *good account* helps them build a *good case*. Toward this end, legal officials focus on victims' veracity and skill as a witness. They subject a witness to tests such as whether her account is consistent from one time to another and whether it is linear, rational, coherent, credible, and persuasive. Will her account withstand a defense attorney's challenge?

When they suspect a "real rape" did not occur, when inconsistencies are found in a victim's testimony, or when they "have a feeling something is wrong" with a victim's story, LE officials and prosecutors give lie detector tests to rape victims.[6] Typically, they represent the practice as helpful to the case. They rarely say they doubt her story.

The Medical Institution

In hospital emergency rooms (ERs) where rape victims are examined, rape victims (and their families and friends) encounter and often clash with medical professionals and law enforcement (LE) and these last two with each other (and with rape crisis personnel). In reviewing the mission, goals, and resources of hospitals, I find organizational frames that prompt medical professionals to view rape victims negatively and treat them unresponsively. As a rape crisis center (RCC) director notes, medical staff sometimes allow rape victims to sit alone without anyone to comfort them, make them wait for hours, and refer to them as "the Rape." What prompts a physician to hide in a laundry closet to avoid a rape exam or to help a child with a cold before a rape victim? Are medical personnel mean-spirited? Some no doubt are. But most are not and yet events like those described in the opening quotes occur. Some orienting frames and activities of ER settings prompt medical professionals to treat rape victims unresponsively. As with the chapter on legal organizations, this one shows how the medical institution and medical professionals' work contexts and jobs *systematically* foster this dynamic. Medical professionals need not "intend" to be insensitive or hurtful to rape victims for their actions to have these effects.

Opinions vary over how a rape victim should be treated in hospitals. Should her circumstances and needs determine her treatment? Should the medical profession? What about law enforcement? If the victim's welfare were the top priority, rape exams would be concerned primarily with a victim's physical and emotional well-being and setting her on the road to recovery. If the medical profession prevailed, rape exams would focus on ameliorative treatment for physical injuries. If the legal institution prevailed, the exam would focus on evidence collection for a possible criminal case. In conflicts over rape exams, the legal institution usually "wins." Rape exams are not *primarily* about victims' well-being and ameliorative treatment. They are first and foremost about collecting physical evidence for a potential legal case.

Medical institution frames assess rape exams in light of the legitimacy standards of the medical profession and hospitals. Their collective mission is to help the sick and injured, thus physicians and nurses evaluate rape victims against this standard. In the general case, they find uninjured victims lacking, prompting the conclusion that rape exams are not medical procedures calling for their professional judgment and skills.

"Rape exams are not medical procedures." Medical professional correctly understand that rape exams are legal procedures—evidence collection procedures for a potential legal case. Reflecting their evidentiary aims, rape kits contain instructions about what the examiner should do and their inclusion of combs, nail clippers, and swabs for collecting hairs, nail clippings, and body fluid samples affirms their non-ameliorative purpose. Prescriptive protocols from prosecutors offend physicians' sense of autonomy and presumed right to determine their relations with patients. A requirement for meticulous and fairly extensive paperwork and chain of evidence practices, over and above the examination and evidence collection, are other aspects of a legal rather than medical procedure.

"We don't understand rape exams" Many ER physicians and nurses do not understand rape exams. Physicians' lack of knowledge is shown in comments by a physician quoted at the start of the chapter who said residents under his supervision "think they have to determine if a *real rape* occurred," although he tells them they do not. His ignorance is shown in a question posed to me at the end of our interview.

> Do I need to go through a detailed history of the sexual act that occurred? … Since I didn't know if I should, I always did. (chief resident in obstetrics/gynecology, white man, age thirty)

This physician, who no longer conducts rape exams (although he supervises residents who do) also said he did not ask the nurse what a victim had said before he entered the room, and he did not know what belonged in the rape exam report. Because he did not *know,* he always "asked the victim everything." Prosecutors shudder over such comments because they want physicians only to document injury and collect physical evidence, *not* to record victims' comments unless they pertain to injury. A physician's muddled record of a victim's account can hurt the legal case against her rapist.

Legal institution workers are keenly aware of physicians' lack of skill in rape exams. One assistant prosecutor complained about this situation. Ironically, the speaker failed to suggest that the prosecutor's office do anything to improve the situation.

> When the victim is taken to the ER, the MDs are not aware of what they're looking for and if the evidence is not obtained immediately, we lose it. The MDs are not trained on how to handle evidence to go to court with. (assistant state attorney, white man, age thirty-six)

"We can't drop everything when a rape victim arrives." Nurses and physicians alike resist treating rape victims as emergencies that deserve immediate attention. Their view of victims as "nonpatient nonemergencies" justifies postponing rape exams until "legitimate emergencies" are resolved. One nurse said her department's triage system places rape victims at the bottom of the list because they are not at risk due to severe illness or injury: "We have to put the serious cases first." Law enforcement objects to the long waits that this system produces for victims and themselves. A deputy sheriff who describes a dislike for waiting acknowledges that rape exams are evidentiary rather than medical procedures and that hospitals do not view them as a high priority.

> My biggest complaint is the ... hours spent in hospital waiting rooms. We may have to wait three or four hours to get them [rape victims] examined and get out of there. ... It's not the other organization's [hospital's] fault because they have to deal with whatever their priorities are. And their priorities aren't collecting evidence. (police detective, white man, age fifty)

A police officer, describing a former arrangement where rape victims entered the regular ER waiting area, said long waiting times also expose victims to scrutiny and harmful curiosity. He approves of a new arrangement that uses a separate facility and specialized nurse examiners because it removes the victim from public scrutiny and reduces waiting time. These virtues are frequently noted regarding Sexual Assault Nurse Examiner (SANE) programs that reduce time in two ways: Exams are done sooner after a victim arrives and nurse examiners are interrupted slightly less often than physician examiners during rape exams (for instance, by being called to another emergency).

> Before, the poor girl would just have to sit there. And there I was, in uniform and all, making her a spectacle to gawk at. They [others in the waiting room] might not have known what was up but they knew something was wrong. ... Now though, it's better ... [I am] hardly ever there over two hours, more like

an hour and a half, where before it was always three and sometimes five or six. (police officer, white man, age fifty-one)

"Doctor-patient privilege is violated!" Many physicians object to the presence of anyone other than victim, physician, and nurse in rape exams. The concepts of professional autonomy and patient-doctor privilege gives them a "right" to private encounters with patients and having others present violates these standards. Some states, for example, Florida and Texas, recommend but stop short of requiring that no one other than medical personnel and rape victim attend these exams.[7] Some communities have protocols that allow RCC advocates to be present. In this case, the RCC has negotiated the right to attend, claiming their presence fosters responsiveness because physicians are less likely to make inappropriate remarks or be rude with them present. Also, they can hold the victim's hand, explain to her what is occurring, and offer her support, all of which victims find comforting. Physicians in these communities do not necessarily comply with the agreement, however. For example, a nurse in one such community said physicians tell her not to call the RCC *until after the exam is complete,* so the advocate cannot attend. In a physician's eyes, outsiders violate assumptions about patient-physician privacy and are deeply resented.

SOCIALLY CONSTRUCTING RAPE VICTIMS

For reasons noted earlier, hospital and medical profession frames orient nurses and physicians to see rape exams as illegitimate annoyances rather than legitimate obligations. Unfortunately, these conditions also affect their views and treatment of victims, fostering unresponsive behavior.

"Rape victims are not true patients!" In the eyes of physicians and nurses, rape victims are not true patients. Legitimate patients are injured or sick and physicians and nurses willingly provide them with emergency medical care. When a rape victim is not physically injured, they view their involvement in rape exams as inappropriate and the uninjured victim as less than a "true patient." These perceptions shape their actions and cause them to dislike interacting with rape victims and to treat them harshly.

"Some are not even real rape victims?" Compounding concerns about rape victims' patient status, medical staff have legitimacy doubts of another kind—whether a victim is a "real rape victim." Although they have an obligation to determine whether a victim tells the truth, medical professionals nevertheless make judgments about this issue. Their judgments range in tone from mildly critical, like the following quote, to quite harsh assessments and actions. An ER nurse expressed doubts about victims who seem like teenagers trying to get away with something, saying such doubts make it hard for nurses to "stay motivated."

Many of our cases are *suspicious* and we don't feel really good about it. ... Some of them [victims] seem more like teenagers trying to get away with something than, you know, real rape victims. That makes it harder for our staff to stay motivated. (ER nurse, white woman, age thirty-five; emphasis hers)

"Rape victims make us uncomfortable?" Rape makes most everyone uncomfortable and medical professionals are no exception. Discomfort can come across to victims as distant, cool judgment rather than skilled concern and care. A comment from a physician at the start of the chapter reflects this claim, "Why should I be called ... to examine a stranger, someone I don't even know, who doesn't want to see me and [whom] I don't want to see?" Another physician expressed his discomfort:

I always had a feeling when I walked into the victim's room that I was not wanted, needed maybe ... but not wanted. I felt like it was an intrusion at a very sensitive time. We all dislike having to do the rape exam; it's a distasteful time. (chief resident in a teaching hospital, white man, early thirties)

Rape exams are discomfiting for nurses too, as reflected in a comment from a charge nurse who said, "Nurses don't feel comfortable with it [a rape exam] because it's legal evidence."

When the nonmedical nature of rape exams makes medical professionals uncomfortable, they communicate this to victims. A physician or nurse who is unsure or feels distaste for the exam often communicates disapproval. As Rebecca Campbell and colleagues (2001) report, even mildly negative comments nearly always harm rape victims.

"Rape cases take too much time ..." Time is a serious issue in hospital ERs that are regularly overloaded with patients, particularly at night and on weekends. Public hospitals have to provide primary care to the uninsured and respond to stabbing, gunshot, drug overdose, and automobile wreck emergencies, and when rape victims enter this setting, physicians and nurses view them as adding fuel to the fire of overload and overwork. Medical personnel, especially nurses, resent the *time* rape cases take, perceiving them as taking away from their more serious duty to treat genuine emergencies. An ER nurse complained this way:

[A rape exam] is *so time-consuming* [emphasis hers]. Our protocol says a nurse goes and stays with the victim throughout the medical procedure. We dread this because on a busy night we lose someone for at least two hours. We'll be up to our necks in real emergencies with car wrecks, stabbings, you name it and the police arrive with a rape victim. Not that I'm not sympathetic; it's a terrible thing. But we have to give [up] one of our nurses to stay with her the entire time and we really need our nurses for genuine emergencies. I'm not saying she [a nurse who stays with a victim] shouldn't do it but our staff resent it … and I can understand why. (ER charge nurse, white woman, age forty-two)

Physicians complain about time also. Physicians who "ask everything" and "collect everything" may indeed be tied up for hours. Yet, according to my research, many physicians spend only about twenty minutes on rape exams because nurses do most of the exam on their own (Martin and DiNitto 1987).

Chain of evidence. Chain of evidence demands take time also. *Chain of evidence* is a term concerning the integrity of legal evidence. Chain of evidence demands require evidence to be protected from tampering, loss, and contamination. Swabbings, scrapings, or other material removed from a victim's body during a rape exam cannot be left unattended; someone must assure it came from the victim and was not altered or left unattended. When LE is on the spot, that is, stays until after a victim is examined, takes possession of evidence after it is collected, and transports it to the appropriate office, all is well. If they fall down on the job, however, as can occur when victims come to the ER without reporting to LE or an officer refuses to take evidence away, or for other reasons, medical staff have the responsibility of protecting it.[8] Problems can also arise when medical staff do things improperly, such as fail to secure the evidence or otherwise violate the legal protocol. At any rate, chain of evidence tasks pose an additional burden for medical staff, and in the usual case, they dislike it.

RAPE EXAMS: SHOULD HOSPITALS BE INVOLVED?

Many physicians want law enforcement to do rape exams, want them removed from the hospital, or want nurses to perform them; they favor anyone but themselves (see the second quote at the start of this chapter). Some nurses feel the same way about giving the responsibility to law enforcement (see later). But rape exams are conducted by medical professionals in hospital settings all across the United States and the practice is likely to continue. Why is that the case? This section reviews arguments for and against hospital's and medical professions' involvement in rape exams. Described variously as "medical examinations where physical evidence is collected," "sexual assault evidence collection kits and protocols," and "rape kits," rape exams have entered the lexicon of organizations that work with victims. The usual procedure includes plucking of head and pubic hairs; collecting loose hairs by combing the head and pubis; swabbing the vagina and rectum to collect semen, blood, or saliva; and swabbing the victim's nose, mouth, and ears. Fingernail clippings and scrapings are collected also, in the event she scratched her assailant, and examiners often retain a victim's clothing because semen, hair, blood, saliva, or other evidence may be attached. Some hospitals take a blood sample from rape victims, allegedly to check for infection or disease, although sometimes victims' blood samples are subjected to an alcohol analysis, a practice that can undermine their status in a legal case down the road. Some hospitals screen victims for sexually transmitted diseases, including HIV, and some offer prophylaxis for a possible pregnancy. But such services are far from the norm.

So, why do hospitals and physicians do rape exams?

FOR HOSPITALS AND PHYSICIANS

The general belief is that rape exams should be done at a hospital by medical professionals. Hospitals are open 24 hours a day, 365 days a year, and they have the necessary equipment, supplies, and professionals with skill and authority to examine women's bodies. As semi-public arenas, hospital ERs can be entered and exited at any time, day or night. Most have lighted parking lots and, often, security guards to protect those who come and go after dark. Little wonder hospitals are viewed as preferred sites for rape exams that must done at 3 a.m. on Saturdays as well as 2 p.m. on Mondays.

Some communities have experimented with private health clinics, county health departments, and other alternative sites, but many find them wanting. Non-ER sites have drawbacks such as being closed, deserted, and dark at night and on weekends. Victim and law enforcement officer may have to wait for the examiner in a patrol car in an unlighted, deserted parking lot. The examiner may arrive first and feel too unsafe or threatened to wait. Convenience and access in addition to feasibility and legitimacy argue for hospitals as rape exam sites.

Medical professionals have the knowledge and skill to identify and respond to physical trauma; thus, they can be helpful to injured victims. Licensed physicians have societal legitimacy to inspect and probe the bodies of strangers, furthermore, including a woman's genitalia and anus. Because these "cavities," as referred to by a police officer, are "entered" during rape exams, the exam is an intimate kind of experience. Most potential examiners—most definitely the police—lack the legitimacy to conduct such an exam. The authority to conduct rape exams is thus granted to medical professionals by the state, and what the state gives the state can take away. The state uses its authority to require medical professionals to perform rape exams.

We know from research that a physician's sensitive conduct of can be therapeutic for victims. According to ob/gyn physician Dorothy Hicks, who founded Jackson Memorial Hospital's Rape Treatment Center in Miami in the 1970s, a physician's reassurance can start a victim on the road of recovery. A physician (or nurse) who comforts a rape victim, tells her she is not to blame, and reassures her that she will be all right can help her recover. Yet, many physicians fail to act this way, and for this way, and for this reason, many states have reduced their reliance on them, a trend that seems to be spreading across the nation. Larger communities with many victims each year have turned to specially trained nurses and specially designated examination sites, either in or near but separate from the regular ER. Law enforcement's wish for better and more timely evidence and the innovation of

SANE programs or their equivalent have spurred this development. In many ways, then, the case for hospitals and medical professionals is compelling.

AGAINST HOSPITALS AND MEDICAL PROFESSIONALS

The case against hospitals and medical professionals is compelling also. In research with others in the 1980s, I identified multiple drawbacks of doing rape exams in regular hospital ERs. Hospital ERs are often hectic, forcing victims to wait hours for the exam, and rape exams are not easily accommodated in the crush of medical emergencies, patient overloads, and staff shortages that are endemic to these sites. Most ERs have only one room with a pelvic table, and exam protocols often require the pelvic room plus physician and nurse to be free. Victims and law enforcement officers may wait for hours for all three to become available. Victims may be stared at as a result of being accompanied by a uniformed LE officer or be required to submit to regular ER admission procedures, which can be upsetting immediately after being raped. Furthermore, hospital ERs are expensive. Rape exams cost up to $1,000 in Florida, for example, and the state refunds a maximum of $250 (until 1999, the maximum refund was $150). Some hospitals bill victims for costs not reimbursed by the state, even though state law forbids the practice if the victim agrees to "cooperate with authorities." However, Florida law does allow hospitals to bill victims for medical treatment provided during rape exams.

Physicians are often untrained in rape exams and many refuse to be take courses to learn about them. As a result, many perform rape exams incorrectly. Fear of adversarial legal proceedings and concerns over professional autonomy make them resistant to finding out more. That rape exams are dictated to them by prosecutors and require extensive documention and protection of the "chain of evidence" are aspects that increase resistance, and physician-patient privilege concerns only make it worse.

ER nurses also fail to comfort and support rape victims. Feeling the pressures of medical emergencies, too many patients, and staff shortages, plus having doubts about victims' truthfulness, they see rape victims as burdensome. Furthermore, their lower professional status means they cannot override rude behaviour by physicians even if they feel empathetic. As a rule, nurses know more about rape exams than physicians do and do more of the exam, but many also are untrained about them or how to treat victims. Many nurses have little true understanding of rape's devastating impact on victims. In most cases, the result of these conditions is that some ER nurses are no more responsive to rape victims than physicians are.

Because physicians' authority is subject to state authority, physicians cannot refuse to do rape exams.[9] Yet, they *can* make victims wait and they *can* treat victims unresponsively, as this chapter shows. No one so far has found ways to prevent these developments, at least on a large scale. Physicians' professional orientation and the medical contexts in which they work make their unresponsive actions probable and understandable, although regrettable.

DISCUSSION QUESTIONS

1. In your view, how important is the "gender issue" in the treatment rape victims receive from the legal and medical establishments? What role does gender play in the way rape workers in the legal and medical establishments respond to rape victims? Should rape workers be exclusively female, or does it not matter?
2. How does the legal institution influence police officers and prosecutors to subject rape victims to "unresponsive" treatment? Can you envision ways to avoid this dynamic?
3. How does the medical institution orient physicians and nurses to view and treat rape victims? What incentives can you imagine for hospitals to treat rape victims more responsively?
4. In your view, is it better to have rape exams done in hospitals by medical professionals or to find other places and examiners for this task?

NOTES

1. My concern is with how organizations, jobs, communities, institutions, and gender *direct* officials to treat rape victims. Individuals have many reasons for behaving unresponsively toward victims; for example, some believe rape myths; fear being raped; resent rape cases' complexity, difficulty, and "messiness"; worry about making mistakes; worry about being accused of wrongdoing; and so forth. And no doubt such conditions prompt a certain amount of unresponsive behavior toward rape victims.
2. Staff turnover in law enforcement and hospitals makes maintaining staff competence and skill difficult. Organizations with few rapes a year have little incentive to train staff in rape work. Rape crisis centers have problems with funding, staff turnover, and burnout, as well as a lack of community support. The public's discomfort with rape and reluctance to support anti-rape initiatives make RCC personnel feel unappreciated and discouraged. Reluctance by police, prosecutors, and hospitals to include them in their networks is also a problem.
3. Frazier and Haney (1996) found that police identified suspects in forty-eight percent of the rapes reported to them but questioned suspects in only one third of those cases, eventually referring to the prosecutor only twenty-two percent (of 569 rapes).
4. Renison and Rand (2003:10); and U.S. Federal Bureau of Investigation, *Crime in the United States*, 2004.

5. I make these assumptions about legal organizations: (1) Leadership directs members to fulfill the organization's official mission; (2) staff are competent to do; (3) legal organizations are (relatively) free of corruption; and (4) staff are no more or less biased than the public about rape victims. My analysis may not apply if other conditions exist. For example, if elected officials use their office to feather their nests or give jobs to friends, or if official goals are intentionally subverted, dynamics other than those I identify will have to be considered.

6. Polygraph tests are notoriously difficult to administer and interpret. If a victim mistakenly identifies someone as her assailant, the polygraph may not detect it if in her mind she is truthful. On the issue of consent, polygraph results cannot determine intent. A victim can fail a polygraph if she says no to the question, "Did you consent to having sexual intercourse with the defendant?" because she may have said words of consent under threat of harm from her attacker. Her blood pressure may rise because, yes, she said the words but did not mean them.

7. The tendency to *medicalize* social problems reinforces the use of hospitals and medical professionals for rape exams. Medicalizing means to treat a social, cultural, or political problem as a health problem that can be resolved by medical treatment. Men's violence toward women can, for example, be viewed as a social, cultural, and political problem related to definitions of masculinity and violence or as a health issue about whose body is hurt via sexual assault. When Americans have a health problem, they consult medical professionals. If rape is a health problem, a hospital and medical professionals are appropriate. They have the equipment, resources, and skills to do rape exams and help victims. They are open around the clock, and they have humanitarian goals that prevent them from turning away anyone in need. Using medical establishments and professionals reflects a lack of alternatives as much as these reasons, however.

8. Nurses are subject to state authority as well as to physicians' authority. Physicians have higher status and influence over nurses; thus, in addition to other conditions that prompt nurses' resistance, resentful/resistant physicians are a factor as well.

REFERENCES

Campbell, Rebecca, Tracy Sefl, Holly E. Barnes, Courtney A. Ahrens, Sharon M. Was-co, and Yolanda Zaragoza-Diesfeld. 1999. Community services for rape survivors: Enhancing psychological well-being or increasing trauma? *Journal of Consulting and Clinical Psychology 67(6):* 847–58.

Dunn, Jennifer. 2001. Innocence lost: Accomplishing victimization in intimate stalking cases. *Symbolic Interaction* 24 (3):285—313.

Frazier, Patricia A., and Beth Haney. 1996. Sexual assault cases in the legal system: Police, prosecutor, and victim perspectives. *Law and Human Behavior* 20 (6):607–28.

Hans, Valerie P. 2000. *Business on Trial: The Civil Jury and Corporate Responsibility.* New Haven, CT: Yale University Press.

Herman, Judith. 1992. *Trauma and Recovery.* New York: Basic Books.

Konradi, Amanda, and Burger, Tina. 2000. Having the last word: An examination of rape survivors' participation in sentencing. *Violence Against Women 6* (4):353–97.

Koss, Mary. 1993a. Detecting the scope of rape: A review of prevalence research methods. *Journal of Interpersonal Violence* 8:198–222.

MacKinnon, Catherine. 1987. *Feminism Unmodified: Discourses on Life and Law.* Cambridge, MA: Harvard University Press.

MacKinnon. 1989. *Toward a Feminist Theory of the State.* Cambridge, MA: Harvard University Press.

Martin, Patricia Yancey, and Diana DiNitto. 1987. The rape exam: Beyond the hospital emergency room. *Women and Health* 12:5–28.

Martin, Patricia Yancey and Marlene Powell. 1994. Accounting for the "second assault": Legal organizations' framing of rape victims. *Law and Social Inquiry* 19:853–90.

Renison, Callie Marie, and Michael R. Rand. 2003. Criminal Victimization, 2002. Bureau of Justice Statistics, Office of Justice Programs. U.S. Department of Justice.

Stenross, Barbara, and Sherryl Kleinman. 1989. The highs and lows of emotional labor: Detectives' encounters with criminals and victims. *Journal of Contemporary Ethnography* 17:435–52.

Tyler, Tom R 1990. *Why People Obey the Law.* New Haven, CT: Yale University Press.

Vachss, Alice. 1993. *Sex Crimes.* New York: Random House.

INTRODUCTION TO: FEMALE SEX TRAFFICKING

Defining the Nature and Size of the Problem

JAN CAMPBELL

This article exposes the vast economic endeavor of trafficking humans for mail-order brides, forced prostitution, domestic servitude, farm labor, camel jockeys, begging, forced marriage, and for harvesting human organs. The horrific exposure that we get from Samarasinghe's work paints a picture of why human trafficking occurs, from the development of commercial prostitution and meeting men's sexual needs to profiteering from the use of bodies, farm labor, and cheap labor.

In historically patriarchal societies, prostitution has been an active part of society despite the attitude that it is immoral and those who engage in it should be shunned. This article shows that the trafficking of humans has focused mainly on women prostitutes, but also has expanded to children, especially in Thailand.

The author discusses the structural and systemic problems in identifying the volume of trafficking and indicates that some data may not show an accurate picture of the problem. Women may leave their homes to legitimately work in another part of the world, only to be trafficked into sexual exploitation. They become "hidden victims" and, as Samarasinghe indicates, the numbers of victims are then underrepresented in the data.

FEMALE SEX TRAFFICKING

Defining the Nature and Size of the Problem

VIDYAMALI SAMARASINGHE

H uman trafficking in the form of slavery has being a part of history as evidenced in the ancient empires of Egypt, Babylon, Greece and Rome. Later, the transatlantic slave trade that spanned nearly four and a half centuries captured and transported thousands of able-bodied men, women and children from the African continent across the Atlantic to the Americas. Even after the abolition of slavery in 1838, the use of 'indentured' labor, transported from the Asian continent by the colonial powers to work in plantations in South America and Asia, had broad similarities to slavery (Tinker, *197 A)*. All or most of the characteristics associated with slavery are also played out in the contemporary human trafficking. Modern forms of trafficking are a flourishing international business involving a chain of people, which includes the victims, local recruiters, corrupt officials, business interests, governments and global syndicates of organized crime.

Trafficking in human cargo, whether the victims are females or males, adults or children, involves the movement of people internally or internationally for some form of work, which may be legal or illegal, and under highly exploitative working conditions. Today, women, men and children are trafficked across borders and domestically for farm work, factory work, domestic servitude, camel jockeys, begging, forced marriage, mail-order brides and forced prostitution and also for harvesting human organs. A fundamental issue in the discourse of trafficking is that while the trafficker is well aware of all the ramifications, the trafficked victims have at best partial information, and at worst none at all. Trafficking basically caters to a demand, created by a scarcity often stemming from the illegal nature of the work and the social stigmatization of the type of work demanded. However, trafficking is also triggered by the need to use cheap labor in order to maximize profits from a range of certain goods and services produced for the market. In all cases, profiteering from the use of bodies, labor and the time of the victims motivates the traffickers.

DEVELOPING THE DISCOURSE ON FEMALE SEX TRAFFICKING

Female sexual exploitation accounts for a significant proportion of the current global flows of trafficking. Female prostitution, separated for the most part from the morally accepted norm of female chastity, has been a global phenomenon since the time of recorded history. Lerner's scholarship on the *Creation of Patriarchy* illustrates that while commercial prostitution was seen as a social necessity for meeting the sexual needs of men, it was also used as a distinguishing marker between chaste women and immoral prostitutes. For example she notes that the Assyrian legal code established that while all chaste women who go out in the streets should veil themselves, "… [H]arlot must not veil: her head must be uncovered." (Lerner, 1987:137). The moral structures of any society are shaped by different socio-behavioral elements, which are perceived to be appropriate or inappropriate by that particular society. Madonnas and whores are thus created to uphold the binary opposites, i.e., respectability and decency of the Madonnas in contrast to the immorality and indecency of the whores. Hence, female sexuality has to be controlled in order to maintain the sanctity of marriage, the legitimacy of children and, by extension, the stability of society. At the same time prostitution is implicitly accepted since the controlled female sexuality within marriage and other stable forms of cohabitation inhibits males, whose sexual demands are expected to go beyond the restricted spaces dictated by stable forms of cohabitation. As Emma Goldman stated in 1917, "… [S]ociety considers the sex experience of a man as attributes of his general development, while similar experiences in the life of a woman are looked upon as a terrible calamity. A loss of honor and all that is good and noble in a human being. The double standard of morality has played no little part in the creation and perpetuation of prostitution" (Goldman, 1917/1970:25). What is embedded as a constant throughout human history is that prostitution is perceived to be immoral and that those who engage in prostitution should be shunned by decent society. Yet it continues to be sought out by a section of the male population creating a space for a thriving clandestine activity. In modern society, where laws are encoded to uphold moral strictures, prostitution is illegal or restricted to specific locations in an overwhelming majority of countries, but the demand for prostitutes seems to be increasing. Thus, given the immorality and illegality of prostitution and social acceptance of the male need for sex outside stable co-habiting relationships, trafficking of women and girls becomes the *modus operandum* of obtaining the supply to meet the demand.

The contemporary discourse on trafficking in women may be traced to the latter part of the nineteenth century when Europe was caught up in the intermingled discourses on prostitution and 'white slavery'. The Contagious Diseases Acts (CDA) enacted in England between 1864 and 1869 was an attempt to subject prostitutes to a set of regulations, including mandatory medical examinations for sexually transmitted diseases and to impose restrictions on prostitutes' freedom to move. The 'Abolitionist' movement spearheaded by Josephine Butler waged a successful campaign to abolish the Act on the premise that regulating prostitution gave it legitimacy and exposed the "official recognition of the 'double standard' of sexual behavior of men and women" (Doezema, 2000:30). Abolitionists noted that when the state regulates or legalizes prostitution, it leads to its acceptance as a social institution and as a legitimate form of work. In that context the state would not have to concern itself with whether or not women are trafficked or coerced (Barry, 1995:237). Early abolitionists equated prostitution of women to their victim-hood as exploited human beings.

In the last decade of the nineteenth century, the International Society for the Suppression of the White Slave Trade was formed and covered conferences periodically from 1899–1913. Member countries signed agreements to maintain surveillance at ports, repatriate women and criminalize the acts of abduction and trafficking (Tambe, 2001). The term 'white slavery' was formally used at the 1902 Paris Conference where representatives of several governments met to draft an international instrument for the suppression of white slave traffic. While initially the term was meant to distinguish the practice from the nineteenth century black slavery, it immediately assumed a racial, gendered image of innocent 'white women' outraging the sensibilities of white racist segments of society (Barry, 1979). This social outrage over 'white slavery' was greatly influenced by the social purist movement and supported by the abolitionists, although some of the abolitionists challenged the often repressive aspects of the social purists (Walkowitz, 1980). The anti-trafficking 'white slavery' campaign had an explicit racial overtone. Grittner explains 'white slavery' as "the enslavement of white women or girls by means of coercion, tricks or drugs by nonwhite or non-Anglo-Saxon men" (Grittner, 1990:5). The emphasis was on the purported transportation of innocent white females for purposes of sexual exploitation by non-whites, and not on prostitution in general. The anti-white slavery campaign withered away in the early twentieth century.

The International Conference of 1921 recommended that the term 'white slavery' be dropped and replaced with "traffic in women and children" (Lazarsfeld, 1938: 437). This new term was also adopted by the League of Nations, which began focusing on trafficking in women after 1921. Prostitution remained the cornerstone of Conventions on trafficking proposed by the League of Nations. Its 1921 Convention raised the age of consent of women from 20 to 21 years, and the convention of 1933 made all trafficking, even of adult women, a criminal activity (Tambe, 2001). The U.N. Convention of 1949 on the Suppression of Traffic in Persons and the Exploitation for the Prostitution of Others in effect had adopted as its foundation the abolitionists' perspectives on anti-prostitution. The preamble to the 1949 Convention declares[1] that prostitution and trafficking in persons are incompatible with the dignity and worth of human persons and endanger the welfare of the individual, the family and the community. It called upon nations to close brothels and punish those who procure for and promote prostitution (Barry, 1995:120). However, although the U.N. Convention of 1949 uses the word 'trafficking' in its title, it did not specifically define the concept of trafficking.

The issue of trafficking is specifically addressed in the 1979 U.N. Convention on the Elimination of All forms of Discrimination Against Women (CEDAW).[2] Article 6 of the Convention directs state parties to take all appropriate measures, including legislation to suppress all forms of traffic in women and exploitation of women for the purpose of prostitution. Children's rights were addressed by the 1989 Convention on the Rights of the Child,[3] in which Article 35 directs the states to take appropriate national, bilateral and multilateral measures to prevent the abduction and sale of or traffic in children for any purpose or in any form. A new urgency for a comprehensive and a stronger commitment to combat slavery-like practices and transnational criminal activity has resulted in a series of new and expanded protocols to address the issue of global human trafficking. The complete set of commitments made by member states regarding human trafficking are embedded in the *U.N. Convention Against Transnational Crime; The Protocol to Prevent, Suppress and Punish Trafficking in Persons, Especially Women and Children*, which supplements the *U.N. Convention and Interpretive Notes on the Trafficking Protocol*[4] Taken together (hereafter referred to as the *U.N. Trafficking Protocol*), these three documents comprise a set of international obligations, which specifically address the issue of human trafficking (Jordan, 2002). The 1990 International Convention on the Protection of the Rights of All Migrant Workers and Members and Their Families, in force only since July 2003 also addresses the issue of trafficking.

The main thrust on human trafficking during the past century and half has been primarily focused on female prostitution. Spurred on by the powerful campaigns of the abolitionists and the social purists the emphasis was on 'rescuing' the female from immoral sexual behavior. Female prostitution was considered as an involuntary activity and women who became prostitutes were thus by definition deemed to be 'trafficked'. This assertion of necessary victim-hood of female prostitutes has since been challenged by different anti-trafficking advocates who argue that some women may choose to become prostitutes and hence cannot be categorized as trafficked. The main thrust of the current trafficking discourse is still focused primarily on the issue of prostitution, which continues to be perceived, by and large, as an exercise based on sexual exploitation of women and girls.

While the supply of trafficked women that outraged Europeans and led to the anti-trafficking campaigns at the turn of the twentieth century came mainly from white Anglo-Saxon societies, the current global female sex trafficking pattern illustrates a shift of the supply lines to developing countries of Asia, Africa and Latin America and the former socialist countries of Eastern Europe and the Soviet Republic. Furthermore, while Anglo-Saxon women no longer play a significant part in the supply side of female sex trafficking, there is a blurring of 'skin colors' of trafficked women since all major racial categories are caught in the web of female sex trafficking flows. Both internationally and intra-nationally, relatively richer and more developed areas demand the supply of trafficked women and a higher premium is placed on lighter skinned women and young virgins. The supply and demand structure of female sex trafficking clearly illustrates the nature of commodification of the trafficked female.

THE NUMBERS GAME

A serious concern of policy makers, donor agencies, NGOs, advocates and scholars who are involved in analyzing the trafficking situations and formulating and implementing empirically grounded anti-trafficking initiatives is the serious lack of accurate statistics on sex trafficking. U.S. Government estimates on trafficking of human beings, as reported in the U.S. State Department annual Trafficking in Persons Reports (TIP), demonstrate the underlying problems in getting accurate data on trafficking in human beings. All numbers quoted by the U.S. Government are estimates and furthermore, there has been a gradual reduction of global human trafficking estimates over the past four years. In 2002 the estimate was 700,000 to 4 million people, reduced to 800,000 to 900,000 people in 2003, and 600,000 to 800,000 in 2004. The 2005 estimate of trafficked persons globally is the same as for 2004 (U.S State Department, 2002, 2003, 2004, 2005). Among them eighty percent of the cases of trafficking concerned sexual exploitation. Of the cases where women were reported to be victims of trafficking, eighty-five percent were said to be trafficked for sexual exploitation, two percent for other types of forced labor and thirteen percent for both types of exploitation (Kangaspunta, 2003).

The United Nations Office of Drug Control and Crime Prevention (UNODC), whose databases on monitoring global trends, routes and volumes of trafficking in persons and the smuggling of migrants are used extensively by organizations engaged in anti-trafficking initiatives derives its statistics of traffic flows mostly from estimates. Unfortunately, once published, the initial estimate is often cited by other publications and becomes credible. Lin Lean Lim notes that since the estimates range so widely they should be treated with caution. For instance, she points out that the figure of 800,000 Thai child prostitutes has been seriously questioned by other sources familiar with the situation in Thailand. The estimate was based on a sample of just one brothel and extrapolated to the 60,000 brothels found in Thailand (Lim, 1998:9). Similarly, Sanghera and Kapur (2000) observe that the common belief that 5,000–7,000 Nepali girls are trafficked across borders to India each year, and that currently 150,000–200,000 women and girls are in various Indian cities, were disseminated in an article published in 1986 and has remained unaltered over the past 18 years.[5] While this is not to say that all estimates are gross exaggerations, fabrications or dated, my own field visits to countries of Asia have shown that trafficking numbers are indeed significant and in some instances, numbers quoted appear to be underestimates.

The problem seems to be in the flawed methodology used, especially the difficulty of tracing the estimate back to the methods (Steinfatt, Baker and Beesey, 2002).

While accurate numbers of trafficking could be obtained best from good field-based methods, several inter-related factors inhibit this process. The most significant road block is the illegality of trafficking, hence its clandestine nature and the intimate, private activity of sexual relationships, compounded by the stigma attached to prostitution. The serious lack of anti-trafficking legislation and law enforcement mechanisms makes the already vulnerable women and girls who become victims reluctant to report trafficking incidents to the authorities. In fact, until very recently, indifference or apathy on the part of the policy makers to the issue of trafficking in women and girls was the rule rather then the exception. Victims of sex trafficking mostly belong to the poorer segments of society who are usually ignored by decision-making political groups in society.

As Tyldum and Brunovskis have shown, two main issues inhibit accurate counting of trafficking victims. First is the problem of a common 'conceptual identification' of a trafficked victim. The second is the 'practical identification' of trafficked victim—of "being able to say this is a victim of trafficking" (Tyldum and Brunovskis, 2005:20). While new international anti-trafficking instruments have constructed more expanded definitions of trafficking, continuing lack of clarity in defining female sex trafficking leads to confusion, both at the theoretical as well as at practical levels (Gallagher, 2001, GPAT, 2003). Indeed, in practice identification of trafficked victims becomes a difficult task since they are enclosed within a 'hidden population' (Heckathorn, 1997), one that refuses to cooperate or gives unreliable responses to questions in order to protect itself since her/his activities are socially stigmatized and/or illegal. Blurred boundaries between smuggling/immigration/trafficking also not only demonstrate problems in conceptual clarity, they pose practical problems in clearly identifying a trafficked victim.

Most governments do not give priority to research and data collection on trafficking numbers or patterns. One gets the impression that any new efforts in this direction, particularly among developing countries, is at the behest of donor agencies which are increasingly pushing anti-trafficking initiatives as a segment of development aid. A significant feature of the U.S. *Trafficking in Persons Act of 2000* is that the U.S. Government reserves the right to impose mandatory non-emergency sanctions on those governments which, according to the annual survey conducted by the U.S. State Department, do not make a significant effort to combat trafficking (U.S. Department of State, 2001). Such policies by major aid donor countries compel developing countries to undertake statistical surveys in order to formulate anti-trafficking strategies.

Apart from structural and systemic problems faced in obtaining accurate numbers of female sex trafficking, the trafficking discourse itself carries with it certain practical problems in identifying a clearly distinct category of trafficking. Firstly, the ideological debate on prostitution between the anti-legalization/abolitionists and pro-legalization advocates would give different numbers of trafficking victims. While the anti-prostitution abolitionists would consider all prostitutes as trafficking victims, the pro-prostitution would want to separate those adult women who enter prostitution voluntarily from women who are forced into commercial sex sector and all child sex workers. Second, there is a more practical difficulty of separating trafficking statistics from migration statistics, and especially in terms of migrant smuggling. 'Smuggling' and 'trafficking', which are often used interchangeably, confuse the issue of separating the numbers between the two categories of human flows. Third, there is also confusion in pinpointing the difference between legitimate migration and trafficking. For instance, women who migrate to Japan for work from the Philippines or Thailand may have official travel papers and employment/fiancée contracts. However, once they reach their destination some of them are forced into sexual exploitation. In such cases, while their mobility as a primary dimension of trafficking is legal, would they be deemed to be trafficked victims since the final outcome of their migration is sexual exploitation? Fourth, there is an element of danger in gathering trafficking data for two reasons. First, some of the female sex trafficking is known to occur in conflict zones, where any type of data gathering on sex trafficking becomes difficult. Second, the increasing control exercised by criminal groups on the sex industry in general makes the efforts of data gathering dangerous for a researcher. Finally, trafficking is generally not incorporated into the national agendas in most countries. Consequently, there are very few state coordinated mechanisms to research or gather trafficking data. Citing a successful anti-trafficking initiative started in 2003 by the Government of Norway, Tyldum and Brunovskis (2005) state that law enforcement bodies were given more resources and were instructed to give higher priority to trafficking for sexual exploitation. The number of cases identified had increased dramatically, although the overall numbers still remained rather low. The question was whether the low numbers were the tip of the iceberg or an accurate number of all cases of trafficking. The researchers also bring up the issue of bias of law enforcement or rehabilitation organizations which could distort the numbers of trafficked persons.

Indeed, while data gathered directly as numbers would give a clearer picture of the volume of trafficking flows, it is obviously an elusive goal. Estimates of sex trafficking, derived through extrapolation is useful in understanding the direction and the nature of trafficking and gives us an idea of the magnitude of the problem faced by the global community. The global network of female sex trafficking flows show that no part of the world is completely free of sex trafficking (Mattar, 2005).

DISCUSSION QUESTIONS

1. How did the international understanding of female sex trafficking develop?
2. How would you define human trafficking? How would you try to identify trafficking victims?
3. Why is it difficult to obtain an estimate of the number of trafficking victims?

NOTES

1. Convention for the Suppression of the Traffic in Persons and of the Exploitation of the Prostitution of Others, adopted by the General Assembly in its resolution 317 (IV).
2. General Assembly resolution 34/180 (A/RES/34/180).
3. Convention on the Rights of the Child, adopted by the General Assembly in its resolution 44/25 (A/RES/44/25).
4. The U.N. Convention Against Transnational Organized Crime entered into force on September 29, 2003, after it received its fortieth ratification in July 2003, nearly three years after its adoption by the U.N. General Assembly in November 2000. The U.N. Protocol to Prevent, Suppress and Punish Trafficking in Persons, Especially Women and Children Entered into Force on December 25, 2003, with 45 countries ratifying.
5. The article that first published these statistics was written by Dr. I.S. Gilada of the Indian Health Association in Mumbai, India, and presented in a workshop in 1986. Subsequently a version of this article was published in the *Times of India,* January 2, 1989 (quoted in Sanghera and Kapur, 2002).

REFERENCES

Barry, Kathleen. 1979. *Female and Sexual Slavery.* New York: New York University Press.

Barry, Kathleen. 1995. *The Prostitution of Sexuality.* New York: New York University Press.

Doezema, Joe. 2000. "Loose Women or Lost Women? The reemergence of the Myth of 'White Slavery' in Contemporary Discourse on Trafficking in Women." *Gender Issues* 18 (l):23–50.

Gallagher, Ann Theresa. 2001. The International Legal Response to Human Trafficking. Paper read at Technical Consultative Meeting on Anti-trafficking Programs in South Asia: Appropriate Activities, Indicators and Evaluation Methodologies. Katmandu, Nepal. September 11–13.

Goldman, Emma. 1917/1970. *Traffic in Women and Other Essays on Feminism,* (2nd ed.). New York: Mother Earth Publishing Association.

Global Program Against Trafficking in Human Beings (GPAT). 2003. Coalition Against Trafficking in Human Beings in the Philippines: Research and Action Final Report. Vienna: United Nations.

Grittner, F.K. 1990. *White Slavery: Myth, Ideology and American Law.* New York and London: Garland Press.

Heckathorn, D.D. 1997. "Respondent-driven Sampling: A New Approach to the study of Hidden Populations." *Social Problems 44* (2): 174–198.

Hugh, Tinker. 1974. *A New System of Slavery: the Export of Indian Labor Overseas 1830–1890.* London: Oxford University Press.

Jordan, Ann. 2002. *The Annotated Guide to the Complete UN Trafficking Protocol.* Washington, D.C.: International Human Rights Law Group.

Kangaspunta, Kristiina. 2003. Mapping the Inhuman Trade: Preliminary findings of the Human Trafficking Database. *Forum on Crime and Society* 3 (1–2):81–103.

Lazarsfeld, Sofi. 1938. *Women's Experience of the Male.* London: Encyclopedic Press.

Lerner, Gerder. 1987. *The Creation of Patriarchy.* London: Oxford University Press.

Lim, Lin Lean. 1998. "The Economic and Social bases of Prostitution in Southeast Asia." In Lin Lean Lim (ed.) *The Sex Sector: The Economic and Social Bases of Prostitution in Southeast Asia.* Geneva, Switzerland: International Labour Organization, 1–28.

Sanghera, Jyoti. 2000 and R. Kapur. *An Assessment of Laws and Policies for Prevention and Control of Trafficking in Nepal.* Kathmandu: The Asia Foundation and New Delhi: Population Council/ Horizons.

Steinfatt, Thomas M., Simon Baker and Allan Beesey. 2002. "Measuring the number of trafficked women in Cambodia." Paper presented at The Human rights Challenge of Globalization in Asia-Pacific-US: The Trafficking in Persons, Especially Women and Children. Honolulu, Hawaii. November 13–15.

Tambe, Ashwini. 2001. Codes of Misconduct: The Regulation of Prostitution in Colonial Bombay, 1860–1947. Ph.D Thesis. American University, Washington, D.C.

Tyldum, Guri and Anette Brunovskis. 2005. "Describing the Unobserved Methodological Challenges in Empirical Studies on Human Trafficking" In Frank Laezko and Elzbieta Gozdiekeds. *Data and Research on Human Trafficking: A Human Survey.* IOM. 17–34.

USDS. 2001. Trafficking in Persons Report 2001. Washington, D.C.: U.S. State Department.

USDS. 2002. Trafficking in Persons Report 2002. Washington, D.C.: USDS.

USDS. 2003. Trafficking in Persons Report 2003. Washington, D.C.: USDS.

USDS. 2004. Trafficking in Persons Report 2004. Washington, D.C.: USDS.

USDS. 2005. Trafficking in Persons Report 2005. Washington, D.C.: USDS.

Walkowitz, J. 1980. *Prostitution and the Victorian Society: Women, Class and State.* Cambridge, UK: Cambridge University Press.

INTRODUCTION TO: HUMAN RIGHTS SEX TRAFFICKING AND PROSTITUTION

Perspectives on Prostitution

JAN CAMPBELL

Alice Leuchtag describes the world of sex trafficking in this article. Introducing the reader to a young girl named Siri provides a face and a persona to the problem. Enslaved children just like Siri are trafficked all over the world, bringing profits in the billions of dollars to the slaveholders.

This article raises consciousness about the trade and introduces us to the realities that this type of slavery is a way of life for many families around the world. Young girls are seen as commodities to be sold and traded like currency. It is unconscionable to think that this extreme form of sexism and objectification of females still exists today. This compelling expose shows us how insidious the problem is, in that it is seen as commonplace by the locals and is promoted to tourists as a viable attraction.

HUMAN RIGHTS SEX TRAFFICKING AND PROSTITUTION

Perspectives on Prostitution

ALICE LEUCHTAG

D espite laws against slavery in practically every country, an estimated twenty-seven million people live as slaves. Kevin Bales, in his book *Disposable People: New Slavery in the Global Economy* (University of California Press, Berkeley, 1999), describes those who endure modern forms of slavery. These include indentured servants, persons held in hereditary bondage, child slaves who pick plantation crops, child soldiers, and adults and children trafficked and sold into sex slavery.

A LIFE NARRATIVE

Of all forms of slavery, sex slavery is one of the most exploitative and lucrative with some 200,000 sex slaves worldwide bringing their slaveholders an annual profit of $10.5 billion. Although the great preponderance of sex slaves are women and girls, a smaller but significant number of males—both adult and children—are enslaved for homosexual prostitution. The life narrative of a Thai girl named Siri, as told to Bales, illustrates how sex slavery happens to vulnerable girls and women. Siri is born in northeastern Thailand to a poor family that farms a small plot of land, barely eking out a living. Economic policies of structural adjustment pursued by the Thai government under the aegis of the World Bank and the International Monetary Fund have taken former government subsidies away from rice farmers, leaving them to compete against imported, subsidized rice that keeps the market price artificially depressed.

Siri attends four years of school, then is kept at home to help care for her three younger siblings. When Siri is fourteen, a well-dressed woman visits her village. She offers to find Siri a "good job," advancing her parents $2,000 against future earnings. This represents at least a year's income for the family. In a town in another province the woman, a trafficker, "sells" Siri to a brothel for $4,000. Owned by an "investment club" whose members are business and professional men—government bureaucrats and local politicians—the brothel is extremely profitable. In a typical thirty-day period it nets its investors $88,000.

To maintain the appearance that their hands are clean, members of the club's board of directors leave the management of the brothel to a pimp and a bookkeeper. Siri is initiated into prostitution by the pimp who rapes her. After being abused by her first "customer," Siri escapes, but a policeman—who gets a percentage of the brothel profits—brings her back, whereupon the pimp beats her up. As further punishment, her "debt" is doubled from $4,000 to $8,000. She must now repay this, along with her monthly rent and food, all from her earnings of $4 per customer. She will have to have sex with three hundred men a month just to pay her rent. Realizing she will never be able to get out of debt, Siri tries to build a relationship with the pimp simply in order to survive.

The pimp uses culture and religion to reinforce his control over Siri. He tells her she must have committed terrible sins in a past life to have been born a female; she must have accumulated a karmic debt to deserve the enslavement and abuse to which she must reconcile herself. Gradually Siri begins to see herself from the point of view of the slaveholder—as someone unworthy and deserving of punishment. By age fifteen she no longer protests or runs away. Her physical enslavement has become psychological as well, a common occurrence in chronic abuse.

Siri is administered regular injections of the contraceptive drug Depo-Provera for which she is charged. As the same needle is used for all the girls, there is a high risk of HIV and other sexual diseases from the injections. Siri knows that a serious illness threatens her and she prays to Buddha at the little shrine in her room, hoping to earn merit so he will protect her from dreaded disease. Once a month she and the others, at their own expense, are tested for HIV. So far Siri's tests have been negative. When Siri tries to get the male customers to wear condoms—distributed free to brothels by the Thai Ministry of Health—some resist wearing them and she can't make them do so.

As one of an estimated 35,000 women working as brothel slaves in Thailand—a country where 500,000 to one million prostituted women and girls work in conditions of degradation and exploitation short of brothel slavery—Siri faces at least a 40 percent chance of contracting the HIV virus. If she is lucky, she can look forward to five more years before she becomes too ill to work and is pushed out into the street.

Though the Thai government denies it, the Health Organization finds that HIV is epidemic in Thailand, with the largest segment of new cases among wives and girlfriends of men who buy prostitute sex. Viewing its women as a cash crop to be exploited, and depending on sex tourism for foreign exchange dollars to help pay interest on the foreign debt, the Thai government can't acknowledge the epidemic without contradicting the continued promotion of sex tourism and prostitution.

By encouraging investment in the sex industry, sex tourism creates a business climate conducive to the trafficking and enslavement of vulnerable girls such as Siri. In 1996 nearly five million sex tourists from the United States, Western Europe, Australia, and Japan visited Thailand. These transactions brought in about $26.2 billion—thirteen times more than Thailand earned by building and exporting computers.

In her 1999 report Pimps and Predators on the Internet: Globalizing the Sexual Exploitation of Women and Children, published by the Coalition Against Trafficking in Women (CATW), Donna Hughes quotes from postings on an Internet site where sex tourists share experiences and advise one another. The following is one man's description of having sex with a fourteen-year-old prostituted girl in Bangkok:

> Even though I've had a lot of better massages ... after fifteen minutes, I was much more relaxed. ... Then I asked for a condom and I fucked her for another thirty minutes. Her face looked like she was feeling a lot of pain. ... She blocked my way when I wanted to leave the room and she asked for a tip. I gave her 600 baht. Altogether, not a good experience.

Hughes says, "To the men who buy sex, a 'bad experience' evidently means not getting their money's worth, or that the prostituted woman or girl didn't keep up the act of enjoying what she had to do ... one glimpses the humiliation and physical pain most girls and women in prostitution endure."

Nor are the men oblivious to the existence of sexual slavery. One customer states, "Girls in Bangkok virtually get sold by their families into the industry; they work against their will." His knowledge of their sexual slavery and lack of sensitivity thereof is evident in that he then names the hotels in which girls are kept and describes how much they cost!

As Hughes observes, sex tourists apparently feel they have a right to prostitute sex, perceiving prostitution only from a self-interested perspective in which they commodify and objectify women of other cultures, nationalities, and ethnic groups. Their awareness of racism, colonialism, global economic inequalities, and sexism seems limited to the way these realities benefit them as sex consumers.

According to the Guide to the New UN Trafficking Protocol by Janice Raymond, published by the CATW in 2001, the United Nations estimates that sex trafficking in human beings is a $5 billion to $7 billion operation annually. Four million persons are moved illegally from one country to another and within countries each year, a large proportion of them women and girls being trafficked into prostitution. The United Nations International Children's Emergency Fund (UNICEF) estimates that some 30 percent of women being trafficked are minors, many under age thirteen. The International Organization on Migration estimates that some 500,000 women per year are trafficked into Western Europe from poorer regions of the world. According to Sex Trafficking of Women in the United States: International and Domestic Trends, also published by the CATW in 2001, some 50,000 women and children are trafficked into the United States each year, mainly from Asia and Latin America.

Because prostitution as a system of organized sexual exploitation depends on a continuous supply of new "recruits," trafficking is essential to its continued existence. When the pool of available women and girls dries up, new women must be procured. Traffickers cast their nets ever wider and become ever more sophisticated. The Italian Camorra, Chinese Triads, Russian Mafia, and Japanese Yakuza are powerful criminal syndicates consisting of traffickers, pimps, brothel keepers, forced labor lords, and gangs which operate globally.

After the breakdown of the Soviet Union, an estimated five thousand criminal groups formed the Russian Mafia, which operates in thirty countries. The Russian Mafia trafficks women from African countries, the Ukraine, the Russian Federation, and Eastern Europe into Western Europe, the United States, and Israel. The Triads trafficks women from China, Korea, Thailand, and other Southeast Asian countries into the United States and Europe. The Camorra trafficks women from Latin America into Europe. The Yakuza trafficks women from the Phillipines, Thailand, Burma, Cambodia, Korea, Nepal, and Laos into Japan.

A GLOBAL PROBLEM MEETS A GLOBAL RESPONSE

Despite these appalling facts, until recently no generally agreed upon definition of trafficking in human beings was written into international law. In Vienna, Austria, during 1999 and 2000, 120 countries participated in debates over a definition of trafficking. A few nongovernmental organizations (NGOs) and a minority of governments—including Australia, Canada, Denmark, Germany, Ireland, Japan, the Netherlands, Spain, Switzerland, Thailand, and the United Kingdom—wanted to separate issues of trafficking from issues of prostitution. They argued that persons being trafficked should be divided into those who are forced and those who give their consent, with the burden of proof being placed on persons being trafficked. They also urged that the less explicit means of control over trafficked persons—such as abuse of a victim's vulnerability—not be included in the definition of trafficking and that the word exploitation not be used. Generally supporters of this position were wealthier countries where large numbers of women were being trafficked and countries in which prostitution was legalized or sex tourism encouraged.

The CATW—140 other NGOs that make up the International Human Rights Network plus many governments (including those of Algeria, Bangladesh, Belgium, China, Columbia, Cuba, Egypt, Finland, France, India, Mexico, Norway, Pakistan, the Philippines, Sweden, Syria, Venezuela, and Vietnam)—maintains that trafficking can't be separated from prostitution. Persons being trafficked shouldn't be divided into those who are forced and those who give their consent because trafficked persons are in no position to give meaningful consent. The subtler methods used by traffickers, such as abuse of a victim's vulnerability, should be included in the definition of trafficking and the word exploitation be an essential part of the definition. Generally supporters of this majority view were poorer countries from which large numbers of women were being trafficked or countries in which strong feminist, anti-colonialist, or socialist influences existed. The United States, though initially critical of the majority position, agreed to support a definition of trafficking that would be agreed upon by consensus.

The struggle—led by the CATW to create a definition of trafficking that would penalize traffickers while ensuring that all victims of trafficking would be protected—succeeded when a compromise proposal by Sweden was agreed to. A strongly worded and inclusive UN Protocol to Prevent, Suppress, and Punish Trafficking in Persons—especially women and children—was drafted by an ad hoc committee of the UN as a supplement to the Convention Against Transnational Organized Crime. The UN protocol specifically addresses the trade in human beings for purposes of prostitution and other forms of sexual exploitation, forced labor or services, slavery or practices similar to slavery, servitude, and the removal of organs. The protocol defines trafficking as:

> The recruitment, transportation, transfer, harboring or receipt of persons, by means of the threat or use of force or other forms of coercion, of abduction, of fraud, of deception, of the abuse of power or of a position of vulnerability or of the giving or receiving of payments or benefits to achieve the consent of a person having control over another person, for the purpose of exploitation.

While recognizing that the largest amount of trafficking involves women and children, the wording of the UN protocol clearly is gender and age neutral, inclusive of trafficking in both males and females, adults and children.

In 2000 the UN General Assembly adopted this convention and its supplementary protocol; 121 countries signed the convention and eighty countries signed the protocol for the convention and protocol to become international law, forty countries must ratify them.

Some highlights of the new convention and protocol are:

For the first time there is an accepted international definition of trafficking and an agreed-upon set of prosecution, protection, and prevention mechanisms on which countries can base their national legislation.

- The various criminal means by which trafficking takes place, including indirect and subtle forms of coercion, are covered.
- Trafficked persons, especially women in prostitution and child laborers, are no longer viewed as illegal migrants but as victims of a crime.
- The convention doesn't limit its scope to criminal syndicates but defines an organized criminal group as "any structured group of three or more persons which engages in criminal activities such as trafficking and pimping."
- All victims of trafficking in persons are protected, not just those who can prove that force was used against them.
- The consent of a victim of trafficking is meaningless and irrelevant.
- Victims of trafficking won't have to bear the burden of proof.
- Trafficking and sexual exploitation are intrinsically connected and not to be separated.
- Because women trafficked domestically into local sex industries suffer harmful effects similar to those experienced by women trafficked transnationally, these women also come under the protections of the protocol.
- The key element in trafficking is the exploitative purpose rather than the movement across a border.

The protocol is the first UN instrument to address the demand for prostitution sex, a demand that results in the human rights abuses of women and children being trafficked. The protocol recognizes an urgent need for governments to put the buyers of prostitution sex on their policy and legislative agendas, and it calls upon countries to take or strengthen legislative or other measures to discourage demand, which fosters all the forms of sexual exploitation of women and children.

As Raymond says in the Guide to the New UN Trafficking Protocol:

> The least discussed part of the prostitution and trafficking chain has been the men who buy women for sexual exploitation in prostitution. ... If we are to find a permanent path to ending these human rights abuses, then we cannot just shrug our shoulders and say, "men are like this," or "boys will be boys," or "prostitution has always been around." Or tell women and girls in prostitution that they must continue to do what they do because prostitution is inevitable. Rather, our responsibility is to make men change their behavior, by all means available—educational, cultural and legal.

Two U.S. feminist, human rights organizations—Captive Daughters and Equality Now—have been working toward that goal. Surita Sandosham of Equality Now says that when her organization asked women's groups in Thailand and the Philippines how it could assist them, the answer came back, "Do something about the demand." Since then the two organizations have legally challenged sex tours originating in the United States and have succeeded in closing down at least one operation.

Refugees, Not Illegal Aliens

In October 2000 the U.S. Congress passed a bill, the Victims of Trafficking and Violence Protection Act of 2000, introduced by New Jersey republican representative Chris Smith. Under this law penalties for traffickers are raised and protections for victims increased. Reasoning that desperate women are unable to give meaningful consent to their own sexual exploitation, the law adopts a broad definition of sex trafficking so as not to exclude so-called consensual prostitution or trafficking that occurs solely within the United States. In these respects the new federal law conforms to the UN protocol.

Two features of the law are particularly noteworthy:

- In order to pressure other countries to end sex trafficking, the U.S. State Department is to make a yearly assessment of other countries' anti-trafficking efforts and to rank them according to how well they discourage trafficking. After two years of failing to meet even minimal standards, countries are subject to sanctions, although not sanctions on humanitarian aid. "Tier 3" countries—those failing to meet even minimal standards—include Greece, Indonesia, Israel, Pakistan, Russia, Saudi Arabia, South Korea, and Thailand.

- Among persons being trafficked into the United States, special T-visas will be provided to those who meet the criteria for having suffered the most serious trafficking abuses. These visas will protect them from deportation so they can testify against their traffickers. T-non immigrant status allows eligible aliens to remain in the United States temporarily and grants specific non-immigrant benefits. Those acquiring T-1 non-immigrant status will be able to remain for a period of three years and will be eligible to receive certain kinds of public assistance—to the same extent as refugees. They will also be issued employment authorization to "assist them in finding safe, legal employment while they attempt to retake control of their lives."

A DEBATE RAGES

A worldwide debate rages about legalization of prostitution fueled by a 1998 International Labor Organization (ILO) report entitled The Sex Sector: The Economic and Social Bases of Prostitution in Southeast Asia. The report follows years of lobbying by the sex industry for recognition of prostitution as "sex work." Citing the sex industry's unrecognized contribution to the gross domestic product of four countries in Southeast Asia, the ILO urges governments to officially recognize the "sex sector" and "extend taxation nets to cover many of the lucrative activities connected with it." Though the ILO report says it stops short of calling for legalization of prostitution, official recognition of the sex industry would be impossible without it.

Raymond points out that the ILO's push to redefine prostitution as sex work ignores legislation demonstrating that countries can reduce organized sexual exploitation rather than capitulate to it. For example, Sweden prohibits the purchase of sexual services with punishments of stiff fines or imprisonment, thus declaring that prostitution isn't a desirable economic and labor sector. The government also helps women getting out of prostitution to rebuild their lives. Venezuela's Ministry of Labor has ruled that prostitution can't be considered work because it lacks the basic elements of dignity and social justice. The Socialist Republic of Vietnam punishes pimps, traffickers, brothel owners, and buyers— sometimes publishing buyer's names in the mass media. For women in prostitution, the government finances medical, educational, and economic rehabilitation.

Raymond suggests that instead of transforming the male buyer into a legitimate customer, the ILO should give thought to innovative programs that make the buyer accountable for his sexual exploitation. She cites the Sage Project, Inc. (SAGE) program in San Francisco, California, which educates men arrested for soliciting women in prostitution about the risks and impacts of their behavior.

Legalization advocates argue that the violence, exploitation, and health effects suffered by women in prostitution aren't inherent to prostitution but simply result from the random behaviors of bad pimps or buyers, and that if prostitution were regulated by the state these harms would diminish. But examples show these arguments to be false.

In the pamphlet entitled Legalizing Prostitution Is Not the Answer: The Example of Victoria, Australia, published by the CATW in 2001, Mary Sullivan and Sheila Jeffreys describe the way legalization in Australia has perpetuated and strengthened the culture of violence and exploitation inherent in prostitution. Under legalization, legal and illegal brothels have proliferated, and trafficking in women has accelerated to meet the increased demand. Pimps, having even more power, continue threatening and brutalizing the women they control. Buyers continue to abuse women, refuse to wear condoms, and spread the HIV virus—and other sexually transmitted diseases—to their wives and girlfriends. Stigmatized by identity cards and medical inspections, prostituted women are even more marginalized and tightly locked into the system of organized sexual exploitation while the state, now an official party to the exploitation, has become the biggest pimp of all.

The government of the Netherlands has legalized prostitution, doesn't enforce laws against pimping, and virtually lives off taxes from the earnings of prostituted women. In the book Making the Harm Visible (published by the CATW in 1999), Marie-Victoire Louis describes the effects on prostituted women of municipal regulation of brothels in Amsterdam and other Dutch cities. Her article entitled "Legalizing Pimping, Dutch Style" explains the way immigration policies in the Netherlands are shaped to fit the needs of the prostitution industry so that traffickers are seldom prosecuted and a continuous supply of women is guaranteed. In Amsterdam's 250 officially listed brothels, 80 percent of the prostitutes have been trafficked in from other countries and 70 percent possess no legal papers. Without money, papers, or contact with the outside world, these immigrant women live in terror. Instead of being protected by the regulations governing brothels, prostituted women are frequently beaten up and raped by pimps. These "prostitution managers" have practically been given a free hand by the state and by buyers who, as "consumers of prostitution," feel themselves entitled to abuse the women they buy. Sadly and ironically the "Amsterdam model" of legalization and regulation is touted by the Netherlands and Germany as "self-determination and empowerment for women." In reality it simply legitimizes the "right" to buy, sexually use, and profit from the sexual exploitation of someone else's body.

A HUMAN RIGHTS APPROACH

As part of a system of organized sexual exploitation, prostitution can be visualized along a continuum of abuse with brothel slavery at the furthest extreme. All along the continuum, fine lines divide the degrees of harm done to those caught up in the system. At the core lies a great social injustice no cosmetic reforms can right: the setting aside of a segment of people whose bodies can be purchased for sexual use by others. When this basic injustice is legitimized and regulated by the state and when the state profits from it, that injustice is compounded.

In her book *The Prostitution of Sexuality* (New York University Press, 1995), Kathleen Barry details a feminist human rights approach to prostitution that points the way to the future. Ethically it recognizes prostitution, sex trafficking, and the globalized industrialization of sex as massive violations of women's human rights. Sociologically it considers how and to what extent prostitution promotes sex discrimination against individual women, against different racial categories of women, and against women as a group. Politically it calls for decriminalizing prostitutes while penalizing pimps, traffickers, brothel owners, and buyers.

Understanding that human rights and restorative justice go hand in hand, the feminist human rights approach to prostitution addresses the harm and the need to repair the damage. As Barry says:

> Legal proposals to criminalize customers, based on the recognition that prostitution violates and harms women, must ... include social-service, health and counseling and job retraining programs. Where states would be closing down brothels if customers were, criminalized, the economic resources poured into the former prostitution areas could be turned toward producing gainful employment for women.

With the help of women's projects in many countries—such as Buklod in the Philippines and the Council for Prostitution Alternatives in the United States—some women have begun to confront their condition by leaving prostitution, speaking out against it, revealing their experiences, and helping other women leave the sex industry.

Ending the sexual exploitation of trafficking and prostitution will mean the beginning of a new chapter in building a humanist future—a more peaceful and just future in which men and women can join together in love and respect, recognizing one another's essential dignity and humanity. Humanity's sexuality then will no longer be hijacked and distorted.

Freelance writer Alice Leuchtag has worked as a social worker, counselor, college instructor, and researcher. Active in the civil rights, peace, socialist, feminist, and humanist movements, she has helped organize women in Houston to oppose sex trafficking.

Alice Leuchtag, "Human rights sex trafficking and prostitution—perspectives on prostitution". Humanist. FindArticles.com. 08 Jul, 2010. http://findarticles.com/p/articles/mi_ml374/is_l_63/ai_96417147/ Copyright © 2003 American Humanist Association Copyright © 2003 Gale Group

CPSIA information can be obtained
at www.ICGtesting.com
Printed in the USA
LVOW03s0159040116

468957LV00014B/285/P